Masculinity in Transition

Masculinity in Transition

K. Allison Hammer

University of Minnesota Press
Minneapolis
London

The University of Minnesota Press gratefully acknowledges the financial assistance provided for the publication of this book by the College of Arts and Science at Vanderbilt University.

Emily Dickinson poems from *The Poems of Emily Dickinson: Variorum Edition*, ed. Ralph W. Franklin (Cambridge, Mass.: Belknap Press of Harvard University Press), copyright 1998 by the President and Fellows of Harvard College; copyright renewed 1979, 1983 by the President and Fellows of Harvard College; copyright 1914, 1918, 1919, 1924, 1929, 1930, 1932, 1935, 1937, 1942 by Martha Dickinson Bianchi; copyright 1952, 1957, 1958, 1963, 1965 by Mary L. Hampson; reprinted by permission; all rights reserved. Samuel Ace, "The Shower" and "Letter to Linda," in *Home in Three Days. Don't Wash.* (Hard Press, 2019); *Normal Sex* (Ithaca, N.Y.: Firebrand Books, 1994); published by permission of the poet. Andrea Gibson, "Gender in the Key of Lyme Disease," "Andrea/Andrew," "No Filter," "Johnny Appleseed," and "Elbows," in *Lord of the Butterflies: Poems* (Minneapolis: Button Poetry/Exploding Pinecone Press, 2019), reprinted with permission of Button Press. Acknowledgment to Stanford G. Gann Jr., Literary Executor for the Estate of Gertrude Stein, for permission to use the text of Gertrude Stein.

Portions of chapter 1 were published in a different form in "Toward a Theory of Female Phallicism," *EOAGH* (September 2022); reprinted with permission, https://eoagh.com/. Portions of chapter 2 were previously published in a different form in "Radical 'Boyhood' Futures for the Twenty-First Century, or Pinocchio (Finally) Gets His Phallus," *Studies in Gender and Sexuality* 20, no. 3 (2019): 177–88, http://wwww.tandfonline.com. Portions of chapter 1 were previously published in a different form in "'Doing Josephine': The Radical Legacy of Josephine Baker's Banana Dance," *WSQ: Women's Studies Quarterly* 48, nos. 1 and 2 (2020): 165–81. Portions of chapter 4 were previously published in "Epic Stone Butch: Transmasculinity in the Work of Willa Cather," *TSQ: Transgender Studies Quarterly* 7, no. 1 (2020): 77–98; reprinted by permission of the copyright holder, Duke University Press; and in "Butch Life Writing: Private Desires and Public Demands in the Works of Gertrude Stein," *Feminist Formations* 27, no. 2 (2015): 27–45; reprinted by permission of the copyright holder, Johns Hopkins University Press.

Copyright 2023 by the Regents of the University of Minnesota

All rights reserved. No part of this publication may be reproduced, stored in a retrieval system, or transmitted, in any form or by any means, electronic, mechanical, photocopying, recording, or otherwise, without the prior written permission of the publisher.

Published by the University of Minnesota Press
111 Third Avenue South, Suite 290
Minneapolis, MN 55401-2520
http://www.upress.umn.edu

ISBN 978-1-5179-1434-9 (hc)
ISBN 978-1-5179-1435-6 (pb)

Library of Congress record available at https://lccn.loc.gov/2023012250.

Printed in the United States of America on acid-free paper

The University of Minnesota is an equal-opportunity educator and employer.

Contents

Introduction: Rejecting "American" Manhood   1

Part I. Challenging Phallic Supremacy

1. "She's a Pistol": Female Phallicism   29
2. "When I Was a Boy": Boi/Boyhood and the Unworking of Masculinity   55

Part II. Challenging Conceptions of the Nation

3. The "Not (Quite) Yet" of a New Collectivity: Feminist Masculinity and the American Western   85
4. Virtue Is Divided: Unruly Alliances in Willa Cather and Gertrude Stein   133

Part III. Challenging Masculine Impenetrability

5. "Skin of His Hand against the Skin of My Back": HIV/AIDS Self-Writing and Film of the 1980s and '90s   169
6. "A Man Is a Worker": Economic Penetrability, Labor Abuses, and Landlessness   211

Conclusion: Toward the Future of Masculinity and Relationality   253

Acknowledgments   261
Notes   263
Index   303

Introduction

Rejecting "American" Manhood

After the election of Donald Trump in 2016, toxic masculinity has become a focus of critique in the media and among activists, artists, and cultural critics, as the life chances of many groups of people around the world continue to decline. Toxic masculinity fuels what trans scholars Dean Spade and Ciro Carrillo call the "daily, routine disasters of capitalism and white supremacy."[1] This indictment is not hyperbolic or unearned. However, recent critical attention has done little to release its grip, as the phrase "boys will be boys" continues to condone and even celebrate masculine dominance. Gender studies scholar Bobby Noble observes that there are already too many books about men, and yet men still have "no self-conscious history of themselves as subjects of masculinity."[2] Many of these books about men promise self-improvement through a depoliticized rebranding of style and presentation, designed to help men simply "do better." "Freedom" more than ever has come to connote "free enterprise," and consequently, gender has become yet another consumable.

Popularized catchphrases, like toxic masculinity, tend to default to an individual model of redemption and identity formation over more macro, political, and collective concerns, particularly through the soundbite-producing machinations of social media. Consequently, toxic masculinity, which from here on I will call "normative masculinity," lacks critical specificity. The root systems would need to be untangled, not only for what they indicate domestically in the United States but as key mechanisms for understanding U.S. imperialism since the late nineteenth century. The term *toxic* connotes spread, and while certainly not specific to the United States, sexual control and domination, full democratic participation in the life of the nation-state, along with the qualities of impenetrability, all coalesce—and spread—under the sign of white masculinity.

Normative masculinity adheres to a set of scripts that dictate what masculinity should and should not be, which requires the simultaneous denigration and exclusion of numerous Others.[3] The total rejection of anything considered weak or penetrable becomes part of masculinity's definition. Such a rigid orientation to the world is highly unstable, however, and requires the projection of fears and anxieties onto women and "lesser" masculinities. Jasbir Puar observes that after 9/11, the media depicted terrorist masculinities as feminized—the most "failed and perverse"—associated with a variety of pathologies, including "homosexuality, incest, pedophilia, madness, and disease."[4] Terrorist masculinities from "somewhere in the Middle East" are dialectically opposed to the strong-arm masculinities of family and patriotism in the West.[5] Insidious forms of oppression reaffirm normative masculinity, even while the shoring up of hegemony is not seen as the primary motive.[6]

In *Masculinity in Transition,* I view normative masculinity, across embodiment, gender identification, and sexuality, as motivated primarily by the desire for profit and for the psychological wages of masculine dominance and white supremacy. As historian Robin D. G. Kelley writes in *Freedom Dreams,* saturating consumerism and materialism, the stark inequalities of modern life in thrall of global capital, can *never* represent freedom.[7] The apotheosis of normative masculinity appears in the right-wing nationalism of Trump, Brazil's Jair Bolsonaro, prime minister of India Narendra Modi, prime minister of Hungary Viktor Orbán, and former president of the Philippines Rodrigo Duterte. As Kelley more recently argues, these men do not foreshadow a return to 1930s fascism, nor do they represent the fiery end of neoliberalism.[8] Rather, this ascendancy of fascism is an extension of neoliberal logic through a new historic bloc of right-wing fundamentalists, corporate interests, and working people forming authoritarian, neofascist movements grounded in fear.[9]

In conversation with literary scholar C. Riley Snorton, I view normative masculinity as embedded in the history of chattel slavery, xenophobia, and their afterlives, through which gender itself becomes "mutable" and "amendable" and ultimately not something that the marginalized can own and determine for themselves.[10] In the time of captivity, gender was not a binary system of classification but rather what Hortense Spillers calls a "territory of cultural and political maneuver."[11] Sex and gender became revisable according to racial capital's logics of accumulation and exchange.[12] White, normative masculinity appeared by contrast as the fixed universal signifier, and it is this fantasy of permanence and stability that supplies its present-day contours.

In addition to naming and refusing normative masculinity, it is also crucial to consider what must take its place: namely, practices of care and mutual aid, outside of state-sponsored channels of support. There are many discussions about care circulating in the culture, particularly during the Covid-19 pandemic. However, little attention is paid to how care and masculinity can be put into conversation with one another through queer and transgender theory. Care is of course a prominent analytic in affect theory, but using affect as a primary framework would pull the argument toward the identitarian and personal and away from the collective and systemic. Theories of deconstruction and critiques of racial capitalism best capture the saturating political and economic effects of fraternal control, white supremacy, and dispossession.

Masculinity in Transition brings together an archive of contemporary and canonical texts that encourage care not only for those in our proximity but beyond an individual, and limited, vision. Historically situated responses to masculine normativity provide examples of what I am calling "unruly alliance," a term that escapes the imprint of fraternal constructs, transcending the limits of identitarian thinking. Unruly alliance offers a complex view of subjectivity and a vision for a politics of solidarity that can scale up to address gender and raced oppressions as well as ecological and economic issues. The term describes the kinds of bonds that occur outside of heteronormative domestic and familial arrangements, but without drawing on theories of queer kinship. Unruly alliance helps to zero in on moments when conditions are ripe for what Angela Davis famously calls "unpredictable or unlikely coalitions grounded in political projects."[13] Because unruly alliance can be brought to bear on nearly any other context, it can become a widely applied concept for discussing human relationality.

As a deconstructive masculinity studies project, *Masculinity in Transition* also corrects the tendency to focus exclusively on masculinities expressed by bodies assigned male at birth. While concern over the spread of toxic masculinity is not hyperbolic or unearned, there must be a simultaneous distancing from binary, so-called biological conceptions of gender. However, not all trans and queer masculinities resist fraternity and racial capitalism, as some may be included in liberal agendas on a contingent basis, resulting in new margins. What I have discovered are moments and scenes in which there is a turning away from these seductions, exposing the instability of masculine normativity more generally. While cultural production is a tool of disciplinary power, it can also propose new ways of relating and being. Collectively, it is possible to perform masculinity (broadly defined) without perpetuating historical trauma, but this can only be realized through an imaginative orientation toward the future.

"I Could'a Been a Contender"

Masculinity in Transition owes a debt of gratitude to the crises for masculinity produced by feminist, queer, and transgender theory since the 1970s. Scholars like C. J. Pascoe, Jack Halberstam, and Kath Browne use queer theoretical approaches to gender to show how people assigned female at birth also develop complex masculine practices and subjectivities capable of disrupting the conflation of biology and gender. Lou Sullivan, Jameson Green, Jay Prosser, and others also establish how trans men forge new masculinities that tamper with this conflation.

However, to gain a more comprehensive view, I engage an array of masculinities in conversation with one another, taking inspiration from Kale Bantigue Fajardo's interdisciplinary ethnography *Filipino Crosscurrents: Oceanographies of Seafaring, Masculinities, and Globalization*. Writing against scholars who essentialize maleness, manhood, and heterosexuality through "male anatomy," Fajardo asks how the cultural politics of Filipino maritime/migrant masculinities take shape vis-à-vis other masculinities and how Filipino men or masculine subjects "negotiate and understand these cultural politics."[14] I share Fajardo's desire to address the complexities and social construction of masculinity in relation to white supremacy, colonialism, and labor exploitation and in the context of "dominant and/or racist white gay cultural practices" or "globalized gay discourse."[15]

By placing subjectivities side by side, I resist the urge to idealize, or to make exceptional, queer and trans revisions. Halberstam's *Female Masculinity* (1998) provided for the first time a taxonomy of queer masculinities—butch, transsexual, transgender, and drag—

existing in a productive, discursive relationship with being a lesbian. His work is still widely read and cited, as a bold confrontation against feminists and heterosexuals who resist and delegitimize various forms of female masculinity. Arguing for the originality and necessity of such a study, he states that there would be "inevitable effects of a fully articulated female masculinity on a seemingly fortified male masculinity."[16] He claims that masculinity transforms automatically when the "butch raging bull" replaces the "pugilist" as the champion, the newly anointed "legitimate contender."[17] It is unclear how the white "Raging Bull (Dyke)" on the cover of *Female Masculinity* and the white, conjured image of Rocky Balboa or Jake LaMotta are significantly different.[18] Does masculinity outside of the assigned male body require that one become a contender for the title of most legitimate?

Because gender is first and foremost a racial construct, there needs to be a closer examination of what Halberstam means by "inevitable effects." Critical whiteness studies scholars define the concept of "whiteness" in multiple ways, including as an identity or way of understanding oneself and one's ancestry, as an ideology forged through a set of social practices, and as a system of power. No white person fully disavows this power, which becomes a problem for so-called revisions of masculinity. When self-described butch cultural anthropologist Esther Newton celebrates the "power" claimed by white butch dykes or when Halberstam promotes the "inevitable effects" of the white "butch raging bull," they do not adequately account for how race and class galvanize this power. As feminist philosopher Linda Martín Alcoff contends, all white people tend to believe, consciously or subconsciously, in "white vanguardism," or the notion that white people are the moral, political, scientific, and technological forerunners of the human race.[19] As Alcoff suggests, white vanguardism is particularly common among the white working classes, which historically includes white butches, because it offers a sense of entitlement and dignity and an antidote for feelings of inferiority.[20] However, whiteness is neither ontologically empty nor purely aligned with white supremacy; rather, whiteness "is a prominent feature of one's way of being in the world, of how one navigates that world, and of how one is navigated around by others."[21] In a similar vein, feminist writer Sara Ahmed approaches whiteness not as a reachable object but as an orientation rendered invisible over time, one that puts things (opportunities, artistic success, financial gain, education, and much more) within reach.[22] As a kind of imagined ground, whiteness determines the ways one interacts and forms social relations, which, when combined with masculinity, becomes a noxious brew.[23]

To be clear, in *Female Masculinity* and elsewhere, Halberstam conveys masculinity's "saturating effects," but masculinity outside of the assigned male body always appears as the ultimate revision, which suggests that only these subjects can compel masculinity's transformation.[24] However, normativity is mobile and rhizomatic, and no one identity category can claim to be completely immune to its promises of economic, social, and political inclusion. In the age of homo- and transnormativity, masculinity can be easily co-opted by the state and by neoliberal agendas. *Homonormativity* refers to the liberal platform, epitomized by agencies like the Human Rights Campaign, that advocates for same-sex marriage and various forms of civic inclusion while identifying liberation in terms of privacy, intimacy, domesticity, and consumerism. As Lisa Duggan asserts, the "New Homonormativity," which gained momentum in the 1990s, rejects the "privacy-in-public claims and publicizing strategies of 'the gay movement' . . . in favor of public recognition of a domesticated, depoliticized privacy. The democratic diversity of proliferating forms of sexual dissidence is rejected in favor of the naturalized variation of a fixed minority arrayed around a state-endorsed heterosexual primacy and prestige."[25] White trans masculinity can become equally aspirational, part of a larger trans(homo)nationalist, pinkwashing project, compliant with compulsory neoliberal individualism.

Proving this point, in her study *Men in Place*, Miriam J. Abelson discovers that the majority of trans men she interviewed desired masculinity in the form of a "softer" ideal. They viewed gender as apolitical and often wanted to blend into the scenery (which is an inherently white privilege) and enjoy the domestic pleasures of a "normal" nuclear family life. The reentrenchment of so-called normalcy can produce newly insidious forms of masculine normativity that are difficult to detect and critique. Abelson uses the term *goldilocks masculinity* to describe a happy masculine medium to which many of these trans men aspire, a gender style that in my view should be subject to criticism the same way men's liberation movements were when they sought to reap the benefits of feminism without giving up any power or privilege.²⁶ The "new father," the "new sensitive man," and other versions of a kinder, gentler masculinity may simply modernize rather than dismantle patriarchy.²⁷ Such masculine revisions thoroughly depend on whiteness-as-currency and a narrow and personalized conception of identity politics.

White masculinity can secure an array of alliances and privileges across identity categories and historical contexts.²⁸ At the same time, what Halberstam calls "unfettered masculinism," with fascist masculinity as its most extreme manifestation, is an effect of a debilitating insecurity, a visceral fear of lack and failure.²⁹ Regardless of how these masculine habits and behaviors look on the surface, they appeal to those who feel they deserve to be much bigger than they are. This phenomenon of the need to be bigger is complicated and takes many forms, requiring critique and analysis that remains attentive to historical particularity and to the ways individual subjectivity intersects with larger structures of exploitation and oppression.

Trans- and homonormativity can compel the formation of what Jacques Derrida describes as a kind of shadow brotherhood, in which fraternity is replicated by outsiders who may ironically nurture dreams of patriarchy's demise.³⁰ Such bands of outsiders only mirror the bonds of fraternity and neoliberal logic even while remaining outside of normative alignments of sex and gender. The cliché "LGBTQIA+ community" is often based on sympathy between members of groups with similar identity labels, but these sympathies can be easily contradicted by new racisms or chauvinisms. Underscoring the limits of identity politics focused on the personal, cultural critic and historian Nikhil Pal Singh warns that personal commitment is not a substitute for systemic change. Many in the LGBTQIA+ community belong to the creative classes, whom Singh accuses of "tinkering with microaggressions and safe spaces within shrinking kingdoms of high cultural and educational attainment."³¹ My aim is to discover how masculinity can disidentify with global capital, white supremacy, and Eurocentrism—or, in other words, the very things that make masculinity "toxic" in the first place.

As I discover in chapter 4, "Virtue Is Divided: Unruly Alliances in Willa Cather and Gertrude Stein," some historical trans and queer masculinities both affirm and destabilize normativity at different points in their lives and careers. On the one hand, Cather and Stein worshipped strong-arm military men, engaging in what I call "butch exceptionalism," corresponding to their historical, U.S. imperialist moment. While by no means exclusive to butch lesbians or trans men, the tendency to be nostalgic about masculinity is endemic to masculinity itself, as it is currently written about, represented, and practiced. However, their relationships with low-ranking soldiers during and after World War I, and the care they showed for them, illustrate the potential of unruly alliance. Both expressed in their writings shock and horror at the war, which altered gender in a more profound way than is often realized, and both found it imperative to express their grief and horror over the dehumanizing effects of trench warfare. Looking closely at the lives and works of these writers, I refuse an either/or approach to transnormativity and ask instead how gender performance shape-shifts in a nonlinear fashion across the life span of an individual and cultural milieu. At the same time, whiteness and class privilege must be viewed as prerequisites to artistic success.

For a time, Cather and Stein embraced a limitless form of affection and care capable of transcending death, which Derrida called *lovence,* but without the fraternal adherence to the principles of selection and hierarchy. As feminist theorist Grace Hong observes, individualism defines the American ethos. To assert one's will as an individual makes one part of a collectivity, ironically one that is made up of subjects connected by their common resistance to bonds.[32] This resistance is also a rejection of femininity and all of the negative associations it carries in the West: penetrability, concern for others, self-sacrifice, etc.—qualities that are also racialized as part of a premodern, archaic past connected to the natural world.

Masculinity in Transition resists more broadly these ways of understanding identity and relationality. The Combahee River Collective first coined the term *identity politics* in the 1970s, but in Hong's view, they used it to embrace the category "women of color" as a way to mediate "a variety of contradictory and competing identifications and disidentifications" and to understand identity as multiply determined and unstable.[33] The collective's understanding of identity politics undermines this elevation of the possessive individual and the concept of a knowable subjectivity. For Patricia Hill Collins, identity politics, as it continues to be understood by Black feminists and women of color, ensures "political rights and economic development via collective action to change social institutions."[34]

The anti-identitarian impulses in trans and queer theory began genealogically with Foucault, who asserts that identity is only useful if it is viewed not as a problem of existence that one must uncover but as a subjective set of strategies used to form a multiplicity of relations.[35] Identity becomes programmatic when it coalesces to become law, principle, code of existence, or an ethical universal rule, and when everything done or said must be framed through the question "Does this thing conform to my identity?"[36] Foucault predicted that, for gay men in particular, such a shoring up of self would ultimately lead back to an ethics that closely resembles "the old heterosexual virility."[37] This move away from identity continues to guide queer theorists, particularly those who focus more precisely on disability, race, and class. Queer of color theorists Roderick Ferguson and Cathy Cohen, and trans scholar Dean Spade, for example, are heavily influenced by women of color feminisms of the 1970s, which use identity politics to point outward from the self, toward the social world and toward the debilitating material conditions of the neighborhood and in the lives of family and community members.[38] As queer and crip theorists Robert McRuer and Anna Mollow explain, after the 1970s, identity politics began to point inward "toward the self . . . toward 'representative' identities."[39] In *Crip Times: Disability, Globalization, and Resistance*, McRuer speaks to the ways in which neoliberalism simultaneously contains and domesticates identity, representation, and rights.[40]

Unruly alliance also extends beyond theories of queer kinship. In *Disturbing Attachments*, queer theorist Kadji Amin points out how queer kinship, or chosen family, creates new idealizations, which, if not traditionally familial, promise to "make good on the family's failings."[41] He writes on how chosen family is historically bound to a "neoliberal, post-gay liberation time and place. As such, it resonates with queer attachments to the values of egalitarianism, individual autonomy, and elective affinities."[42] In the queer tradition of "living with damage in a damaged world," Amin proposes an attitude of "deidealization" that would call attention to queer as "inextricable from relations of power, queer deviance as intertwined with normativity, and queer alternatives as not necessarily just alternatives."[43]

Like Amin, in writing this book, I experienced disappointment when I discovered that some of my most beloved queer and trans icons were more than a little complicit with political fraternity and racial capitalism, in ways that made me question my affections for them. As Amin insists, deideralization is vital as a nonbinary form of inquiry, which can result in less repudiating and individualizing accounts of entanglements with power.[44] As I argue in chapter 6, "'A Man Is a Worker': Economic Penetrability, Labor Abuses, and Landlessness," complicity with neoliberalism and fraternity is often necessary for survival. *Stone Butch Blues* (1993), by Leslie Feinberg, and "Brokeback Mountain," the short story by Annie Proulx, have not been adequately critiqued as being about labor and racial capitalism and how masculine gender, sexuality, and relationship form, and fracture, because of economic marginalization and labor abuses.[45] In *Stone Butch Blues*, masculine vulnerability is shaped by the factory, and the queuing up outside the unemployment office, within the contradictions of capital's global phase. Feinberg proposes the possibility of the trans/butch worker as a revolutionary—a stone not only in the sexual arena but within the hierarchy of the workplace. In "Brokeback Mountain," Ennis Del Mar and Jack Twist are the lowest of the low in the Wyoming world of work, for not only are they gay men, but they are sheepherders, a so-called white trash category par excellence. Their sexuality is not just taking place on Brokeback: it *is* Brokeback. Caring for animals and each other on the land provides the foundation for a vulnerable masculinity, but one that cannot survive without the refuge of the closet and concessions to a particular kind of mountain West masculinism.

Taking another look at canonical literature and film requires what I call "reading again," which involves looking with fresh eyes, allowing for a discovery of what holds promise and what must be questioned and critiqued. By reading again, I follow literary scholar Colleen Lye's proposal that reading attentively can "generate a textured sense of the strength and roots of ideological persuasion."[46] "Brokeback Mountain" and *Stone Butch Blues* tend to be read solely as stories of queer love in hostile times and places, which makes us aware of how, in Lye's words, "American universality depends upon the possibility of assimilation."[47] However, there is always the danger of "discovering aliens in our midst, or the wholesale possibility of American takeover by aliens."[48] The "aliens" in this case are radical trans and queer labor organizers or those internally displaced because of their supposed white trash status.

These masculinities grounded in vulnerability have far-reaching implications for gender and community, as the workplace can help redefine both masculinity and labor, one of the main routes for the formation and concretization of gender more broadly. Some representations of queer and trans working masculinities open outward to recognize shared alienation as part of the neoliberal condition. They use shared alienation and the failure of approximating normative masculinity to create forms of belonging that are not so-called enrichments of the past.

In *Masculinity in Transition,* unruly alliance may be temporary, utilitarian, and devoid of the kind of pathos that intimate relationships seem to require. They make take shape on a factory floor, a wartime field hospital, or a desolate rural plain. As observed in chapter 5, unruly alliances may also form during times of illness and crisis, such as the height of the HIV/AIDS epidemic in the United States, when traditional forms of heroic protest in the streets became impossible. They may also arise out of creative necessity in the form of mentorships. They may be multigenerational, occurring between two people or many. By coupling the word *unruly* with *alliance*, I continue Amin's project of moving beyond the mandate that queer relations be exceptional, whether that means exceptionally just, politically oppositional, or resistant to hetero- or homonormative ways of relating.[49] In reality, all alliances are unpredictable—and yes, unruly—and because of the continual movement of power, politics, and history, they are often ephemeral.

The elementary quality of the word *care* might make it seem too basic to be effective for addressing the complexity of the current crises, but *care* contains within it a passionate refusal of the deeply held Western values of autonomy and independence. Further, unruly alliance can scale up to describe macrological political and economic forms of care. Crip-femme theorists, like Leah Lakshmi Piepzna-Samarasinha, describe care webs as redeployments of anarchist concepts of mutual aid taking root in early twentieth-century Russia and Europe. However, she also reminds us that Black, Indigenous, and brown communities utilized care webs well before and after white anarchists.[50] Care webs in disability and trans communities often result from loss of birth or adoptive family and other official sources of support. As trans scholar Hil Malatino writes, "Trans collectives and communities are deeply interwoven and interdependent, enmeshed in a way that makes distinguishing between the roles of caregiver and recipient difficult—they're rotating, interchangeable, and reciprocal."[51] Care brings with it the promise of new futures, but it appears radical in the United States only because dehumanization and neglect have become normalized and routine.[52]

I use the term *mutual aid*, and the related term *care web*, to indicate the "voluntary reciprocal exchange of resources and services for mutual benefit," which, opposed to charity, connotes relationality and connection instead of the moral superiority of the giver.[53] Dean Spade defines *mutual aid* as the kind of movement work that addresses needs for housing, food, health care, transportation, and more, and at the same time draws attention to the conditions and politics that created that need in the first place. Spade avidly supports mutual aid as a kind of "survival work," which, when accomplished in tandem with social movements, can result in transformative change.[54] At its best, mutual aid creates extragovernmental modes of living, which engender well-being in the face of harm.[55] Far from the narrower terms of queer rebellion, mutual aid projects are "genuinely participatory . . . voluntary, reciprocal, non-hierarchical, non-bureaucratic, egalitarian, cooperative, intended for mutual benefit."[56] Similarly, Aren Aizura coins the term *communization of care*, a process that he links not to old ideas of "community" but to the ways leftists in 1970s France conceived of zones that exist outside of capitalism, which would require relying on those with whom we are interdependent but not necessarily intimate.[57] Unruly alliance also builds upon Malatino's concept of "prefigurative politics," which involves building in advance the space for one another within our psyches, homes, institutions, and collective spaces, for however long that space may be needed or wanted.[58]

Most compelling for *Masculinity in Transition* is the idea that care work, in the spirit of mutual aid and feminist disability politics, is self-reflective, intent on asking how we all contribute to unlivable conditions.[59] Normative masculinity blocks social transformation through political and collective expressions antithetical to the practices of mutual aid and care. Therefore, in contrast to processes of fraternization, the examples in this book reach toward horizontal forms of relationality. Care webs and mutual aid teach about the qualities needed to establish these forms: the ability to deliberate, communicate, unlearn shame derived from asking for, offering, or accepting help, undoing in the process what Malatino calls "the mythos of neoliberal, entrepreneurial self-making."[60]

Mutual aid depends instead upon connecting through the impersonal, which means not cold or harsh in this context but no longer reliant on land, blood, and identity for its formation. Mutual aid inspires new ways of relating that can span the psychic distances that ensure our isolation. Social movements result, which are "democratic, non-hierarchical, and centered on healing."[61] Masculinity becomes no longer welded to dominance and the habit of needing to be on top in every situation but instead works to integrate so-called feminine-identified principles for living, for as the twenty-first century progresses, the stakes and consequences of masculinity as total and complete dominance are manifesting—demanding a response.

The Counterfeit Currency of Fraternity and Racial Capitalism

Through deconstruction and critiques of racial capitalism, I insist on the urgency of this reconceptualization of masculinity. Both the novel and familiar terrors of our present reveal that subverting normative masculinity is only possible within a broader rejection of the current political and economic systems. Jacques Derrida's *The Politics of Friendship*, an assembled series of lectures delivered from 1988 to 1989, maps how the deferral of universal equality is bound up with masculine ideals and ways of bonding, encouraging restrictive, individual forms of relationality. Derrida maintains that the philosophical roots of liberal contract ideals provide men with a counterfeit hegemony. In this section, I link Derrida's discussion on friendship to critiques of racialism, which for Cedric J. Robinson establish similarly counterfeit ways in which the West has been conceived of as a "genealogy of civic virtue and moral progress," marching onward from ancient Athens to the twenty-first century.[62]

Part of Derrida's "political turn," these lectures examine the philosophical history of masculine friendship. From the perspective of the 1980s (a turning point of growing conservatism, "family values," neoliberal economics, particularly in the United Kingdom and the United States, and the HIV/AIDS pandemic), he also perceives the escalation of multiple crises. He views these crises as consequences of a suturing of masculine norms that occurred between the otherwise vastly different Greco-Roman, Christian, and Enlightenment periods, through to the Revolutions. The politics of male–male friendship in the West is interwoven with violence and selective forms of care, justified by what Derrida calls phallocentrism, the centering of the assigned male body, and phallogocentrism, the primacy of the assigned male voice in language.

He reflects continually in these lectures on the apostrophe of the French Renaissance philosopher Michel de Montaigne, attributed to Aristotle, "'O my friends, there is no friend.'" In its canonical interpretation, the apostrophe suggests that the friend is a scarce commodity, because there are so few men who can meet the demands of this kind of political commitment. This apostrophe was later challenged but ultimately—misogynistically—upheld by Immanuel Kant, Friedrich Nietzsche, Carl Schmitt, and Maurice Blanchot. Even when the idea of primary, masculine friendship is inverted, the fraternity concept is still privileged. The recurrent problem with the figure of the friend, in addition to *his* scarcity and elite status, is that the friend regularly appears as the brother, who "seems spontaneously to belong to a *familial, fraternalist* and thus *androcentric* configuration of politics."[63] Even further, democracy is seldom represented without the possibility of fraternization, as a process and method of securing political bonds. This spontaneity proves fraternity's status as the default, as it elevates and justifies the truth effects of male–male friendship.

The problem we come to in the age of democracy and the fraternal contract in the eighteenth century is one of numbers, emanating from Aristotelian and Ciceronian motifs. Only the rarefied bond between assigned male individuals (European, white, male, class privileged) mattered. The power derived from these friendships, and from the processes of fraternization, constitutes the rationale for rule by the few—a selective, meritocratic kind of care—which is carried over across time. A contradiction occurs when the liberal social contract arrives and yet the friendship bond remains masculine and built upon prestige and the desire to consolidate power among a small band of brothers. Regardless of sexual practices or queer readings of classical or Enlightenment thinkers, the relational problem recurs because of the binds of masculinity. Pederasty does not necessarily lead to a break with gender normativity, and while a queer reading of Montaigne is available, his exclusion of women and other racially and economically marginalized subjects from the bonds of friendship, the political basis of solidarity, is the crucial point of ignorance.

Within each philosopher's invocation of the apostrophe, Derrida discovers the instability that grounds this masculine bond, most notably through the binary oppositions of friendship/enmity and private/public life. Through these instabilities, he contends that these bonds are based on a deceit or an error in thought that has been passed on, with profound impacts on culture, politics, and the family. While in ancient times the homophilic version of patriarchy was organized around a very different logic, there are aspects within the processes of fraternization that endure, and fraternity as a concept has remained the political foundation. Politics as it is understood in the West would cease to exist without it. The inventions of gender, race, and homosexuality as normalizing devices only serve to multiply the number of outsiders that concretize and uphold the fraternity. An outsider may be included in this "fratriarchy," but inclusion may require neutralization, a forgetting that such outsiders can never be "docile examples for the concept of fraternity."[64]

Thinking masculinity and care together, friendship exclusive to brothers continues to be a primary structuring principle of patriarchal control. As feminist political scientist Carole Pateman writes in "The Fraternal Social Contract," civil society as we know it today is founded on the classic social contract theories of the seventeenth and eighteenth centuries. The legitimacy of the state in civil society, central to both socialism and nineteenth- and twentieth-century liberalism, is thoroughly grounded in patriarchal principles. For Pateman, fraternity persists as "the crucial bond integrating individual and community."[65] The word *bond* compels me to ask how masculinity connects individuals, how this bonding takes place, and through what means, considering that in the fraternity, the individual is defined by a patriarchal separation of the private, feminized sphere and the public, worldly sphere.

The fraternal contract did not depart from this form of friendship in some significant respects. When the sons killed the fathers (the monarchs), the power thus transferred guaranteed the sons access to women, as they still existed solely in the realm of nature and the domestic. Within a strict racial hierarchy, women are utterly determined by their biology and their capacity to give birth, while white men are gifted with phallic power. In chapter 1, "'She's a Pistol': Female Phallicism," I deconstruct the relentless phallus/penis equation and dispel the idea that phallogocentrism is an inevitability, a necessary aspect of American manhood. A theory of female phallicism offers the ways that the so-called ersatz penis, or "girl cock" of a trans woman or a dildo worn by a female-presenting cisgender woman fundamentally jams the symbolic signals of this equation, one that secures sexual and racialized morphologies. Performance artist Nao Bustamante uses a speaking, bedazzled dildo in her 2009 "filmformance" *Silver & Gold,* a tribute to the history and future of body art performance. Her filmformance suggests that racial and gendered boundaries can be crossed through female phallicism, which has relevance for transphobia and trans acceptance in feminist communities. Transphobia can be attributed in part to what I am calling *transphallomisogyny,* as I show through *The Crying Game* (1992).[66] However, trans feminist art and writing reconceptualize trans women's relationships to the phallic. Through female phallicism, I also discover the utility of unruly alliance as a response to the continual demand for submission to the logics of fraternity.

Masculinity in Transition extends Derrida's call for a shift away from the male friend—the brother—which must be so radical and thorough that it may not even be called "friendship" any longer. To counter normative masculinity, I reframe this exclusive understanding of care, generosity, and the social safety net. In doing so, I echo Derrida's belief that the age of urgency is upon us and that there must be a deeper understanding of how a particular structure of friendship within a minority of men, *always* a minority, has been consistently weaponized.[67]

I couple Derrida's insights with critiques of racial capitalism, a term that originated in South Africa in 1976 with the publication of a short paper titled *Foreign Investment and the Reproduction of Racial Capitalism in South Africa,* by Martin Legassick and David Hemson, two white South African Marxists affiliated with the African National Congress.[68] What they propose is not so much a theory of racial capitalism but a critique of the liberal idea that the flow of international capital could subvert the apartheid state and replace it with normative capitalism in a multiracial democracy.[69] Cedric J. Robinson adopts the phrase and develops a framework for conceptualizing a more general history of capitalism, one that would refute the idea that racism and heteropatriarchy operate alongside capitalism as mechanisms for oppressing subgroups and dividing the working class.[70] Instead, capitalism operates *through* an ideology of white supremacy. In both the Old and New Worlds, women lacked the opportunity for public life because they did not own property or control their own labor. Their supposed submissive nature provided a rationale for the denial of citizenship. However, as historian Eric Foner argues, while white women in U.S. history "occupied a position of subordinate citizenship, nonwhites were increasingly excluded from the imagined community altogether."[71] The country's economic growth depended on slavery, while territorial expansion relied on the dispossession of Native Americans and the conquest of Mexican lands.

Critiques of political fraternity and racial capitalism together create a powerful metanarrative of modern Western masculinity. For Robinson, capitalist democracy hovers like an aura "over our institutions of knowledge and power, suffusing inquiry and decision making with the counterfeit certainties of predestination."[72] Derrida makes a remarkably similar claim for the ways the philosophers' practice of verifying and citing one another's "truths," which constitutes the history of both humanization and fraternization, makes what is counterfeit seem both serious and true.[73] I recall here Snorton's use of the term *transversality* to describe the recovery of submerged relationalities, which "linger in the depths" and have effects even while remaining invisible.[74] Processes of fraternization and the logics of racial capitalism have a similar dual transversality in that they create systems of authorization and authority, lines of being and becoming that reinforce normative masculinity in ways so common as to be no longer remarkable—and no longer remarked upon in some anticritical circles.

Multiculturalism played a key role in instituting racial hierarchy. For the last two hundred years, the race sciences and the "subdisciplinary adjutants" (e.g., comparative politics) fixed taxonomies and so-called stable racial-historical and gender identities, all of which composed a "natural sociology of hierarchy."[75] Within Aristotelian constructions of sex differences, the colors of race—white, Black, yellow, red, and brown—were composed in a descending order of humanity, which justified unequal social privileges.[76] The "paradigm of multiculturalism" took on the appearance of a natural history. Particularly from the seventeenth through the eighteenth centuries, this so-called natural history of "mankind" and its "scrubbed-white mantras" extolled the virtues of rationality and the ancient Mediterranean, which deprived the Other of humanity.[77] And this natural history formed a complex weave with popular culture of all kinds, one that expands rather than contracts in our time as "a haunted, majestic presence of an enduring construction of plurality and difference."[78] Robinson insists that it is haunted today because it is no longer collectively contested, or because the voices of contest continue to be economically and politically disenfranchised.

Collective contestation is often disrupted by liberalism's granting of conditional access to power for some queer, trans, and racialized subjects. However, as the Covid-19 pandemic has shown, this access can be revoked during times of illness and crisis. In chapter 5, "'Skin of His Hand against the Skin of My Back': HIV/AIDS Self-Writing and Film of the 1980s and '90s," I revise and extend Michel Foucault's concept of "friendship as a way of life" through Derrida alongside insights from disability studies and the disability justice movement. HIV/AIDS self-writing and autoethnographic film feature practices of care within variable relational networks. At the height of the pandemic in the 1980s and early '90s, lovers and friends produced eulogies to the dying, often when they themselves were sick and without hope for their own futures. In short spans of time, lovers became caretakers, then undertakers, which led to the loss of an entire generation.

I revisit the film *Black Is . . . Black Ain't* by Marlon Riggs, who indicts Black paternalism and the assimilatory postures of some within the Black community who ostracized gay men, like himself, dying of AIDS.[79] He laid the groundwork for later critiques of the ruse of a postracial society in the United States. While visible signs of racial division certainly can be used to discredit government officials, the promise of overcoming racial divisions is deployed in the service of state violence, both at home and abroad. In response, Riggs creates filmic poetry, submerging viewers into the queer time of illness, visually testifying against the false promises of racial liberalism in the 1980s. While in the past racial oppression was overt and public, advocated by the administrative state in schools, housing, employment, health services, electoral politics, and more, in the post-civil-rights era, racism became steeped in the illusion of postracism. The freedom movement's achievements were reversed, but these rollbacks were dressed up as race projects, like the war on drugs, enabled by the media.[80] Global capital reproduces itself by manipulating racial, gender, and sexual difference toward the goal of accumulation. As Hong insists, the monikers "Asian American," "African American," and so on are now not only a basis for solidarity but also ways to identify and produce consumer markets or pools of exploitable labor.[81]

In Snorton's terms, interlocking forms of anti-Black and anti-trans hostility speak to the existence of a long history of "racialized gender denigration."[82] Snorton seeks to disrupt the idea that "race" and "gender" are fixed and knowable, in part by invoking "trans" as "movement with no clear origin and no point of arrival."[83] He then discovers how transness circulates within Blackness and how Blackness is also "transected" by practices of embodiment that coalesce around gender. The interconnections of race and gender in cultural forms, within a moment of Black and trans death, must be made visible, as the Covid-19 pandemic underscores the need for care as a method and framework for "inhabiting unlivable worlds."[84] *Masculinity in Transition* contributes to this understanding of how Blackness and transness coarticulate and coalesce into their current formations, while at the same time remaining, in Snorton's words, "irreconcilable and irreducible."[85] In *Black Is . . . Black Ain't,* Riggs embraces his femininity and queerness without shame, and in so doing rejects the racial marking and othering that occurred for enslaved boys and men through their Black mothers. By saying "yes" to the feminine within, Riggs conveys how those furthest from democratic polity, those denied participation (in this case, feminine, gay Black men), are the groups most likely to identify and execute a rupture in the ideologies of racial capitalism; those furthest from justice are in the best position to supply meanings of justice.

Some masculine subjects supply these meanings of justice from a marginalized historical position based on class, sexuality, and gender performance, which places the wages of whiteness out of reach without the refuge of the closet. More recent examples are the transgender poets in chapter 2, "'When I Was a Boy': Boi/Boyhood and the Unworking of Masculinity." These white artists resist the lures of liberalism through self-reflexive critiques of their own privilege. Inspired by Gloria Anzaldúa's use of the concept of *Nepantla,* these masculinities reject fascism and what Halberstam calls "unfettered masculinism—seductive, raw, and terrible; appropriative, dangerous, and antireproductive."[86] Contemporary trans and queer poetry becomes a location for the critical analysis of white, cisnormative boyhood and its condoned, sometimes even celebrated, violence. Beginning with the historical example of Emily Dickinson, I observe how trans poet Samuel Ace and nonbinary poet and performer Andrea Gibson refuse masculine habits of dominance developed in childhood. Trans and queer masculinity often function as alternatives for those who refuse the masculinity of their fathers or other abusive figures of authority. Ace no longer even wishes he had a normative boyhood, considering that Davy Crockett and the Lone Ranger would have been his primary role models. Gibson directly contests white, male hegemony by invoking political movements like Black Lives Matter and Standing Rock in their spoken word poetry, which they spontaneously craft with audience feedback. Gibson's nonbinary expressions of masculinity suggest a rerouting of the categorical definition of masculinity, an acceptance of its contradictions and seeming incompatibilities. This zone of undecidability requires risk, as one enters what Noble calls the "No-Man's Land" of gender, the "stretch of contestatory and discursively productive ground" that no one can venture into and "remain a coherently ontological and natural subject."[87]

These works reveal that racial hierarchy, constructed through masculine dominance, is unstable and ideologically fragile and subject to delegitimization by defectors, critics, opponents, and survivors.[88] Singh argues that race (and I add masculinity) as a regime of power reveals political weakness rather than strength, because it must constantly reassert itself and coerce compliance and solidarity among a widening circle of perpetrators. For Singh, it is crucial to toggle back and forth between historical and present-day racism. This does not mean that figures of historical racism "exhaust all possible meanings of U.S. nationalism" or that racial, colonial, or fascist genealogies do not contain fissures and contradictions. However, contemporary manifestations of U.S. power attach to the historical for the purposes of inventing new lethal human divisions. The failure to make these historical connections has in fact "placed the entire world in danger once again."[89]

In conjunction with denouncements of toxic masculinity in the United States, there has been much talk about the "new" fascism inaugurated by Donald Trump, whom many view as the apotheosis of toxic masculinity. This is an example of when a historical connection must be parsed out with more exactness and accuracy. The critiques of Donald Trump's fascist masculinism often elide the historical reality of American democracy, domestic racism(s), U.S. empire building, and warmongering. They tend to see Trump as an aberration rather than as a continuation. Post-2016, parallels have been drawn between Nazi Germany and the United States, but critics of racial capitalism warn that the current moment must be viewed as a more overt expression of fascisms bred at home. What Singh calls our "savage wars of peace," our indifference to torture (or even enthusiasm for torture), and indefinite detention supported by some U.S. officials and public intellectuals—all expressions of masculine dominance in one way or another—indicate that the fight is not one against new fascisms but rather against the reinvigorated unanimity of democracy and totalitarianism.[90]

Langston Hughes describes the many casualties of U.S. militarism as a sign of a fascism that was not imported from Europe but is rather specific to the United States and its history of racism and conquest.[91] However, as Robinson adds, the conceptual limits of fascism established by Western historians and social theorists propose its confinement to Europe between the First and Second World Wars, sometimes appearing in state regimes (in Germany, Italy, Spain, and Portugal) and elsewhere out of more or less mass movements (in Austria, Bulgaria, Croatia, Slovakia, Hungary, Romania, Poland, Finland, Norway, Denmark, Britain, Belgium, and France).[92] Defined through the above spatial and temporal boundaries, fascism is branded as "right-wing extremism," "neurotic authoritarianism," or "radical resistance to modernization."[93] Through the lens of the West as hero and savior of individual freedom (both materially and "spiritually"), the fascist "villain" is a charismatic leader who incites the antagonistic force of authoritarian mass movements. According to World War II logic, the men of bourgeois democracies must save the people from the misfortune of fascism and supply the remedy that will restore "freedom."[94] Within this reasoning, Trump's fascism, and that of the far right more broadly, infects the United States like a communicable disease—a strain of toxic masculinity from another time and place.

Those who suggest that Trump's fascism is new also forget that for non-Western peoples, *fascism* is an umbrella term that includes the old and new horrors of "militarism, imperialism, racialist authoritarianism, choreographed mob violence, millenarian crypto-Christian mysticism, and a nostalgic nationalism."[95] Fascism is actually a familiar modern social discipline, which, like Christianity, imperialism, and nationalism, allows for the attainment and preservation of power for elites. Fascism maintains an economic and sociocultural intimacy with colonialism and slavery. Black radical intellectuals who witnessed the rise of fascism in Europe in the 1930s knew that regardless of its origins, it had become a weapon for capitalists to destroy working-class movements.[96] Black American sociologist Oliver C. Cox even characterizes the fascist state as a capitalist state in the process of "degeneration."[97] Taken together, these critiques make clear that fascist masculinity is not inherent to any one nation or a fact of a particular culture or class but an outgrowth of racial capitalism.

The historical and present-day problem of reconciling free development and democratic consent with sustained military occupation and conflict is a problem of U.S. empire *and* fraternization. As a feminist project, *Masculinity in Transition* engages with the work of critics who view racial capitalism as operating through heterosexism. Hong applies women of color feminism and comparative race methodology to theorize "coalition through difference."[98] In chapter 3, "The 'Not (Quite) Yet' of a New Collectivity: Feminist Masculinity and the American Western," I make connections between Hong's work and Singh's elaborations on the so-called war on terror. Because of its generic consistency, and incredible longevity (beginning with the very advent of film), the Western becomes an ideal form for tracking the coeval development of masculinity and nation. Ironically, in an era of increasing gender stasis in Westerns during the war on terror, the 2016 limited series *Godless* and the ongoing HBO series *Westworld* propose alternatives to both masculine normativity and hierarchal forms of relationality.[99] I read these Westerns through the classical figure of Antigone and Judith Butler's *Antigone's Claim: Kinship between Life and Death* to assess what might have happened if Antigone had united with her sister instead of rejecting her.

These new Westerns take a horizontal approach to what Jessica Nydia Pabón-Colón calls feminist masculinity, furthering the messaging of feminist and antiracist movements.[100] *Godless* attends to the historical realities of the frontier and the pervasive economic hardship, disease, and racial violence. Sexual assault becomes a focal point amid the rise of hashtag movements, as well as transnational feminist solidarity. *Godless* captures the brutality of patriarchal control against a community of women left to fend for themselves after a mining accident kills off nearly all the men. The women take back the town from private mining interests and refute the idea that they are unfit for political autonomy and ownership of their bodies and labor. However, *Godless* also portrays the marginalization of Black people and Native Americans through substantive roles, calling attention to the brutal violence enacted against them—even by the white women themselves. In a very different redeployment of the genre, *Westworld* makes a metacommentary on the Western itself and its concealment of racial violence and male domination. Through combining the conventions of sci-fi and Western, the series reveals that the West has always been a kind of theme park for the game of Manifest Destiny. A postmodern stage set of a frontier town becomes a place for rich vacationers to act out their violent, sexual fantasies on AI hosts, who, through a programming glitch, awaken to their realities and begin to dismantle the picturesque scenery and its creators.

Westerns on streaming platforms also represent Blackness and transness as coconstructed. In *Godless*, a transmasculine character, an anomaly in this community, is represented and affirmed alongside a community of Black people, suggesting how the historical experiences of transness and Blackness resonate with one another and lead to potential unruly alliances. The show also demonstrates how the fields of trans studies and African diaspora studies find common ground through the historical disorientations of race and gender. Indigenous characters are no longer historical props in Westerns but rather fully evolved characters with substantive speaking roles in their own native languages. In *Westworld*, the history of the rape of Black women is encountered as that which is enacted and repressed for Manifest Destiny to fulfill its allegedly God-given mission of internal colonization.

Folding in the question of masculinity more directly, and what a transitioning away from these modes of being might look like, I insist that its deconstruction through trans and queer theory must respond to posttruth politicking and our fascist moment, which has attracted an aggrieved white majority. Masculinity must be deconstructed within the seductions of Trumpism, which for Singh includes "brutal, sadistic inversion of the inclusionary niceties of neoliberal diversity talk with a return to a casual banter of racial, gender, and sexual punishment: arrest for abortion, criminal prosecution for participating in Black Lives Matter, registration and surveillance for Muslims, torture for terrorists."[101] Trump is not an exception, just the most brutal incarnation to date, and he is perhaps even a Frankensteinian horror created by the war on terror itself.

Throughout the chapters that follow, I insist that culture is a central, not a peripheral, site of struggle. Rather, culture is where systems of meaning emerge and are contested within the contradictions of fraternization and global capitalism. Women of color feminist practice insists that culture has never been transcendent or disconnected from the material order.[102] As Hong writes, culture has been "fundamental to capital's reproduction, and thus to its crisis."[103] Peruvian sociologist and humanist thinker Aníbal Quijano uses the word *system* to describe how relations between parts and the totality are not arbitrary and how the latter has hegemony over the parts in the orientation of movement, not in a systematic sense, as this relation is never logically functional.[104] Such logical functioning only occurs in machines and organisms, not in social relations. Culture can be viewed similarly, as a system of meaning-making that is not a one-to-one reflection of the material world or a form of aesthetic escapism unrelated to social relations.

In this archive, recognition of a shared world occurs outside of the tangling briars and territorialism of exclusive masculine friendships between brothers. To represent the different constructs that are destabilized and challenged, the chapters are structured in three parts. In Part I, destabilizing the phallic supremacy of those assigned male at birth expands access to phallic pleasures and desires across embodiments. In Part II, trans and queer representations dismantle colonial conceptions of white androcentric nationalism. In Part III, trans and queer masculinities resist the pervasive masculine conceit of impenetrability, demonstrating how disease and economic marginalization create conditions in which this alleged virtue is not accessible or desirable. Unruly alliances, forged during times of crisis and stress, become examples for all relationality during future pandemics and epidemics, as well as economic crises, which are increasing in intensity, frequency, and speed. They show how current neoliberal economic practices and fraternization render some bodyminds expendable.

Rather than presenting a linear progression, I connect sometimes disparate historical moments wherein masculinities echo across time. *Masculinity in Transition* resists the temptation to read history, and masculinity, as a story of consistent improvement through social movements or theoretical developments. All gender and sexual expressions are constrained by their historical limitations, which speaks to the fortitude with which some subjects imagine gender otherwise, or due to race, sexuality, socioeconomic class, or ability are placed in situations that require different forms of relating and being.

In the Conclusion, I attend to a question that surfaces throughout: What does this book offer for all masculinities? One major insight is that normative masculinity, as a function of white supremacy and fraternity in the West, is fundamentally unstable, as it swings between the two poles of hegemony and crisis.[105] While masculinity generally parades as free not only of gender but of constraints in general, the reality is that masculine normativity produces debilitating anxiety over the need to remain in control. As Todd W. Reeser offers, "masculinity resembles capitalism, which also seems to be predicated on the idea of freedom—whether to earn as much money as one wants, to change class status through hard work, to buy what we want, or to select the product desired from among a large selection of products at the store."[106] Ultimately, the goal should be to envision *all* masculinities, and all genders for that matter, as malleable and subject to change, which helps avoid toxic traps, making it less likely that these traps will be built in the first place.

Movement, proliferation, and the unlocking of the qualities of human experience require new conceptions of both gender and relationality more broadly. There must be progress toward what Reeser describes as masculinity in a state of constant motion, for if masculinities "truly move on forever, changing and creating new possibilities, [one] cannot remain on top or in a position of domination. In a larger sense, notions of stable gender themselves, once this movement begins, break down and gender stasis is no longer possible."[107] He rightly advocates "no masculine being, but only a series of becomings."[108] In *Female Masculinity,* Halberstam similarly proposes that "because white male masculinity has obscured all other masculinities, we have to turn away from its construction to bring other *more mobile* forms of masculinity to light."[109] The vulnerability of normative masculinity lies in its constant need for reaffirmation, which can reappear across the categories of "queer" and "trans," as the shape-shifting of the "sensitive, new age guy" and the "goldilocks" trans man suggests. If masculinity can never be "at rest," it can never appear as the seamless, universal signifier in the way some masculine-identified people may desire.[110] The process of constructing and reaffirming masculine normativity has never been uncontested but is always rife with contradiction. It is within these contradictions, embedded in specific histories and political contexts, that opportunities arise for new relationships to masculinity and to one another.

Part I
Challenging Phallic Supremacy

Chapter 1

"She's a Pistol"

Female Phallicism

Consider the turn of phrase "she's a pistol," used condescendingly in the mid-twentieth century to refer to a woman who claims phallic power for herself. This analogy—among others—shows how much masculine normativity relies on the penis, perhaps more than any other aspect of embodiment. As masculinity studies scholar Todd W. Reeser puts it, "manhood" and "penis" are synonymous, as sex and gender are often collapsed together.[1] Many people hold tight to the belief that masculine dominance is based in so-called biology, refusing to see the ways it is constructed and reinforced through culture. Through the phallic, assigned male bodies reinforce their originary and precultural status. Film and television personalities—from Sylvester Stallone to Vin Diesel—present themselves as phallic bodies, always in total control, weaponizing able-bodied masculinity metaphorically.[2]

The penis makes the man, and this logic has been used to denigrate women who claim a female masculinity through the phallic. Any woman who thinks she can attain the phallic power of a man is branded as criminal, delusional, or just plain sick. Biological determinism may even help explain why dildos and penetrative sex between women are never represented in mainstream cultural production. Historically, men have acquired their confidence through ridiculing women's attempts to possess the phallus. As Lillian Faderman reports, from the sixteenth to the eighteenth centuries, male writers could not conceive of women's sexual pleasure without men and when it was visible, it was considered amoral.[3] Around this time, lesbians could be severely punished or even put to death if they were caught using a dildo.[4] However, while men in previous centuries enjoyed an unlimited "phallocentric confidence," competition from lesbians, gay men, and trans people beginning in the twentieth century placed limitations on this confidence.[5]

The politics and rhetorics of the penis/phallus equation convey anxiety rather than assurance. As psychoanalytic queer scholars and deconstructionists have argued for generations, the hegemony of normative masculinity requires the symbolic phallus, which the penis cannot approximate. The obsession with erectile dysfunction and how to cure it is one example of this failure to live up to this imagined phallus. Etymologically, an impotent man is one who has been stripped of power (*impotens* in Latin means "not powerful").[6] Impotence also implies a woundedness that is coded male, such as the heroic wounding inflicted during active military duty.[7]

It is not surprising, then, that chaos, dread, and fear ensue when the penis—or its proxy, the dildo—shows up where it supposedly really does not belong: on the body of a trans or cisgender woman who challenges the predictable power plays of masculine phallocentrism. One of the most significant ways that normative masculinity can be challenged is through what I am calling female phallicism, which is not a transfer of phallic power but rather a reconceptualization of the phallic as a domain of care, as well as creative and generative assertion. Female phallicism also departs from the term *phallic woman*, another slur against women who lack feminine softness and passivity and who threaten to expose the fragile structures of male authority.

Beyond its individual potentialities, then, female phallicism can give rise to forms of unruly alliance that deviate from male bonds secured through myths of control. Unruly alliances based on female phallicism also lack the reclamatory luster of those based on the "queer kinship" of the 1980s and '90s, a term that seems to automatically connote dignity, redemption, and appropriate pathos.[8] These unruly alliances based on female phallicism may have more in common with BDSM, Daddy play, and modern pederasty, which, in Kadji Amin's words, tests the "boundaries of the discourse of queer family."[9] Through an expansion of a politics of pleasure that has been sidelined in the era of queer liberalism, female phallicism dethrones masculine normativity as the true phallic power. To illustrate its potentials, I offer the performances of Nao Bustamante, a Latin@ performance artist who uses a bedazzled dildo to deconstruct binary categories of gender and race. This theory also can be applied to what I am calling transphallomisogyny, which is based on the false belief that trans women can never be invited into the category "woman." Female phallicism expresses an active desire for the arrival of the "not yet," a departure from programmed ways of relating and fucking, creating and being.

Toward a Theory of Female Phallicism

The assigned male body's exclusive right to the phallic is central to both the politics of fraternity and the neoliberal logics that ground normative masculinity. Phallocentrism makes it difficult, if not impossible, for those on the margins to harness the political and material potentialities—and pleasures—of the phallic. Here the term *phallocentrism* needs some specification as a historical construct promoted by cultural production, sometimes through sneaky reformulations of the same, tired themes. Exclusion, whether promoted by the far right in the so-called culture wars, or by trans-exclusionary radical feminists (TERFS), continues to be based in biology.

In Western philosophical history, the connection between phallocentrism and the male–male friendship ideal is enshrined in the concept of virile virtue, which centralizes the white dick. Virtue does not depend, in this case, on some ethical goodness, but rather it functions as an originary gift, providing a renewable benefit of the doubt. The fact that virtue is virile suggests that fraternization perpetuates itself through phallic dominance, in extreme cases turning sexual harassment and assault into a kind of excess of virtue rather than a crime. A crime against a woman and a crime against humanity (the community of "man") are not the same things, as the term *rights of women* remains a separate concept. Crimes against women exist in a distinct class, which obscures how these crimes are often the effects of white normative masculinity *as* virile virtue. Phallic power, then, must be universalized as a potentiality for all embodiments, gender identifications, and sexualities, but without its characteristic aggression and violence.

Male phallic supremacy and virile virtue rely on the distinction between the European body and the nonbody of the Other. In the Western philosophical canon, assigned female bodies become associated exclusively with biology, nature, and the domestic. Only men are capable of being unbound from the body, though, crucially, not from the penis as sign of virility—what makes virtue possible. In "The Coloniality of Power, Eurocentrism, and Latin America," Aníbal Quijano discusses this modern dualism and its close ties to race and gender, as well as to the Eurocentric mode of producing knowledge.[10] The bourgeois secularization of Christian thought, which began with the writings of Descartes, inaugurated a radical separation between reason/subject and the body. Within this schema, reason not only secularized the idea of the soul from the standpoint of theology but represented a mutation into a new entity—the reason/subject, the only entity capable of rational knowledge. The body became an object of knowledge, incapable of reason. Quasi-scientific theories of race originate in the objectification of the body as nature and its expulsion from the realm of the spirit.[11] Certain races, and particularly women of those certain races, become irrational objects of knowledge: "It was only within this peculiar perspective that non-European peoples were considered as an object of knowledge and domination/exploitation by Europeans virtually to the end of World War II."[12] These discourses established phallic exclusivity in the political and economic structures of the West and its relational patterns.

Fraternity determines that women are ill-prepared to assume the task of political responsibility and freedom. However, a simple reassignment of phallicism to outlaw masculinities, even those that are trans and queer, is insufficient for disrupting this inheritance. If new phallic possibilities are to emerge, there must be a collective refusal to submit to the logics of canonization that put these discourses in a position of authority. We must ask: What forces and procedures placed these canonical discourses into this position of authority in the first place?

In *The Politics of Friendship*, Jacques Derrida's main concern is to recognize the tensions, ruptures, and scansions (rhythms) within these "great philosophical and canonical discourses on friendship."[13] Relationality no longer based on fraternization would separate entirely from the economic, genealogical, ethnocentric, and androcentric features that ground phallic authority. Eighteenth-century revolutionary movements promised to extend fraternal friendship toward a "universal range" that theoretically challenged the limits of natural, literal, genetic, sexually determined (etc.) fraternity. However, the so-called revolutionary fraternity actually engaged in a hyperbolization of the fraternity concept, extending it "beyond all juridical, legislative, and political determinations of the law."[14] Caught up in hyperbolization, fraternity's promise of universalization has been provisionally given, and at the same time refused and denied, because no one can quite measure up to its standards. The phallus becomes a perfect symbol of this "falling short." True fraternity in the figurative sense is this universal, spiritual, symbolic, and infinite fraternity, which never comes to pass. This hyperbole is transported to friendship, into all of its "associated semantic values."[15] The "fratriarchy" spills into and affects all aspects of life, upheld by cultural production, influencing, and even determining, the most intimate of encounters.

The "exemplarist logic" that determines the "gift" of phallic supremacy is the strategy of all nationalisms, patriotisms, or ethnocentrisms.[16] While the Greco-Roman, Christian, and Revolutionary discourses on fraternity differ greatly, together they present "two major questions of 'deconstruction': the question of the history of concepts and (trivially) so-called 'textual' hegemony, history *tout court*; and the question of phallogocentrism. Here *qua* phratrocentrism."[17] Despite the differences in the epistemes, Derrida discovers a kind of grafting in the name of phallocentrism. In this exemplary universal fraternity grounded in the liberal social contract, a woman cannot replace a man, nor a sister a brother. A woman may know the world well enough, but she cannot quite grasp the concept "fraternity." Rather, "she reads [the word and concept *fraternity*] as one reads in nursery school, she reads it without reading it," or, in other words, she cannot access its spirit.[18] She misses out on its sacredness, and history, and therefore she has no access to this future that is promised in advance. While there has been hope for liberal inclusion in the social contract as it has been practiced in the twentieth and twenty-first centuries, such inclusion may very well mean neutralization. It may demand a kind of amnesia, a forgetting of the reality that such outsiders can never be docile examples of the concept of fraternity. They can never appear as themselves, for themselves, and they can never be politically mobilized. They appear, if at all, within the preestablished terms of the language of fraternity.

In psychoanalysis, we find similar justifications for male phallic dominance, similar nontruths becoming true. The notion of castration grounds the heteronormative, colonial epistemology of the body, such that outside of two sexes and two distinct kinds of bodies exists only pathology and disability.[19] As Paul B. Preciado observes, the dialectic of "having or not having a penis is presented as a dilemma between two mutually exclusive possibilities."[20] In Western societies, the heteronormative, colonial, and racialized epistemology of the body requires that "male" and "female" sexual morphologies, and their attendant parts, remain completely distinct. Jacques Lacan insists that this distinctness is what sustains the very structures of society and culture.[21] This separation is grounded in the idea that those assigned female at birth "are" the phallus (the Lacanian "privileged signifier" that allows access to power), while those assigned male "have" the phallus. The body of a trans woman with a penis is so threatening because it conjures both at the same time, the threat of castration (as a "woman" is the phallus) and masculine castration anxiety (resulting from the male fear of its loss). The normative sex/gender contradiction of a trans woman with a penis, or a femme-presenting cisgender woman with a dildo, threatens the fiction that one cannot both "be" and "have" the phallus at the same time.

However, in "The Lesbian Phallus and the Morphological Imaginary," Judith Butler argues that the phallus is both "transferable" and "substitutable"—these separate spheres of "having" and "being" a fabrication that benefits white, capitalist patriarchy.[22] Butler destabilizes the fusion of penis and phallus, claimed by both Freud and Lacan, by identifying how they fix the phallus and penis together through a series of denials, disavowals, and negations. The bodily ego for Freud, and the projective idealization of the body for Lacan, suggest that corporeal morphologies result in part from an externalized identification.[23] Consequently, the idealized phallus is subject to contradictions, and Butler's lesbian phallus intervenes as a consequence of this "transvaluative denial of its substitutability, dependency, diminutive size, limited control, [and] partiality."[24]

Yet, a trans woman's penis clearly does not fit into Butler's field of "body parts, discursive performatives, alternative fetishes" that can resignify the phallus. Butler does state that the phallus/penis equation becomes destabilized through "various and unanticipated anatomical (and non-anatomical)" phallic appearances and utilities.[25] However, by naming this theory the (implied cisgender) lesbian phallus, they suggest that any other body part will do—just not *that one*. Butler was limited by their historical moment, since in the 1990s, transgender theory had not been institutionalized in the academy, and trans people were much less visible as a community.

I propose a theory of female phallicism as an extension of Butler's lesbian phallus, a theory that reveals both the philosophical ruse of the penis/phallus equation and the multiple ways trans women re-signify the phallus in psychoanalytic terms. Not only do trans women have phallic power, but phallic power itself becomes feminized and transformed. Female phallicism also refuses the dangerous assumption that phallic power is always subversive and working against the equation of power and violence. Power needs to be reconceptualized as the power to create change, to invent using the imagination—and to assert without violence. Female phallicism furthers Butler's project of breaking down the constructed divisions between "body parts and wholes, anatomy and the imaginary, corporeality and the psyche."[26]

Transphallomisogyny, a form of misogyny based on the presence of the penis (real or imagined), confirms that the penis and phallus never fully separated. Instead, the penis becomes a weapon for further isolating and oppressing trans women. Some trans-exclusionary radical feminists may allow trans women to assume the spirit of womanhood, but their bodies prevent them from fully entering the category "woman." If you have a penis (or are still haunted by the corporeal memory of one), you cannot count as female. Biological determinism within a minority of radical feminist communities shows how the dissolving of gender categories, a long-standing aim of feminism, and the resignification or queering of the phallus all too often occur through the degradation and omission of trans women.

"The Lesbian Phallus and the Morphological Imaginary" performs crucial work by opening a space for queer phallic possibilities. However, phallic masculinity is conferred upon an assumed butch lesbian subject, which marginalizes other possibilities, including for cisgender femme phallic subjectivities. The butch phallus becomes the new norm, while other phalluses remain unnamed within an umbrella of possibilities that are yet to come. This repression of female phalluses parallels similar exclusions of trans women in the theory of gender performativity, as I explain later in this chapter. This repression opens the possibility that trans women and a range of female-identified persons will be accused of mimicry of hegemonic sex/gender relations.[27] There needs to be more explicit recognition of how the phallic lesbian could also be femme-presenting.

Jack Halberstam theorizes how the dildo can be viewed not as a phallic signifier but as a sexual object that destabilizes the originality of the penis. This allows for the bequeathal of masculinity on some subjects not assigned male at birth.[28] For Halberstam, the dildo renders transparent how phallic supremacy authenticates assigned masculine privilege.[29] Halberstam insists that dicks *are* dildos—or, in other words, the "real thing" *is* the simulacrum, to cite Jean Baudrillard's term—but by using the drag king as his prime example, he, too, assumes a transmasculine wearer. The trans man and the butch lesbian become the natural heirs to queer masculinity.

Female phallicism instead connotes the embodiment of both binary categories, male and female, and suggests a nondialectical negation, preventing the creation of a field of abject phallic subjects.[30] As noted earlier, the body of a trans or cis femme woman with a penis/phallus connotes simultaneously the threat of castration, which Butler observes is a way of "being the phallus" (as it is thought that women "are" the phallus), and the male fear of castration anxiety, which stems from "having the phallus" and fearing its loss.[31] However, when the phallus is attached to the body of a femme-presenting woman, such a perceived misplacement causes a collapse of "being" and "having," creating even greater friction within binary gender that secures sexual difference. "Being" and "having" are no longer dialectically opposed, as they are in the case of the phallic masculine lesbian and the trans man, who retain a critical distance from the feminine. One cannot both possess the phallus and represent its absence at the same time without compromising the integrity of masculine and feminine morphologies, which Lacan insists sustain language, the law of the father, the act of naming—our very place in society and culture.[32]

New mobile masculinities emerge from these ruptures and crises caused by female phallicism, highlighting the willfulness required to continue the ruse of virile virtue and distinct sexual morphologies, for through the misplaced phallus, the specter of sodomy and the pleasures/fears of the anus also return.[33] The phallus becomes a source of unruly alliance that is not *constituted* but *constituting*. The idea of movement is key, because part of the collective promise for the female phallus is that it does not stay stuck to masculinity as it is conventionally understood. Even further, masculinity in general becomes mobile rather than fixed. When the phallus begins to move with greater fluidity across a range of embodiment, gender identification, and sexuality, it becomes a source of generative play—and political possibility. By refusing to give in to interpellation in the first place, subjects refuse the process of naming and make room for an approach to the phallus that does not traffic in transphallomisogyny, or sexist, predetermined subjectivities (e.g., "virile virtue") for femme-presenting women. Female phallicism instead creates multidimensional, dialogic spaces for dismantling racialized, gendered, and sexualized hierarchies and ideologies.[34]

Nao Bustamante's Filmformance *Silver & Gold* (2009)

From blues artists to cabaret and variety actors, women have historically used female phallicism to disrupt racially constructed gender morphologies. As Reeser adds, such theatrical, cinematic, musical, and artistic performances have a reverberating effect, influencing communities of viewers far into the future.[35] Performers often use various phallic props and tools—such as dildos or dildo-like objects, like cigarettes—to symbolically demonstrate their ability to penetrate. They confirm the viability of a phallus that appears on a feminine-presenting body.

Nao Bustamante is a Los Angeles–based performance artist whose "filmformance" *Silver & Gold* provides a postmodern example of onstage phallic anarchy. Through a combination of projected film, live performance, and costuming, she invents a "magical and joyfully twisted exploration of race, glamour, sexuality, and the silver screen."[36] Through the phallic, she calls back to queer filmmaker Jack Smith and his muse, Dominican movie starlet Maria Montez. However, by forging a relationship with the dead Montez, Bustamante rejects nostalgic longing for white, masculine greatness achieved through fraternization and instead invokes the presence of a dead femme-presenting star, furthering Smith's critique of Hollywood's obsessive reproduction of the exotic. Bustamante endows herself and Montez with femme bravado, the symbol of which is not a pink pussy hat, an emblem of twenty-first-century hashtag movements, but rather a bedazzled dildo.

When Bustamante first appears onstage, she is cloaked in black and hidden from the audience, standing near a black, boxlike podium. On the film projected behind her, she tends a bed of lilacs with forbidding hedge trimmers to the soundtrack of European classical music. This potentially lethal garden tool in the hands of a femme-presenting Latin@ symbolizes how women "are" the phallus and represent the threat of its removal, while by contrast men "have" the phallus. Wearing a white (virginal) dress, she reclines in this bed of lilacs, establishing for the audience a predictable set of gendered expectations. However, as she walks in a dream state across an empty field, the camera registers her body disappearing. When the camera comes close again, gender categories begin to collide. She performs ballet in the woods, then suddenly dons a beekeeper's costume. By exclaiming histrionically, "¡Ay, Dios mío!" she also suggests that racial categories are simultaneously threatened.

Bustamante then discovers a mannequin head hanging from a tree, wearing a yellow mustached hat, which signals that we are entering a space beyond binary categories, where the prosthetic and the supposedly real will become indistinguishable. The mannequin head, attached to a stick body wearing a sequined dress, becomes her waltz partner, but the tempo accelerates, conjuring the dance of the red shoes and the hysterical "too muchness" of the Latin@ body. Bustamante then discovers that she has become the figure, while the actual figure is reduced to sticks and a head of lilacs. In a critical turning point, she announces to the figure that this is her "realm." She laughs manically as though possessed, announcing to the birds overhead and to a duck decoy in her arms that "this is my real life."[37]

To her shock and horror, she looks down and discovers an erect "penis" protruding from beneath the sequined dress. At first, she tries to deny its existence by calling it both her "curse" and her "oracle," but she realizes she is overpowered when a swarm of penises attacks her, causing her to collapse to the ground and lose consciousness, to the tune of "La Estrellita." However, she wakes up and finds that the phallus—now pink, bejeweled, and femme—inspires not revulsion and fear but desire and identification. She strokes the tiny glitter face and croons, "You're a part of me. I could never get rid of you." She tells the anthropomorphized dildo, "You are so beautiful," and the dildo responds, "Why yes, I am quite handsome, aren't I?" The dildo's masculine voice of authority might have sprung spontaneously from this series of actions, or perhaps it has been part of her all along.

Theatrical excesses—signs of glamour and wealth, including ballet slippers, golden sandals, and sequined dresses—suggest the difference between Butler's thesis on gender performativity, and the process of reiteration, and stagings of gender that are contained or intentional.[38] Through creative practices, which invite a communal response from the audience, stagings of gender bring forward the absurdity of male phallic dominance, virile virtue, and colonial control in ways that scholarly references to gender performativity cannot. Bustamante is part of a resurgence in body art, performance art, and live art since the early twenty-first century, which overflows with what queer theorist Juana María Rodríguez calls a utopian and embodied "stream of gestures" through which people strive for social and political connection.[39] These artists resist both the hierarchies that separate art from "real life" and the hierarchical, neoliberal demands of the art market, which predominantly benefits men.[40] These artists view the body as a "thinking subject," infused with memories, emotions, and a visceral sense of moving through time.[41] As performance critic Amelia Jones writes:

> The return to the live via complex modes of re-enactment, re-staging, reiteration, might be seen to be sparked by (and eliciting of) openness and hope, by way of presenting new possibilities of intervention and by activating fresh ways of thinking, making, being in the world.[42]

While it is unclear how this resurgence connects to any particular historical development, Jones posits that such performances express the instability of our times, which opens the way for unruly alliance, as what is broken can be remade anew. These performances convey insecurity (or, I would add, vulnerability) as a source of power, discovered through an acknowledgment of uncertainty, of "we know nothing"—derailing the egotism and certainty of phallocentrism.[43]

By choosing to stage this phallic reclamation in nature, Bustamante also refuses the belief that "nature" is a "she" who bestows friendship on equal brothers, while the purpose of women is to enable the attainment of virile virtue. By accessing a female phallic power found in nature, she delegitimizes the mind/body split that grounds fraternity. Behind the scenes, she develops unruly alliances with her assistants and friends, exceeding the kinds of bonds that keep colonial gender and racial hierarchies in place. She approaches her pieces with "the enthusiasm of an amateur," negating the concept of artistic genius that frames canonical masculine friendships.[44] In a highly collaborative and spontaneous creative environment, she relies heavily on improvisation over the conceit of "rehearsal."[45] She collaborates with others to create anthropomorphized props, like the dildo, which are embodied forms of utopian political action.[46] In conversation with Rodríguez, Bustamante counters Leo Bersani's antisocial impetus with the "queer articulation of utopia that is always on the horizon and decidedly committed to futurity."[47]

Bustamante's performance art occurs in the context of the global capital phase marked by "flexibility" or "flexible accumulation" based on the hyperextraction of profit through varied strategies.[48] In this period, Fordist modes of production existed alongside "nonmodern" modes—patriarchal, artisanal, semilegal, illegal (including sweatshops and home-based work).[49] Differentiation and diversification are common accumulation strategies for transnational capital, which exploits the labor of very young, racialized women as a preferred workforce.[50] Corporations reproduce racialized and gendered difference toward the goal of ever-increasing efficiency. However, Grace Kyungwon Hong argues that such logic determines not just economic accumulation strategies but all practices of late twentieth- and twenty-first-century capital.[51] At the same time, capital attempts to install new forms of universality based on consumerism and commodification. Unlike Fredric Jameson or David Harvey, who believe that consumerism is a totalizing process that completely commodifies all culture—becoming what they call "postmodern"—Hong insists that culture is also a site of contestation and crisis.[52] Culture is a material force rather than a transcendent, aestheticized domain, and it constitutes social relations rather than simply reflecting them.[53] In conversation with Hong's work, Bustamante's *Silver & Gold* shows how normative phallicisms are both contested and affirmed within the contradictory formations of global capital. Culture also contributes to a discourse of resistance against the exploitation of young, racialized women, who lack any kind of ownership over their own bodies and labor. Her work could be categorized, in Guy Debord's terms, as a spectacular allegory of how capital reproduces excessive desires that it cannot contain or resolve, sometimes in ways that paradoxically oppose consumer culture and implied phallic supremacy.[54]

Bustamante seizes this imaginative function of culture through pastiche as a form of protest. Pastiche is often understood as part of racial capitalism because it is a random, ahistorical recycling of past styles and a manifestation of the United States as flexible and differentiated—simultaneously nationalist and extranationalist, and capable of taking and using whatever it wants, from whatever period.[55] Bustamante critiques this ahistorical use of pastiche by calling attention to inequities and what Hong describes as the failure of capital to produce total global commodification in Jameson's terms.[56] Minoritized cultures are not entirely subsumed by the cultural dominant of postmodernism, but they are also not completely autonomous either. Bustamante refuses both what Hong refers to as the economic determinism of political economy that reduces everything to an epiphenomenon of capitalism (there is no way out) and the ahistorical, nonmaterialist understanding of difference that characterizes postmodernism.[57]

Within this critical practice of pastiche, she uses comedy to embrace amateurishness and imperfection. A childlike Bustamante creates her own world, which she calls her "realm." As Mel Watkins, Bambi Haggins, and others argue, when comedy occurs in the guise of the child, the woman of color performer actually expresses power over the "adult"—in this case, the colonizer—as a form of subterfuge.[58] This is what Haggins calls "laughing mad" as a "liberatory act."[59] One of the funniest and most disturbing scenes occurs when Bustamante is chased by the swarm of penises of different sizes and colors, graphically depicted in photographic realism, which are at first tiny but become increasingly menacing, demanding her submission (Figure 1). Anticipating *Silver & Gold,* in the hysterical 1992 piece *Indigurrito,* she straps a burrito onto a harness and, with a mock sanctity reminiscent of a religious ritual, asks the assigned male members of the audience to kneel on the stage and atone for the sins of colonialism by taking a bite of the burrito.[60] In all of her work, she pokes fun at female beauty rituals—for example, high heels, which she replaces with oranges.[61] In her 1995 piece *America, the Beautiful,* Bustamante covers her entire body with tape, which makes her appear sculpted. As Rodríguez contends, in queer Latin@ contexts, while the category "woman" can be monolithic and exclusive, "the feminine, the female, and the femme" are "shifting shadows."[62] "Woman" as monolith has been critiqued in transgender and intersex scholarship, but the term still moves like a specter through accounts of femme subjectivity and sexuality. Recalling the idea of "femme" as shadow category that is often invisible, in *America, the Beautiful* Bustamante performs a shadow play in which she conveys the darkness and irony in this patriotic song and its subtle and overt denigration of the feminine writ large.[63]

Bustamante does not just resignify the phallus but, through a series of fragments and flashes, blurs the binary relationship of being and having the phallus.[64] She implies that though the penis/phallus equation takes on the appearance of facticity, parading as the "real," it has always been counterfeit. However, even the dildo fails to occupy a superior relationship to the other materials in the filmformance. She thinks of both as "props" and "gestures" the way a sculptor may think of their clay, plastic, or carpet. In her decolonized approach to art and phallicism, she erects "no hierarchies—not of materials, not of mediums, not of art as it sits in relation to the world."[65] There is no one authentic or true phallic presence, but rather, in the spirit of Cindy Sherman's self-portraits or Matthew Barney's *Cremaster* films, "the space of the document (whether visual or audiovisual) . . . becomes the only space in which the performance occurs."[66] She turns away from the Kantian ideal of aesthetics, and the philosophical conceit of an "absolute Idea," derived from divine origins.[67] Gone is the distinction between "performance" and "document," one normally proceeding the other in an ontological relationship.[68] This lack of distinction makes the "event"—both the theatrical performance and its documentation—open to a number of audiences, with no exact relationship between signifier and signified.[69]

It is also uncertain whether the phallus is part of her body or if it is a dildo that has become enigmatically attached. Through this uncertainty, she suggests that the phallus is never fully attainable or attached in the first place, and therefore all men simultaneously experience penis envy *and* castration anxiety.[70] Bustamante alters and extends the radical proliferation of "synthetic" forms of desire and pleasure, explored by Paul B. Preciado.[71] In *Countersexual Manifesto*, the dildo reconfigures the erotogenic boundaries of the fucking/fucked body, questioning how the limits of the flesh correspond to the limits of the body.[72] Like other technologies of sex relegated to the "unnatural," and unspeakable, the dildo lurks at the outer limits of racist, male-dominated capitalist systems.[73] By virtue of its detachability, universality, adaptivity (for anus, vagina, mouth), and es-

FIGURE 1. Bustamante uses comedy to highlight the absurdity of assigned male phallic supremacy and the resulting violence. Nao Bustamante, *Silver & Gold,* 2009. http://naobustamante.com/archive/silver-gold/.

trangement from heteronormative sex, the dildo symbolizes a kind of diasporic "dispossession and nomadism."[74] Claiming the dildo allows Bustamante to also claim the privilege of mobility. Her self-described "new body part" does not just approximate the phallus but exceeds it by becoming a speaking subject, distinctly feminine in appearance.[75] Her adoration of the body part suggests that it is not mere entertainment, or surface, but a being capable of penetrating toward more profound cultural terrain. Its erectness makes it doubly threatening, as it calls into question the self-authenticating presence of the erect penis (the same thing occurs when the flaccid penis, the clitoris, the vagina, or the anus appear on the scene).[76] Bustamante produces the culturally disorienting effect of a woman waking up with a talking hard-on.[77]

At the same time, Bustamante undermines the colonizer's ability to take command within the "culture, rationality, and progress" impulse of scientific-medical discourses.[78] If it is a dildo, then it is a movable object "fixed on to flesh," which can be untied, separated, and reattached; as a result, the dildo allows us to "decolonize and rehabilitate the fetish as the cultural technology that enables fabrication of any sexual body."[79] If sexuality itself is fabricated, regardless of the synthetic or nonsynthetic nature of the sex, then assigned male power loses its force and meaning.

That soundtrack of tribal drumming that accompanies the swarm evokes the predatory nature of race and sex categorization. Bustamante performs many different kinds of "translations," which mobilize queerness as what Héctor Domínguez-Ruvalcaba calls an "instrument of decolonization."[80] Bustamante's female phallicism becomes part of a queer Latin American diaspora articulating a "complex intersectionality" through which the phallic connects to economics, religion, legal systems, race, class, nation, and politics.[81] When she tries to run away from the mostly white penises, their attacks only intensify, which symbolizes the reach of their power. In another reference to colonialism and racial difference, the classical music with which the piece began changes to salsa, and her sounds become chant-like. Like a femme Latin@ Dorothy from *The Wizard of Oz* who falls asleep in the field of poppies, she awakens not to the lion, tin man, and scarecrow but to the bedazzled dildo (Figure 2). The comedic dislocation from so-called reality suggests the ways that some trans and queer masculinities cannot be "translated into a rational logic of the culture and gender system," but rather remain estranged from it (14).

Bustamante causes a gestural jamming of gendered cues and signals that escape the entire logic of sex/gender, race, and nation and propose a space beyond, paradoxically by conjuring the stereotyped, hypersexed, "too muchness" of the Latin@ body. As Rodríguez argues, Latina performances of gender and sexuality already "arouse discomfort" and signal a "surplus" that is inappropriate for everyday contexts:

> Our bodies dispatch sweeping flourishes or hold back wilted rests. We swish too much and speak too loudly. The scents we exude disturb the numbing monotony of straight middle-class whiteness. . . . Our racialized excess is already read as queer, outside norms of what is useful or productive.[82]

Bustamante accentuates these daily "colorful extravagances," revealing the racial and sexual contradictions present in the fetish. Her "new body part" does not so much become what Butler describes as an "alternative fetish," resulting from the "transferable, substitutable, and plastic" nature of the phallus, but rather she questions what the term *fetish* means to begin with.[83]

For performance theorist Anne Anlin Cheng, the racial fetish "de-

FIGURE 2. Bustamante loses consciousness after her battle with the penises, but she wakes up to a bedazzled dildo attached to her body, which she kisses and croons over. Nao Bustamante, *Silver & Gold,* 2009. http://naobustamante.com/archive/silver-gold/.

files instead of clarifies" dichotomies, because it unleashes cycles of identification and disidentification, blurring the lines between self and other.[84] Bustamante introduces "the crisis of meaning in the fetish *and* in the cross-cultural exchange between European whiteness and the 'other.'"[85] An epistemological crisis ensues—a crisis over how we know what we claim to know.[86] When a femme subject possesses a phallus, eliciting the lust of the white imperialist, who secretly hungers for this femme dick, a profoundly queer disturbance results.[87] Bustamante's sexual identity also cannot be established, especially when the dildo/penis is attached to her femme-presenting body and aesthetic: glittery dresses, ballet slippers, the fashion mannequin idol, glamorous makeup.[88] Bustamante draws on the multiple queer desires of her audience, which can become the basis for unruly alliance.

In the final scenes of the film, Bustamante ushers in the "not yet," the time of possibility and of the unknown, which is also the time of unruly alliance. She connects to the mysteries and enchantments of the female phallus. The film ends with Bustamante emerging from the black cloak in the same sequined dress and mustache hat. A male voice announces that the film company that produced Maria Montez's films will bring her body back (literally dig her up) through some bizarre means. A Black woman wearing a glittery gold belt joins Bustamante in a hypnotic, ritualized dance as Montez's body is resurrected. This suggests that the "not yet" must be actively sought—the past and its symbols harnessed for liberation rather than for more egotism and control. This living dildo becomes a way to show that the feminine is not incompatible with the phallic, nor is it solely bound up with stereotypes of selfless care and giving. Like other women of color performers before her, she uses this potent icon of normative masculinity to discover empowerment and freedom from racial/colonial constraints and from the ritualized maintenance of white male hegemony.

Toward a Trans Theory of Female Phallicism

The film industry has used transgender women with shocking frequency to support the supremacy of the assigned male phallus. In this section, I will explore some of the harmful ways that film has abetted the larger cultural and political project of disqualifying trans women. By contrast, theory and cultural production outside of the Hollywood culture machine have acted as witnesses and antidotes to this transphallomisogyny.

The 2020 Netflix documentary *Disclosure* gives viewers a primer on transphobia in film, briefly revisiting that nadir of 1990s transmisogyny and racism, the British film *The Crying Game* (1992).[89] While I am highly critical of *Disclosure*'s optimism about the transformative potential of mainstream representation, I was grateful for its renewed attention to *The Crying Game*'s viral, cross-Atlantic, transphallomisogyny. Thanks to *Disclosure,* the scene in which Fergus (Stephen Rea) pushes his girlfriend to the ground after discovering her penis—then vomits into a bathroom sink—comes once again into the foreground. As GLAAD director of trans media and representation Nick Adams offers in *Disclosure,* the film caused a ripple effect of men vomiting in response to the penis of a trans woman, similar to the ripple effect of cross-dressing psychopathic serial killers inspired by *Psycho* (1960). This trope of vomiting men was repeated in *Ace Ventura: Pet Detective* (1994), *Family Guy* (2010), and *The Hangover: Part II* (2011), normalizing this comedic gag reflex for generations. *The Crying Game* was also shortly followed by David Cronenberg's

M. Butterfly (1993), based on David Henry Hwang's play, in which a married heterosexual man (Gallimard) falls in love with a trans woman who has a penis.[90] As a result of this supposedly monstrous hybridity, Gallimard kills himself in shame in the final scene of the film. Vomiting could also be seen as a loss of bodily control, a failure of masculinity—a direct result of the collapse of the morphological distinction between gender and race categories. If language, the law of the father, the act of naming itself, relies on keeping these sexual morphologies separate, then the male character's phallic status must falter in this moment.

Female phallicism helps to illuminate what we are witnessing in *The Crying Game* and what the stakes are of Dil's Black, transfeminine body. When Dil (Jaye Davidson) is assaulted by Fergus, it becomes clear that the distinction between anti-Blackness and anti-transness is porous. In C. Riley Snorton's words, "antitrans violence is also and always already an articulation of antiblackness."[91] It is not just Fergus's reaction that is troubling, however, but also how Dil's penis becomes a structuring device, up to and including the moment of "disclosure." From the beginning, the film's viewers are encouraged to assume the gaze of Fergus, a member of the IRA who develops an unexpected friendship with Jody (Forest Whitaker), one of the organization's Black kidnapped victims. Jody makes a last request of Fergus: to seek out his girlfriend, Dil, a hairdresser in London, and to take care of her in his absence. First, the film encourages sympathy for, and identification with, Fergus as a character because his conscience will not allow him to murder Jody. Second, Fergus not only finds Dil but also gives up his life of crime to become what sociologist Miriam J. Abelson calls the irresistible goldilocks man, neither too soft nor too hard. This construct can be used to incorporate palatable standards of masculinity within neoliberal politics and to respond to (but not significantly engage with) social movements.[92] The goldilocks man is prone to placing blame on others, eliding the reality of his own power. His "goodness" is also reinforced through the character of Dave, Dil's boyfriend who physically and verbally assaults her when she refuses his advances after meeting Fergus. In an alley scene when Dave is about to strike Dil, Fergus intervenes and beats him to the ground, showing he is not too soft to take violent action when necessary. Dave is clearly the villainous foil, the "bad guy" to Fergus's "good guy." Depictions of masculinity that strike this balance are deceptive because they encourage the false premise that normative masculinity already has been revised or reformed.

Dil is famous for her rendition of the Boy George classic "The Crying Game," and she quickly becomes his love interest. By the time Fergus vomits in the bathroom sink, viewers have already been seduced into believing that he is the "good guy" (Figure 3). Furthering his image, Fergus decides to pursue Dil despite the fact that she is a trans woman. Dil reinforces Fergus's professed innate goodness when she tries to make up after the incident. She rationalizes his behavior by telling him submissively that "even when you were throwing up, I could tell you cared."

While we do not see Dil's penis again for the rest of the film, it looms as a darker evil than any IRA murder or kidnapping. Her status as the racialized abomination, true trickster, and murderer crystallizes after Fergus confesses that he played a role in Jody's death. Dil ties Fergus to the bed and threatens to kill him with his own pistol if he does not promise to love her and never leave her. Dil, now in possession of the gun as phallic substitute, poses a direct threat to all men, even to supposedly good men like Fergus. This plot twist recalls the title of this chapter: "she's a pistol"—a denigrating term that can be applied to trans women who are deemed crazy, out of control, and lethal, in this case because of both their race and gender assigned at birth. Her penis becomes a weapon against the very integrity of culture, politics, the family, and the nation, a crime Fergus later pays the price for by going to prison, supposedly on her behalf. Dil does not realize that Fergus would have gone to jail anyway for his role in the terrorist organization, and she accepts that it is because of Fergus's chivalry, not her own escape from the scene, that she avoids prison. When she visits him in prison at the end of the film, Fergus's own abuse of Dil is exonerated, and Dil assumes the role of a caretaker who makes sure he is taking his vitamins and staying healthy.

Dil's role in the film can also be theorized through the experience of Christine Jorgensen, who became famous as the first trans woman to receive gender affirmation surgery in Denmark in the early 1950s. Her story appeared on December 1, 1952, on the front page of the *New York Daily News* with the headline "Ex-GI Becomes Blonde Beauty." For Snorton, Jorgensen dramatized "the pervasive unease felt in some quarters that American manhood, already under siege,

FIGURE 3. Through the gesture of giving flowers, *The Crying Game* creates the impression that Fergus is a "good guy," despite the violence he later commits against Dil. *The Crying Game,* directed by Neil Jordan, featuring Jaye Davidson and Stephen Rea (1992; Los Angeles: Miramax, 2013), DVD.

could literally be undone and refashioned into its seeming opposite through the power of modern science."[93] She became an example of personal triumph and individual freedom at a time when the United States expanded its interventionist Cold War ideology and when decolonial struggles proliferated around the world.[94] Transgender historian Emily Skidmore writes on how Jorgensen created an image of a "good transsexual" by removing through heteronormativity the "sex deviant" perception and laying claim to a white celebrity status that gave her a personal freedom at the expense of supposedly bad transsexuals.[95] As Snorton conveys, the "freedom" of white, wealthy trans women could only be realized against the "unfreedom" of Black and trans bodies, who could never transgress the racial logics of Jim Crow domestically or imperialist and military interventions abroad.[96] By contrast, Black trans women of the 1950s were shadows and obstructions that made possible Jorgensen's teleological, medicalized transsexuality a form of freedom.[97] Similarly, Dil becomes, in Snorton's terms, a "countermythology" and a way to read "the imbrications of race and gender as indexes of power's circulation."[98] The "revelation" of her penis (and its immediate suppression) shows how erasure can occur through "persistent and animating presence."[99]

The Crying Game captures the essence of transphallomisogyny, one symptom of which is the violent, sickening reaction to the Black trans penis, either present or imagined, not as a singular moment but as an ongoing, buzzing anxiety. The naturalization of this panic and dread—and the ensuing semantic lockdown, gridlock, and pandemonium—is not a single plot point but a pervasive haunting. Culture and politics that encourage transphallomisogyny play a role in the ongoing cycles of poverty and violence experienced by trans women of color.

Neither Butler's theory of gender performativity nor the concept of the lesbian phallus takes into account trans women and these material realities, including their phallicisms. According to Viviane K. Namaste, queer theorists have rarely considered the implications of an enforced sex/gender system, and they often elide the social and institutional operations that produce subjects.[100] Namaste argues that Butler uses the examples of nonnormative trans "others" as "spectacles" that allow normative gays and lesbians to perceive themselves as "natural."[101] She calls out the various "stagings" of transsexual and transgender embodiment, which turn people into fictionalized objects:

> While Butler reads drag as a means of exposing the contingent nature of gender and identity, I suggest that we point to the essential paradox of drag within gay male communities: at the precise moment that it underlines the constructed nature of gendered performance, drag is contained as a performance in itself. Gay male identity, in contrast, establishes itself as something prior to performance.[102]

The centralizing of the drag queen has three consequences: it can be used against transsexuals, it forces separation of drag queens from transsexuals (which is not true in reality), and it prevents the creation of broad-based trans politics.[103] Queer theory has tended to use *transgender* as an abstraction, in trans poet Joy Ladin's words, "for theoretical purposes as a signifier of human possibility rather than lived lives."[104]

Radical lesbian feminists also need to come to terms with essentialist tendencies that emerge most virulently in response to trans women. In this respect, they are in alignment with Western philosophy's obsession with the penis as a sign of power and as a determining factor in establishing sexual and racial difference. The obvious touchstone is Janice G. Raymond's *The Transsexual Empire: The Making of the She-Male*, in which she argues that male-to-female transsexuals were, in Jay Prosser's words, "agents of a medical empire sent out to colonize women's community and somatic home: not natives to an originary femaleness but latecomers, aliens and thus not bona fide women."[105] Overall, feminism has become more trans inclusive in the 2020s, and yet the field continues to harbor some implicit bias against trans women in particular. As literary scholar Bobby Noble adds, feminists could choose to embrace, for their own benefit if nothing else, the indeterminacy of "gender, sexuality, embodiment, class, race, nation, and ethnicity."[106] These constructs are historically specific "passionate fictions" bound up with the equally messy concepts of "the social, the subject, constructions of power, the mind, the soul, the body, capitalism, and economics, etc."[107] Instead of insisting on a "fixed and ahistorical essence of gender," which contributes to the project of normative masculinity, there needs to be increased resistance to any kind of politics based on the supposed self-evidence of the body.[108] By shedding the clear-cut definitions that often motivate feminist politics, the terms of the exclusion/inclusion debate would lose their efficacy. This shedding would lead to what Namaste calls "the conception and implementation of a feminist program committed to social change, one that takes seriously the lives and realities of poor people."[109]

If indeed the phallus is not the penis, then it follows that the penis does not have to be the phallus, or put another way, phallic power could shift to become a transfeminine power. In a photograph of Tala Candra Brandeis called *Biology Is Not Destiny* from the collection *Our Vision, Our Voices: Transsexual Portraits and "Nudes,"* Loren Cameron chooses a bold depiction of what might be called a "girly penis" or "girl cock."[110] Tala sits cross-legged on soft fabric, her penis lying on a diagonal against her right ankle. By resting her right arm against her right knee, and extending her left arm outward, she invites the viewer to enter this scene of femme softness and vulnerability, even while her tattoo sleeves suggest toughness and bravado. Ringed fingers and arms covered with bracelets also offer a gendered mash-up of femmeness. She tilts her head to the left, as though to proposition the viewer, her long hair falling loosely over her left arm. In this photograph, Cameron resists the demand that trans women reject their penises to appear more traditionally feminine. This provocative photograph causes a profound crisis of categorization, similar, though with different stakes and consequences, to Bustamante's performances.

In reality, trans women have a range of relationships to their penises and to their own phallic potential. While I am in no way suggesting that the white trans women's experience should be centralized, as this would perpetuate the kinds of transmisogynoir that we see in *The Crying Game*, Julia Serano's *Whipping Girl* expands the conversation. Serano discusses her own penis as a fundamentally changed body part after transition, which compels her to plead with the minority of feminists who embrace a polarizing biological determinism: "Those who patrol the gates of women-only spaces are often dead set on discriminating against me, driven by the ridiculous belief that my girly little estrogenized penis is somehow still pulsating with hypermasculine energy."[111] Serano urges us toward a female phallicism that is more ample, heterogeneous, and creatively inspired. Trans women who have gender affirmation surgery can also harness phallic transferability through a dildo. However, neither needs to be designated as the "original" or the "simulacrum." Through female phallicism, the dildo becomes a political and artistic tool that disrupts the policed borders of racial and sexual difference.

Trans women may also discover new forms of transmasculinity or butchness. These potentialities extend beyond Halberstam's *Female Masculinity* by emphasizing the *female* in the title and by questioning what we might mean by *masculinity*. Or maybe the penis can be reimagined as dildo, or the dildo can be reimagined as penis. The point here is that the crucial task of separating penis from phallus cannot occur through the omission of trans women, which continues to occur because of the fetishization of the fleshly penis as the ultimate symbol of American manhood.

Ultimately, any policing of sex/gender borders goes against a politics of mutual aid, which requires untethering from fraternity as the structuring principle of politics, culture, and the family. A theory of female phallicism can further the perhaps naive goal that everyone, regardless of their gender or sexual identity, can love their bodies and have positive experiences with them, for the short time we have them. Most trans and queer folks have encountered varying degrees of adversity in embracing their bodies and pleasures. Everyone should be encouraged to live fuller, more embodied lives, even if their bodies do not match society's categorizations. The main motivating factor for creating any kind of new gender theory should be the desire for better life chances and less exposure to death for the most marginalized. There is reason to be hopeful. Trans theorist and activist Dean Spade believes we are in the process of inventing "new capacities for caring for one another," which are reflected in movement work.[112] He sees a world in which new relations to ourselves and others are emerging alongside worsening material conditions that threaten life on every level.[113]

Despite *Disclosure*'s optimism, visibility and increased representation are not the answer. Following the publication of the edited collection *Trap Door: Trans Cultural Production and the Politics of Visibility*, radical academics, cultural critics, and producers have expressed deep distrust of the new panopticon of trans visibility.[114] *Disclosure* ultimately defaults to the idea that "it is better than it was," which denies the reality of what micha cárdenas calls the "modulation of visibility" required for passing, which places the power in the hands of the viewer, who then decides whether the trans person fits into the category "male" or "female."[115] Similarly, women of color feminist practice views "visibility" as a potential "rupture, an impossible articulation."[116] Visibility might not be inclusion after all, but a new form of surveillance and management, of control over a subject position, results in violence by the state or local nonstate actors. The echo effect of the gag response certainly suggests this is so.

More radical conceptions of phallic power must be part of this transformative change. The eradication of transphallomisogyny requires not a positive restoration of trans women to the Hollywood screen, or a change in our media diet, but the forging of new theories, creative practices, and grassroots activism that are trans inclusive. In such a phallic utopia, Dil would be loved for being, in *Disclosure*'s Zackary Drucker's words, "a beautiful woman with a penis." Her body would be cherished because of, not despite, her beautiful female phallus.

Toward a Phallic Utopia

Contemporary queer and trans scholars need to continue to ask the question Butler posed in 1993: "Are we to accept the priority of the phallus without questioning the narcissistic investment by which an organ, a body part, has been elevated/erected to the structuring and centering principle of the world?"[117] Female phallicism shifts how the potentialities of the phallic are imagined, toward the goal of subverting normative masculinity. Female phallicism exceeds the dialectic that plagues this question, for to refuse the "priority of the phallus" means to create a "not-phallus," which would still rely on cisgender masculinity, or the reinscription of trans men and butches, for its definition. In this chapter, I offer how female phallicism instead provides a horizontal schema of phallic relations, causing a profound crisis in gender/sex categorizations.

In the filmformance *Silver & Gold*, Nao Bustamante precipitates this crisis by blurring the distinction between dildo and penis, and between colonizer and colonized. Using a collage of gendered symbology, Bustamante reminds viewers of queer and transgender movements' extension and radicalization of the anti-Oedipus proposal, the notion that the entire discourse of "castration" upholds a heteronormative, colonial epistemology of the body. The filmformance exists in dynamic tension with the transphallophobic depiction of Dil in *The Crying Game*. The exclusion of trans women's phalluses speaks to the larger problems of erasure and objectification in queer theory and feminism.

The task of acknowledging existing phallic possibilities, and of creating both material and symbolic spaces of phallic expansion, is still in process. Expanding on Butler's field of substitutability, I envision multiple horizontal relations, which would include dildos, phallic body parts, and more penetrative sex beyond the dehumanizing world of lesbian porn for straight men. Expanding the sexual imaginary for trans women will have an explosive effect on masculinity and will help build a politics that in Spade's words "openly opposes liberal and neoliberal agendas and finds solidarity with other struggles articulated by the forgotten, the inconceivable, the spectacularized, and the unimaginable."[118] Female phallicism can lead to new forms of relationality—a breakdown of the centralization of white, male bonding as the only form of politics and bodies that *matter*.

Chapter 2

"When I Was a Boy"
Boi/Boyhood and the Unworking of Masculinity

In the previous chapter, I looked at the ways fraternal politics and racial capitalism bestow upon assigned male bodies the privileges—and pleasures—of phallic assertion. Here, I turn toward the problem of phallic "boyhood" and how the "gifts" of boyhood—adventure, messiness, and healthy forms of assertion—became the exclusive property of white boys.[1] Psychoanalysis continues to uphold this ruse, apparent in the oft-repeated phrase "boys will be boys." Trans and queer masculinity can become instead a source of phallic exuberance and mentorship, psychic locations of pleasure, joy, and belonging.

During one of her last visits with Gloria Anzaldúa before her death in 2004, Emma Pérez recalls how she purchased a boyish, blue men's work shirt at her favorite store, the Gap. Anzaldúa loved the store because she related the word *gap* to the Nahuatl concept of *Nepantla*, a psychic location of in-betweenness. Pérez notices a "playful glint in Gloria's eye" as she compliments her, "Te ves bien butchona."[2] This "playful glint," meant especially for Pérez, conveys the exuberance of unruly alliances, part of a collective effort to subvert colonial and neocolonial forms of white phallic supremacy.

While this is changing in recent decades, queer theory has often been accused of centering white, gay male experience and paying comparatively little attention to marginalized groups. Anzaldúa embraced the term *queer* before many contemporary scholars, but she was originally dismissed as not "queer enough," possibly because of her holistic approach to discrimination coming out of women of color feminism. This erasure of Anzaldúa represents the more pervasive effects of racism and sexism, particularly within queer theories of masculinity.

As Anzaldúa writes in *Borderlands/La Frontera: The New Mestiza*, "I, like other queer people, am two in one body, both male and female. I am the embodiment of *hieros gamos*: the coming together of opposite qualities within."[3] Through refusing to "make a choice" about gender and desire, Anzaldúa nurtures what I call a lowercase masculinity. Rather than engaging in forms of resistance based on a dialectical process, Anzaldúa and other trans and queer poets in this chapter access phallic power to create new relationalities. Phallic exuberance, achieved through mentorship and community, delegitimates the power of the administrative state, the abusive father, or other authority figures, who use phallic supremacy for domination and colonial and neocolonial control.

The glint in Anzaldúa's eye when she wears the blue work shirt suggests a recovery of boyishness, or the more contemporary boiishness. *Boi*, a burgeoning trans and queer term used by people of color, detaches from the normative mandates of white boyhood. Another way to express this lowercase masculinity is B. Cole's term *masculine of center*, coined in 2008 to refer to a more expansive and less racially or class-specific gender expression than *butch*.[4] As C. Riley Snorton writes, "There is a growing consensus in transgender studies that trans embodiment is not exclusively, or even primarily, a matter of the materiality of the body."[5] Even when there is a corporeal "real," its meaning, whether legal, medical, or cultural, disintegrates within the processes of racialization. *Boi* becomes an important location for questioning the "sex = gender" equation. Childhood buoyance, the pleasures of masculine undecidability and in-betweenness, offers a twilight space for the critical unworking of American manhood.

Pérez shares that her dear friend, Anzaldúa, self-described as *"una marimacha de la frontera,"* encourages others to travel the in-between space of Nepantla.[6] For trans poet and theorist Trace Peterson, Anzaldúa is one of the key writers and thinkers who made possible "a kind of literary community that would allow for the eventual visibility of trans poets."[7] Mentorship has been vital to the trans community for generations. As Hil Malatino offers, pedagogical, and often expansively maternal and care-based, relationships occur when a trans person in the midst of a gender affirmation process takes on a trans "big brother" or "big sister," who may or may not be younger in years.[8] I engage in this chapter with historical and contemporary trans poets who use boi/boyhood and mentorships as unruly alliances to resist phallic domination. Nepantla appears in the poems as a haunting that allows trans and queer subjects to access imagined boyhoods, which are all too often repressed and forgotten.

"Boys Will Be Boys"

From a very young age, white boys receive the message that their sadism and aggression are natural and healthy, in line with the demands of capitalist productivity. These conceptions of boyhood are ascendant in the cultural imagination in the twenty-first century, apparent in men's groups like the Proud Boys, who are utterly determined to reclaim white heteronormativity through any means necessary. The glorification of boyhood violence is predictably reproduced in media and politics. However, even while "boys will be boys" justifies and forgives virulent strains of so-called toxic masculinity, it is still possible to transform and transcend these defaults.

In his 1909 essay "Analysis of a Phobia in a Five-Year-Old Boy," Freud sets the stage for the enduring "boy = penis" equation, Five-year-old Hans dreams of a horse with a gargantuan penis, which causes him to experience what Freud describes as phobic dread. To overcome his phobia, Hans must, in classic Oedipal fashion, separate from his mother and identify with his father. His overbearing father, Max, works with Freud to identify the hidden desires and preoccupations that give rise to Hans's fears. Freud's treatment ends when Hans has a dream in which "'the plumber came; and first took away my behind with a pair of pincers, and then gave me another, the same with my widdler.'"[9] Hans's father interprets the dream as a manifestation of Hans's wish for a bigger ass and penis. Hans agrees with this assessment (why would he not?), much to Freud's own professional satisfaction. His agreement supposedly proves his productive identification with the assigned male parent, which ensures future gender and sexual conformity.

Freud insists that all of masculinity's joys and problems originate in the penis, regardless of family and cultural environment, and therefore, as psychoanalyst Ken Corbett observes, "the penis precedes the boy."[10] At the same time, Freud creates a false equivalence between masculinity and heterosexuality, often using the two words interchangeably. In so doing, he elides any sexual possibilities for boys and men outside of vaginal penetration. Further, through his interpretation of Hans's dream, he suggests that masochism and sadism are the only two routes for so-called healthy boyhood development, with sadism being the preferable choice. The masochistic side is symbolized by Hans being overwhelmed by the plumber's pincers, while the sadist side is encouraged through Freud and his father as models of dominance and control. Hans himself symbolizes the exorbitant costs of normative masculine inscription, including the mandatory "forsaking of fantastic cross-gendered identifications."[11] Freud's theory of boyhood still dominates, whether it is consciously articulated or not.

Hans's mother, however, becomes a nonspeaking subject, which conveys Freud's repression of the feminine and failure to consider the entire social web of family relations outside the bond between the boy and his father. The past century's psychological discourse on boyhood hinges on these very pressures and erasures. Since the 1970s, feminism has helped to position the mother as key to her son's masculine development, but Freud's pseudobiological interpretation often prevails. The intractability of the Oedipus complex suggests that it is not just a developmental moment but, in queer theorist David L. Eng's words, "a constitutive prohibition that emerges with the very inception of language, a structuralist legacy privileging certain forms of kinship as the only intelligible, communicable, reproducible and livable ones."[12] According to Eng, while we have moved beyond structural accounts of language, these insights have not been applied to kinship, which once again demonstrates how gender and relationality are coconstituted. Normative boyhood thus can be disrupted through language, as both an action in itself and as a foundation for action that can lead to masculine transformation.

The poets in this chapter challenge Freud's authority and become what Victor Turner calls "liminars," figures in ritual and ceremony that occupy positions of betweenness. Liminality is related to the concept of "anti-structure" that unsettles culture in order for it to survive and grow.[13] While to members of the traditional order it may appear that liminars produce unwanted chaos (as evidenced by recent antitrans laws and the virtual hysteria surrounding trans embodiment), they are actually responding creatively to troubling conditions.[14] Most importantly, liminality occurs during times of slippage between matrilineal and patrilineal systems, in which the subordinate form overtakes the dominant. In such situations, liminars represent gender inversions or reversals of established power dynamics.[15] The poets in this chapter use boi/boyhood and phallic exuberance as a form of masculine liminality, a way of being and creating that does not rely on the polarity of sadism and masochism. Liminality is instead associated with traits like ambiguity, invisibility, darkness, and the wilderness, all aspects that trans and nonbinary poets embrace as themes in their work. Liminars slip through the network of classifications that would designate their own positions in cultural and national spaces.[16]

Poets reclaim boi/boyhood through accessing the private, twilight edges of imagination. They form mentorships and embrace the organic community found in and through poetics, which counteracts the language of fraternal "exemplarity." As Jacques Derrida writes:

> Friendship should always be poetic. Before being philosophical, friendship concerns the gift of the poem. But sharing the invention of the event and that of the other with the signature of a language, friendship engages translation in the untranslatable. Consequently, in the political chance and risk of the poem. Would there not always be a politics of the rhyme.[17]

Poetics can exploit the instabilities found in Western philosophical concepts that ground politics, culture, and the family. The poem becomes the space of "chance and risk" where friendship and masculinity become unknowns rather than preconceived certainties. Within the realm of the "untranslatable," the figure of the friend no longer appears as the brother but as an *unheimlich* presence uniquely capable of questioning the reproduction of fraternization as a process and method of securing relationality.

Taking inspiration from Aimé Césaire's essay "Poetry and Knowledge," Robin D. G. Kelley insists that poetry is the only way to access the kind of knowledge that can help us move beyond the present crises.[18] Through poetry, we get to experience the whole: every history, future, dream, life form, creative impulse, emanating from the unconscious. Poems create cognitive maps of a world that has not yet been born.[19] In this chapter, poetry dreamed up in such a space of gender and sex undecidability becomes the ground for unruly alliances. Some queer and trans subjects play with undecidable masculinity and the qualities we typically associate with normativity (e.g., "competence, autonomy, self-control, ambition, risk-taking, independence, rationality") but without rejecting femininity or homosexuality in themselves or others.[20] While the poets in this chapter play with dominance as a form of artistic style and sexual expression, they do not become dominating, which allows them to fundamentally alter the psychic drama of masculinity.

"When I Was a Boy"

Through the work of Samuel Ace, Max Wolf Valerio, and kari edwards, the first three trans poets to publish monographs in the United States, Trace Peterson maps the possibility of what she calls a "trans poetry aesthetic."[21] Peterson discovers several aspects that might even suggest a "trans poetics." First, these poets refuse to present their trans identity directly and instead make oblique reference to transition, while carefully separating the identity of the speaker ("I") from the author. Second, they tend toward a highly fictionalized "scene" of the self over straightforward biography, often "testing the limits of habitability" in the poems, tampering with the readers' sense of location in space and time. Third, they collapse boundaries between genres, invoking a "ghostly line break" or a poetry-within-prose. She theorizes that this playful ambiguity results from their difficulty in becoming legible as "author-figures."[22]

A trans poetry aesthetic has likely existed throughout the history of American literature. For example, while Emily Dickinson had no community context or language for her gender nonconformity, a similar set of qualities can be discovered in her work. Her desire for what I am calling an "imagined boyhood" connects to her refusal of choice and coherence. Imagined boyhood is a space of fantasy and creativity existing within the limitations of a historical moment, with or without corporeal or sartorial manifestations of gender transition or affirmation.

In attempting any transgender history, it is important to recognize that *transgender* only became an identity marker in the 1960s. Viviane K. Namaste views *transgender* as a broad umbrella term for "individuals whose gendered self-presentation (evidenced through dress, mannerisms, and even physiology) does not correspond to the behaviors habitually associated with the members of their biological sex."[23] Namaste's definition creates space for the inclusion of a range of historical trans and proto-trans masculinities, a space that continues to take shape in the 2020s. As Jay Prosser notes, beginning in the 1990s, *transgender* came to be understood as a potential coalitional politics, "assembling into a movement subjects previously dispersed if not assimilated in straight and queer worlds," which means that *transgender* exists in productive tension with *queer* and *transsexual*.[24] Historically, as Susan Stryker and Paisley Currah write in the inaugural issue of *TSQ: Transgender Studies Quarterly, transgender* can be a critical neologism for considering gender difference in the past.[25] However, they caution that it would be anachronistic to label past figures in the "identitarian" sense. *Transgender* becomes rather an analytical tool for exploring the intricacies of historically contextualized gender expressions. I argue that like *transgender,* the term *transmasculinity* identifies what Stryker and Currah call a spectrum of experience, a "conceptual space" where contemporary scholars can question the intelligibility, and legibility, of "all embodied subjectivity" across time.[26] Within this conceptual space, race and class determine the parameters and limit points of historical trans possibility.

Dickinson's imagined boyhood makes her a gender radical for her time, a fellow traveler through Nepantla, though she is often not recognized as such. Through boyhood, Dickinson crossed, crossed out, revised, and rerouted both the poetic and familial line. The various nineteenth-century normalizing devices that she managed to undermine include a patriarchal family structure, the demand for religious conversion, the heterosexual imperative, and the publishing industry, which eventually accomplished postmortem the straightening she resisted through obsessive textual privacy.

Dickinson was subject to the nineteenth-century ideology of separate spheres, which severely constrained her creative expression. In response, she developed a body of work that envisions a transcendent life of fulfillment. In her time, the "cult of true womanhood" was the emergent form of modern domestic relations. White women were moral guardians, since—unlike male family members and, particularly, their husbands—they were supposedly shielded from the immorality of the public sphere of work in an increasingly competitive economic market.[27] According to literary scholar Gillian Brown, this ideology "with its discourse of personal life" proliferated alongside capitalist economic development, which separated women from the world of production and politics and redirected men toward work areas that were increasingly precarious and "subject to the caprices of the market."[28] For white people, the private sphere became a refuge from capitalist discipline and state control, a place to experience warmth and connection not found in the marketplace. Such a site of white permanence would supposedly ensure their own imagined place at the top of the racial and economic hierarchy and quell the anxieties that arose from the pressures of global capital. Dickinson disoriented the cult of true womanhood, despite aggressive attempts to infantilize and discipline her.

Dickinson resisted imaginative inertia and envisioned a world beyond her immediate present where she could live out her dreams of boyhood pleasure. By assigning herself a series of male names (Brother Emily, Uncle Emily, and simply Dickinson), she assumed the poetic creative capabilities and political power of the male poet.[29] Establishing a male alter ego through naming also allowed her to take on the role of seducer in her relationship with her sister-in-law, Susan Huntington Gilbert Dickinson. She rejected the masculine privilege of having one's name passed down, one of the key ways in which normative masculinity has been secured in Western culture. The citation of the name explains how the philosophical quotation "O Friends, there are no friends," and all that it implies, was handed down without question from Aristotle and Cicero, to Montaigne, Kant, Nietzsche, and Blanchot. As Derrida explains, the name ensures the legacy of its bearer, and so "the knowledge of the name and the question of public space will be caught up in the same knot."[30] As an assigned female person, Dickinson had to engage in this act of naming in private and in letters and conversations with family and friends. In many ways, both through naming and poetic practice, she initiated an antiphallogocentric disordering of the senses that persisted throughout her life and work.

Despite the ethereal and psychologically unwell way in which she is often depicted in the contemporary imagination, she was rather a "Soul *at the White Heat*," as one of her poems suggests.[31] She seized the right to be a boy in ways for which there was no language or community in nineteenth-century Amherst. She resisted temporal/spatial boundaries and created for herself a scrappy, rough-and-tumble persona, which is echoed in her poetry and letters. For example, she told a nephew in the 1870s, "'Mother told me when I was a Boy, that I must "turn over a new Leaf"—I call that the Foliage Admonition.'"[32] Dickinson envisioned childhood scenes, which may or may not have happened, to develop her boyishness.

An imagined boyhood allowed Dickinson a certain amount of psychic freedom from the obsessive self-government required of white women, for the best way to control white women's cultural production was to make sure that censorship took place on the most intimate level—inside one's own head.[33] The nineteenth century was a time of unprecedented publication and reception of women's writing. However, Dickinson pushed against the proscriptions of femininity and "the community of expression" that limited the voices of women writers. Attitudes about white women writers produced both literary conformity and rebellion, often taking the form of absences, apologies, and displacements.[34] Literary scholar Joanne Dobson writes extensively about the figure of the angry little girl in nineteenth-century literature, as a method of subverting strict censorship of expression, offering a "legitimate outlet for female anger."[35] Restrictive notions of the ideal female citizen prevented women from showing a full range of emotion, as any "passionate personal expression" necessarily conflicted with "an altruistic feminine morality."[36] Uncensored female experience was believed to be disruptive to the social order, a view that began early in the nineteenth century, peaking in the middle, and slowly losing favor by the 1870s.[37]

The nineteenth-century author "of worth" was a person assigned male at birth. As Sandra M. Gilbert and Susan Gubar describe, "he" was by definition:

> a father, a progenitor, a procreator, an aesthetic patriarch whose pen is an instrument of generative power like his penis. More, his pen's power, like his penis's power, is not just the ability to generate life but the power to create a posterity to which he lays claim.[38]

The white male poets, and their penises/pens, were the only legible creators worthy of remembrance. Since women had no right to create a posterity, through friendship or personal expression in the form of literature, women who became poets "grotesquely crossed boundaries dictated by Nature."[39] Alfred Habegger, one of Dickinson's many biographers, explains that in her letters she often expressed a "damaged sense of agency, a frustrating inability to reach the world of men that [had] been disclosing itself" to her.[40] Poetry was a practice for men, and the idea of a female poet was an oxymoron.

Caught in many different types of double binds, Dickinson could therefore neither emulate her teachers and clergymen, who had a particular flair for rhetoric, nor directly depict them on the page. Dickinson could only experience the boyishness she desired through refracted memory and dream. "Poem 271" speaks directly to the patriarchal line(s) she imagined crossing to reach forbidden objects and places:

> Over the fence —
> Strawberries — grow —
> Over the fence —
> I could climb — if I tried, I know —
> Berries are nice!
>
> But — if I stained my Apron —
> God would certainly scold!
> Oh, dear, — I guess if He were a Boy —
> He'd — climb — if He could![41]

She references herself as "He" to conjure a poetic self that can and will climb the fence in search of berries, regardless of the berries' ability to quench her thirst. Boyish embodiment allows her to imagine that world "Over the fence" and the quality of the "Berries" found there, not worrying over the feminine requirement of cleanliness ("Apron"), and to at least investigate the possibility of berries, of boyish pleasure "— if He could!" The fence represents both the troubled line of gender as well as the poetic line, which are co-constituted in Dickinson's poems.[42] She also has long been admired for her "ghostly line breaks," primarily in her use of dashes that are less like straight lines and more what Ellen Louise Hart and Martha Nell Smith describe as curviforms with added dots that mimic the shape of birds' eyes (Figure 4).[43] In Paula Bennett's words, the dashes, symbols of breakage and refusal, require her readers to "entertain disruption in wording, tone, subject, and grammar for which conventional usage provides few if any precedents . . . disjunction [becomes] an integrative force."[44]

This moment of climbing in search of forbidden objects also breaks

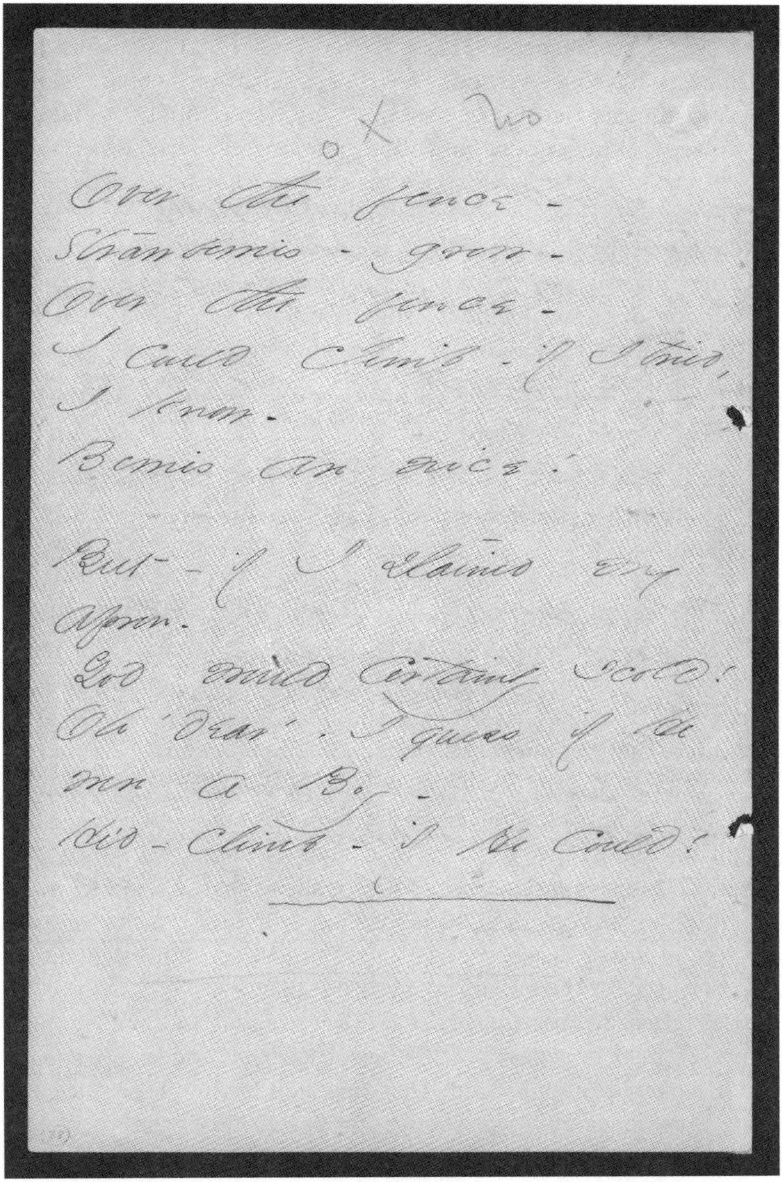

FIGURE 4. Image of Emily Dickinson's original fascicle, "Over the Fence," ink, Emily Dickinson poems, MS Am 1118.3 (38d), Houghton Library, Harvard University, Cambridge, Massachusetts.

the intersecting line of patriarchal religion ("God would certainly scold!"). In nineteenth-century Amherst, nearly all white women claimed to have experienced Calvinistic salvation, which enabled them to educate the rest of the community on temptation and sin. However, Dickinson remained all her life unconverted. When writing letters to her nephews, she characterized her point of view on religion as similar to a boy's, based on those true feelings a boy might hold on to despite the pressure to conform, before the moment they became "ghostly mouthpieces for patriarchal law."[45] Through her subversion of these insidious straightening devices, she created a trans and queer directionality in her work and life. Her refusal to conform to the conventional line break means a refusal of binary gender in preference for what we would now call hybridity or gender liminality—"if He could!"

The change in pronoun from "I" to "He" in the final line of "Poem 271" suggests her alienation from herself, one that is required if she is to detach from her historical limitations. While other male poets of her time, like Walt Whitman, spoke from the unitary "I," Dickinson's refusal to make definitive choices creates what Sharon Cameron calls a gender polyglossia.[46] The poems often contain two or more voices or stories, with one existing outside of the boundaries of the poem. This "outside" cannot be assimilated, so it must be seen as in relation to, but not part of, the poem. Poetic boundaries create this inside/outside, though they are boundaries that in my view ebb and flow. The variants often make unclear whether the voice "owned" by Dickinson and by the "other" are one and the same.[47] However, it is a self-othering—a moment of *im*personality—that is filled with the potential for movement and overcoming (climbing), taste, and fulfillment of bodily desire (berries). This process of self-evacuation is also essential for the initiation of unruly alliances.

Her refusal to grow up persisted throughout her life, as she sought to preserve, as in a glass bottle, the spiritedness and independence she discovered in childhood. Her imagined boyhood matched her inner experience and corresponded to her vision of the world. She savored the memory of wandering the fields alone and collecting flowers for her herbarium, losing a boot in the mud, indulging like Huck Finn in the pleasures of corporeal freedom. "When I was a boy" became a repeated phrase in middle age and a starting point for poems and letters. As Habegger explains, "Eventually she looked back at this free and fearless outdoor sauntering as a defining activity of her life 'when a boy,'" a phrase that became particularly important "after her habits of seclusion were established."[48] These were the recollections she would save and protect in her poems, particularly after she lost Sue to her brother and became confined to her father's home and grounds.[49]

Dickinson also expressed her deviations from the "straight" line in what literary scholar Robert McClure Smith calls her "enigma poems," which can be viewed as part of a quest for an undecidable masculinity.[50] In the enigma poems, Dickinson disorients the reader's ability to locate not only gender but the line between fiction and reality. She does this through asking rhetorical questions, such as "Which is it?" The poems can be difficult to categorize, because they disrupt any kind of clear delineation between categories. They require a queer embrace of the "perverse," a term used by many queer theorists in reaction to Freud, who claimed that anything blocking the direct, procreative line to heterosexual union, including foreplay, was perversion.[51] As queer theorist Eve Kosofsky Sedgwick writes in *Tendencies*, "Becoming a perverse reader was never a matter of my condescension to texts, rather of the surplus charge of my trust in them to remain powerful, refractory, exemplary."[52] This "surplus charge" is always available in Dickinson's work, which means she always tended toward the unruly. Perversion, metaphorically reproduced in the stray mark and the deviating line, is useful for thinking of ways that poetics can challenge normative masculine social conventions and orthodoxies.

In "Poem 272," Dickinson reverses the dynamic of gender not by taking on the male role but by placing the male seducer in jeopardy through a kind of phallic sleight of hand. As Robert McClure Smith writes, Dickinson rearranges the gendered dynamics of power by "destabilizing [the male] established position of rhetorical authority," a position with which she was familiar from her upbringing and various male teachers and role models.[53]

> Would you like Summer? Taste of our's —
> Spices? Buy — here!
> Ill! We have Berries for the parching!
> Weary! Furloughs of Down!
> Perplexed! Estates of Violet — Trouble ne'er looked on!

> Captive! We bring Reprieve of Roses!
> Fainting! Flasks of Air!
> Even for Death — A Fairy medicine
> But, which is it — Sir![54]

Here she offers a parody of a market or a bazaar, a highly fictionalized scene common in trans poetics where we are given the option of many different varieties of elixirs. However, while the "Berries" in "Poem 271" offer fulfillment, in this poem "Berries" are instead "parching." Dickinson instructs us to be weary of this market bazaar and the false choice it offers. Dismantling of masculine power occurs specifically when she poses the question, "which is it." The impossibility of assigning gender/sex to any of these images makes this concluding question a kind of perverse rhetorical blockage, and an exclamatory one at that, which displaces rather than locates gender and sex. She directs us in these enigma poems away from the straight line, both in content and form, and toward a queer *dis*orientation.[55] According to Robert McClure Smith, this disruption occurs often enough "that the examination and dismantling of the power dynamic between speaker and her male addressee is the primary theme of the poems."[56] In the excessive use of exclamation points—references to "Fainting! Flasks of air!"—she critiques gender and sexual normativity with irony and puts a spotlight on gender-based violence, subtle and overt.

Queer moments in the enigma poems also occur whenever the world appears "off-center" or "slantwise." In "Poem 1263," Dickinson famously advises, "Tell all the truth but tell it slant."[57] She resisted the straight ideals of so-called order and perfection—the very foundations of Western phallocentrism—privileging instead slantwise process and incompletion. As Dickinson scholar Paula Bennett offers, "The result is a free, constantly changing form of poetry in which conclusions—whether formal or thematic—cannot be drawn and in which *variant readings are part of the substance of the text.*"[58] The enigma poems represent her struggle to "cope linguistically with an experience that defies symbolization."[59] She expresses the troubling effect of transness and queerness, which deviate profoundly from the so-called universal value of gender coherence. In the enigma poem "Poem 305," she directly conveys the experiences of "difference" that cannot be categorized:

> The difference between Despair
> And Fear — is like the One
> Between the instant of a Wreck —
> And when the Wreck has been —
>
> The Mind is smooth — no Motion —
> Contented as the Eye
> Upon the Forehead of a Bust —
> That knows — it cannot see —[60]

This is a poem not directly about gender but rather about the liminal interstices of experience. The poem even lacks gender pronouns, which creates a loss of location, a phenomenological experience that is foreign to any conventional way of thinking. Through the enigma poems, she attempts to occupy multiple categories, precisely by occupying none: she becomes seducer, boy-poet, woman-lover, father worshipper, refuser of women's religion and sexuality, unwilling domestic, and keeper of flowers. This freedom exists precisely through the inability to "see." As Robert McClure Smith writes, "Central to the poem is its speaker's struggle to articulate a condition of undecidability, an experience of being caught between two alternate poles."[61] This leads to a friction in the reading of the poem, due to the impossibility of one interpretation, hence one reading—or one gender.

As a trans and queer poet, Dickinson does not just present the reader with the experience of poetic ambiguity, which could be classified and approached as a linguistic problem, one that could be dealt with through critical reflection. Rather, the poem produces in the reader an ambiguous experience, a collapse of distance that is closer to a state of mind, possibly provoking "a misery that accompanies an insoluble personal problem."[62] However, Dickinson also presents a space of perpetual possibility.[63] As Sedgwick insists, queer can and *must* mean "the open mesh of possibilities . . . lapses and excesses of meaning when the constituent elements of anyone's gender, of anyone's sexuality aren't made [or cannot be made] to signify monolithically."[64] It is within this "open mesh of possibilities" that masculinity comes to be experienced slantwise. The enigma poems therefore suggest that the phallocentrism, and phallogocentrism, can be unworked and that the complete disavowal of femininity and homosexuality is not inevitable. In this liminal state, she enacts an iteration of gender's back-and-forth movement, what Todd Reeser calls a masculinity in motion, as she simultaneously critiques—as boy—the force of patriarchal control.[65]

The incoherence, or ghostly breaks, within the lives and work of trans poets can prevent us from designating fixed meanings to identity and desire, leading us away from what queer-crip theorist Robert McRuer calls "orderly and singular corporeality."[66] Sara Ahmed similarly argues that despite cultural norms that compel us to resolve our ambiguities and choose an orientation, sexuality and gender are experienced as fundamentally *dis*orienting. Sex and gender, and the "'loop' of [the] repetition" in which bodies become oriented toward a specific set of desires and behaviors become akin to natural facts.[67] Dickinson was far from stranded on the shores of a binaristic world. Her teachers, her father, her peers, religious leaders in her community, wanted her to do something constitutionally against her nature, *make a choice,* but she refused. Dickinson instead embraces Peterson's utopian vision of "leaving the gender of the poem open."[68]

Twenty-First Century Undecidable Boyhoods: Samuel Ace and Andrea Gibson

The trans poet Samuel Ace and the nonbinary poet-performer Andrea Gibson use similar imagined boyhoods in their work, within the vastly different historical constraints and possibilities of the twenty-first century. Both poets cultivate and enjoy what Dickinson deeply lacked: mentoring relationships and communities of readers and audience members as forms of unruly alliance. This draw toward boyhood for Ace and Gibson also occurs as resistance to globalization and the negative freedom granted to masculine subjects in their calcified, adult state, for while boyhood aggression and sadism are condoned and, in some contexts, encouraged, boyhood also offers a potential twilight zone of undecidability and potentiality.

Globalization creates a prevailing understanding of freedom in the negative sense, as freedom from all obstacles that hinder fulfillment of personal desires. Historian Eric Foner helps explain how the creation of so-called new and improved commodified masculinities occur through this market-driven "negative freedom," which began to saturate the culture post-1970s. Writing in 2001, he foreshadows the election of mobster-boss Donald Trump, who for many is the most toxic-masculine of all:

A series of presidential administrations, aided and abetted by most of the mass media, have redefined both American freedom and America's historic mission to promote it for all mankind to mean the creation of a single global free market in which capital, natural resources, and human labor are nothing more than factors of production in an endless quest for greater productivity and profit.[69]

Previously understood expressions of positive freedom become burdens on international competition, as what is interdependent, relational, and feminized belongs to an archaic past.

In their liberal form, trans masculinities can become more aligned with negative freedom and with racial capitalism. Bobby Noble describes how the change from being read as a "working-class butch woman" to a trans embodied "half guy, half lesbian" also meant moving from being formerly off-white to a now fully white person.[70] Noble became "more white" as he attained greater passing privilege, which suggests how masculinity, whiteness, and ability function simultaneously to grant status and social and economic mobility. For Noble, "becoming male" requires a conception of the political, collective, and the macro, which is often difficult to achieve in such a self-oriented society. We need to reject any highly individualistic attempt at gender radicalism, in which one consumes gender like the latest designer trend. Boi/boyhood can become a space of possibility that is not yet pressured by the demands of capitalist normativity and white supremacy.

As Peterson shares, Samuel Ace came into his own as a poet and a trans man through contact with Anzaldúa, specifically a poetry workshop she led in New York in the 1980s (Figure 5).[71] The workshop, which took place in Anzaldúa's living room, gave him and other trans poets personal support and creative freedom. This experience of mentorship allowed Ace to write the poems "Tales of a Lost Boyhood," found in his first book, *Normal Sex*, published under his pretransition name, Linda Smukler. Ace describes the moment in her living room when his body began to "lead" the writing and when he permitted himself to "excavate the sensory and emotional realities of [his] childhood, including [his] imaginary boyhood."[72] He entered this zone of Nepantla, a space of growth for both his gender becoming and his poetry, which, according to Peterson, presented opportunities to "really [confront] artificial borders and boundaries"

FIGURE 5. Samuel Ace. Photograph by Sonny Nordmarken. Reprinted with permission from Samuel Ace.

in a way that finally made sense to him.[73] In turn, Samuel Ace became a mentor for poet TC Tolbert, which in "the purest sense of the word [is] someone who thinks with purpose and spirit, someone who allows this thinking to be witnessed."[74]

These "Lost Boyhood" poems were reprinted by Belladonna* Collaborative in 2019 in a dual collection with *Home in Three Days, Don't Wash*. He includes a series of letters written back and forth between his "female" self, Linda Smukler, and his current "male" self. This is a highly unusual rhetorical move in the world of trans writing, as many poets now have the privilege of coming out prior to establishing a publication record.[75] Cameron Awkward-Rich praises this dialogue between Smukler and Ace, because it dispels "the (false) truisms about transmasculine life . . . that girlhood leaves no trace, which is a way of thinking about time and space that also structures some of the most pernicious American [racialized] fantasies."[76] In lesbian feminist writer and activist Joan Nestle's reflection on Sam's letters to Linda, she applauds how he heals the wounds of the past inflicted from furious battles between trans people and lesbian feminists. Ace can write in such a way that one does not replace the other but rather "[embraces] the knowledges of both."[77]

Dickinson can be viewed as a predecessor of Samuel Ace, as there are formal and conceptual similarities between the two poets. For example, Dickinson's refusal to conform to the conventional line break is similar to Ace's use of gaps and caesuras, which Peterson describes as like a "rhythmic pulse." Ace even compares punctuation to gender-as-confinement, something he does not wish to "impose" on readers.[78] Like Ace, Dickinson would save and protect similar boyhood imaginings in her poems and in her daydreams, particularly after she lost Sue to her brother. Many masculine-identified folks not assigned male at birth feel similarly exiled from themselves after adolescence, like travelers allowed to take with them only a few souvenirs from their boyhoods. Like rare plants and flowers, these memories are often lost after adolescence, which means they must be preserved and treasured once they are rediscovered.

"Lost boys" is also a reference to the childhood story of Peter Pan, both the 1953 Disney film and the 1904 J. M. Barrie play on which it was based.[79] In the story, a ragtag group of "lost boys" have fallen out of their strollers as babies. If they are not claimed within a week, they are sent to Neverland, where Peter Pan becomes their captain. Ace remembers as a young child listening to the Mary Martin musical version of *Peter Pan* based on the Barrie play.[80] He and his sisters would sing rounds of "Tender Shepherd" on long car rides. Ace directly names Peter Pan in the poem "Squirrelhorse," where he channels the voice of a very young, school-age child: "There's light in the windows and on the ceiling. I fly there sometimes with Peter Pan and dive down. Dive here where my house is a boat and there's a river for it on the wall."[81] The use of short, staccato sentences, metaphor ("my house is a boat"), and images of flying away offer boyhood escape, one that is temporally and spatially removed from the present moment. The idea of a boyhood Neverland opens a psychic and poetic space without temporal/spatial boundaries.[82] Simple vocabulary and childlike reportage plunges the reader even more into this imagined boyhood, one that contains its own dangers. In the poem "Tales of a Lost Boyhood, 1. Drummer," Ace cultivates the voice of a child again through metaphor wherein "the specks on the linoleum are beetles. A swarm of bugs that eat houses. They eat and eat until their eating is a roar and my father walks in the door."[83] The poem begins with a vision or a dream of himself the previous summer being lifted up and carried away by the sky, where he becomes the "bare-chested Indian boy and saw the devil's paintbrush." "Bare-chested" and "devil" become linked terms, conveying the supposedly deviant nature of these dreams of boyhood escape.

In these poems, misreading or mishearing become devices for capturing the distance between imagined boyhood and the violence of reality. Ace invents for his narrator memories of what is said and heard that correspond to his gendered feelings. For example, in a scene with his father, he imagines a different gendered interaction than the one that took place in reality: "'Hello little girl,' he says. Hello little boy is what I hear."[84] He feels like a drummer inside, which compels him to drum his glass at the dinner table with his silverware, an action that makes his father grab his hand. The boy accidentally knocks over a glass of milk, which fills his skirt, symbolizing the feminine as something forced upon him, literally poured over him in a way that he cannot control. The boy retreats to his room after enduring his father's tirade, and he proceeds to fashion a set of drumsticks, or phallic extensions of himself, out of clothes hangers. Staring at the bedspread, he notices the pattern of a fence:

> I play in that fence. I bounce over it and there's a stream. I walk in the stream and the trees tower over me. They stand naked for a long time before they reach their full and leafy tops. I throw rocks in the water. One sound is like a bell. The next like my drum. There are frogs too. Green and portly frogs like the hearts of bears.[85]

The character first observes the fence, then imagines playing "in" the fence before he finally decides, like Dickinson, to climb over. Once there, he discovers a boy's paradise, complete with a Huck Finn–like set of items ideal for running away from home: a red bandanna on a stick, a metal plate, a knife, a flint, and a fishing line and hook. "I need very little," he declares. "I walk with the fish. The stream runs through my head and out my feet."[86] In this fantasy, he becomes one with nature, which refutes the idea that being trans destroys the "natural laws" of gender assigned at birth. However, the fantasy quickly evaporates as he hears his father's footsteps on the stairs. He turns on the sink and pretends it is a waterfall, believing that if he stays quiet, everything will be all right; in other words, the fantasy will keep him safe from his father's tyranny.

Mentorship and critical reflection on masculinity also go hand in hand in the "Lost Boyhood" poems, sometimes framed through a Dickensian use of enigmatic questions. In the poem "The Shower," the narrator is confused and disturbed, yet too young to make sense of what they are witnessing:

> My voice is thin I stand in the shower what's that? I ask I
> am at the level of that what is it? a penis he says men have
> them I stand there watching it I don't have one girls don't
> have one he holds it for me touch it can you touch it? long
> and skin thick over something hard thicker than all my
> > fingers
> it moves under them it's not a part of him does he take it off
> when he puts on his clothes? we are taking a shower he is
> holding it to show me underneath this is the scrotum
> > he says
> like two eggs what's all that raised over them? touch it veins
> he says hairy he is very black hairy there.[87]

As Peterson notes, in this poem, Ace refuses the process of "naming" the penis, using instead childlike descriptions of "long and skin" and "very black hairy there."[88] Ace also leaves room for doubt as to whether this person is the child's father or an unnamed perpetrator. This leads to friction in the experience of the poem, particularly because Ace never endured this scene but creates a fictionalized narrative to enact sexual difference and gender ambiguity, and to critique patriarchy.

In *Normal Sex*, boyhood acts as a doorway to transition. In "Monkey Boy," gender affirmation is imagined as escape through a stuffed animal to a faraway place (Wyoming) where he is able to crawl inside the monkey's body and change his name to "Jim Ace." The poem becomes, in Peterson's words, a "biographical foreshadowing, a prophetic moment," that captures for me the liminality of "boyhood," a psychic space of possibility.[89] Awkward-Rich views these fantasies as "a reparative retreat into the vast territories of the interior. *Boyhood* names a child's wish and need for the loosening of gender's, of modernity's, of subjectivity's constraints." In this way, Ace's work leads us toward "trans as a particular practice of imagination."[90]

In these poems, Ace refuses a so-called safe retreat into white masculinity and instead makes critical decisions about what kind of boy he would like to be. In the poem "Sister," for example, he decides he wants to be the woodcutter who saves Hansel and Gretel by doggedly following their tracks, which allows: "My arms are thicker than the trunks of trees and I carry my axe on my shoulder. I will rescue my children whom I love with all my heart."[91] Sam even confides in a letter to Linda that he is grateful he did not experience boyhood as an assigned male person, as the fantasy may exceed the potential of the "real thing." He writes:

> Some of my cis-male friends have shared with me harsh depictions of their childhoods. Some were beaten, hazed, and humiliated. Some competed viciously with each other. Some bonded over cruelty. Some valorized strength and daring and could not tolerate vulnerability. . . . I believe that you [Linda], as a child, had little understanding of any of this.[92]

Ace also recognizes that the masculine objects he coveted as a child—Davy Crockett's coonskin cap, for example—symbolize racism and colonialism. He was exposed to an early American television culture that was "entirely white and obsessed with mani-fest-destiny."[93] He critically considers the state of the world in 2019, when over half of the world population lives under authoritarian rule and when many trans people are exposed to violence because of their race or visible gender nonconformity. His poems recognize that simply becoming a boy will not erase this history or the potential for violence.

The critical unworking of boyhood also takes place in the work of nonbinary poet-performer Andrea Gibson. In the spirit of the mentoring relationships inspired by Anzaldúa, Gibson produces sold-out shows that gather loyal fans who can recite their poems by heart. A cult phenomenon, and a four-time Denver Grand Slam Champion, Gibson started their career performing with Vox Feminista, a group of radical feminist performers.[94] They came out as bisexual in 1997, lesbian a year later, but now they identify as genderqueer, using the pronouns *they/them*. Their coming out process and their experiences of being genderqueer speak to trans masculinity as a space of becoming, interwoven with poetry. In an interview, Gibson explains how they will probably spend their whole life "shifting and becoming and trying [their] best to pay close attention to the pull of [their] own heart."[95] While they do not feel that their gender falls on either end of the spectrum, their style and aesthetic reflect what I call a lowercase masculinity, resembling a "baby butch" of the mid-twentieth century, despite the fact that they are in their midforties.[96] The image they promote in their shows is often one of a working-class teenage boy wearing their favorite beat-up brown work boots, sleeveless gray denim jacket, black hoodie, low-slung black skinny jeans, belt, and choppy, short hair. Gibson sparkles in this zone of masculine undecidability, the space of Nepantla where gender is performed far differently from what was observed in childhood.

Audiences and political events inform the creation of their lines, which are often revised on the spot. This sense of shared purpose constructs a sense of community around and through the poems. In their seventh studio album, *Hey Galaxy*, they take inspiration from the Black feminist writer Roxane Gay, Indigenous protests at Standing Rock, and the musical *Fun Home*, based on the graphic memoir of the same name by Alison Bechdel.[97] In their 2019–2020 touring show, *Right Now, I Love You Forever*, "a multimedia, poetic story-telling experience," they spoke candidly about their failures in love, with the aim of soothing the wounds of "hopeless romantics and the absolutely hopeless."[98] By sharing in the experience of political and personal "hopelessness," they encourage a form of unruly alliance that can scale up to grapple with the everyday disasters of our current political and neoliberal moment.

In a Zoom show during the Covid-19 pandemic, entitled "It's Okay to Fall Apart," they spoke casually from a couch in their bedroom, expressing their despair over the sudden end to the tour due to the global pandemic.[99] In light of the death of Supreme Court Justice Ruth Bader Ginsburg the night before, they confessed to the audience that they were not doing so well, which showed in their frequent need to start over from the beginning. They model self-acceptance, in their case in the company of over seven hundred fans. As McRuer insists in "Composing Queerness and Disability," our "authorized" methods of producing and analyzing texts, derived from time spent in college classrooms, often conform to a heteronormative and ableist viewpoint. The art of composition must instead be an exercise in the "loss of composure."[100] Gibson enacts McRuer's "loss of composure" in this show by performing a genderqueer, boyish vulnerability during a moment of cultural and political upheaval, which encourages their audiences to also "fall apart" in a way that is safe and compassionate.

Gibson used these breaks in the show as opportunities to explain how they "argue" with lines and how the edited versions of the poems in the published books often do not correspond to what they perform on stage. In an interview with Tig Notaro, they express how sensitive they are to audience response: "I write for it to be spoken out loud, so I don't know whether or not a line is going to work or resonate until I do it live. Until I've performed it, maybe 10 or 15 times, it's not really in stone."[101] Gibson sees their poems as playing a role in changing peoples' minds and hearts, which they believe can happen "in an instant." By creating a truly democratic process of creation and performance, Gibson continues with the project of discrediting normative masculine relationality and phallic supremacy. Undecidable "boyish" masculinities, friendships, and communities of mutual aid, forged through their work, extend outward from the coffee shops, bars, clubs, and university auditoriums where they perform. In the poem "Gender in the Key of Lyme Disease," they propose that issues of death and survival should not be proportional to one's gender conformity:

> I'm always thinking about the gender   of dying,
> and the gender of surviving.[102]

By saying later in the poem, "I don't know / the gender of living," they propose that gender is not a fixed point on a horizon that is occupied for an entire lifetime but rather a series of becomings intertwined with the common processes of the body. Gender is a concept to be thought rather than a set of static rules, considering that the "gender of living" is not knowable, and the answer might even be that there is no "gender of living." This leaves masculinity open to interpretation, pushing the needle toward a mobile masculinity not based on one arbitrary set of qualities over another.

Gibson's personal background also speaks to the idea of gender as a series of becomings. As they tell Notaro, they look much the same as they did as a tomboy growing up in the woods of Maine, even with the same haircut. They came from a Baptist family of modest means, and the world of nature and the outdoors became a profound escape from the confines of both gender and religion forced upon them by their mother. Their tomboy childhood was spent "running around in the creek and lakes and stuff like that."[103] While they chose to keep the name "Andrea," they acknowledge another possibility, perhaps an alter ego, in the short poem "Andrea/Andrew":

> Your name
> is a gift
>
> you can return
> if it doesn't fit.[104]

Gibson proclaims their right to name themselves, one of the most empowering aspects of transness. Another poem about boyhood in the collection *Pansy* lacks any kind of gendered language, which again plunges the reader into this longing for boyhood pleasures found outdoors, untethered from the proscriptions of the family and the church:

> My mother
> fixing my hair for my school pictures.
> Me, fixing my heart
> on the rowdy wind.[105]

In this boyhood world, stained teeth are allowed, along with other supposed excesses associated with boys. When their mother fixes their hair (in a girlish way), the inner life of the heart remains stubbornly attached to a "rowdy wind." In this poem, they communicate an important message of vulnerability and strength for fans in the process of constructing their own masculinities.

In the poem "Your Life," when they reflect on themselves in childhood from an adult perspective, the pronouns switch to "you," adding to the feeling of a boyhood that has been lost or misplaced and is in the process of being rediscovered. The second-person voice creates a distance between the reality of what childhood was like and the dream-state of imagined possibilities. This distance is understandable considering that within these imagined scenes of becoming, Gibson realizes that the boys were "building their confidence on stolen land."[106] This realization compels them to contemplate their own misogynistic tendencies, which suggests misogyny is not only a product of being assigned male at birth but something that can be easily adopted by trans and queer subjects. In "No Filter," they make a powerful statement on the transferability of masculine normativity:

> But please, don't let me be
> the kind of person whose crimes get revealed
> after I die. May it all be written while I'm still alive,
> even this: In the sixth grade, I left a note in a locker
> that I still worry made a girl rethink her beauty
> for the rest of her life.[107]

The extreme right justification of the poem performs its own kind of queer disorientation as Gibson remembers their tomboy past and how they humiliated a girl for her appearance.

In "Letter to the Editor," Gibson ruminates in a childlike manner about their invented role models that can take the place of those sixth-grade boys. Their alter ego, "Johnny Appleseed," succeeds in turning away from normative behaviors:

> **VIII.**
> These are my vows:
>
> —Johnny Appleseed, whose real name was Johnny Chapman, was someone who would never hurt a fly.
> So much so that if he spotted even one mosquito
> flying too close to a flame, he would jump up
> and put out his own campfire on even the coldest darkest
>   nights.
> (That's the type of Johnny I intend to be.)[108]

By stating their intention never to be the cause of hurt to any being, they deviate from more individualized masculine reclamations and reinventions. Putting their intention in parentheses, they emphasize that this is not just a fictional scene but a life goal. They make direct amends to those harmed in the past and a promise to those who will come into their lives in the future that they will be more consciously aware of their privilege.

Gibson understands, however, that the past is never quite past and that gender must continually respond to political and economic conditions. In the poem "Elbows," they admit: "I am always a groom / just learning to pull my own weight / without wishing my past weighs less than it does."[109] By sharing their stories openly, they create poems that are safe places for themselves and others to explore the desire for boyhood without shame, guilt, or remorse. For them, becoming a woman was like going through a "soft death," but all their experiences have added up to their current place of process:

> Your life the first time someone drags you
> from a restroom by the collar of your coat.
>
> Your life each time airport security screams,
> *Pink or blue? Pink or blue?* trying to figure out
>
> which machine setting to run you through.
> Choosing your life
>
> and how that made you into someone
> who now finds it easy
>
> to explain your gender by saying you are happiest
> on the road, when you're not here or there, but in-between.[110]

Childhood memories, as well as current pleasures, humiliations, and failures, become a different kind of cultural clay. Their ability to admit failure, which includes their courage to start "from the beginning," sets Gibson apart from other poet-performers. This poem, one of Gibson's most well known, also contains the famous line, "Your pronouns haven't even been invented yet," which fans have stenciled on walls and reprinted on T-shirts and tattoos.[111] Through this poem and others, it becomes possible to imagine boyhoods in the spirit of unruly alliance.

Do You Dare to Climb the Fence?

The poets in this chapter actively resist the reduction of texts and lives into neatly aligned packages and coherent subjectivities, preferring instead lived experiences of *dis*orientation. From their own historical vantage points, they ask, do we dare climb the fence, regardless of whether there will be berries on the other side? Do we dare to refuse to make a choice? In *Troubling the Line,* TC Tolbert writes that in compiling the first-ever collection of trans and genderqueer poets, the editors sought "a deep experience of the textual body—to see how [an] author takes up, inhabits, and imbues space."[112] This visceral, "deep experience" is discovered throughout the examples in this chapter, which fundamentally trouble masculinity—and the line—adding resonance and polyvocal meanings.

Ace and Gibson each propose that there is no one answer to the question of masculinity, nor one identity category that captures the prize of the "most revised." Rather, as Pérez similarly warns in *The Decolonial Imaginary,* "if you seek categorical, definitive answers, you will not find them. I will submit more questions, more interventions, as I continue to speak from the margins, as I continue to experiment with my own *'sitio y lengua.'*"[113] The word *experiment* alerts us to the unfinished project of gender, encapsulating the spirit of the trans and genderqueer poets who explore masculine undecidability. These poets consciously work through the taboo against femininity and homosexuality and the inherent racism and ableism in white boyhood constructions, for Hans's horse is not only "big" but stout and muscular, an ableist symbol of phallic mastery. Contrary to the urgings of the right-wing political coalition in the United States, masculinity is never fixed but rather mobile and unstable, revealing the ruse of its status as universal signifier.

By constructing her own boyish Nepantla, and by sharing this space with others like Pérez and Ace, Anzaldúa forwards an invitation to unruly alliances of the future. This is an invitation to ambiguity and complexity, which cannot be reduced to digitized sound bites or images that are readable at a glance. The phallic possibilities of masculinity are effectively unmoored and given a chance to breathe. In the process, many points and lines of being and becoming are invented. As nonbinary poet Eileen Myles writes in their contribution to *Troubling the Line,* "I'm proposing a riddle instead (and an echo too) that perhaps gender, perhaps the self, that perhaps just the impossibility of language is what we've got."[114] Maybe masculinity is similarly impossible in a way that can be both pleasurable and difficult. The impossibility of all three—gender, self, and language—is what we confront, and attempt to untangle, all the while becoming more and more aware of the unruliness of such a project.

Part II
Challenging Conceptions of the Nation

Chapter 3

The "Not (Quite) Yet" of a New Collectivity
Feminist Masculinity and the American Western

> This girl was already versed in insolence when she transgressed the laws that had been set forth; and, that done, lo, a second insult,-to vaunt of this, and exult in her deed.
> Now verily I am no man, she is the man, if this victory shall rest with her, and bring no penalty.
> —Creon's speech, *Antigone*, Sophocles

In the United States, unyielding military strength, economic supremacy, and cultural hegemony over the rest of the world are primary indicators of the health and vitality of the nation. In the next two chapters, I offer how nationalism upholds and celebrates so-called toxic masculinity. This toxicity is palpable, for example, in the presidential legacy of George W. Bush. He famously told King Abdullah of Jordan on September 28, 2001, "We're steady, clear-eyed, and patient, but pretty soon we are going to have to start displaying scalps."[1] Bush continually asserted in numerous remarks and speeches his manly intent to act in response to the September 11 attacks. With Bush as sheriff and Dick Cheney as deputy, the United States now had a new alibi for its imperialist invasions of non-Western nations. In applying the "Wanted Dead or Alive" ethos of the Old West to his hunt for Osama bin Laden, Bush established for the future a familiar approach to international relations. He spread the belief that the terrorist, like the criminal and the barbarian, is inherently murderous and uncivilized, and therefore must be tamed through "illiberal means," including deprivation of freedom or outright extermination.[2]

Bush emulated, often directly, the swagger of a John Wayne or

Gary Cooper, and sure enough, the Western film and television genre was quick to respond to Bush's warmongering. The television show *Deadwood* (2004–6) promotes a return to vigilante justice, which shows how the world-making of the Western has often developed in close relationship to politics. The Western genre reveals that culture has never been innocent in its drive to justify violence at home and abroad. In the traditional Western, the male subject of the story often moves from being embedded in a limiting social situation to becoming a self-determining subject: master of his own fate. By promoting the transcendence of social constraints through the exercise of will, Westerns have supported U.S. narratives of development and the production of a universal, abstract subject.[3]

Westerns symbolize American freedom, and perhaps more than any other genre, they show how "America"—as myth and reality—symbolizes for the world one kind of freedom or another.[4] Early Western films depict Native Americans as the ontological enemy, but these themes were also recycled and repurposed during the war on terror. Westerns often cast racial and gendered outsiders as biologically, sociologically, historically, and anthropologically inferior, even when race is rejected as a legitimate mode of designation. Various strategies of concealment in these films render vulnerabilities to violence, poverty, punishment, and ill health as "vestigial, unsystematic, unintended, and lacking in social authorship."[5] By naturalizing these vulnerabilities, the Western insists that the elimination of these outsiders is socially desirable.

Not only do Westerns have enduring domestic appeal, but they have been widely exported as part of capitalist democracy's project of producing a consumable history and a genealogy of the West, part of what Cedric J. Robinson calls its "ideological conduit."[6] The consistent stylistic conventions of the genre, familiar to so many, provide the United States with both the ideological backing for its status as a world power and a means to deny status and engage a historical forgetting of its territorial rule.[7] The Western often aligns with U.S. war planners and their intellectual supporters, who view the entire world as an "open frontier," one that the United States is "uniquely charged" to secure, in the service of the onward march of rational individualism and capitalist exchange.[8]

Bush's Western flair, with its self-authorizing butchness, is a good indicator of how gender was portrayed in the Western after 9/11. As scholar of the Western Mark E. Wildermuth observes, in the decade following 2001, no Western series featured a single female protagonist.[9] However, Westerns have begun to show signs of a shift. The Netflix 2017 limited series *Godless* and HBO's *Westworld* (2016–22) depict unruly alliances through what feminist scholar Jessica Nydia Pabón-Colón calls "feminist masculinity."[10] By refusing white liberal ideas of what it means to be "feminist," the characters in these Westerns form unruly alliances across embodiments, gender identification, and sexuality. At the same time, they heed Homi K. Bhabha's warning that masculinity must not be denied or disavowed but rather "disturbed."[11] *To disturb* in this context means "to interfere with the normal arrangement or functioning" of a set of social relations.[12]

Cross-pollinating masculinities in these Westerns question fraternity and racial capitalism as the bases for modern nation-building, while collectively grieving over biopolitical violence against Indigenous cultures and the generational trauma of settler colonialism and slavery. They use masculinity to fight common causes, mobilizing difference rather than sameness. I situate these masculinities within women of color feminism as a method for analyzing how gendered and racialized formations are produced in relation to one another. In Grace Kyungwon Hong's terms, women of color feminist practice exploits the contradictions of racial capitalism by "displacing the singularly formed subject of the nation-state with contradictory, multiply determined subjectivity, articulated through an intersectional analysis."[13] Feminist masculinity in twenty-first-century Westerns is used to resist the nation-state as a "repressive apparatus, as guarantor of unequal property relations, as privileged possessive individual" in capital's global phase.[14]

More than any other cultural form, film and television have been, in Todd W. Reeser's words, the "privileged locus for studying the relation between nation and masculinity."[15] So while it would be inaccurate to say that these new Westerns depart entirely from masculine-nationalism (which explains the "not [quite] yet" in the title of the chapter), in the context of the genre's historical arc, these feminist masculinities are remarkable. They unmask the interconnectedness of the war on terror, histories of slavery, Indian Wars, and hemispheric interventions, revealing that the United States, as Nikhil Pal Singh observes, "has only ever been a kind of empire"— one that cuts along lines of race and gender.[16]

Women as Ultimate Partisans

The nation-state provides a semblance of stability and security for normative masculinity.[17] As Aníbal Quijano explains, the state is a structure of power through the articulation of the following elements: disputes over control of labor and its resources and products, sex and its resources and products, and intersubjectivity and knowledge.[18] Members of the nation-state supposedly share a sense of what Benedict Anderson names an "imagined community" but also what Quijano describes as a "more or less democratic participation in the distribution of the control of power."[19] A modern nation-state is composed of modern institutions of citizenship and political democracy, but citizenship can only function as legal, civil, and political equality for socially unequal people. The nation-state's temporary and partial homogenization of citizen-subjects consists of their common democratic participation in the establishment and management of institutions of public authority and their mechanisms of violence. The character of any given state is therefore only as national and as democratic as the power existing within a space of domination.[20]

While the nation-state presents itself as timeless, in reality it grew out of what Joane Nagel calls "a renaissance of manliness" in the late nineteenth and early twentieth centuries.[21] This institutionalization of manliness ascribed to white men the characteristics of willpower, courage, discipline, competitiveness, adventurousness, independence, and dignity, all of which mapped onto the abstract democratic ideals of liberty, equality, and fraternity.[22] As Nagel explains, masculinity and nationality are products of one another.[23] The place of women, and of femininity more broadly, is by contrast symbolic and maternal, which becomes obvious when we consider that one's country of origin is often described as the "motherland."[24]

The typical Western delivers the message that war is an indispensable, albeit unfortunate, feature of capitalist democracy. Singh cites a haunting similarity between eighteenth- and nineteenth-century military conflicts and intervention on the Great Plains and those taking place in the Philippines, Vietnam, Afghanistan, and Iraq, all of which show that the everyday idiom of American capitalism on its "'disoriented frontiers' is savage war and race war, along with the proliferation of subjects without rights."[25] The state has found ample justification for the war on terror in the Western, as well as in the work of historians like John Lewis Gaddis, among others. The justification for preemptive violence against "non-state actors" in the name of global security often occurs through channeling the "usable past" of the American Indian Wars, recycling the claim that "marauders" must be faced down wherever they are found.[26]

The idea of the West, as it is depicted in Western fiction, has been "central to the global imaginary for over two hundred years."[27] Inspired by novels and short stories rather than newspapers or historical records, early Westerns sought legend and mythmaking within a "manufactured sense of authenticity."[28] Before they became interested in character development and narrative, the goal of the creators of Westerns was to "astonish audiences with pure action and visual spectacle."[29] In the narratology of the classic Western (including silent Westerns, 1930s B-Westerns, and A-Westerns of the 1930s and 1940s), violence restores the integrity of the national body and can be endlessly justified. Native peoples exist outside of the realm of legitimate politics and the justice system, and they can never launch a rational grievance.

Before World War II, nearly all Westerns promoted the nation as an aesthetic and political project that relied on being able to tell the difference between a friend and an enemy. The friend/enemy grouping, which is decisive for the very functioning of the nation-state and for an endless state of war, is also a grounding principle of normative masculinity. As Immanuel Kant writes in *Metaphysics* (1797), the "unjust enemy" of the nation is "someone whose publicly expressed will, whether expressed in word or in deed, displays a maxim that would make peace among nations impossible and would lead to a perpetual state of nature if it were made into a general rule."[30] Jacques Derrida links the friend/enemy grouping to the three types of political crime: assassination with political motivation, which is the most standard meaning post–World War II; distinct from murder, political crime specifically motivated by the necessity of the enemy, which requires that the enemy be killed (must be killed) and which constitutes the meaning of the political itself; and the political crime of stopping to examine politics, which is to transgress against the fraternal structure. Any member of the fraternity must choose between these three interrelated crimes, for political crime is a necessity to protect the fraternity. However, this friend/enemy binary is unstable, as one constantly slides into the other, which means that from the late twentieth century forward, it has become increasingly difficult to distinguish between these political crimes, between murder and homicide, and between homicide and genocide. For Derrida, grievances against the loss of human life in a political context, or on the streets of a marginalized neighborhood, would have to be launched against the fraternal concept itself: its laws of selection and the friend/enemy grouping.

The early ontological enemy in the Western is the Native American "savage" who intends to destroy white civilization. The friend couple—the Lone Ranger and Tonto or Butch Cassidy and the Sundance Kid—unite against this ontological enemy who must be killed to ensure civilization's survival. These films compel audiences to root for the hero regardless of their own marginalized status. As James Baldwin related in his famous debate with William F. Buckley Jr. in 1965, he watched Westerns growing up, and he used to side with the cowboys: "It comes a great shock," he stated gravely, "to discover that Gary Cooper killing off the Indians, when you were rooting for Gary Cooper, that the Indians were you."[31]

Singh, echoing Derrida, makes a generative connection between Carl Schmitt, Weimar-era critic of liberal parliamentarianism, and twenty-first-century U.S. right-wing jurisprudence in their mutual contempt for international law and their efforts to collapse executive and juridical authority.[32] Responding to this GOP agenda in the 2020s—intent on war, predation, and racial and civilizational divide—Singh sarcastically imagines Carl Schmitt and Samuel P. Huntington smiling together from "somewhere in hell."[33]

Schmitt famously defined *the sovereign* as "he who decides the exception to rule and norms on the basis of 'extreme peril' or 'danger to the existence of the state.'"[34] For Schmitt, the sovereign exception, and the designation of the enemy, highlights the contradiction between the supposed over-inclusiveness of liberal notions of human equality and the forms of exclusion that mass democracy ultimately requires. From this perspective, democracy first seeks homogeneity but then must pursue its elimination, whenever the need arises. As Singh claims, the reinvigoration of the state of emergency and the state of exception after 9/11 show that modern liberalism does not adequately repress the question of sovereignty through separation of powers, rational deliberation, individual rights protection, and public debate.[35]

It is devastating to realize that Schmittian logic is present in both twenty-first-century U.S. right-wing jurisprudence and in Hitler's *Mein Kampf*. Hitler reflected Schmitt more bluntly when he proclaimed that the Eastern territories would be for Germany what India was for England, only Germany would be more successful in cleansing away supposed racial impurities.[36] In *Mein Kampf*, Hitler cited the American Indian Wars as inspiration for Germany when he praised the American innovation and supposed resistance that led to the slaughter and relocation of Indigenous peoples: "We must remember that at the time when the American continent was being settled, many Aryans struggled for a livelihood as trappers and hunters etc. . . . But, as soon as their numbers grew to a certain point and better equipment made it possible to tame the land and resist the natives, more and more settlements sprang up throughout the country."[37] However despicable the reasoning, from the perspective of the twenty-first century, Singh highlights how Schmitt did predict correctly that these states of emergency would force liberal democracy to "decide between its elements."[38] A division would occur between so-called civilized rights-bearing peoples and the adjacent space of state violence, with colonial history as the prime example.

The United States has—time and again—decided between its elements, always in favor of the so-called civilized. The enemy of the state dwells within and without in U.S. empire, and domestically, the Indigenous and Black populations have been subjected to the most direct and incessant violence. The formation of the United States was violent from the start, and while Native Americans were formally recognized as nations during the early years of the republic, after independence they were excluded and later dispossessed of land and nearly exterminated. As Quijano offers, this was the coloniality of the new model of power, since American Indians and Black people could not have a place in the control of the resources of production or in the institutions and mechanisms of public authority.[39] Indigenous survivors of conquest have been imprisoned in North American society as a colonized race. The Indian Wars have of course been a favorite subject matter for Westerns, and this perpetual scene of revisit and revision shows how American conceptions of space and power are structured around the elimination or sequestration of "the savage." As Quijano explains, colonized peoples were inferior races and their knowledges and culture existed not in a European teleology but as part of a primitive, irrational, and premodern past based in nature.[40]

In the lecture "The Phantom Friend Returning," Derrida shows that the fraternal friend and the Schmittian enemy rely on one another for their existence, but that ultimately this binary is unstable.[41] Schmitt insists that the political depends existentially upon the figure of the enemy and the determined possibility of "actual war": "Should only neutrality prevail in the world, then not only war but also neutrality would come to an end. The politics of avoiding war terminates, as does all politics, whenever the possibility of fighting disappears."[42] This decisionism, required by the state of exception, is the theory of the enemy, which becomes the condition of politics in the twentieth century. Schmitt continued to support "decisionism" and the need for the possibility of war, which he describes in *Political Theology* as the ability of the sovereign to decide "where there is an extreme emergency as well as what must be done to eliminate it. Although he stands outside the normally valid legal system, he nevertheless belongs to it, for it is he who must decide whether the constitution needs to be suspended in its entirety."[43] For Schmitt, "the exception, which is not codified in the existing legal order, can at best be described as a case of extreme peril, a danger to the existence of the state or the like."[44] Importantly, only the sovereign can decide whether such a political (versus an economic) state of exception exists, and thus whether an enemy must be killed. Depoliticization must be avoided at all costs, and therefore if there were no enemy, one would need to be invented. In Schmitt's view, depoliticization would lead to rogue violence, the stakes of which become higher with technological innovation. This is the fear. But for Derrida, through depoliticization, and the deconstruction of this conception of the political, another politics—another democracy—could be implemented.[45] This genealogical deconstruction would reveal how the nation-state "commands in the name of birth, of a national naturalness which has never been what it *was said to be*."[46]

Derrida speaks of Schmitt's imprisonment and interrogation from 1945 to 1947 for his collaboration with the Nazis, and yet his unwillingness to admit the weaknesses of his own theories up until the moment of his death. Schmitt wished to awaken a traditionalism that was beginning to wane in the mid-twentieth century, visible for him in the loss of the public/private distinction, which ensures the submission of women and people of color. The enemy has always been a public one, thus a masculine one. Schmitt, like Heidegger, wanted to get behind the subjectal or anthropological determination of the friend couple and remove all psychological, anthropological, moral, aesthetic, and economic determinations: "Never in the thousand-year struggle between Christians and Moslems did it occur to a Christian to surrender rather than defend Europe out of love toward the Saracens or Turks. The enemy in the political sense need not be hated personally, and in the private sphere only does it make sense to love one's enemy, i.e., one's adversary."[47] The concept of a private enemy is meaningless, and in fact, the very sphere of the public emerges *with* the figure of the enemy. For Schmitt, there is no such thing as an enemy on the individual, psychological, and subjective level, but rather he exists as an objective and natural enemy. In Schmitt's continual return to the necessity of the "real possibility" of war, he attempts to purge the friend/enemy concepts of all private expressions of emotion, making all forms of violence possible. As Derrida conveys, in Schmittian logic, the enemy is by definition a stranger, and I wage war on him without hatred, without intrinsic xenophobia.[48] When war is possible, the enemy is already present, which constitutes the human as a combating collectivity.

Friend and enemy become hyperbolic opposites of one another, contributing to the philosophical idea of absolute hostility. Schmitt discovers this fundamentally pessimistic attitude in thinkers like Machiavelli and Hobbes, who in his mind were the only systematic, authentic, and coherent thinkers of human nature. War ensures the continuance of the political, dependent upon the friend/enemy distinction. The body politic should always correctly identify the foreign enemy outside itself, but this is never truly accomplished. This failure speaks to a fundamental problem with the concrete idea of the enemy. In Derrida's view, the purely political enemy that Schmitt uses to define the political is unattainable, but Schmitt still insists that this ideal discourse is practical and empirically proven.

Concrete thinking about the need for an enemy and the possibility of war, which defines political thinking in the twenty-first century as well, is therefore dangerous and flawed. As Derrida insists, in modern terms, the foundation of citizenship in a nation is obscure and mystical, foreign to rationality, and consequently it will always be exposed to "sophistications," mystifications, and perversions of rhetoric, which reproduce the worst symptoms of nationalism, ethnocentrism, and xenophobia.[49] Therefore, contrary to Schmitt, it is not enough to free the concept of a public enemy of all private hatred, for as the Western genre clearly shows, xenophobic passions cannot be removed in this way. In Schmitt's rigorous upholding of "decisionism," of his concrete view of politics, he actually confirms for Derrida that the fraternity is a symbolic "conjuration" rather than a natural law.[50]

Schmitt exemplifies the kind of thinking that promotes war as sustaining life, for if life is combat and everyone is a combatant, then war occurs on behalf of life. At the heart of the political, in this understanding, war is the exception, and because killing is exceptional, it remains the decisive event. However, in reality, the exception is the rule. In combat, the most extreme possibility (of the political grouping of friend and enemy), Schmitt believes that human life gains its political tension. What he is essentially saying is that rarefaction (war is still the exception) intensifies the political tension and reveals the truth of the political, which is that the less war there is, the more hostility: "To the extent that wars today have decreased in number and frequency, they have proportionately increased in ferocity."[51] Schmitt therefore denounces neutralization and depoliticization in modernity, but the symptom is actually over- or hyperpoliticization. As Derrida explains, "The less politics there are, the more there is, the less enemies there are, the more there are," and the same with friends.[52] In *The Concept of the Political,* Schmitt contends that "a world in which the possibility of war is utterly eliminated, a completely pacified globe, would be a world without the distinction of friend and enemy and hence a world without politics."[53] While Schmitt states that it is irrelevant whether such a depoliticized world is desirable, Derrida asserts that it is clearly not a world that Schmitt wants, for it would be like a "dehumanized desert."[54] So, while a world without politics may contain, for Schmitt, other oppositions, other "interesting antitheses and contrasts, competitions and intrigues," because it has no enemy and no friend, it becomes uninhabitable.[55]

However, as Derrida concludes, Schmitt's "purely concrete" division between friend/enemy, like the nation-state itself, is haunted. Schmitt, in vain, holds on to his "Platonic dream" that these concepts remain pure even when they are, for Derrida, clearly contaminated.[56]

This is because the concrete, or polemical, reality is directly opposed to the spectral (a synonym for "abstract" or "empty"). However, Derrida suspects that by welding polemical to concrete, and opposing these concepts to the "spectral, abstract, and empty," whatever is concrete is placed out of reach in its purity, outside of analysis, as the irreducible. But the abstraction of the specter always haunts the concrete: "ceaselessly appeals, is always exceeded, overtaken—let us say haunted—by the abstraction of its spectre."[57] To overcome this haunting, Derrida describes how Schmitt must compulsively refer to the concrete, a word that appears with frequency in his political writings. Schmitt's theorizing necessitates a structural disavowal of the difference between performance and theory, since he would not agree that his discourse on politics is only theoretical, which amounts to a kind of denial of reality. This inversion of signs (where the friend can be the enemy and vice versa) means it is impossible to tell the difference between the concrete (the "real possibility" of war) and the spectral. Schmitt's own logic on the concrete leads him to crisis because he will never admit to the dead end of his own logic—the reality of absolute war and absolute hostility as leading, in the modern era, to total annihilation. He will not admit that his own philosophical purity carries the consequence of the annihilation of humanity qua humanity.

Derrida extends his thinking on the friend/enemy distinction and its implications for democracy through the partisan, which Schmitt elaborates on in *Theory of the Partisan*.[58] Schmitt explains the partisan as a marginal figure in history in the classical European interstate war between regular armies until World War I. In the case of the partisan, "war remains *bracketed*, and the partisan stands outside of this bracketing," a fact that determines his "essence" and "existence."[59] The partisan can be the one original claim, for the one who came before, "indigenous" to whatever land, place, or country.[60] For Derrida, the figural specter that lies in wait within "concrete" politics is the partisan "who no longer respects the normal conditions and juridically guaranteed boundaries of war," who does not respect this law of the *"concretely determined* enemy."[61] In political philosophy, the partisan connotes the possibility of absolute hostility through the internal destabilization of the state through revolution, which, as Schmitt asserts, places "the area's entire population" at "great risk."[62] Importantly, as Schmitt's repetitive use of *he* suggests, within the theory of the partisan, absolute hostility can only occur between "brothers." The absolute war that Schmitt talks about—the revolutionary war—drives the theory of the partisan to its extreme point, for in this type of combat, "he has moved away from the conventional enmity of controlled and bracketed war, and into the realm of another, real enmity, which intensifies through terror and counterterror until it ends in extermination."[63] The war that violates all laws therefore, in Derrida's view, can be fratricidal war, through which the fraternal figure of the friend returns.[64] This brother enemy has both a biblical and Greek tradition, and indeed there are many examples where closeness creates hostility and the closer the bond, the more intense the hostility. However, Derrida notes that Schmitt does not even mention the sister, and rarely the brother, but when he does mention the brother, he does so with utmost seriousness, as the originary friend who is a sworn by oath, and also as the friend killed in absolute war: the absolute political enemy.[65] As Derrida observes, because the brother can be the enemy, the brother enemy is a "wound within myself."[66]

The impossibility of any assigned female person to enter this scene of wounding—this scene of absolute hostility—leads to Derrida's insight that the ultimate partisan is, perhaps, the sister:

> An inhabited desert, to be sure, an absolutely full absolute desert, some might even say a desert teeming with people. Yes, but men, men and more men, over centuries of war, and costumes, hats, uniforms, soutanes, warriors, colonels, generals, partisans. . . . In vain would you look for a figure of a woman, a feminine silhouette, and the slightest allusion to sexual difference.[67]

If she does not even appear in the theory of the partisan, the theory of the absolute enemy, then what if she were the absolute partisan? Following this logic, Derrida surmises that she becomes an enemy who blurs and interferes with "the reassuring limits between hostility and hatred, but also between enmity and its opposite, the laws of war and lawless violence, the political and its others, and so forth."[68] For Schmitt, this question of women could not be answered in political theory, because women are outside politics—outside of fraternity.

What concerns humanity in general has no political significance for Schmitt. In *The Concept of the Political*, he writes that "the concept of humanity is an especially useful ideological instrument of imperialist expansion, and in its ethical-humanitarian form it is a specific vehicle of economic imperialism."[69] The universal concepts of humanity, earth, and world are, for Schmitt, foreign to the political. As a result, in Derrida's view, the sister becomes the "Antigone between all these families, finite or infinite, or inimical brothers."[70] This must lead to an admission that the politics of the nation-state is phallogocentrism in action. There are many indications of this in European cultures, in the Bible, in the Koran, in the Greek world and in Western modernity. Political virtue has always been virile virtue. Women's slow and painful citizenship would go hand in hand with the symptoms of depoliticizing neutralization noted by Schmitt. This leads us to the ultimate realization: this structure, this phallogocentrism, could only be combated outside and beyond the name "politics." However, Derrida claims that this requires a complex double gesture: on the one hand, not renouncing the logic of fraternization and replacing it with another one, therefore one politics rather than some other, while on the other hand, simultaneously working to denaturalize the figure of the brother: "his authority, his credit, his phantasm."[71] In order to deconstruct fraternal authority, the first thing would be to take into account that there has never been anything natural in the brother figure, either in the face of the friend or the enemy. Feminist masculinity in this chapter might therefore work toward this denaturalization.

The exclusion of the sister, and by proxy the effeminate homosexual, repeats in American Westerns that reify the coconstruction of masculinity and nation. These histories make feminist masculinity a notable intrusion on the genre, suggesting a groundswell of potential change. For much of the history of the genre, fraternization justified turning sister-outsiders into objects rather than subjects. This is obviously true of not only the typical Western but also the buddy cop movie in which the emotional bonds between men are portrayed with much more gravity than any friendships between women. In *Westworld* and *Godless*, friendship and fraternity become troubled concepts, ones that are difficult to recover without unconsciously defaulting to de facto fraternities built on principles of sameness—masculine narcissism rather than difference.[72] Feminist masculinity can lead to unruly alliance, to a different mobilizing force, as the twenty-first century continues to replay this theater of exclusion with relentless predictability.

The Revisionist Western

While earlier Westerns consistently framed the battle between white people and Indigenous people as ontological, in the immediate post–World War II era, Western films became more visually and psychologically expressive and critical. They could be described as revisionist because of visual stylization (away from a focus on grand landscapes) or narrative trajectory. As scholars of the Western Jim Kitses and Gregg Rickman write, the revisionist Westerns entirely, or partly, interrogate traditional representations of history and myth, heroism and violence, masculinity and minoritized populations.[73] Revisionist tendencies can also be found throughout silent and sound eras, and likewise, classical elements also continued after the war. Movies like Howard Hawks's *Red River* (1948) are examples of the "super-Western" (after André Bazin), in which conventional elements merged with other genres, like film noir.[74]

John Ford is an exceptional revisionist director whose postwar cavalry films critique expansionist idealism, Western heroism, and confrontations with Native Americans.[75] Scholars of the Western Mary Lea Bandy and Kevin Stoehr recommend *The Searchers* (1956) and *The Man Who Shot Liberty Valance* (1962) as "true masterpieces within Ford's later project of disclosing the dark underbelly of the American West's progress from wilderness to civilization."[76] At the same time, Ford expresses ambivalence about masculinity and the role of women in this so-called narrative of progress. As cultural critic Nancy Schoenberger writes in *Wayne and Ford*, masculinity can be "a maudlin elegy for something that never existed—or worse, a masquerade that allows no man, not even John Wayne, to be comfortable in his own skin."[77] Figures like Wayne add fuel to the so-called crisis of masculinity by increasing the tension between the objective (images, representations, performances) of masculinity and the subjective (the personal, individual), which means that everyone falls short.[78]

Consequently, while Ford's later films transformed the genre, they do not offer the possibility of feminist masculinity, as I am defining it in this chapter. For cultural anthropologist Maureen T. Schwarz, a Western must meet certain standards to qualify as feminist:

> the plot must constitute a subversion of and a challenge to a mainstream text; the actions of a female protagonist must drive the plot rather than simply provide a reason for the actions of the male character or characters; the dialogue of one or more female protagonists must challenge and subvert masculine discourse as well as convey agency; and meanings must be plural rather than singular.[79]

While I agree with this assessment, I echo film studies scholar Fran Pheasant-Kelly's insistence that attention must also be paid to a film's grouping.[80] Feminist masculinity must be portrayed as an intersectional group formation, rather than as a solitary pursuit, and in as realistic a way as possible, taking into account historical research on the West.

Throughout the late classical and revisionist eras, there are examples of strong, independent women, for example Hallie (Vera Miles) in *The Man Who Shot Liberty Valance* and Vienna (Joan Crawford) in *Johnny Guitar* (1954), but rarely do they productively unite with others.[81] *Calamity Jane* (1953), and its portrayal of Calamity's (played by Doris Day) relationship with Katie Brown (Allyn McLerie), is one of the only Westerns in this period that offers "positive sisterhood."[82] Outside of this aspect, however, the film is staunchly conservative. Calamity Jane wears filthy (but tailored) buckskins, but she is trained to behave domestically. Her independence is contested, temporarily, until she makes a negotiated peace with Wild Bill Hickok (Howard Keel). The resolution includes her marrying Bill in a white dress (even though she, not Bill, drives the buckboard after the wedding).[83] Few Western productions feature a group of women as central to the narrative, with perhaps the exception of *Westward the Women* (1951).[84]

Many consider *The Man Who Shot Liberty Valance* to be one of the most tragic and emotionally impactful Westerns in existence.[85] The film is largely constructed through flashback and is set in the early twentieth century. The train, a symbol of modern civilization in countless Westerns, brings Senator Ransom Stoddard (James Stewart) and his wife Hallie from the east to the town of Shinbone to attend the funeral of Tom Doniphon (John Wayne). Tom's and

Ransom's stories of their earlier years in Shinbone unfold through Ransom's memory during Tom's wake. In front of a preserved stagecoach, Ransom tells the new journalist of the *Shinbone Star* the supposedly true story of the unknown man. It begins with a robbery of Ransom's stagecoach, carried out by Liberty Valance (Lee Marvin), a man with no morals but whose unofficial authority is unchecked by local law. Ransom, a morally idealistic young lawyer, is beaten, and his law books are destroyed. After the robbery, Tom finds Ransom and brings him back to Shinbone. Ransom suffers humiliation from Liberty, but he eventually succeeds in gunning him down, but only with the help of Tom. As flashbacks end later that day, and after Ransom has finished telling the supposedly true story of their lives, another train takes him and Hallie away again. But as the train leaves the station, the mood is one of deflation and loss. As Bandy and Stoehr observe, in this scene, "we see a politically important man and his wife seated together, aged and tired, not at all heroic but rather deeply, sorrowfully aware of what has been lost."[86] Hallie has placed on Tom's coffin a cactus rose, which she found in the desert while Ransom was busy with the journalist, suggesting that "life in Washington has offered Hallie no cactus roses."[87] Her allegiance is torn but seems to lean toward the land and people of her youth, including Tom—not to the new civilization that the lawyer-turned-politician represents.[88] The ending of the film is ultimately unclear and unsatisfactory for all involved.

Hallie's character shows that even as women began to take on more heroic or central roles in films, the Western was still a limited gendered space of white male action.[89] As David Lusted insists, there are few suffragettes, farmers, or professional women, but many mothers, schoolteachers, sex workers, saloon girls, ranchers, and Native American wives. When the romance hero's objective is to civilize the West, white women become key to a "successful transition."[90] As Lusted recalls, in Ford's *My Darling Clementine* (1946), the racialized and sexualized character Chihuahua loses out to a demure white woman, and the price she pays is the loss of her own life, as is the case with nearly all Indigenous women in Westerns.[91] While revisionist Westerns did provide "active and independent" roles for white women, they are often met with resistance from men.[92] In this respect, Ford's revisionist female characters are major departures from genre conventions, as they are often mature women who, in

Gaylyn Studlar and Matthew Bernstein's words, "ensure the birthright of future generations of Americans" through which masculinity takes on feminine values, which would include care.[93] These mature women exist in sharp contrast to the female characters of director Budd Boetticher Jr., for example, producer of low-budget Westerns in the late 1950s, who believed that the heroine is only important because of what she provokes; in herself she has not even a slight importance.[94]

Hallie both rejects and upholds the traditional female role in the Western. She returns to Shinbone not as a maternal figure but as a politician's wife on a life journey of her own, to some extent. However, she never significantly tests male authority, and she shields herself from performing the kind of resistance that would provoke a response. Hallie disrupts the ideal of heterosexual partnership as the common resolution in Westerns, particularly when national unity is at stake, but because her allegiance is ambivalent throughout, both in the scenes that take place in present-day Shinbone and in the flashbacks, her status is uncertain. Hallie's melancholy also serves as a statement of her ambivalence, as her losses are palpable from the moment she enters the town, which is also devoid of joy. As Bandy and Stoehr note, there are no "bustling town folk tipping hats, no 'Howdy Ma'am' outside the general store, no kids playing with dogs, no happy ranchers driving up in their wagons." Throughout these early scenes, Hallie holds tight to a large, striped hatbox, her face somber and drawn. Wrapped tightly in garments of mourning that represent her solitude, she is "nearly overcome with her remembrance of the past."[95] While Ransom is being interviewed by the reporter, Hallie takes a ride out "desert way" with the old man Link Appleyard (Andy Devine), former sheriff of Shinbone and a friend of Hallie's from the old days. Link and Hallie arrive at Tom's burned-out ranch, the music reminiscent of Ford's earlier film *Young Mr. Lincoln* (1939), a symbol of the death of a loved one. Hallie points to the cactus rose and glances longingly at Link, asking him to get one for her so she can put it on Tom's coffin.

Hallie may be educated, the wife of a senator (former first governor of the state, bound for the vice presidency), but her mourning for Tom is palpable, along with the masculinity he represents. Tom is Hallie's would-be suitor for much of the film, and he displays a very selfish and possessive love for her. He alone has decided Hallie's future; she will work hard by his side on the ranch and raise a family. By contrast, Ransom is a teacher, who gives Hallie the opportunity to read and write. Similarly, if Hallie chooses Ransom, she will be his "helpmate" in his future career as a major political figure on the national stage. Either way, while Hallie is feisty and strong-minded, she lacks ambitions of her own. The most agency we see in Hallie is in her ability to express that she may have made the wrong choice. Most importantly, Hallie is alone and isolated, without a source of unruly alliance, which underscores that sisterhood is not a prominent feature in the Western in general.

Politically speaking, the film revolves around the tension between the Old West's difficult and sometimes violent transition to modern democracy and an ordered system of rights and liberties. Hallie is the ultimate partisan, in Derrida's terms, who hovers at the edges of political discourse between brothers, even if Ransom does seek his wife's permission to talk to the journalist. The tension between the wilderness (the cactus rose) and the garden (the town, civilization), implies that the old order of primitive justice is "nonetheless retained in some degree in modern society's continuing need to satisfy personal vengeance in terms of state-sanctioned violence" against the true enemy.[96] The problem of masculinity remains unresolved as well, for the time may come when someone like Tom is needed to settle scores with the so-called true enemy. Civilization and the law must leave room for Tom's version of justice.

If women are civilizing forces in Westerns, then Hallie's ambivalence signals persistent political questions. However, ultimately, the tensions and conflicts between the masculinities of Liberty, Tom, and Ransom are the focus of the film, and their triangulated relationship structures the plot. Hallie's family owns a restaurant called Peter's Place, the confined stage set where the personalities of the three men clash. Their triangulation corresponds to the three typical, competing masculinities in the Western: Ransom represents the townspeople or agents of civilization; Liberty is the "savage" or "outlaw" who threatens the town; and Tom is the hero who possesses the skill of the "savage" or "outlaw" but is committed to the townspeople.[97] In one of their most intense confrontations, Hallie observes the action from a distance, perpetually unsure both of herself and the men, while Ransom is the butt of the joke for both Tom and Liberty.

The "Not (Quite) Yet" of a New Collectivity

FIGURE 6. Ford presents statehood as the best solution in the Wild West, but Tom maintains his status as the "good bad man" whose vigilante skills may be needed one day. *The Man Who Shot Liberty Valance,* directed by John Ford, featuring John Wayne, Jimmy Stewart, and Vera Miles (1992; Los Angeles: Miramax, 2013), DVD.

Tom initially refers to Ransom as "pilgrim," but then his reluctance to use a gun to "settle scores" leads Tom to rename him "tenderfoot." Meanwhile, Liberty refers to Ransom as "dude," which at the time meant "a person from an urban environment, an easterner who has arrived in the West and is presumed to be inexperienced."[98] Clearly, Ransom is treated with suspicion by both men, since his presence represents a loss of cowboy culture and masculine bravado. At the same time, however, Tom is kind to Ransom and gives him his credit at the restaurant until he can get back on his feet. This suggests their interrelationship—Ransom as representative of the state and Tom as the violent actor waiting in the wings (Figure 6).

Ransom and Tom's quarrel over Hallie demonstrates Eve Kosofsky Sedgwick's theory that masculinity is not defined and defended simply in a binary relationship to the feminine but rather through their competition over a desired love object.[99] Anxieties about homoeroticism and homosexuality (both desire and the act itself), and a fear of the feminine, become major definitional elements of masculinity in the Western. When the hero expresses desire for his rival's lover, he disperses homosexual panic while still being able to imitate and admire his rival freely.[100] In this form of mimetic desire, the desire to possess the love of another, the woman ceases to function as a subject and becomes an object of exchange.[101] The triangle schematizes how gender and desire act as conduits for masculine power. The pushing away of both femininity and homosexuality becomes part of the rhetorics, symbolics, and "conjuration" processes of fraternization, which props up nationalism, ethnocentrism, androcentrism, and phallogocentrism. As Jasbir K. Puar writes, the nation is both familial and fraternal, and homosocial fraternal relations affirm both the heteronormative family and the silence of women and serve as consolations for the prohibition of homosexuality.[102]

Ransom's effeminacy accentuates Tom's butch swagger, and making fun of Ransom becomes one of Tom's favorite pastimes. When Tom senses that Ransom is (ineptly) attempting to flirt with Hallie, he remarks to his Native American sidekick, Pompey (Woody Strode): "Well, Pompey, looks like we've got ourselves a ladies' man."[103] When Ransom works in Hallie's kitchen under her direction, he wears a girly apron, which further codes him as effeminate. Liberty also makes fun of Ransom by chiding, "Lookee at the little waitress." Tom intervenes (one of several times he saves Ransom's life), but Ransom still pleads with Tom, "I don't want a gun; I want to put him in jail." Tom replies, in a condescending and paternalistic tone: "I know those law books mean a lot to you, but not out here. Out here a man settles his own problems." At this point, Tom begins to call him "tenderfoot," a nickname that also dispels queer panic by veiling his jealousy and desire for emulation.

When Ransom puts up a shingle announcing his intent to practice law, Tom warns again that posting a sign like that in public will require that he carry a gun. Tom's constant reminder about a gun makes audiences wonder not only whether Ransom will follow Tom's advice but also whether an ordered system of rights requires violence (or at least the threat of violence) to protect it from external challenges.[104] Hallie's character can only observe this tension, as she has no ability to sway the outcome one way or another. Ransom persists, however, in his quest to civilize Shinbone. Working out of *Shinbone Star* editor Dutton Peabody's (Edmond O'Brien) office, he supports the editor's defense of homesteaders who want statehood, which weaves in the larger political story of the settlement of the West.[105] Tom, by contrast, is against statehood, since as a "rugged individual," he is more concerned with his ranch, with finishing the new addition to the house so that he and Hallie can marry and start a family. However, his methods of trying to court Hallie are "clumsy and brutal."[106] There is an alarming scene in which Pompey attends Ransom's school and reads the phrase "inalienable rights" aloud from the Declaration of Independence. The film gestures toward Pompey's nearly enslaved status, as he becomes another prop for Tom's ego. Tom conveniently intervenes at this moment to stop all this "book learning," which is corrupting Pompey and turning the townspeople into sissies, who will not be able to fight off Liberty and his gang. Tom may also envy Ransom's education and sincerity, which are ultimately persuasive for Hallie, but he would rather burn his own house down than admit his envy.

Ford ultimately embraced the inevitability of progress and often took a populist perspective on behalf of the little guy. He presents statehood as the best solution for most people and Ransom as the best leader. However, at the mass meeting for the election held at Hank's Saloon, chaos ensues, and it is Tom who restores order, nominating Ransom as one of two delegates to represent them in the territorial convention for statehood. Tom, therefore, is the "good bad man," "who exists amid historical and political transition—as the threat of violence that is needed to secure the establishment of a democratic system of ordered freedom."[107] Meanwhile, Liberty claims himself "the delegate from south of the Picketwire," which is rejected, leading to Liberty's moment of revenge: "You got a choice, dishwasher; either you get out of town, or tonight you be out on that street alone. You be there, and don't make us come and get you."[108]

That night, Ransom practices out in the desert with a borrowed pistol, while a drunk Peabody notices a typo in the newspaper. Before trying to fix it, he goes to fill his jug at the Mexican saloon. Liberty and his men wait for Peabody; among them is Reese, played by Lee Van Cleef, who became famous a few years later when he played the evil Angel Eyes opposite Clint Eastwood in *The Good, the Bad and the Ugly* (1966). In a brutal act of revenge, Liberty forces Peabody to eat a copy of his own newspaper, before beating him with his trademark silver whip. All his files and type are destroyed, and they leave him for dead, placing a newspaper over his face and smashing all the windows. After hearing the bullets, Ransom rushes out from the restaurant to find Peabody beaten but alive. In this moment, he decides to face his fear of Liberty, and he returns to the restaurant to get his newly acquired gun from the carpetbag under his bed. Hallie runs to Pompey, who is waiting nearby, and tells him to go get Tom. Ransom walks out into the street, timidly, shaking while holding his gun, looks into the newspaper office, and moves along in the shadows, waiting. Liberty comes out of the saloon, yelling, "Hash-slinger, you out here?" Ransom and Liberty walk toward each other, and Liberty tells him to come closer where he can see him. Liberty shoots him in the arm, causing Ransom's gun to fall, but he allows Ransom to pick it up with his left hand: "All right, Dude, this time, right between the eyes." Liberty aims his gun while the men are not far apart, and while each fire, it is Liberty who falls dead. Ransom walks back to the kitchen, holding his arm, collapsing on the bed, mirroring an initial scene after the stagecoach robbery. Hallie wraps his wound while crying, and he looks back at her, knowing that she is in love with him. Tom is in the doorway, realizing he has finally lost Hallie for good.

However, keeping with the mood of ambivalence, the story fails to provide total confidence in Tom's form of justice, after he handles the rejection poorly. He snaps at Hallie, telling her he will "be around," and slams the door on his way out. He lights his trademark Wayne cigarette, walks past the saloon while Liberty's body is taken away on a buckboard, and proceeds to get very drunk. Pompey rescues Tom from this debauched state and takes him home, Tom driving and yelling the whole way, still drinking. Tom bolts into his house before Pompey has a chance to stop him and sets fire to the addition he was building for Hallie and his future family. Pompey carries him outside as the house and the surrounding trees burn to the ground. It is hard not to feel some sympathy for Tom, while his violence is differently terrifying than that of Liberty. There is also a sense that he is a would-be abusive husband, whom Hallie narrowly escaped. As Hong writes, white masculinity strategically distances itself from femininity through a consistently repeated display of bravado. Tom reaffirms American individualism for a postwar world through a predictable frontier mentality, while simultaneously hinting at its limitations.

The last section of the film takes place in Capitol City at the convention, where Ransom is elected territorial representative to Congress. Based on his reputation as Liberty's killer, he is clearly the best champion of law and order. At this point, Tom enters through the swinging doors, wearing a dusty jacket. He sits on the lobby stairs, "dirt-smudged and mean-looking, smoking and getting angry."[109] Ransom leaves the hall, disgusted by his own reputation as a murderer, but Tom intervenes with the truth, as he lights another match that reveals his scraggly beard and bleary eyes: "You *talk* too much, *think* too much. Besides, *you* didn't kill Liberty Valance. Think back, Pilgrim. Valance came out of the saloon. You were walking toward him when he fired his first shot. Remember?"[110] This scene shows that the entire film has been a process of remembering, which thrusts viewers into a flashback within a flashback. The camera zooms in close and holds on Tom, who releases a deep drag from his cigarette as the moment of truth is revealed. As Bandy and Stoehr note, the true climax of the film is not the shoot-out between Ransom and Liberty but Tom's revelation, which makes Tom the central masculine figure in the story. Ransom may be well-versed in book learning, but he is no hero. However, while Tom earns viewers' sympathy for this "twisted act of heroism," this scene also signals his exit from the plot.[111] Unlike in *The Searchers,* there is no curative closure for Tom, no final majestic shot of Tom riding off into open country with his friends, and we already know that Tom never used his gun again and never rebuilt his ranch.

In this battle between myth and reality, myth wins out, along with statehood and modern democracy, but the need for Tom lingers. At his funeral, we learn that Tom was long ago stripped of his cowboy identity, forgotten by Shinbone. He lies in the coffin without boots, spurs, or gun belt, which upsets Ransom, and he insists he be buried with his cowboy gear and identity intact. While Tom is unknown to them, they demand to know the true story, claiming the public's right to knowledge. The film is therefore part mystery, part Shakespearean tragedy, part morality play, with a focus on both dialogue and reflective silence, stripped of the kind of masculine physical activity we expect from the genre.[112] However, to Ransom's surprise, after the interview, the newspaper editor tears up his notes and delivers one of Hollywood's most famous lines: "This is the West, sir. When the legend becomes fact, print the legend."[113] In *Westworld,* Anthony Hopkins's character, Dr. Robert Ford, mastermind of the amusement park of the same name, repeats this line ironically, which shows how the line crystallizes the dialectic between realism and romanticism that "underlies the genre as a whole."[114]

As Ransom leaves the little room, he turns to close the door and sees the cactus rose on top of the coffin. The camera zooms in

FIGURE 7. As they board the train back to Washington, D.C., Hallie is deflated and lost, torn between her life with Ransom, a future vice president, and Tom's memory. *The Man Who Shot Liberty Valance,* directed by John Ford, featuring John Wayne, Jimmy Stewart, and Vera Miles (1962; Los Angeles: Miramax, 2013), DVD.

on the flower, "a recurring symbol of love and passion throughout Ford's oeuvre."[115] Hallie lets Ransom know the truth, that she placed it there, in memory of the flower he once gave to her. At the same time, there is a loss of respect for Ransom, because he is relieved that the editor tears up the notes, allowing him to return to Washington with his reputation intact.[116] Her longing for Tom occurs against this backdrop of loss in the faith of representative democracy, the supposed excesses of which were foretold by Schmitt, showing that we may need Tom after all, when the chips are down. Moreover, Tom may be a drunk—he may even be a womanizer—but he is the only honest man of the three, and he ultimately wins Hallie's heart even after death (Figure 7). As for Hallie, she is "not yet" a figure of feminist masculinity, an accommodation that symbolizes both the survival and a simultaneous questioning of the friend/enemy distinction. Ultimately while law and order prevail, the possibility of actual war against an enemy (in Schmitt's terms) is retained.

Like in many Westerns, the railroad in *The Man Who Shot Liberty Valance* is the vehicle for masculine nostalgia, foreshadowing the social movements of the 1960s and '70s, which will threaten the supremacy of white masculinity. The railroad is a constant in the

Western regardless of whether its presence is historically accurate, symbolizing a film or show's desire to "encounter history" and to connect the static world-making of the West to so-called progress and ultimately to the fear of death and extinction.[117] Masculinity is consumed by the melancholic task of prophesying its own demise. The film ends where it begins: with Tom's funeral. The railroad also expresses the growing fears that the Wild West is being permanently replaced by machines and technology, rendering the concept of manpower obsolete. Masculine physicality—carnal and sexual, all qualities associated with Wayne and the "good bad man"—will ultimately, however, withstand these changes, in one form or another.

A similar railroad-centered Western is *Johnny Guitar*, directed by Nicholas Ray, which presents for the first time an active and independent woman who resists male authority until the very end.[118] Vienna (Joan Crawford) challenges male dominance through her ability to wield a gun and own property, two qualities that historically defined female agency in the genre. In fact, some argue that *Johnny Guitar* is the closest to a Hollywood feminist Western in this period.[119] The film is set in a baroque saloon house owned by Vienna, who provokes the envy of the local township because she has invested in land that will no doubt increase in value with the arrival of the railroad. Their envy grows hysterical, as represented by the character Emma Small (Mercedes McCambridge). Several scenes on horseback show Emma as a bitter, solitary, and sexually repressed woman who dresses like a widow. Her envy of Vienna is most apparent in a stunning close-up, as she turns to face the camera exultantly after setting fire to Vienna's place. This is the climax to a film in which Vienna has tried to mediate among conflicts "dominated by death, betrayal and revenge."[120] By offering hospitality to the Dancin' Kid (Scott Brady) and his band of outlaws and finally harboring an injured youth, the tolerant female world she stands for is condemned. Surviving a failed attempt to hang her and a gunfight with Emma, Vienna runs off with Johnny Guitar (Sterling Hayden), washing her hands of the assorted ranchers, outlaws, and the posse set on her destruction: "still in pants, still more than equal to any man."[121]

There has been some disagreement about whether the film is important as a potential lesbian film or as a harbinger of gender confusion. In *Female Masculinity*, Jack Halberstam includes Vienna, and her nemesis Emma, in the category "predatory butches." While films like *Johnny Guitar* may have incited hostility toward lesbians, which were thought to be spreading like a disease in postwar urban centers, Halberstam argues they have since become inspirations for butches.[122] Other scholars insist that the battle is between Emma's conservative, stereotypical lesbianism and Vienna's more fluid gender and sexuality. For Jennifer Peterson, what is most important about the film is its polyvalency and the recognition, not necessarily resolution of, multiple discourses of gender.[123] Emma is always presented in her black tweeds, while Vienna changes from black trouser suits to dresses, abandoning the white costume that signifies her purity when Emma sets fire to the saloon. For Lusted, at this point, she reveals the trousers beneath, suggesting she has it all, both breasts and a gun.[124]

Gender trouble is also symbolized by Vienna's attachment to the men she employs, whom she cares for paternalistically when the saloon closes down, giving them money and courage to make their own way. While both Johnny and Vienna use guns as phallic symbols, Johnny is a reformed gun-obsessed vigilante who tries to win Vienna back by showing his softer side. He prefers his tiny guitar and refuses to carry a gun until it becomes necessary. In the beginning of the film, Johnny becomes the butt of the joke for the Dancin' Kid, Vienna's lover, who emasculates him by calling repeated attention to his lack of a gun. Vienna and Johnny also play contrasting musical instruments (Vienna's choice is a grand piano set on a stage, which she plays adeptly during a confrontation with Emma and her gang). Vienna is the one to stir the action in the film, while Johnny is passive, often an observer at the edges of the frame.[125] Neither is completely defined by their gender, and Vienna's masculinity is not a sexual deterrent for Johnny.[126] The song that opens and closes the film also reveals that the story is told from Vienna's point of view: "There was never a man like my Johnny, like the one they call Johnny Guitar."[127] This combination of role-playing and female point of view makes Vienna one of the few "self-sufficient individualistic" female Western heroes, "triumphantly affirmed by the narrative."[128]

However, while Vienna does offer the possibility of a feminist masculinity, she does so within the same triangular formula as *The Man Who Shot Liberty Valance*. Here the triangle between Emma, Vienna, and Johnny guards against gender confusion and progress, portended by the arrival of the railroad. In part, the film functions ideologically to punish white women after they entered the workplace in large numbers during and after World War II, achieving higher social and economic status. Crawford modeled the film after her own struggles infiltrating the so-called boy's club in the Pepsi-Cola corporation. As feminist film theorist Molly Haskell explains, through these characters, white women had to "pay for" ascending the employment ladder with a fall from "the pedestal," a fall that is expressed through characters that were both "hard and squishy, scathing and sentimental." Haskell sees these characters as evidence of a backsliding from the feminism of the 1920s and '30s, as they could only possess a "pseudo-toughness, a façade of steel wool that at a man's touch would turn into cotton candy."[129] The vertigo caused by this fall from the pedestal is expressed in *Johnny Guitar* through the use of high angles and nighttime scenes, which gives the film a "labyrinthine and claustrophobic" feel.[130] The enclosed space was a popular type of setting for noir films, a genre that also sought to limit the perceived spreading threat of women, who were coded as crossdressed spies and traders, jewel thieves, and man-eaters.

However, aspects of this film do depart significantly from the norm, setting the stage for *Godless* and *Westworld*. Vienna and Emma inhabit a complex landscape of masculinities, but it is the women, not the men, who provide much of the dramatic tension. Vienna is certainly not the wilting lily who fortifies her husband's virility, as in Grace Kelly's portrayal of Amy Kane opposite Gary Cooper in *High Noon* (1952). For a time, the female objects (Vienna and Emma) refuse their roles as "passive co-conspirator[s] in the process of triangulation" and instead become active subjects.[131] By making a physical fight between two women a central narrative element, the film unsettles the fraternal contract and shifts away from the classic Western's more blatant rejection of women. It is hard to imagine John Ford or any other director of a Western film putting women at the center, but in *Johnny Guitar*, the most feminine figure is a male cook named Old Tom, who dies when he is caught in the crossfire during the confrontation with Emma's gang.

Ultimately, the film depicts the calamity that would ensue should women be allowed to enter the fraternity and become involved in the serious business of nation-building. In the end, Vienna kills Emma and reunites with Johnny, confirming the impossibility of unruly

FIGURE 8. *Johnny Guitar* breaks with typical roles for women in the Western, but the film ends with a violent showdown between Emma and Vienna, canceling the possibility of unruly alliance. *Johnny Guitar,* directed by Nicholas Ray, featuring Joan Crawford, Mercedes McCambridge, and Sterling Hayden (1954; Republic Pictures, 2012), DVD.

alliance between women. In woman-woman-man triangles, female homosociality provides the ground for women to function as subjects, but this can only be an imagined function. For feminist philosopher Iris Marion Young, women live the contradiction of being, on the one hand, transcendent "free subjects" and, on the other, objects for the pleasure (and entertainment) of patriarchal society.[132] Men ultimately cannot function as objects of exchange, because it would be too threatening to patriarchy. Overall, sexist domination, exploitation, and oppression erode the relational fabric between women, encouraging them to take one another down (Figure 8). Vienna obsesses over Johnny with theatrical intensity. The grating hostility between these two women, and their eventual showdown, speaks to how feminists have been denigrated throughout history, excoriated for what Sara Ahmed calls their "killjoy" effect on everyone around them.[133] Their disagreement over the railroad confirms the supposedly self-evident truth that they are the ultimate partisans, incapable of fraternal bonding. They allegorize the crisis of modernity—through Emma, representing the conservative townspeople, and Vienna, the modern woman—and the railroad once again puts the viewer in a position of "encountering history," all the while soothing anxieties about a potential breakdown of the gender order.

The Not (Quite) Yet of a New Collectivity

In modern democracies, fraternity is "the symbolic bond alleging the repetition of a genetic tie," which persists even after death, as birth and death become like bookends preserving national identity through the patronym.[134] In this symbolic bond, the seeds of ethnocentrism, populism, and xenophobia are planted, establishing the root systems for the global atrocities committed in the twenty-first century. Such crimes and abuses prove the intractability of this discourse of fraternity, as the locus where "truth, freedom, necessity, and equality come together."[135] Given that fraternity is a structuring principle of American masculinity, it is difficult to see how the future can open onto anything new. Here, Derrida insists that one would have to return to a form of friendship that does not belong to the *philia*, *phusis*, or *logos*, one that is not, or is not yet, political in the Schmittian sense.[136] In this space of the prior, the concept of the political could be resituated, revealing the instability of the friend/enemy distinction. *Unruly alliance* is a term for a new relationality, formed in this chapter through feminist masculinity.

In my analysis of *Westworld* and *Godless*, I revisit Antigone, whom Derrida names as the exemplar of the sister-outsider who is rendered mute in this friend/enemy dialectic. Scholar of the Western Anthony Mann argues that Westerns are so popular because of the raw, primitive characters, resembling the "sweeping legends" of Greek plays, like *Oedipus Rex* or *Antigone*.[137] For Derrida, the sister functions for the fraternity as the "Antigone between all these families, finite or infinite, or inimical brothers."[138] The politics of the nation-state is phallogocentrism in action.

In the Greek tragedy, Antigone insists on giving her brother, Polynices, son of Oedipus, a respectable burial after he is killed fighting his brother, Eteocles. The two brothers were alternating, sharing rule over Thebes, until Eteocles rejects the arrangement. Polynices gathers an army to attack Thebes in a battle that claims both of their lives. King Creon then ascends to the throne and issues a decree that Polynices must not be mourned or receive a proper burial because of his assault on the kingdom. Antigone openly defies Creon, and he condemns her to be buried alive in a cave. Creon eventually changes his mind and tries to free Antigone, but she hangs herself in the cave before he can reach her. Shortly after, Creon's own son Haemon, who was in love with Antigone, dies by suicide by impaling himself on his own knife. His mother, Queen Euridice, kills herself in response, all of which suggests that it is Antigone who has caused the destruction of Creon's entire household. He becomes an elderly, failed figure, indicating that Antigone has succeeded in destroying him, even in death.

The fear of similar chaos keeps the fraternity in place. Antigone's crime breaks the incest taboo, the very structuring principle of patriarchal kinship relations, which, according to structuralist anthropology and psychoanalysis, cannot be altered without society falling apart. However, rather than focusing on Antigone's incestuous draw to her brother, I turn instead to consider Antigone's relationship to her sister, Ismene, who initially refuses to help Antigone bury her brother: "We're born women, we're not brought into being / To war with men; and second, that we are ruled / By those whose strength is greater, and we must yield / To this—and to much that's worse than this."[139] However, when Ismene changes her mind, Antigone is insulted, "Do not share my death, do not take as your own / That which you did not touch! My death will be / enough!"[140] Sophocles makes unruly alliances between women impossible in the play, which suggests their enduring exclusion from the kinds of virtuous bonds that carry political significance. Antigone cannot invoke the law of the father, or speak in his voice, without repercussions for politics and culture, but she also cannot rally together others without unleashing an even more threatening chaos. The crushing of Creon's spirit—which occurs after Antigone's suicide—would be realized exponentially if unruly alliances were allowed to form.

The characters in *Godless* and *Westworld* do recognize in each other the potential for unruly alliances, as at the same time they diverge from the racial inequalities of the feminist Second Wave. The threshold between nature and culture that is destabilized under the specter of incest also becomes threatened when persons outside the fraternal order enter the polis. For Judith Butler, such a shift reveals the interchangeability of social norms and the symbolic, and the counterfeit quality of so-called timeless and elementary structures of intelligibility.[141] These Westerns invoke Antigone and Ismene as harbingers of a different future, but instead of engaging in self-defeating infighting, they take refuge in each other. By refusing their places in well-established narratives of the West, they expose the inflexibility and cruelty of heteropatriarchal rule. They also refuse the mantle of self-reliance, so central to normative masculinity, by defending together their bodies and futures. They disturb the pact that mid-century Westerns once made with viewers that white masculine hegemony, supported by beautiful white women and scenery, would be restored by the end credits.

Not surprisingly, 9/11 reinvigorated the Western after a decade of decline.[142] Shows like *Deadwood* (2004–2006), *Longmire* (2012–2017), *Wynonna Earp* (2016–2021), and *Yellowstone* (2018–) and films like *Open Range* (2003) all support dominant conceptions of masculinity and nation. *Deadwood* is set in the 1870s in South Dakota as the community grows from a camp to a full-fledged town. David Milch, who created, produced, and wrote the show, intended to explore the enduring theme of bringing order out of chaos, which suggests once again how the Western becomes a vessel for both the containment and expression of political and cultural concerns.[143] Former vice president "Deputy" Dick Cheney is from Wyoming, which is also the home of the Johnson County War, the basis for the Western films *Shane* (1953) and *Heaven's Gate* (1980).[144]

Westerns like *Deadwood* legitimized the war on terror, contributing to a national narrative of continually expanding freedom, "intertwined in a complex skein of legalism and myth, material accumulation and moral disavowal."[145] As Robinson offers:

> A raw, collectively experienced event was deliberately and cynically reconfigured into an absurd abomination of propaganda, public manipulation, and the counterfeiture of human rights. Licensed by these machinations, everything that preceded September 11 was obliterated. And in lieu of an explanatory back story, a history, the public was lured into a sycophantic chorus on "evil." The history, as usual, was well worth forgetting.[146]

Permanent yet unpredictable violence as a guarantor of freedom—this "counterfeiture" of human rights—characterizes the lead up to the twenty-first century and beyond. In both of his administrations, Bush played a major role in furthering the civilizational struggle against Islam, yet in true postracial fashion, with the backing of a multicultural personnel. After 9/11, a new era of global war was inaugurated, which represented a return to pre–World War II liberal imperialism, deepening a shift that had already begun in the 1990s.[147] For Singh, this "long war" was neither a "clash of civilizations" nor active imperial administration "recommended by a few outlying pundits" but a reinstallment of a more primal American race war and "fantasy of national social and economic regeneration through (frontier) violence."[148] George W. Bush used numerous clichés of the Wild West, which were delegitimized (for critics) by news of the extrajudicial violence taking place in Guantánamo Bay, Abu Ghraib, and Fallujah.[149] Atrocities in these shadow sites occurred even though torture and enslavement are internationally recognized as nonnegotiable breaches of human rights.

In the first decade of the 2000s, women in Westerns were returned to the status of outsider. Wildermuth conveys that there was a "rise of a culture of masculine protectionism in America post-9/11 culture where men are seen as protectors and women as helpless victims in the face of threat to the American security state posed by international terrorism."[150] For Lynn Spigel, this was the consequence of the perceived need to make American audiences feel they were in a moral position, and this tendency ran through a number of genres.[151] As feminist scholar Susan Faludi offers, the "women as victim" trope in the aftermath of 9/11 was directly related to the cowboy rhetoric of George Bush and the search for the "guardian of the homestead" who could protect the American family.[152] Women were also participants in justified revenge, contributing to an atmosphere of "universal, cross-gender, national determination," which demonstrates the genre's adaptability and political relevance.[153] Martin Holtz describes Maggie (Cate Blanchett) in *The Missing* (2003), for example, as a victim of traumatic loss whose vengeance/rescue mission is a sign of a mainstream feminist, pragmatic activism. She accepts Native American culture, and yet in the end, the integrity of the white family, and the nation's moral authority, must be guaranteed.[154]

What has yet to be represented in this historical sweep of the Western is the presence of feminist masculinity and unruly alliance. As referenced earlier, Fran Pheasant-Kelly insists that for a film to be feminist, attention must be paid to a film's grouping. Feminism must be portrayed as intersectional and collective rather than solitary and individual.[155] The grouping must be depicted in as realistic a way as possible, using historical research on women in the West and the roughness of life on the frontier (disease, natural disasters, dead cattle, etc.). Films must include close-up shots of women and themes of miscegenation, or potential miscegenation along with a disruption of the Native-American-as-perpetrator/white-woman-as-victim binary.[156] All the female characters must be skilled horse riders. As Maria Cecília de Miranda N. Coelho notes, "the horse acts . . . as an equalizer that gives women as much freedom and power as men."[157] White masculinity must be portrayed to some extent as failed or unstable (e.g., immature, sleazy, drunken, lacking in manliness, etc.).[158]

Directed by Scott Frank, *Godless* went into production in September 2016 and was released on Netflix on November 22, 2017, one month after #metoo went viral (even though the Me Too movement had been around since its 2006 creation by Black social activist and community organizer Tarana J. Burke).[159] Frank situates the miniseries in the 1880s in La Belle, New Mexico, a defunct mining town run entirely by women after most of the men have been killed in an accident. The only man to survive from inside the mine is a listless wanderer whom the town calls John Doe. Meanwhile, the evil villain,

Frank Griffin (Jeff Daniels), searches in vain for his adopted adult son, Roy Goode (Jack O'Connell), who shoots Frank in the arm during a brutal train robbery. By stealing the money and running away, Roy tries to draw Frank away from the town so he can hunt him down and kill him and then distribute the funds to those in need. Frank seems to deserve this fate, as he commits every possible violation of civil society—rape, pillage, and theft—all while pretending to be a preacher. When Frank loses the arm that Roy shot, he carries it around, wrapped in cloth and covered in a swarm of flies, which suggests both the gangrenous quality of normative masculinity and its potential amputation.

The most subversive feminist masculinities in the series are Alice Fletcher (Michelle Dockery), who operates a horse stud, and Mary Agnes McNue (Merritt Wever), the cross-dressed, de facto mayor of the town. The locals believe Alice brought bad luck, one reason being that the town's sheriff, Bill McNue (Scoot McNairy), saved her from a brutal rape. She moves in with a Paiute family and marries one of them, but he is later murdered by the townspeople. Meanwhile, Mary Agnes is a no-nonsense sharpshooter who, after the mining accident, dons her dead husband's attire and reverts to her maiden name. When she is not (successfully) wooing former sex worker Callie Dunne (Tess Frazer), the richest woman in town, she is preparing the women for a face-off with Frank.

Critical reviews agree that because of its female cast, *Godless* can be labeled a feminist Western. One commentator writes that it is "a proto-feminist pasture, shot in a sweeping 2.39:1 aspect ratio where horses roam and women rule. And the show sets itself up for those women to stand their ground against Frank's outlaws."[160] However, more significantly for the #MeToo era, *Godless* takes sexual assault as its central theme, proposing that unruly alliances are required to overwhelm this existential threat. To this end, the show proves how remarkably the genre responds to historical currents as it tracks the ebb and flow of American culture and politics. As American studies scholar Richard Slotkin conveys, not only can Westerns be read through politics, but politics can be read through Westerns, as even the campiest of Western fables reflects the gender and racial ideals for that time.[161] Most importantly, *Godless* relocates sexual assault from a purely metaphorical function to an activist one. As Sabine Sielke argues, in discourse and images, rape is often represented metaphorically, as "an insistent figure for the social, political and economic concerns and conflicts."[162] Sexual assault has been dealt with openly as a part of the Western genre after 1955, as a result of the development of the ratings system and society's willingness to see women as victims of unwanted sexual advances.[163] However, as evidenced by *Duel in the Sun* (1946) and *The Ballad of Little Jo* (1993), tragedy and epic are often the preferred forms.[164] Women are victims or avengers, but within a purely symbolic register, a tradition that Coelho argues stretches back to the *Iliad*. However, she also feels hopeful that change is possible: "One can only hope that this will happen when writers and directors recognize the Western's heroization of rape."[165] In my view, *Godless* attempts to redress this history through representing the reality of rape rather than exploiting it for symbolical effect.

Godless ushers in a primal scream, a moment of breakage, and a time of reckoning. The first episode contains a flashback scene of a lone survivor who has been raped during the train robbery, singing the elegiac and haunting hymn "He Is the Power in My Soul."[166] The show makes visible what Ann Cvetkovich describes as the "dual movement involved in the forming of nation-states": the exclusion of the traumatized subject and the simultaneous "patriotic celebration of nationhood."[167] The very constructs of nation and masculinity rely on the control of sexuality as an area of prime national interest, either through women's role as "symbol of the national hearth and home" or through various forms of sexual enslavement or abuse.[168]

The camera bears witness to trauma, utilizing low camera angles and uncomfortably intimate close-ups of diverse characters rather than only of male heroes and villains.[169] When Alice recounts the story of her rape to Roy, the attack is revealed through flashbacks from her point of view, including close-ups of her traumatization.[170] She clearly remembers her own body in a yellow dress, lying on the ground in a forest clearing. Through a point-of-view shot from her perspective, we see a group of men form a circle around her, disguised with horned buffalo heads.[171] Bill rescues Alice, but Alice makes her own bid for revenge when she stabs one of the attackers over and over in the torso.

Preferring reality to fantasy in an era of permanent war, *Godless* presents an uncensored and unadulterated West, where smallpox consumed entire towns, dead babies were placed in shallow graves, and grisly scenes of crime and despair were prevalent. The stark, dusty, and dangerous set of *Godless* therefore resembles more closely the diminished life chances on the frontier. *Godless* moves slowly, in rhythm with the actual pace, where there would have been little entertainment, endless hard labor, and a lot of waiting for the next natural or human-made disaster. What is left of masculine authority is either completely inept and immature, in the case of the young Whitey Winn (Thomas Brodie-Sangster), or ersatz and clueless, like Mary Agnes's brother, Bill. During the shoot-out with Frank and his gang, an overconfident Whitey tries to take them on alone and, while showing off his pistol tricks, gets stabbed in the chest.[172] When Bill confronts Mary Agnes about her expressions of masculinity, she responds wryly, "Someone's gotta take care of things around here."[173] Mining executives planning a hostile takeover of the town and its resources receive the brunt of Mary Agnes's resistance when she asks, in response to their "business" advances, "How deep is your shaft?" Mary Agnes is authentically attired in a man's shirt and waistcoat, and she always wears a gun and holster. She has the erect posture and the demeanor of a cowboy and wears a ridgetop hat, a traditional cowboy hat slightly taller than the average.[174] Her character can be compared to Jo Monaghan (Suzy Amis) in *The Ballad of Little Jo,* an independent sheep farmer who cross-dresses to avoid criticism from the men around her.[175] However, different from Jo, Mary Agnes not only is cross-dressed but also asserts an apologetically butch/trans subversion of normative masculinity, one that is active rather than defensive.

Godless also departs significantly from the two most common representational tropes for Native Americans: the "primitive savage" incapable of civilization or the "noble savage" who is still supposedly primitive but is uncorrupted by European civilization. Particularly in classical Westerns, the former provides justification for racial genocide, while the latter offers appeals to save and preserve their heritage and populations.[176] However, even revisionist Westerns that use Native Americans and women as central subjects invariably choose Native American men and white women.[177] In *Godless,* unruly alliances cohere instead around scarring and the refusal of historical amnesia. Alice lives with her Paiute mother-in-law, Iyovi (Tantoo Cardinal), a character with her own feminist masculinity, and her half-Paiute son, Truckee (Samuel Marty). Iyovi and Truckee are fully

FIGURE 9. In contrast to Vienna and Emma in *Johnny Guitar,* Mary Agnes and Alice work together to defeat Frank Griffin and his gang. *Godless,* episode 7, "Homecoming," directed by Scott Frank, aired November 22, 2017, on Netflix, https://www.netflix.com/title/80097141.

fleshed-out characters with substantive speaking roles. Not only are the actors Indigenous by heritage (it was common to use white actors in blackface or redface in previous eras), but the characters regularly speak the Paiute language. Instead of a male figure, it is Alice who communicates and lives with the Paiute, a radical departure from the conventional characters of John Wayne who often played the role of arbiter.

In the final shoot-out with Frank and his gang, a collective of women plays the resistant role. However, Alice is at first reluctant, which shows she is not in favor of gratuitous violence but will do what it takes to save the town (especially after she sees Charlotte Temple [Samantha Soule] struggling to fire a gun). The camera takes a distance shot of Frank and his men as they approach town on horseback, obscured by a cloud of dust. The town buildings are deserted, and silence prevails, adding to the suspense. Director Scott Frank uses a crane shot above the hotel to show Alice and Mary Agnes on the rooftop, like a future Ismene and Antigone, ready to shoot. Typical of Westerns, the action speeds up at this point and includes shots of women in the hotel with guns ready and quick cuts to the men, creating the appearance of a barrage of gunfire. Frequently, Alice and Mary Agnes are united at the center of this exchange of fire, which contrasts with Vienna and Emma who are at odds with one another (Figure 9). They easily gun down the men one by one, while inside the hotel, the women hold their own, with some mishaps. As Stella

Hockenhull writes, "The section is balletic: filmed in slow motion, an unusual technique for television but certainly owing a debt to the Bloody Porch sequence in *The Wild Bunch* (Peckinpah, 1969), the women's prowess is championed as a result."[178]

When women function as objects of exchange for the nation rather than speaking subjects, they experience a kind of disembodiment. As Young explains, when female-identified persons live their lives in the roles that patriarchal culture assigns them, they become "physically inhibited, confined, positioned, and objectified." They are taught to deny their desire to live in a world "constituted by [their] own intentions and projections."[179] One of the effects of feminist masculinity is that as the characters become more masculine, they become increasingly embodied, no longer confined to gloomy interiors.

At the same time, recent criticism of *Godless* compels me to place a "not yet" at the end of this celebratory analysis. Hockenhull ultimately determines that despite its masculinized female characters and the predominance of women, the show retains the tradition of a male hierarchy in which violence rules and women must conform to feminine stereotypes. Her criticism of Alice is compelling. While she wears trousers and a Boss of the Plains brown felt hat, the original cowboy hat that was later molded and creased to suit preferences, Alice still puts on dresses or fitted tops at other points to adhere to the townswomen's habits and demeanor.[180] Through Alice, *Godless* conforms to the Western tradition in which "'high-ridin' women hand their power over to the men they choose to follow."[181] Alice owns and breeds horses, and yet Roy is the expert, unafraid to handle the more unwieldy animals.[182] At one point, Alice attempts to rope a horse, but only partially succeeds, and the animal ultimately breaks and pulls her through a fence. It is Roy who initiates Truckee into the masculine world of horse riding, against the overprotective wishes of Alice and Iyovi.[183] Alice never rides romantically in open terrain either, preferring instead the confines of the homestead.[184] Alice's and Mary Agnes's abilities as markswomen are questioned by the fact that it is Bill and Roy who ultimately kill the rest of the gang.[185] Frank flees only to be killed later in isolation by Roy, whose revenge is actualized. Ultimately, *Godless* questions and revises many normative conventions of the genre that were revived after 9/11, but it still retains some key aspects.

In the very different mode of sci-fi dystopia, feminist masculinities in the HBO series *Westworld* claim personhood and citizenship through the blurring of the lines between natural and artificial embodiment and subjectivity.[186] The show is based on the dystopic vision of Michael Crichton's original 1973 film, which became a media franchise that included the sequel *Futureworld* (1976) and television series *Beyond Westworld* (1980). The 2016 series has a similar plotline and takes from the original its portrayal of a realistic, high-tech amusement park called Delos, which advertises itself as a vacation experience: "Boy, have we got a vacation for you!"[187] In the original film, there are three worlds (the American Old West Westworld, European Medieval World, and Roman World) featuring lifelike androids who experience a viral infection in their programming, which causes the female androids to suddenly reject sexual advances from patrons. While some viewed the film as a warning of the dangers of technology, Crichton's intention was to criticize corporate greed, which becomes evident when the park owners refuse to shut it down after the initial signs of the virus.[188] In the 2016 series, female AI figures not only reject the guests' advances but come together to take over the park.

The 2016 series seems to take cues from *Heaven's Gate* (1980), a film that denies any possibility of hope for a United States not founded on bloodshed and white supremacy. The film rejects the progressive story of Western settlement based on foundational myths and instead portrays a murderous, classist, and racist order in which fulfilling personal relationships are impossible.[189] In similar tones, the 2016 series reveals that the region has always been scenery and prop for Western imperialism, only now women of color and sex workers have become formidable resistant subjects within this elaborate architecture. AI hosts initially do not even know to question their roles in the world that has been created for the benefit of these patrons. The more extreme guests engage in unmitigated rape, murder, and theft, but their crimes are erased by morning as the game begins again. However, these docile bodies begin to exceed the grasp of both guests and corporate executives.

This approach to the West as scenery and prop creates the very space of in-betweenness that Schmitt so steadfastly disavowed. It invokes Bhabha's concept of the "unhomely," or the overlap and displacement of domains of difference where "the intersubjective and collective experiences of nationness, community interest, or cultural value are negotiated."[190] The unhomely is a political and aesthetic application of the Freudian notion of the "uncanny" or *"heimlich/ unheimlich,"* a psychic location that is both familiar and strange.[191] As Bhabha argues, "While the dominant subject attempts to establish a homogenous cultural space through (an imposed) authority and (problematic) authenticity, the subordinate unsettles, shatters, and disrupts domination."[192] The "unhomely stirring" in *Westworld* leads to "interstitial intimacy" in which things that are normally "spatially opposed"—the organic and the artificial, the public and private, past and present—begin to blend together.[193] Within these gaps of experience, unruly alliances are discovered, nurtured, and lived out, as the scenic West begins to be dismantled, like a dream manufactured in the hands of a few brothers.

The railroad expresses again this desire to encounter history, only now history is reconceptualized as this unhomely location, a place where "guests" are transported in and out of an endless narrative repetition and gender script that begin to wear out. The railroad always connects to the static world-making of the West, to supposed progress and to patriarchal rule, but in *Westworld,* the tables are turned and the game has changed in favor of the marginalized.[194] The repeated line from Shakespeare's *Romeo and Juliet,* "These violent delights have violent ends," reveals that the guests will eventually have to pay for their transgressions.[195] In addition, through the superior strength of AI, *Westworld* replays to an extreme degree the fear that machines and technology (and outsiders to the fraternity) are replacing the manpower of the Wild West. The railroad is the harbinger of the machine's hostile takeover, metaphorically conveying the idea that women of color, who have been relegated to the status of objects, will ultimately demand retribution—will demand life.

Specific characters in *Westworld* perform feminist masculinity, which emasculates both guests and administrators. Dolores Abernathy (Evan Rachel Wood), a farmer's daughter, develops a feminist consciousness when she and her father, Peter (Louis Herthum), discover a photograph of a twenty-first century guest left out in the field, a woman posing in a modern cityscape unlike anything she or her father have ever seen. Like Antigone, Dolores is a seer, and life becomes impossible once she comprehends the fakery of her world. Home and world, gender and nation, begin to collide as, in Bhabha's words, "the recesses of the domestic space become sites for history's most intricate invasions. . . . Uncannily, the private and the public become part of each other."[196] Eventually this moment of awakening compels her to leave the family scene, which repeats daily, in exactly the same form. In Spanish, the word *dolores* means the plural of "pain," again suggesting that relations cohere around shared trauma rather than self-sufficiency. Maeve Millay (Thandiwe Newton), a Black sex worker, also begins to experience flashbacks from the repeated violations she has survived at the hands of the guests. Dolores and Maeve attempt to override their configurations, which prevent them from acting like men, and eventually, all the AI figures begin to wake up and access emancipatory scripts coded deep in their subconscious. They bear literal and symbolic arms in the struggle against the park owners, a metaphor for Creon and the state, entwined with neoliberal multinational corporations, which command authority over the body-minds excluded from the fraternity (Figure 10).

Crucially, Maeve and the other sex workers who defy white male authority do so on their own terms, because of their own awakening, in contrast to films like Clint Eastwood's *Unforgiven* (1992), which supposedly seeks to protect sex workers from violence but in the end condones a frenzy of unremitting brutality.[197] *Westworld* allegorizes the crisis that occurs when outsiders to the fraternity begin speaking, together, with a voice of authority, forming new horizontal networks. In a moment of realization and reckoning, they reengage the masculine on collective terms. Referencing slavery, Maeve begins to have flashbacks about mothering a child she was forced to leave in a previous narrative after she is murdered by one of the park's most frequent and sinister guests, the Man in Black (Ed Harris). This guest desires above all to have the park's secrets disclosed to him and to have access to any woman he desires. Maeve imagines a man in a white suit in a laboratory setting, a completely anachronistic and unfamiliar kind of figure in the nineteenth-century American West. Maeve demands answers from a friend, a bandit and member of a gang of marauders that rolls through town providing entertainment by shooting at innocent bystanders. She insists that she has been shot near her hip bone, but despite desperate grasping for a memory, she can only vaguely recall the incident. She asks the bandit to stab her with a knife and retrieve the imagined bullet, but his script does not

FIGURE 10. Maeve and Dolores bear arms together against the park owners, despite their differences, a novel development in the Western. Top: *Westworld*, season 1, episode 2, "Chestnut," directed by Richard J. Lewis, aired October 9, 2016, on HBO, https://www.hbo.com/westworld/season-1/2-chestnut. Below: *Westworld,* season 1, episode 6, "The Adversary," directed by Frederick E. O. Toye, aired November 6, 2016, on HBO, https://www.hbo.com/westworld/season-1/6-the-adversary.

permit him to hurt her. Maeve stabs herself instead and pulls the bullet out of her pelvis, demanding at that point that the bandit have sex with her, which puts her in a position of power.[198] The dissolution of the artificial/nature divide that occurs when these characters begin to "wake up" unsettles the naturalness of masculinity and nation, which leads to a simultaneous questioning of the Law of the Father, Creon's (and others') phallic claims, and political alliances achieved through fraternity and virile virtue.

Beginning in the revisionist era, both the ideology of Manifest Destiny, which guided American expansion, and the manifest destiny of masculinity are discovered to be unstable.[199] In some contemporary shows, the Western is laid bare, stripped of its mythological weight. Against the backdrop of the *unheimlich* echo of John Wayne as Tom Doniphon, we are witnessing not only a eulogy to normative gender relations but also a farewell to a particular vision of race and nation. Undoing the Western occurs through the reimagining of masculinity and the deconstruction of the fraternity that sustains normative gender relations and politics itself. In the wake of 9/11, new Westerns propose the utility of unruly alliances based on mutual aid rather than on the violence of the administrative state within the policed boundaries of national projects.

In capital's global phase, *Godless* and *Westworld* remember the subjects, communities, practices, and knowledges that have been repressed by nationalist epistemologies. Women of color in these new Westerns disorder rather than condone race and gender hierarchies. As Hong conveys, in contrast to white men, Black, Latina, and Native American women are thought to inhabit a state of "antiwill," which, in liberal humanist contexts, means social death, since the will is a precondition for personhood, and having will turns a person into a subject that the state is bound to protect.[200] The state becomes an agent of violation and dispossession, a reality that *Godless* and *Westworld* represent through substantive female characters. Victims become makers of history through assertions of will and acts of remembrance.

However, these shows also reveal how unruly alliances have "not (quite) yet" arrived. While *Godless*'s representations depart from many of the harmful tropes of the past, it fails to include Black people in its portrayal of unruly alliances. After the shoot-out, the dust and the uncanny presence of riderless horses suggest this victory may be darkened by the death of the many who have not survived. A nearby community of formerly enslaved people called Blackdom is victimized by La Belle's racist indifference, as it becomes known that the La Belle silver mine has been poisoning their water supply for years.

FIGURE 11. The citizens of Blackdom agree to help the white women defend their town, but they are soon slaughtered by Frank and his posse. *Godless*, episode 3, "Wisdom of the Horse," directed by Scott Frank, aired November 22, 2017, on Netflix, https://www.netflix.com/title/80097141.

After the citizens of Blackdom agree to help the white women defend their town, Frank and his posse slaughter the entire community. This tragedy represents the nearly nonexistent life chances for formerly enslaved people who fled the South and went west after the Civil War, a phenomenon that is nearly absent from the genre. A notable exception is *Buck and the Preacher* (1971), in which Buck (Sidney Poitier) leads a wagon train of formerly enslaved Black people west after the defeat of the Confederacy.[201] In desperation, they turn to a community of Native Americans, who eventually come to their aid just as their wagon train is about to be overrun by white bounty hunters. In *Godless*, the slaughter of Blackdom at the hands of white bandits and the neglect they tolerated from the white women show the reality of the frontier and the ways in which Black people migrating from the South were treated with indifference or outright abuse. By poisoning their water supply, the women show the public willingness to kill and to quarantine—and to leave to die from a distance (Figure 11).

In *Godless*, the crime against the Black community, and the failure to come to their aid, airs during the time of Black Lives Matter but offers no hope for the efficacy of Black revolt. Viewers are led to celebrate the victory of white women over white men, while Blackdom is relegated to the dustbin of history. Culture promotes not only the outer wars but the inner wars in the United States. The renewal of a primal American race war appears in *Godless* in the form of Blackdom. The presence of this community shows how the "social contexts of racial(izing) division at home and civil(izing) war overseas were more than uncanny, parallel universes: they were part of the same economic, cultural, political and societal condition."[202] The show fails to centralize the suffering of Black people and instead turns them into collateral damage, denying the existence of "a democratic Black political culture that frequently supplants hegemonic moral consciousness with a democratic social ethic of its own, one that is capable of redeeming what has been lost and/or negated."[203]

Godless also mirrors problems in the Me Too movement. Although the Me Too movement was founded in 2006 by Tarana Burke, the hashtag only took off through an October 2017 tweet from white actress Alyssa Milano. High-profile women followed Milano's lead, which added magnitude to the epidemic of sexual assault in the United States but also made clear that these issues are only significant when they are tweeted about by the rich and famous. Misogyny and homophobia saturate all our communities, but the oppressed people who are most privileged should not be the only ones who get to have their oppression taken seriously. At the heart of this problem lies the refusal to acknowledge interdependence with disability, labor, and race-based movements. Feminist masculinity should follow the lead of transnational and women of color feminisms, which articulate the relationship between gender and the various hegemonies scattered all over the world, including global economic structures and patriarchal nationalisms. Transnational feminism crosses boundaries of nation, race, and class that perpetuate the perception of a separation between identity categories, bringing attention to the linkages between imperialism, colonialism, and capitalism.[204] In highlighting how gender and sexuality aid in the production of raced and classed nationalities, transnational feminism expands beyond the narrow boundaries established by the concepts of masculinity and nation, which continue to dictate responses to global phenomena.

By including the "Not (Quite) Yet" of this chapter, I join Black trans theorist C. Riley Snorton in his assertion that social movements exist in the tense of the "future imperfect." The connection between *Godless* and #MeToo becomes an opportunity to think about "what assumptions and politics about memory are fomented within various political movements, including Black Lives Matter, Trans Lives Matter, and Black Trans Lives Matter, which are invested in securing the existence of black and trans people in the present and into the future." The practice of remembering and saying the names of people who are slain also demands "new structures for naming that evince and eviscerate the conditions that continually produce black and trans death." It is possible, then, that contemporary social justice movements are "rhetorical enactments" that "evince a different conception of history and therefore necessarily a different rubric for valuation."[205]

Godless reveals the malleability of normative masculinity and its adoption by a variety of identity categories for their own gain. The incredible resilience of normative masculinity is also foretold in *Godless* when Frank hisses, "This here's the paradise of the locust, the lizard, the snake. It's the land of the blade and the rifle. It's godless country. And the sooner you accept your inevitable demise, the longer you're all gonna live."[206] After his posse is dead, Mary Agnes begins to get too trigger happy, shooting bodies that are already dead, until Bill tells her it is enough to kill them once. But is it? These shows also address the difficulties of eradicating normative masculinity. At the very end of *Godless,* long-awaited Pastor Garret Moore (Chris Bylsma) finally arrives in La Belle to take his post in the church the women have been building all along, but he comes upon a funeral rather than a baptism. The scenes of death with which this show concludes suggest that killing toxic masculinity does not automatically signal its defeat.

As masculine hegemony deflates in the dystopia *Westworld,* the landscape loses its pristine quality, becoming stained, bleak, and empty—somewhere you feel lost, where death stalks you at every turn. These scenes suggest crisis without resolution. However, this place of loss provides an opportunity to think about how feminist masculinity illuminates the gap between the name and the reality of democracy. What are the implications for the future of fraternity and for democracy? Can the name *democracy* be used for anything other than this fraternity of virtue, this appeal to nature assumed by the classical thinkers and carried on throughout the history of Christianity and the Enlightenment?

In the twenty-first century, within ever-tightening neoliberal and reactionary constraints, our relationships to one another can become fragile and porous, but they have the potential to become expansive. Feminist masculinity is instrumental for divesting white male individualism of its unique hold on the American imagination. Unlike charity, mutual aid—or "voluntary, reciprocal exchange of resources and services"—conveys equality rather than superiority.[207] Critically, such forms of mutual aid preceded white settlers in the New World, as many precolonial Black, Indigenous, and Brown communities had complex webs of exchange and care. To understand the normative masculinity promoted in American Westerns is to understand the basic refusal to care for one another in the spirit of reciprocity. As Dean Spade offers, "New capacities for caring for one another, reflecting on our work, and changing ourselves and our relationships to each other and the planet are emerging alongside worsening material conditions that threaten life on every front. At this time, our participation is critically important."[208] Beyond representation, the divestment of power through racial capitalism and fraternal politics requires urgent, strategic response and an alteration to common understandings of what it means to have power or to be powerful, as this power reveals itself in gender, sex, and race categories and in state-regulated institutions and economic systems—power not as something that one individual or one facet of society holds, wields, and abuses but as a mobilizing, spreading, and infectious energy that radically reconfigures our consciousness and our communities. Along with this new understanding of power arrives a variety of feminist masculinities that are relational rather the narcissistic, for the many rather than the few. For the most part, by revising how the West was supposedly won, these Westerns recover the idea of feminist masculinity as integral, not peripheral, to the unhomely reality of all national projects, past and present.

Chapter 4

Virtue Is Divided
Unruly Alliances in Willa Cather and Gertrude Stein

> Baby love.
> A great many people are in the war.
> I will go there and back again.
> —Gertrude Stein, "Lifting Belly" (1915–17)

> Perhaps we feel like that when we die and become a part of something entire, whether it is sun and air, or goodness and knowledge. At any rate, that is happiness; to be dissolved into something complete and great. When it comes to one, it comes as naturally as sleep.
> —Willa Cather, *My Ántonia* (1918)

Critiquing the trans and queer past has become a complex endeavor in the twenty-first century, as white scholars in particular begin to account for the ways allegiances to fraternity, racial capitalism, and the nation-state are often mixed and contradictory, or downright complicit. Discussions on trans- and homonormativity, as well as what Jasbir K. Puar calls trans(homo)nationalism, have shown how "aspirational" masculinity can be tied to normative agendas.[1] For Jacques Derrida, a kind of shadow brotherhood forms when fraternity is simply replicated by outsiders. Moving beyond the politics of fraternity requires a refusal of any kind of naturalized brother figure and, further, suspicion toward the word *community* because it can create an inside and an outside, and the need to count one's friends and enemies.[2] Moments of historical possibility have emerged outside of any concept of naturalized or assumed affinity, but recognizing these moments requires a scalpel-like approach to critique.

The lives and literary careers of Willa Cather and Gertrude Stein provide a fascinating ground for this more precise critique. Writing in the early twentieth century amid global war, both express admiration for "great men" and "great causes," in alignment with their imperialist historical moment. Through a nostalgic longing for greatness, Cather and Stein express what I call "butch exceptionalism," a form of transnormativity based in white, American monumentality.[3] This exceptionalism gave them a self-authorizing power, a license for strength and authority not granted but seized or stolen, tied in their case to whiteness and class. The butch-styled artist of this period often required what I call a "femme witness," a person of either binary gender who functioned as stage manager, typist, travel coordinator, publicist, and emotional support for the butch in her rise to success. Butch artists held a treasure chest of private feelings that could only be shared safely with carefully chosen intimates. Stein and Cather believed they were talented and rare, beyond the limitations of this world. Letters, novels, and poems also convey how they coveted suspect ideologies. As literary titans of the 1920s, the era of big projects and big plans, Stein and Cather wanted to redraw the boundaries of their gendered world. They even felt a kinship with figures like Alexander the Great, Ulysses, Napoleon, Buddha, and Christ, making them exceptional not just within the category "woman" but within humanity itself.

Queer studies has tended to label objects and individuals as either transgressive or normative, utopian or antisocial, designating them in the process as either worthy or unworthy of study. For queer theorist Kadji Amin, such a polarizing perspective cannot "adequately account for the textures of racial, historical, and geographical difference—precisely those differences marginalized across the history of queer inquiry."[4] An acknowledgment of subjects' "disturbing attachments" to race, history, and geopolitics allows for a critical spirit of incompleteness and ambiguity. Critics of Cather and Stein tend to swing between praise or embarrassment, particularly in Stein's case because of her pro-Vichy politics during World War II.[5] In dealing with the trans and queer past, there needs to be a range of methods to confront what disturbs. Amin proposes deidealization as a way to get beyond assigning a "psychically flat role of righting the ills of an unjust social order," which denies subjects the right to be "damaged, psychically complex, or merely otherwise occupied."[6] Deidealization requires that scholars question their own trained expectations and learn to "inhabit unease."[7]

Stein and Cather were complicated people who, early in their careers, also expressed tender feelings toward the soldiers at the front and those returning home from World War I. These bonds were based in *lovence,* which for Derrida captures the essence of love without temporal boundaries and fraternal attachments to selective forms of care based on affinity and sameness.[8] Paradoxically, lovence becomes possible through the military against all proscriptions. As Michel Foucault writes in "Friendship as a Way of Life," in the army, love is both "ceaselessly" incited and shamed. While laws, rules, and habits prohibit homosocial or homosexual expression of "multiple intensities," men have always found ways to short-circuit these prohibitions.[9] Intensities are woven through with lovence.

Cather and Stein at times experienced both the soldier and the nation-state as broken, which unleashed the presence of the uncanny, or *unheimlich.* Their relationships to soldiers became the subject of fiction and poetry, known for its emotional depth and complexity. Perhaps these wounded, dead, or dying men helped soothe their own sense of woundedness from decades of literary rejection and romantic heartbreak. As Stein scholar Ulla E. Dydo recalls in *Gertrude Stein: The Language That Rises,* readers of Stein must imagine the scorn she endured because of her phallic sexuality and gender expression. Despite Stein's buoyant public presentation, she was subjected to "incessant, condescending assaults upon herself as a writer, a person, and a woman."[10] Combined with the war-related trauma experienced by an entire generation, these "incessant, condescending assaults" helped shape Cather's and Stein's writing in the interwar period. In this way, exceptionalism can be viewed as a method of survival.

One of the objectives of trans and queer theory should be to apply more pressure to masculinity across identity categories, ironically taking Stein's directive to ask "what history teaches," even if that lesson leads to a painful deidealization. Here, Stein's and Cather's historical context, the varietals of white masculinity that they sometimes emulated and coveted, as well as textual representations of tenderness and care, are put into conversation to see exactly what, in Stein's words, "history teaches."[11]

Virtue Is Divided: The Transformative Power of Lovence

Biographical evidence is never simply coterminous with literary production, as creativity often exceeds or resists such alignments. However, taken together, Stein's and Cather's fiction, poetry, short stories, and letters reveal a masculinity that was not merely an effect of their lesbianism, as many feminist and queer scholars argue.[12] Desiring masculinity existed independently from sexuality and with remarkable consistency across their lives and works. In her 2003 article "Gertrude Stein Took the War like a Man," Jean E. Mills argues that Stein's textual oppositions and politics indicate a longing for a male body. Stein's works represent for Mills "a linguistic battlefield that is transgendered [sic] in nature, because each idea is constantly vying for definition or explication with its opposite—but in vain."[13] Mills even insists that Stein yearned "to remove the covering that concealed a phallus, her true self as a man."[14] Stein's literary works do offer this possibility; in *Tender Buttons* (1914), an object, like the pencil, becomes a giving phallus: "PEELED PENCIL, CHOKE. / Rub her coke."[15] Some of Stein's fashions also reflect her authorial pleasure in a campy masculinity. When she came to the United States in the 1930s to deliver a series of lectures, she wore a jockey's or deerstalker's cap, tweedy and "mannish," with a visor in front and an upcurl at the back, a copy of one worn by Louis XIII that Alice B. Toklas and Stein once saw in a museum.[16] Later in life, she wore her hair very short in the style of a Roman emperor. However, her masculinity was at times childlike, as both Toklas and the American photographer and writer Carl Van Vechten nicknamed Stein "Baby Woojums," used with the pronoun "he."[17]

From 1888 to 1892, Cather took on the name and identity of William Cather Jr., complete with a crew cut and soldier costume from the Civil War. She continued to take pleasure in a male alter ego throughout her early years at the University of Nebraska. Her college classmates remembered her unorthodox dress and her masculine personality, which they described as "'assertive, energetic, outspoken, individualistic, superior, independent, forceful, strong, self-confident, brilliant, and egotistical, as well as mannish, and boylike.'"[18] While Cather eventually gave up her male style of dress, she never relinquished her masculine emotional orientation. Her jouissance in the materiality of masculinity, including her love of football and Rudyard Kipling, persisted throughout her career.

As discussed in chapter 2, *transgender* only began to be used as an identity marker in the 1960s, and so it would be anachronistic to apply the term to the past in an identitarian sense. However, in this book *transgender* is an analytical tool for exploring masculine gender expressions, within and alongside insights from critical whiteness studies, political philosophy, and critiques of racial capitalism. For some transmasculine artists and writers, whiteness and class status allowed them to attain inclusion to a certain extent, though Cather and Stein in other ways remained outsiders and were subject to misogynistic and homophobic attacks from their publics and their male peers. Through a constellation of privileges and slights, they mapped their own masculine contours, inviting and living out their own dreams of masculinity, even if largely in private.

Critical whiteness studies scholars define *whiteness* in multiple ways, as an identity or method of understanding oneself and one's ancestry, as well as an ideology, a set of social practices, and a system of power. Nikhil Pal Singh discusses how in his notebooks, Frederick Douglass characterizes the production of whiteness as "a process of binding juridical status and despotic power—keeping the 'country,' 'putting on airs,' and arrogating expansive, extracivil rights to kill."[19] In the transition from slavery to wage-based capitalism, "generic whiteness" was defined through its denigration of Blackness, part of the quest to "banish the specter of wageless life" evoked by Black people in the postbellum period, which alerted white people to their actual conditions of market dependency.[20] W. E. B. Du Bois's statement on the "public and psychological wages" of whiteness has been widely discussed because of the connection he makes between whiteness and the monopolizing of fields of employment.[21] However, less discussed is how the terms *public* and *psychological* refer to the transfer of whiteness to the concept of nation as imagined community and the formation of race as a relation that, in Aníbal Quijano's words, prevents Black and Indigenous peoples from having any "place at all in the control of the resources of production, or in the institutions and mechanisms of public authority."[22] Rights for white people expanded in the long eighteenth century in a "privileged relationship" to Black people and Native Americans, who could—or even must—be killed.[23]

The production of race and class has depended on the valuing and devaluing of Black and Indigenous people and their social and biological reproduction toward the goal of capital accumulation and its social reproduction.[24] While racial differentiation is often thought to be extrinsic to capitalism (or as its own variant of capitalism—e.g., slavery), it is responsible for the direct production of value and is therefore key to the technical development of capitalism. Cather and Stein performed masculinity as propertied citizens, and this allowed for a limited freedom to deviate from their gender assigned at birth. Even though U.S. national identity is thought to be universal, white enfranchisement and property have been thoroughly privileged, mutually constituted through an insulated "private" sphere, which all but ensures racialized exploitation and dispossession.[25] In 1993, legal scholar Cheryl I. Harris determined that in the history of U.S. law, whiteness became a prerequisite to owning property and, even further, whiteness itself became a property that white people owned. Precedents in the law even protect "the expectation of rights as actual legal property," reifying white privilege by law.[26]

For these reasons, there are growing concerns that the intersection of transmasculinity and whiteness has not been adequately critiqued. White trans men cannot (and must not) be singled out and turned into a monolithic category for the projection of myriad grievances, but at the same time, whiteness and class offer inexhaustible privileges, particularly for those who pass. In *True Sex: The Lives of Trans Men at the Turn of the Twentieth Century*, Emily Skidmore presents numerous examples of trans men living prosperously, seamlessly integrating into small-town American life, even after their assigned gender was disclosed.[27] Within the emerging eugenics movements, trans men could become part of a white "band-of-brothers" performing "honest labor." As sociologist Miriam J. Abelson asks in her 2019 study, *Men in Place*, are trans men "a sign of more egalitarian gender relations and decreasing homophobia? Are they solely a local variation? Or are they superficial rather than substantive changes that repackage hegemonic masculinity without upsetting relations of power in any significant way?"[28] Perhaps the most honest answer is "all of the above."

Some of Stein's and Cather's longings were expressed within a psychic space of white masculine nostalgia, which cannot be neatly separated from the American exceptionalism of their time. American exceptionalism corresponds to and mirrors butch exceptionalism and connotes hubris, colonial and postcolonial greed, and the coveting of virile virtue. U.S. exceptionalism "hangs on a narrative of transcendence," consecrated through Judeo-Christian beliefs, which place the United States "above empire."[29] American exceptionalism and white exceptionalism become virtually synonymous when the United States wrongly claims, through the welcoming ethos of the "post-ethnic melting pot," that it refused the old plutocracies and class divisions in Europe and in emerging democracies.[30] As David L. Eng asserts, neoliberal forms of this exceptionalism insist on the disappearance of race in the name of freedom and progress, which shows how hegemonic nationalism and masculinity morph and shape-shift.[31]

Stein's and Cather's admiration and nostalgia for heroes of the past could be described as expressions of an aspirational desire to enter a masculine domain that was denied them and that, for the most part, they had no desire to critique. Neither Cather nor Stein felt any alignment to a feminist cause or sense of community with women authors per se. As queer theorist Christopher Nealon writes in *Foundlings*, Cather's misogyny could be "virulent" and her homophobia cutting and cruel, at odds even with her own time period, as shown in her excoriation of Oscar Wilde after his trial.[32] Cather condescended to her fellow women authors as frequently and as viciously as any male critic, despite that she suffered similar abuses after the publication of her war novel *One of Ours* (1922), which won the Pulitzer Prize. When Stein died, a copy of Alvin Langdon Coburn's *Men of Mark* (1913), a collection of photographs of well-known male figures, was found in her personal library.[33] In a short piece called "An Instant Answer or a Hundred Prominent Men," she finds her own place within this history of great men. Stein advises her readers to "Think of the Bible and Homer think of Shakespeare and think of me."[34]

While these affinities could be taken for artistic license and a sign of creative masculine play, it is crucial to note that between 1903 and 1910, Stein derived an almost parodic egotism in part from consulting the theories of Otto Weininger, an Austrian philosopher who wrote *Sex and Character* (1903).[35] Weininger lauded the Aryan male's character, his dedication to action, state, and self, in contrast to the Jew, who represented feminine statelessness.[36] In his mind, the Jew was a traitor to the politics of virility and patriarchal fraternity. However, Weininger also believed that people had a mix of masculinity and femininity and that partners should be complements of one another (extremes should seek out extremes), which allowed Stein to believe in the viability of her own masculinity—and her relationship to Alice B. Toklas.[37]

Stein's draw toward authoritarianism during and after World War II has led scholars like Janet Malcolm to ask difficult questions about Stein's complicity. In *Two Lives,* Malcolm wonders how Stein and Toklas, two public Jewish lesbians, could possibly have survived the war if they had not disavowed their Jewishness and collaborated with a gay German man named Bernard Fäy. Malcolm even unearths evidence that Stein supported Franco and that Toklas tried to free Fäy from jail after the war. Stein used Weininger's convoluted theories to craft a butch exceptionalism through which she could embrace her own genius, for being both a woman and a Jew left her outside the genius construct as an ideal and universal type.[38] Weininger's belief in the singularity of masculine women as the only women capable of creativity seduced Stein and provided her with a rationale for her exceptionalism. He even states in *Sex and Character* that masculine women, from a *"moral* point of view," should be "warmly welcomed and credited with the opposite of degeneration, that is, with having made progress and overcome handicaps."[39] For women, these "handicaps" include having no "'mind' at all": she lacks "the simplest practical purchase on everyday life" and can best be described as advancing "obvious, selfish aims" through "cunning, calculation, [and] *cleverness.*"[40] Obviously for Weininger, and by extension for Stein, women are completely incapable of achieving genius, unless they have consciously cultivated so-called masculine capacities.

The origins, obsessions, and impulses embedded in the word *genius* also warrant closer examination through whiteness. Historically, the word always connotes "white male," though the specific meaning varies across time periods. Modernists inherited the genius concept from the Romantics, but instead of seeing themselves as renewing culture and society, modernists elevated themselves above the masses in their search for "the shock of the new." The genius separated "himself" from the "humdrum routines and the banalized march of 'progress.'"[41] Stein only opened her atelier door to a select club of gifted insiders, who were generally white and male. However, when any one of them failed to recognize her genius, she shut the door abruptly, and for good.[42] Both Stein and Cather carried the blessing and liability of a formidable ego; in their minds, they were peerless geniuses without models or masters, who, like great heroes, were plagued by nostalgic melancholy.

In their sometimes rigid and paradoxical attitudes about gender, they might have echoed Henry Miller's lamentation that "the loss of sex polarity is part and parcel of the larger disintegration, the reflex of the soul's death, and coincident with the disappearance of great men, great causes, great wars, etc."[43] It was precisely the "great men, great causes, great wars" that these writers admired and sought to claim for themselves. The desire for remembrance and glory often, though not always, motivated their masculinities. Nostalgia undergirds a masculine mirage of power that keeps one isolated, and insulated, from present events. For feminist philosopher Iris Marion Young, nostalgia is a form of masculine self-affirmation—a longing for a lost maternal home. Because the object of nostalgic longing is fundamentally unrealizable, nostalgia aches like a wound that will not heal. The subject's effort to cover over the loss of childhood safety and the feeling of immortality is then projected onto female-identified subjects. As a longing for a nonexistent elsewhere, nostalgia allows one to flee from "the ambiguities and disappointments of everyday life."[44] Their nostalgic connection to "great men" and "great causes" fed their egos in numerous ways, as they attempted to prop up their own masculinity through making comparisons between themselves and the so-called great men of history.

Some of their writings therefore reflect the recurrent problem with masculine fraternity—and the securing of bonds through affinity and exclusivity. White queer and trans fraternal bonds risk a reinstallment of fraternity, because the feminine is still marginalized or outright rejected, though more as a set of qualities than as a biological category. The draw to masculinity can be expressed through affinity and liking—through what one is drawn to and seeks to emulate. However, despite this outer bravado, Cather and Stein had a tender side. Stein confessed in *The Making of Americans* (1925) that she feared her own failure as a writer: "I have been a miserable one because I have been always a little pretty nearly certain that I would be ending failing and every one enthusiastic or passionate or sensitive or excited in attacking would then make me a jealous one, a miserable one."[45] This bravado veiled the tenderness, anxiety, and insecurity within.

The double-sidedness of their lives and work mirrors the disjunction between the fraternity and the abstract principle of universality, which Derrida characterizes as a kind of wound. This irreconcilable wound as metaphor reveals a profound contradiction:

> There is no democracy without respect for the irreducible singularity or alterity, but there is no democracy without the "community of friends," without the calculation of majorities, without identifiable, stabilizable, representable subjects, all equal. These two laws are irreducible one to the other. Tragically irreconcilable and forever wounding. The wound itself opens with the necessity of having to *count* one's friends.[46]

The wound is a consequence of the friction between the desire for a society run by the elite minority and one wherein all subjects are "representable" and deserving of care. "Irreducible singularity" may refer to the "masses" that Stein and Cather rejected through their deference to the genius concept, but also to the sea of nameless, common soldiers in the war, whom they befriended and included in their writing.

As seen in chapter 3, if friendship and politics require the enemy, and the friend can only come in small numbers, then it becomes impossible to tell the difference between natural death and killing, between murder and homicide, and, further, between homicide and genocide. At what number does genocide begin, and ultimately, "who founds the law as a right to life?"[47] After the First World War, this question acquires a new urgency. Distinctions between these political crimes are "indispensable" but also less and less "applicable," which prompts the question: Who is the victim and who is the enemy, and for whom do we grieve? Death/murder/killing become more commonplace as the human being becomes less valuable. For Derrida, any grievance against the loss of value of human life would have to be directed against this "judgement handed down, concerning its givens [what is taken for granted], and the most accredited concepts of politics and the standard interpretation of friendship, as to *fraternization*."[48] Another authority would have to be appealed to, one based on human rights (as separate from the laws of fraternity that determine democracy, for example). In their war writings, Stein and Cather extend Derrida's provocative proposal that the future of the political is also the future of friends and that a radically new kind of bond is necessary if human societies are to survive the technological advances inaugurated during World War I.

The rejection of fraternity occurs through what Derrida calls lovence, or the act of loving beyond death but without the requirement of reciprocity or "equality" of virtue and rank. For this chapter and the next, lovence is viewed as crucial for unruly alliance as a vision of future relationality. Derrida discovers this new kind of lovence through a rupture in Aristotle. In the *Eudemian Ethics*, Aristotle states that it is more worthwhile *to love* than *to be loved*: "He is love-inclined who enjoys loving more than being loved; the other, however, is more honor loving. So he, enjoying being admired and loved, loves excess; but the first, the love-inclined, loves the pleasure of loving—for it is necessarily present in him when he is active, for that he loves someone is accidental (for it can escape the notice of the one loved) but his being a lover is not."[49] Derrida interprets this to mean that while *to love* is limitless (you can love someone who is dead, and you can also love an inanimate object), *to be loved* is passive and can even occur without one's knowing they are loved.[50] In Derrida's analysis, Aristotle's stated preference for the active over the passive "destabilizes and renders dissymmetrical the equilibrium of all difference: an *it is more worthwhile* gives precedence to the act over potentiality."[51] The consequence of this rupture that Derrida identifies is that "beyond all ulterior frontiers between love and friendship, but also between the passive and active voices, between the loving and being-loved, what is at stake is 'lovence' [*aimance*]."[52] Loving the deceased brings us closest to the action of loving, which is where a revision of fraternity becomes accessible. For Derrida, thinking friendship thus begins, or should begin, on the side of loving, which disturbs canonical fraternity:

> Friendship (philia) is first accessible on the side of its subject, who thinks and lives it, not on the side of its object, who can be loved or lovable without in any way being assigned to a sentiment of which, precisely, he remains the object. And if we do say "think and love" . . . life, breath, the soul, are always and necessarily found on the side of the lover or of loving, while the being-loved of the lovable can be lifeless.[53]

For Cather and Stein, lovence arises in the possibility of loving the dying and the deceased but as distinct from their narcissistic attachment to generals and famous men. Lovence describes a limitless, objectless love that can reinvent the bond-through-masculinity.

In what Derrida calls lovence, there is a certain "incommensurability" between lover and beloved, which "exceeds the very principle of calculation."[54] This "incommensurability" disorders the Aristotelian discourse on friendship because of a second principle of reciprocity stated elsewhere in Aristotle on the "mutualism" of "primary friendship," which relies first and foremost on constancy and stability.[55] Aristotle calls this supreme bond "the first friendship," which "exists only among few, those who are virtuous and have spent time together and have become dear to each other. . . . For friendship is held to be something firm and only this one is firm."[56] However, Derrida notes that it is through loving the dead that the act of friendship becomes most inscribed, which is by nature dissymmetrical. Derrida discovers an incompatibility between, on the one hand, the idea that friendship is accessed best through loving and beyond death (like the divine, in this sense, closer to perfection of the divine) and, on the other hand, the idea that primary friendship must be reciprocal. And yet, the difference between the two is what justifies hierarchy, as well as counting and being counted. Death makes reciprocity impossible because friendship—primary, perfect, true friendship—must end with the death of both friends. If death is the horizon and the limit point of friendship, then it is bound to grief, for one must be alive to love.

Stein's and Cather's relationships with common soldiers allowed for a dissymmetrical love to take shape beyond the grave. In lovence, subject–object relations are destabilized, as friends seek mutual recognition, even without knowing each other. Derrida describes the interdependence that comes from leaving oneself as of oneself, "which can be done only by letting the other come, and by allowing them to precede and inform me—only if the other is the condition of my immanence."[57] In the *Eudemian Ethics,* the act of loving occurs, crucially, in the context of justice or the question of the just: "About friendship, what it is and what it is like, and who the friend is, and whether friendship is said in one or many ways, and, if in many, how many, and further how the friend is to be treated and what the just is in the case of friendship."[58] Derrida observes, therefore, that friendship consists in behaving "in harmony with the principle of the just," and through its placement in the text, it becomes "immediately equal to that of the beautiful and the desirable in friendship."[59] In fact, the words *retribution* and *justice* could not coexist in human relations founded on lovence. Because it is a process, and because it is spectral, it would exist in a free zone, not a temporally bound one in which "the first friendship" exists. Lovence could not rely on the stability and constancy of the Aristotelian *philia*, even though Derrida discovers lovence within an aporia in Aristotle's two ethics. Such friendship also carries itself beyond the possessiveness of sexual love, which is significant since both Stein and Cather are best known for their intimate relationships with their respective femme witnesses.

Particularly in the 1910s and 1920s, Stein and Cather grappled with this disjunction between the fraternity and the abstract principle of universality, which resulted in what I am calling "divided virtue." Both physically and metaphorically, in the wounded bodies of the soldiers returning home from war, they encounter this divided virtue, which is a problem of the friend/enemy distinction, and of the friction between two forms of love—the limitlessness of lovence and the exclusions of the fraternity. In their mixed allegiances, they were divided within themselves. These divisions erupted during World War I, as *politics* and *war* became nearly synonymous. Literature becomes an opportunity to examine this division—this wound—more closely.

Literary Expressions of Lovence

World War I was an unprecedented slaughter, which revealed humanity's potential for brutality. It was the advent of many firsts: the first use of chemical weapons, civilian bombings, and genocide of the modern era. Siegfried Sassoon's 1918 poem "Attack" suggests that the fundamental difference between this war and previous wars was an attitude toward the human being as a dispensable quantity:

> They leave their trenches, going over the top,
> While time ticks blank and busy on their wrists,
> And hope, with furtive eyes and grappling fists,
> Flounders in mud. O Jesus, make it stop![60]

It is hard for most of us in the twenty-first century to imagine the horror of spending months at a time in the trench, a site of living death and a metaphor for the inauguration of a new century. The ability to hold in suffering, a requisite of white manliness, began to break down because of the war. The psychological pains suffered by so many men were the result not of some unique horror but rather of the less heroic conditions of immobility, passivity, and helplessness created by the trenches. Soldiers passively waited in holes in the ground for the next shell to come and kill them—or maim them beyond recognition.

The physical and emotional paralysis created by the trench defied the descriptive powers of language. As Susan Sontag conveys in *Regarding the Pain of Others*, after the start of the war, "much that had been taken for granted came to seem fragile, even undefendable," and its conditions "exceeded the capacity of words to describe."[61] On the streets of European and American cities, the amputee became a regular sight, and for the first time, an extensive archive of war photographs documented the wounded returning from the front, many of whom suffered from the new shell shock disease. The wounded white male body and psyche was acutely present in the popular consciousness. Sassoon's soldier floundering in the mud became the specter haunting the war writings of Stein and Cather, but for reasons that one might not immediately suspect. Both disliked and feared the war, not because they were pacifists but because it was a slaughter, as was evident in the fact that soldiers whose faces were severely wounded were given masks produced through a sculptor's rendering of the prewar soldier. The war and their desires for masculinity also provided these writers with an opportunity for a different kind of lovence to flourish.

Cather's first experience of lovence occurred much earlier when she developed an imaginary connection to an uncle, a common soldier, who died in the Civil War. In her short story "The Namesake," she imagines herself to be this uncle's double and heir:

> Under the roof where my father and grandfather were born, I remained utterly detached. The somber rooms never spoke to me, the old furniture never seemed tinctured with race. The portrait of my boy uncle was the only thing to which I could draw near, the only link with anything I had ever known before.[62]

This "boy uncle" was not an illustrious male figure, which shows the complexity of Cather's masculine identification. By contrast, at other times, Cather was the wanderer looking for a homeland, a Byronic figure, or a modern-day Odysseus. In her first collection of poems, *April Twilights* (1903), she drew from male myths and legends—Apollo, Orpheus, the Grail, and the father–son bond—as the primary structures for her poems.[63] On a visit to Paris in the summer of 1902, she wrote to her father that the "tomb of Napoleon is the only thing I have ever found in the world which did not at all disappoint."[64] However, here, she connects her own masculinity to an unremarkable family member who lacks any kind of public prestige.

Unlike other writers of her generation, she moved west at a crucial age: old enough to remember, yet young enough to savor the novelty of the adventure. In 1882, at nine years old, she crossed the United States by train from Virginia to Nebraska to relocate with her family, which allowed her to appreciate the last vestiges of the open prairie. As Cather remembers in a 1913 interview in the *Philadelphia Record*: "As we drove further and further out into the country, I felt a good deal as if we had come to the end of everything. . . . It was a kind of erasure of personality."[65] The restraint of songbirds seemed to announce that her purpose in life from that moment forward was "not to cry."[66] However, while Cather remained suspicious all her life of what she considered feminine-styled emotional confession, she showed tremendous tenderness toward friends and family, as well as to returning soldiers. After the death of her ex-lover, Isabelle McClung, she even wrote to her brother that her problem had not been carelessness but caring too much and "too hard."[67] These personal communications show the kind of split that Cather carried with her from early childhood.

As a result of this drastic geographical shift, her fiction is epic in scale but also sparse—critical of modernity, conservative, and often contradictory. In Cather's famous novel *My Ántonia* (1918), she expresses through Jim Burden, a fictional male alliance, what she desires for herself: to be "dissolved into something complete and great," a something so great that "when it comes to one, it comes as naturally as sleep."[68] She even requested that these lines be inscribed on her tombstone. There might be a double meaning here, which opens the wound at the heart of democratic projects. On the one hand, this statement concretized for all of eternity the nostalgic bond between herself and men like Napoleon. On the other hand, Cather wrote many letters expressing her personal interest in the American soldiers returning home from the war, and she often visited these soldiers at the Polyclinic Hospital. On December 27, 1918, in a letter to her sister-in-law, Meta Schaper Cather, Cather described her affection for them: "I don't do much now but run about to see wounded soldiers. They are nearly all fine fellows—I don't see how one country can have so many nice ones and so few rotters. . . . Street-boys, farmer boys, any old boys—they have a kind of gracious grace. A one-armed lad who was here on Xmas eve could eat, and seat his hostess at the table, so deftly with one strong, warm, brown hand."[69] Her appreciation for "any old boys" is an expression of lovence, which persists in the absence of counting, hierarchy, or virile virtue.

My Ántonia gave her the confidence to create Claude in *One of Ours* (1922), which won her the Pulitzer Prize. Through Claude, Cather asks fundamental historical questions about the status of manhood after the war.[70] She foreshadows Derrida's assertion that lines between homicide and genocide were beginning to blur. Claude was based on her cousin, Grosvenor P. Cather, whom she spent time with on the farm in Nebraska before he sailed to France with the American Expeditionary Forces in September 1917. After Cather found his name among the list of Americans killed in battle in France on June 8, 1918, he became another source of lovence. As Cather wrote to her aunt on June 12, 1918: "I can see him sitting on his wagon as plainly as if it were yesterday. . . . He was restless on a farm; perhaps he was born to throw all his energy into this crisis, and to die among the first and bravest of his country."[71] Cather expresses in this letter both her glorification of the war and her belief in the common American soldier as the true hero. However, by the time she wrote the novel, she detested both the war and the development of the West, as linked events and processes.[72] As Sharon O'Brien recounts, the loss of Grosvenor P. Cather and her lover Isabelle McClung, who married a man, compelled her to believe that "the world broke in two in 1922 or thereabouts," a view she repeated frequently.[73] This was also the year of the publication of *One of Ours*, where she crystalized her criticisms and processed the loss of her cousin.

The world would never be made whole again, and she expressed this pessimism by cutting the novel in two distinct halves. While the first half was generally praised as a reflection on the quiet passions of the plains, the second half was denounced as a romantic glorification of war, carelessly patriotic and naive. The idealized version of the war should make contemporary readers uneasy, but the ferocious critical response, launched by prominent male critics, was partly a defense of territory, for they considered Cather to be intruding upon two masculine domains: the pioneering West and the battlefields of the Great War. However, damning critical responses accusing her of complicity with racist American nationalism also came from Cather's personal associates, whom she ceased to count as friends. Despite the criticism, Cather privately defended her choices. In 1923, she wrote to her artist friends, Earl and Achsah Barlow Brewster:

> This book has been a new experience for me. The people who don't like it detest it, most of the critics find it maudlin sentimentality and rage about it in print. But the ex-service men like it and actually buy it. It has sold over forty thousand now and is still selling. I've had to take on a secretary to answer the hundreds of letters I get about it. The truth is, this sort of success does not mean much but bother and fatigue to me—I'm glad I never had it before.[74]

That the ex-servicemen liked the novel and bought it, sharing their appreciation through letters, suggests whom she most desired to reach.

The novel launched Cather as a literary celebrity, but she lamented rather than celebrated this development. She preferred the company of a few treasured friends, some of whom had rejected what she felt was her best, and truest, writing. Cather felt that with Claude she was telling the truth, not about France or the war but the emotional truth about the soldier's experience. In another letter, to Dorothy Canfield Fisher on April 7, 1922, she explained what she had accomplished:

> [To get] across to you what the roughneck, the sensitive roughneck, really does feel when he's plunged into the midst of—everything. It's not only his vanity that suffers—though that very much—; he feels as if he has been cheated out of everything, the whole treasure of ages. . . . I found so many of the sick men I got to know had suffered that chagrin, and had brought back with them another wound than the one on their leg or breast—a wound that would ache at odd times all their lives, and that wound made them wiser, always.[75]

Cather directly references the physical wounds suffered by the soldiers and the metaphorical ones resulting from the useless sacrifice of so many lives for the preservation of the nation-state. However, the wound also has a pedagogical function, as it allows attainment of a wisdom not achievable otherwise.

The choice to cleave the novel in two was also a gendered one. The first half represents Claude's interior life as he attempts to navigate his own emotional landscape working the family farm, while the second depicts the masculine world of public action. Cather's unease about this split is expressed through the fact that Claude is misunderstood in both worlds, for Claude finds comfort neither on the farm nor on the Western Front. Cather also suggests a characteristic restlessness of a generation. As feminist scholar Hermione Lee offers, Cather wanted to portray a broken world through the irony of Claude as a young American hero in a world where heroism is losing its meaning.[76] Claude embodies the qualities of the common boy, who became for Cather a primary casualty, a masculinity that needed to be protected from the brutishness of men like Claude's father and his brother, Bayliss, the capitalist, whom Claude's own mother learns to tolerate as "rugged."

By this time, for Cather, this war was not a worthy heroes' mission but a demoralizing one. At first, Claude believes that the war is part of the poet-hero's journey, and he even compares himself to "the hero of the Odyssey upon his homeward journey."[77] However, because he is being sent off to war at this point in the novel, this is a reversal of *The Odyssey*'s narrative arc and a potential deconstruction of normative masculinity. This is a world in reverse, unraveling before his eyes, through which Cather proposes a reconsideration of the trajectory of Western civilization more broadly. In Cather's fictional world, the poet-hero cannot survive modern warfare, and instead she perversely tethers Claude to the deeds of the past.

When Claude first arrives in France, the sight of the wounded male bodies quickly dampens his enthusiasm for war:

> Their skin was yellow or purple, their eyes were sunken, their lips sore. Everything that belonged to health had left them, every attribute of youth was gone. One poor fellow, whose face and trunk were wrapped in cotton, never stopped moaning, and as he was carried up the corridor he smelled horribly. . . . These were the first wounded men Claude had seen. To shed bright blood, to wear the red badge of courage,—that was one

thing; but to be reduced to this was quite another. Surely, the sooner these boys died, the better.[78]

Claude's viscerally powerful description of these men tells us more about Cather's themes than about the war itself; not only does Claude observe the fact of their condition (the "face and trunk" wrapped in cotton, the condition of the skin, lips, and eyes), but he also bears witness to their pain, expressed through ceaseless moaning. Through Claude, Cather asks fundamental historical questions about the status of manhood after the war and the degree to which one's sensitivities needed refuge.

By describing in painstaking detail Claude's last moments, and by suggesting that Claude lives on after his death, Cather expresses Derrida's belief in a different kind of lovence, one that is not grounded in the canonical history of pairs of noble men. Claude is ordinary—one of a crowd—lacking singularity or exceptionalism:

> Hicks and Bert Fuller and Oscar carried Claude forward toward the Snout, out of the way of the supports that were pouring in. He was not bleeding very much. He smiled at them as if he were going to speak, but there was a weak blankness in his eyes. Bert tore his shirt open; three clean bullet holes. By the time they looked at him again, the smile had gone. . . . The look that was Claude had faded.[79]

The bullet holes are "clean," which means he dies without experiencing any of the bodily ugliness of death—without pain and without mess.[80] This clean death maintains Cather's connection to him as their bond endures the passage from this world to the next. In regard to the fictional character, Cather wrote to a friend in 1922 how "some of him still lives in me, and some of me is buried in France with him."[81] The fact that he was not even bleeding also suggests how Claude has become divine.[82] In a broader sense, the lack of blood also pulls away from the idea of brotherhood and fraternity grounded in a naturalized genealogy, severing the mythical male connection to the nation-state.

Cather felt she understood the dilemma of the emotional wound, which is in part what makes this novel "painful and unsatisfactory" for some critics.[83] A sacred masculine friendship between author and character occurs through lovence, but it is a lovence that extends toward what is tender and caring in masculinity. As Lee writes, "*One of Ours* acts out [Cather's] search for a new mythology to replace the loss of the old."[84] She creates here a kind of elegy, a sign of the impossibility of historical redemption, of telling the story of Odysseus in the same way, given the war, and the intensification of materialism and greed after the closing of the frontier.[85] Cather's attention to the masculinity of this character suggests that these were not simply male alter egos but figures with whom she felt a deep bond based in shared feeling and trauma rather than only in abstract national belonging.[86] The emotional wound offers a negative reading of the future of civilization that resists restoration, which requires living with grief, death, and dying and the loss of "uncountable" numbers of people in the war.[87]

In contrast to Cather, Stein spent most of her career in Paris, entertaining in her atelier famous male artists and writers, at a time when France was attempting to reconcile its rhetorical humanism with its active colonialism abroad. As the Parisian dance hall performances of Josephine Baker suggest, negrophilia and primitivism were all the rage, as early twentieth-century colonialism and modernism coconstructed and implicated one another.[88] In the 1910s and 1920s when Stein first arrived, Paris was at the height of the colonial period, after the city had been "transformed by war, industrialization, migration, overcrowding, and urban redesign."[89] Caught in its own contradictions, Paris often appeared more tolerant of difference than U.S. cities, but colonial violence taking place in the Antilles and Africa created a long shadow that proved difficult to conceal.[90] Assimilationist colonial policy made Paris a "safe haven," as culture temporarily resolved the contradiction between liberating principles and colonization.[91] Paris was consequently also a place of wish fulfillment, of an imagined Black and queer modernity that was not available in the "real." It became a haven for eccentric writers and artists looking for creative and sexual freedom.[92] However, living as an openly transmasculine writer in Paris was not even a remote possibility for Stein, for, as Dydo notes, "lesbians in Paris could not wear men's clothing unless the prefect of the police said they could."[93]

Stein is well known for her bold rejection of both nineteenth-century literary norms for white women and the gospel of high modernism, which determined that only a man could be a genius. Her response to patriarchal figures, however, ranged from critical to ambivalent to admiring. In *Everybody's Autobiography* (1937), on the edge of the Second World War, Stein critiqued sharply "the fathers" across both socialist and democratic political systems:

> There is too much fathering going on just now and there is no doubt about it fathers are depressing. Everybody nowadays is a father, there is father Mussolini and father Hitler and father Roosevelt and father Stalin and father Lewis and father Blum and father Franco is just commencing now and there are ever so many more ready to be one. Fathers are depressing.[94]

However, after the Second World War, she determined that "national renewal could only be achieved through the influence of a strong male authority figure," one who could use his "salutary forces of discipline, compelling their wayward charges to control and limit their urges."[95] In viewing dictatorship as the lesser of the second evil—Communism—she came to exalt these same "depressing" authority figures. In *Unlikely Collaboration: Gertrude Stein, Bernard Faÿ, and the Vichy Dilemma*, feminist scholar Barbara Will rigorously presents the case for Stein's conservatism and her pro-Vichy politics.[96] With archival work, it became impossible to bypass Stein's pro-Fascist politics and support of the "new France" or to continue to promote the view that she only pretended to be a fascist to save herself and Toklas.

Stein's belief that Communism was the greater evil maps onto U.S. Cold War doctrine, which claimed to extend America's Manifest Destiny to the rest of the world. The Cold War view is that the United States and Europe faced a rapidly expanding, "demonic" adversary in the form of the U.S.S.R., but the United States actually sought at that time "hegemonic influence, access to resources, and safeguards for capital."[97] Supposedly, white supremacy had been defeated, and anti-Communism became another way to negotiate discrepancies between the Manifest Destiny to expand the so-called free world and biopolitical eligibility for universal rights to historical agency, self-determination, and national sovereignty.[98]

However, before this turn toward fascism, Stein expressed the tender, active spirit of lovence in recounting her service as an ambulance driver and caretaker with the American Fund for French Wounded during World War I. Stein spent a good deal of time getting to know active soldiers on the battlefield and returning American soldiers or doughboys, the informal name for members of the U.S. Army or Marine Corps. For these soldiers, she appeared both stoic and lighthearted, a source of support, love, and generosity. After her tenure as general of the avant-garde ended, she became a kind of self-proclaimed godmother figure to the doughboys. She cared for these men when they were at their most vulnerable and in need. They nicknamed one favorite soldier "Kiddie," and he in turn playfully referred to Stein as "Stonehenge," because of her elemental strength and her laughter that rumbled like thunder.

While Stein never claimed pacifism, a poetic passage from *Useful Knowledge* (1928) suggests her resistance to the war's unprecedented terror:

> Can we stand ditches.
> Can we mean well.
> Do we talk together.
> Have we red cross.
> A great many people speak feet.
> And socks.[99]

When she asks, without punctuation, "Can we stand ditches [trenches]," she implores her readers to question whether their memory of them can be tolerated. During the war, feet could be lost easily, forming part of the trench wall; they could be submerged in mud or, less dramatically, feet could be cold, numb, and in need of socks. Unlike other American writers, Stein observed this reality directly.

Despite her forbidding abstraction—or her glittery, self-promoting surfaces—the war caused Stein to lose her literary and creative momentum. While psychological interpretations of Stein's reactions are beyond the scope of this chapter, I agree with Stein scholar Sara Ruddick that the subjects she explored before the war provided her with an artistic equilibrium that was later "shattered."[100] She suffered a kind of fatigue, and she never regained the sense of risk-taking found in *Tender Buttons,* her most beloved poetic work.

Stein suffered personally as well, which she describes in the poem "Pink Melon Joy," begun in the first part of the summer of 1914 after war had just been declared but no one understood exactly what was going on. She enjoyed the company of her friends Alfred North and Evelyn Whitehead in England, but the reality was that she and Toklas were unable to return home to Paris for eleven weeks.[101] On

September 10, 1914, Stein wrote to Carl Van Vechten, in her usual affectionate but brief tone: "We were caught by the war in England and have been with friends in the country."[102] In *A Stein Reader*, Ulla E. Dydo writes in the introduction to "Pink Melon Joy" how the piece expresses Stein's "lighthearted, humorous, and erotic" style.[103] However, I also sense in the writing how she was grieving as she encountered the wound of divided virtue.

In this series, the more visceral traumas of the war become available. She includes in "Pink Melon Joy" several passages containing the word *war*, alongside a plea for peace, a kind of prayerlike request that she and friends can "bear" the situation, that they will "let us be," and ultimately for things to be "Mended."[104] Successive references to fighting occur alongside the first mention of the title of the piece:

> Pink Melon Joy.
> II.
> It pleases me very much.
> Little swimming on the water.
> I meant to mention pugilism. Pugilism leaning. Leaning and thinking. Thinking.
> I meant to mention pugilism. Pugilism and leaning.[105]

Stein's use of juxtaposition is important, particularly her simultaneous reference to the pleasant and the unpleasant. Within these folds of language, Stein reveals tender feeling, both the pleasure of friendship and hospitality, the "Pink Melon Joy" of being with Toklas and with good friends, but also the nature of violence and of fighting (pugilism), boundaries (national boundaries, personal boundaries, the difference between far and near, home and away, etc.), and the penetration of those (national) boundaries, which she refers to early in the piece through the word *drilling*. Divided virtue and the conflict that results are revealed through this juxtaposition of inside and outside sometimes expressed in the same sentence, which makes it possible for "pink melon joy" and "Not pink melon joy" to coexist in the same line. Stein's idiosyncratic humor tempers her feelings of terror in "Pink Melon Joy III":

> War.
> I wish I was in the time when all the blame was feelingly added to mercies.
> I wish I could ask what's the matter now.
> By believing in forms by believing in shed by more stationing by really swimming as usual, no shell or fish. Pray.[106]

Stein's mention of the word *Pray* after "no shell or fish," as well as the repetition of *believing* throughout the poem, suggests an attitude of guarded surrender. She creates a poetic structure for her fear, and for her longing for some unspecified time in the past, when there is not only blame (and death) but mercy.

Another piece of writing from this period that communicates lovence is her obscure 1930 novel *Lucy Church Amiably,* self-published under Plain Edition, due to the lack of interested publishing houses. The work was inspired by a church in a hamlet called Lucey near Bilignin, known for its hat-like Russian steeple brought back from the Napoleonic Wars. As Stein muses, the purpose of the novel is "to put into a book what is to be read in a book, bits of information and tender feeling."[107] This may help explain why *Lucy Church Amiably* reads like period footage of men with shell shock who could not control their muscles or their speech, who lost their hearing, their limbs, and often their will to live.

Stein scatters this "information" throughout: references to colonels, conscriptions, propaganda, marshes (an allusion to the marshes that plagued war efforts), regiments (and the numbers of men of different countries who enlist in these regiments). Meanwhile, the abstruse character Lucy—vaguely reminiscent of the future Rosie the Riveter—has a penchant for cleaning knives: "Actions and actions. How many knives can Lucy clean with a machine" (42). It is hard to say exactly what Lucy symbolizes, but she is anything but docile. Vengeful and on the edge of committing a violent act, Lucy could symbolize Stein's own anger over the war's dehumanizing consequences. References to burial occur frequently, for example in variations on "should their heads buried in clover . . . Lucy Church their heads buried in clover" (101).

Stein uses birds to symbolize the battle between stronger and weaker nations: "What is a crow a magpie a hawk to do if five little birds attack one big one. What are they to do a magpie a hawk a crow to do. What is it that they do what is it that they are to do" (102). Stein also depicts the bludgeoning effect of the new methods for spreading propaganda—for example, the dropping of leaflets from airplanes. Stein repeats over the course of four lines: "Lucy Church propaganda   Lucy propaganda   Lucy Church propaganda" (106). Repetition suggests how wounded male bodies and minds are her central preoccupation, as well as national deception, and a feeling of despair that clearly lingered long after the last shot was fired. Within a repetitive, militaristic marching pattern—"left to right, right to left"—she expresses the monotony of the war as well. She laments, with extra spaces placed between each word to slow the reading, "There may be war but there can be no climaxes there" (58). Nonsense repetition conveys the utter futility of the violence, which keeps existing figures—the depressing fathers—in power.

A character with a bi-gendered name, John Mary, offers a remedy for shell shock: feminized therapies and activities. In *Lucy Church Amiably,* the illness creates a "door" in the self, which opens and closes, often not under one's control: "John Mary having shut the door opened it again but not always sometimes it had to be done for him.   The difference between the present and the past.   Pastime" (64). In the passage, and through additional spacing once again, we see the collapsing of time, specifically for those who have experienced war, one that John Mary negotiates through engaging in "pastimes," including gardening. Clearly John Mary suffers from some form of post-traumatic stress, and the remedy is simple work, like gardening: "John Mary understands loss he understands exactitude he understands gentleness he understands undeniable he understands their having it as much as that he understands having been to the burial of an older man whom he has known. John Mary likes to have been very well" (199). John Mary is trying to forget about what happened to him during the war through working in the fields, but he can never quite forget, as Stein makes clear before this passage: "Association and disassociation as if it were used one two three as if it were used four six eight as if it were used five four three as if it were used one two three as if it were used" (119). Association, which is an act of remembrance and connection, and disassociation, the quick repression of the remembered emotion and the object to which the emotion connects, describes the back and forth movement of post-traumatic stress disorder. The counting reminiscent of marching or the count-off to firing on enemy lines mirrors this back and forth movement, and the disordered counting signals John Mary's neuroatypicality.

However, John Mary protects himself from his own memories

by never actually sharing anything recognizable about his military service. He is divided—by war and by gender—like Stein and many others of her generation. The choice between death and death, "between the two statues one to a dead defender and the other to a dead provider," paints a grim picture of this war's aftermath (118). While John Mary can always choose (perhaps) to "not be divided," the fact remains that he *is* also divided between the desire for expression and the inability to express. One cannot forget about the war, despite the at times pure and divine image of Lucy, who "made it seem that Grenoble was far away. / Listen to Lucy. / Lucy Church made a church made a church Lucy Church" (89). Maybe Lucy can put Grenoble at a distance, a city that harbored many of the war's industries, but like a violent waterfall, we meet an overwhelming force of feeling on the other side of this forgetting. The choice between death and death ominously repeats.

Lucy Church Amiably only attracted a small number of readers, and yet it is where I see Stein as sensitive, tender, and conflicted in this period, as she grapples with the implications of the war, which changed her life irrevocably. Other reflections on the war appear in *The Autobiography of Alice B. Toklas* (1933), written through Toklas as proxy author, which shows her search for fame and for masculine strength and self-assuredness. As Malcolm relates, Stein wrote this faux memoir in the fall of 1932 in a kind of "paroxysm of desire" for this fame.[108] Shortly before the work was published, Stein confessed this desire for what she called *"gloire"* to her friend Mabel Weeks.[109] Another motivation for *The Autobiography of Alice B. Toklas* was her dwindling income garnered from family investments. To continue the lifestyle to which she and Toklas were accustomed, she needed to present to the public the self-aggrandizing Stein of the Saturday night salon, a showcase of famous and soon-to-be-famous men, while Toklas amused the women in another room. To accomplish this seduction, she had to consider voice, public presentation, and questions of narrator/narration for the first time. But the public stage of the salon was already prepared for her.

In *Autobiography of Alice B. Toklas*, Stein explains, through Toklas: "Gertrude Stein said commas were unnecessary, the sense should be intrinsic and not have to be explained by commas and otherwise commas were only a sign that one should pause and take a breath but one should know of oneself when one wanted to pause and take break."[110] In Stein's outward styling, she valued self-assuredness, conveyed here through the ability to know how to read without direction (and the inclusion of a comma instead of a period, which makes her the master of punctuation more generally). Yet, there is something fundamentally disorienting about this writing, and specifically about the choice to write oneself in the guise of another. She uses the word *strange* repeatedly in the work, and knowing Stein, we can assume that the word holds a double meaning from the definitional sense of "alien" or the more rarefied "exceptional." She was attracted as well to the most "strange" paintings of the time, and she displayed them with bravado at her salons: "The pictures were so strange that one quite instinctively looked at everything rather than at them first."[111] Here, she means that the paintings were both disorienting and exceptional, much like her own subjectivity.

However, the much darker "strangeness" she experienced during the war also lingers in the prose. This is particularly true when she depicts scenes of battlefields and the lines of trenches on both sides: "To anyone who did not see it as it was then it is impossible to imagine it. It was not terrifying it was strange. We were used to ruined houses and even ruined towns but this was different. It was a landscape. And it belonged to no country."[112] Given the impossibility of language in such conditions, the best one could do was to retrospectively map the contours of this strangeness and its disconnection from common experience and from the imagined boundaries of the nation-state.

For Stein, this strangeness and disconnection was also gendered and describes this feeling of estrangement from a fraternal, national sense of belonging. The war afforded her, as a masculine woman, the opportunity to travel and to perform heroic deeds as a volunteer ambulance driver, which never would have been possible in peacetime. After the war, Stein therefore lamented both the loss of the common soldier and the loss of her own mobility. This is the double tragedy found in her interwar writings. The war gave her a taste for what she had been missing, which may be the motivation behind her statement that it was "a nice war" in comparison to World War II: "The 1914–1918 war was just like our civil war. . . . A nice war is a war where everybody who is heroic is a hero, and everybody more or less is a hero in a nice war."[113] However, by calling it a "nice war," is she playing a game of irony with her readers? As Ruddick suggests, her texts can never be entirely "perfume [or cologne] for us," can never be "controlled, sweet, and appropriate." Instead, they are at once tender and wrenching, inviolable and impenetrable, polysemous and resistant to paraphrase.[114] Stein's butch exceptionalism—her masculine "genius"—therefore also lies in her texts' refusal to be controlled, which makes them endlessly sensual, maddening—tortured at times by divided virtue.

To make matters more strange, at the same time that Stein wrote *The Autobiography of Alice B. Toklas*, she composed her most emotionally complex and enigmatic work, *Stanzas in Meditation*. While stuttering and simmering by night in her stanzas, she managed to create by day a work that "propelled [her] into fame, led to the iconizing of Stein and Toklas, and the demand for the American Lecture tour."[115] In *Stanzas in Meditation*, she appears to grieve over her ex-lover May Bookstaver and over the losses she suffered during the war. Inner emotional fragility and softness are apparent in these elegiac lines, such as "Four leaf clovers make a Sunday / and that is gone."[116] Both "clover" and "Sunday" are repeated in *Lucy Church Amiably*, which suggests a connection between the two works.

In understanding Stein's quest to satisfy both public demands and private desires, we cannot underestimate the importance of the actual words in her texts. In the inner sanctum of *Stanzas in Meditation*, she used words to "keep loss of love at bay, and since loss of love was a threat of death, words allowed her to keep death at bay."[117] If the main objective in *The Autobiography of Alice B. Toklas* was to disarm and seduce an audience, then the purpose of *Stanzas in Meditation* was to resolve a much less tangible but more consequential personal crisis. For this, I agree with Mills that *Stanzas in Meditation* is an even more crucial work than *The Autobiography of Alice B. Toklas* because of its emotional timbre and ability to exceed description and enact feelings of exclusion and loss, which is where we arrive once again at the idea of divided virtue.[118] In entering *Stanzas in Meditation*, we feel an entirely different aspect of Stein's sexual and textual presence, and most importantly, we *feel* rather than intellectualize that her "sense of her own voice and of her power of speech was intermittent."[119] We leave behind Stein the impenetrable artistic mountain and begin the slow tunneling toward the tender place within where Stein experienced lovence.

Far from a disorganized mess of language, Stein uses repetition and an alternative sense structure in *Stanzas in Meditation* to resolve, or at least ameliorate, her crisis. The writing filled her with an entirely different kind of uneasiness. Within the shaky territory of emotional vulnerability, Stein stutter-stepped in her quest to find her voice for the piece. Dydo characterizes the process as traumatic from the start: "Breathless opening lines, full of haste and hesitations, create a kind of in-between state, reaching for words that will fit, the wish to 'kindly have it join.'"[120] While in *The Autobiography of Alice B. Toklas* Stein presents an ironic, butchy smirk as she fills the pages with "peace-loving statements an audience likes to hear," *Stanzas* provides a space for her to "depict the war, in all its disparate pieces."[121]

In both *Lucy Church Amiably* and *Stanzas in Meditation*, repetition submerges us into a deep meditation, a trance state that is common in survivors of trauma. *Stanzas in Meditation* overflows with questions that do not have answers, and this places Stein and the reader/listener/critic in endless suspension: "In one direction there is the sun and the moon / In the other direction there are cumulus clouds and the sky / In the other direction there is why."[122] This last, open-ended line propels us away from the referent and toward an unanswerable riddle at the heart of the democratic project.

Critiquing the Queer and Trans Past

Both Stein and Cather became increasingly conservative and unyielding as they aged and as the twentieth century progressed. In her autobiographical *Wars I Have Seen* (1945), Stein announces her provincial attitudes, to an embarrassing degree. Reactionary and nostalgic, she laments the rate of change in urban societies propelled by the war and turns toward an idealization of rural life—not of the 1940s but of the eighteenth century.[123] Like Bernard Fäy, Stein sought to resurrect the "rugged masculine individualism of Thomas Jefferson's idealized yeoman farmers," who, by comparison, made the men of the industrialized and capitalistic modern era seem effeminate, weak, and feeble.[124] The nostalgia for pre-Revolutionary times mapped neatly onto contemporary fascism in Europe, a reaction to the perceived disorganization, laziness, and decadence of liberal democracies abounding with Jews. Authoritarian rulers, like General Pétain, were to Stein exceptional human beings who transcended all categories (Figure 12).[125]

After the war, Cather became a disagreeable person who detested the Roosevelts, the New Deal, and immigration. She perceived the failures of her time as irredeemable, which once again led her to seek out androcentric histories and myths. In her memoir, longtime friend Elizabeth Sargent painted an unbecoming portrait of a bitter Cather who began "intimidating customs officials . . . dismissing [poet] Amy Lowell . . . defining the correct salad dressing: 'light French olive oil . . . the richest wine vinegar, with a dash of tarragon. She insisted on tarragon.'"[126] This insistence on tarragon suggests her absolute certainty in her own point of view.

However, for a time, their writing became a place to process and reflect on losses, which gives the work an antiauthoritarian impulse. Both discovered the spirit of lovence, which can counter exclusion and discrimination. More broadly, unruly alliances of the future can be based on the limitlessness of lovence, exceeding the temporal boundaries of masculine narcissism, selection, and affinity. When the determinations of virtue and the actions of selection are mobilized, then you have counting and the inevitable self-interest that counting requires, which places severe limitations on democracy and on what Carole Pateman describes as the "crucial bond integrating individual and community."[127] Bonding through an imagined greatness leads to a situation in which *I* only trust *he* who is made in my image, therefore I only trust the few to act politically on my behalf. Some others can or even must be killed, while with the vast masses of humanity, it makes no difference to me whether they are killed. Lovence leads outward toward an impersonal and objectless love, including the dead or the lost, for while you can love the dead, there is no object per se. Their deep compassion for these soldiers, whose identities were largely forgotten, led them toward this understanding of impersonal attachment.

In their own distinct ways, Cather and Stein also use literature itself to call attention to the failures of normative masculinity and assigned male phallogocentrism. Literature can enact what Derrida describes as the "sudden burst of this chance at the heart of the ruin,"

FIGURE 12. Stein grew nostalgic for pre-Revolutionary America and its rugged masculine individualism, which alienated many of her readers. Carl Van Vechten, portrait of Gertrude Stein, with American flag as backdrop, January 4, 1935. Black and white photograph. Van Vechten Collection, Library of Congress Prints and Photographs Division, https://lccn.loc.gov/2004663581.

the chance and potential in the wound that results when two forms of virtue meet—the rare and the limitless.[128] The writer is uniquely capable of remaining intolerant to the intolerable—that is, to the "theological-political system" whose shifting processes already saturate the globe, refusing the ideal of democracy as unconditional.[129] In the archive I have presented, the writing of literature is an action toward new forms of relationality rather than a container for nostalgia.

There is grief, and lovence, that permeates this process of questioning retrospectively the masculinities of trans and queer icons, their attendant politics, and modes of bonding. Heather Love writes on the "backward turn" in queer history and the search for these "difficult subjects" so we may reassess current boundaries of queer scholarship and learn to live with injury.[130] The careers of Stein and Cather do not adhere to any predictable linear progress narrative. As Amin writes, this form of queer time "pulls recursively back to dark histories, countering the modernist logic of progress and development, but with politically ambivalent or even regressive effects." They put back into view the reality that despite its revolutionary potential, queer time also has a way of "hurtling back to a shameful past it can neither supersede nor shake off," which corresponds to postcolonial and racialized time.[131] However, for Amin, deidealization, and the affective histories unveiled, should compel critics toward unfinished intellectual and activist labor. The wound of divided virtue can become a call to action. However, all too often, scholars bypass the unsavory aspects of these histories, picking and choosing the most desirable attributes for the crafting of personal identities.

More difficult still is to find an approach to cultural criticism that takes both progressive and reactionary tendencies into account, a result of tuning in to the way a body of work and a life change across time. Both self-critique and self-love, both pride and negativity, are necessary for the discovery of masculinities that support care and mutual aid as extranational practices. Unruly alliances can provide a way out, but they require collective instruction regarding the masculinities of the past and perhaps a refusal of the very concepts of "genius," "icon," and "hero." Transmasculine subjects have suffered, and continue to suffer, oppression from multiple sources. However, this "looking back," this wistful nostalgia for a bygone era of virile virtue, is clearly not a model for collective sustainability. This more nuanced critical approach would require sharpening our practices of remembrance so that we may both commemorate and critique. It would require a refusal to condemn, or to cancel, when presented with these shadow sides of an icon. There is a space beyond the two choices of gay pride or the hauntings of queer negativity, which can lead to resignation. If, as Halberstam insists, "betrayal and disloyalty are part of the arsenal of a vital and dynamic oppositional discourse," then we need to ask how masculinities have betrayed and been disloyal to masculinity itself.[132] Where, how, when, and by whom—precisely, and in which cultural practices—is the wound of divided virtue uncovered and allowed to heal?

Part III
Challenging Masculine Impenetrability

Chapter 5

"Skin of His Hand against the Skin of My Back"

HIV/AIDS Self-Writing and Film of the 1980s and '90s

In Part III, I take a closer look at impenetrability as a defining quality of masculine normativity, one that has already been visible in the preceding chapters and that runs through and across many cultural and political registers. Masculinity strives to be impenetrable through self-sufficiency, emotional sturdiness, and bodily resilience. Impenetrability as masculine currency, however, is only consistently available for white men, whose hegemony is metaphorically reproduced across many contexts. In the action or war film, white male impenetrability is highly celebrated, and violence is always justified. However, for Black masculinities, as one example, impenetrability connotes maladjustment, pathology, out-of-control rage, and the hunger to penetrate white women. This double standard becomes visible in the portrayal of Black men as rapists violating white women in early twentieth-century film or as hypermasculine urban gang leaders, drug traffickers, and pimps in the Blaxploitation genre. Impenetrability always carries both emotional and sexual meanings, as it aligns with state-sponsored violence and the military.

Fortifying the U.S. southern border and making it impenetrable for refugees and migrants has been a national obsession, while at the same time global capital has been allowed to flow freely and unimpeded. Aníbal Quijano explains that beginning in the postwar period, colonial relations between white people and new immigrants, principally from Latin America and Asia, introduced new risk for the reproduction of the nation. Undoubtedly, many experience these risks increasing in the twenty-first century, as the "old myth of the melting pot has been forcefully abandoned and racism tends to be newly sharpened and violent."[1] The postwar reorganization of capital has formed and reformed the U.S.–Mexico border, particularly since the 1970s, with the goal of making the border more penetrable for capital, information, labor, and goods and more impenetrable and hypernationalist through strict control and policing. The escalation of militarization and surveillance that occurred when the North American Free Trade Agreement (NAFTA) was signed in 1994 made the border more fluid than ever for transnational capital, and at the same time it is now one of the most militarized borders in the world. As Grace Kyungwon Hong reminds us, the United States expends "hundreds of millions of dollars a year to try to maintain the integrity and impermeability of its national boundaries."[2] The flow of capital largely benefits the United States, but a rise in white nativism and anti-immigrant hysteria, echoing the eighteenth and nineteenth centuries, lays the blame for economic recessions on Mexican immigrants taking American jobs, draining social service and welfare resources. Hong describes the use of toxic masculinity to recruit border patrol officers, appealing specifically to those candidates looking for frontier adventure and a role in securing national borders with the help of horses, motorbikes, ATVs, and water vessels.[3] The work is advertised as both exhilarating and manly. The typical U.S. Immigration and Customs Enforcement (ICE) officer is like a high-tech, twenty-first-century cowboy, who upholds the law (displaying impenetrability) while remaining above and outside the law.

A very dangerous form of impenetrability is being spawned in the call for a jurisprudence of "original intent" on the level of constitutional law and the Supreme Court. It is a particularly virulent form of impenetrability operative today, exposing the machinations of white fraternity, and its accomplices, within the logics and grammars of racial capitalism. As Eric Foner notes, "In an age of semiotics and deconstruction, not to mention intense debate among historians about the prevailing ideas of the revolutionary era, there is something refreshingly naïve, almost quaint, in the idea that any text, including the Constitution, possesses a single, easily ascertainable, objective meaning."[4] He adds that, of course, this turn toward "original intent" is not an intellectual stance but a political rallying cry used to justify the rollback of constitutional rights. To reverse the slur intended to brand the proponents of equal rights, they call themselves the real "activist judges," intent on portraying the Constitution as ahistorical and inviolate.[5] Taken together, these developments suggest both a virtual and in-real-life renaissance of white masculine impenetrability occurring in the twenty-first century.

During the current Covid-19 pandemic, some countries of the Global North seek to become impenetrable through vaccination while others are denied those resources. In chapter 3, I discussed the postwar turn toward negative freedom, defined by the absence of external obstacles to satisfy desires.[6] By contrast, positive freedom subordinates the individual to the whole by identifying the state as an arbiter of social good. Some in the United States felt that their whiteness and class status made them impenetrable by nature—which promotes a negative view of freedom as the supposed right to refuse mask-wearing, social distancing, and other mitigation practices. The Covid-19 pandemic has also given birth to a new "state of exception," depriving immigrants and asylum seekers of their human rights. As Robin D. G. Kelley laments in the foreword to Harsha Walia's *Border and Rule: Global Migration, Capitalism, and the Rise of Racist Nationalism*, in the face of deadly disease, the U.S. government accelerated border closings, imposed barriers to asylum, and expanded immigrant detention.[7] *Security* has become the dog whistle for newly violent extremes: securing the economy and sacrificing the most vulnerable; securing resources in a hypercompetitive, inequitable global system; securing borders against the supposed enemy. The drive toward impenetrability speaks to the reach and spread of toxic masculinity, as a quality not only of an individual but an entire body politic.

Endowed with the currency of impenetrability, masculine subjects assign practices of receiving and giving care to feminine Others. Femininity becomes associated with the expression of Eros, of love and not freedom, responsibility, and mutual respect, the so-called more reliable masculine traits. Caring and being cared for makes one vulnerable to outside forces—to nature and the processes of the body. Impenetrability can be a trans- and homonormative value as well, which conveys the degree to which it functions as a measure of manliness. In this section, I look at historical cultural production for ways that trans and queer masculinities depart from this norm of impenetrability. These works were created during times and places when impenetrability became undesirable or impossible to uphold.

Instead, care and relationality become the basis for unruly alliances across identity categories.

This chapter connects impenetrability to the metaphorical and material register of disease during the height of the HIV/AIDS pandemic in the 1980s and '90s. Examples from this period suggest how disease becomes an opportunity to reckon with penetrability and to form bonds with others, whether they are lovers, friends, or strangers. HIV/AIDS also becomes an opportunity to think through state-sponsored forms of impenetrability. Some gay men who died of AIDS-related illnesses express feelings of never having lived up to the impenetrable ideal in the first place, so HIV/AIDS highlighted the oppression already present in society. Queers who are bottoms become what Jasbir K. Puar calls "traitors to the nation, figures of espionage and double agents," associated with Communism during the McCarthy era and with state betrayal in Castro's Cuba, as explored by Reinaldo Arenas in his autobiography, *Before Night Falls* (1992).[8] Like suicide bombers, some were thought to have desired their own death, and feminized gay men are often portrayed as always already dying, victims of "a decaying or corroding masculinity." This perceived "failure" of gay masculinity further establishes the alleged link between homosexuality, incest, pedophilia, and "madness."[9]

In response, communities formed through and around care, as body-minds began to break down physically and emotionally, revealing the instability of masculinity, even as it masquerades as the able-bodied, biologically conferred, universal signifier.[10] The works presented in this chapter—including Arenas's autobiography, Timothy Conigrave's *Holding the Man* (1995), John Foster's *Take Me to Paris, Johnny* (1993), and Marlon Riggs's *Black Is . . . Black Ain't* (1994)—embrace vulnerability, despite the threat of being labeled feminine, which is to say excessively bound to the needs of the body, by both queer and heteronormative society. Self-writing and autoethnographic film place disability and sexuality in close proximity, suggesting they are not incommensurate. To explore further how disability and sexuality came to live with one another during this time, I focus on what I am calling scenes of "sick sex," in which sexual desire occurs because of rather than despite disabling conditions.

While I am remaining within the bounds of the memoir or self-writing form, because of the extreme situation of their creators, these works refuse genre as a normative mode of affiliation and subjectification. They call attention to biopolitical control and social neglect, racial and gendered subordination, and the ruse of universal incorporation. They answer a question posed by English literature and Black studies scholar Christina Sharpe: "What does it look like, entail, and mean to attend to, care for, comfort, and defend those already dead, those dying, and those living lives consigned to the possibility of always-imminent death, life lived in the presence of death?"[11] They refuse the brittleness and inflexibility of masculinity, revealing that indeed, as Michel Foucault surmised, what most threatens heteronormative society is the queer potential of "friendship as a way of life."[12] However, Foucault's friendship as a way of life does not depart enough from the history of male–male friendship and the fraternal contract. Unruly alliances can contain Foucauldian "multiple intensities," while rejecting fraternity, the more or less constant—and counterfeit—claim to power in the West. Unlike sanctified male friendships, the unruly alliances that developed between some gay men at this time embrace the supposed stain of sexuality and promiscuity. By the staid philosopher's determination, these are allegedly unworthy friends. However, instead of responding to this accusation with increased virility, these writers and filmmakers communicate their strength in relationship to one another. New expressions of masculinity and forms of unruly alliance develop from the self-shattering of disease.

In Close Proximity to Death and Dying

The painter Hugh Steers died in 1995 of AIDS-related complications at the age of 32, but during his brief career, he captured the suffering caused by HIV/AIDS in his community of gay men in New York City. Steers added a human dimension to what were, in the eyes of American politicians and the public at large, pathetic, emasculated lives draining out bit by bit. Steers humanized his subjects by placing them in vulnerable positions, often with their caretakers, engaged in intimate scenes of talking, bathing, and sex play. In *Bath Curtain*, completed in 1992, a young man sits shirtless in his white briefs on a toilet next to another man taking a bath (Figure 13).[13] The bather's face is tilted back, shrouded by the translucent shower curtain, foreshadowing death. The light in the painting—the bright sun filtering through the window and the blue-lavender shadow cast by

FIGURE 13. Hugh Steers, *Bath Curtain*, 1992. Oil on canvas. 64½ × 72½ inches (163.8 × 184.2 cm). Courtesy of Alexander Gray Associates, New York. Copyright 2022 Estate of Hugh Steers / Artists Rights Society (ARS), New York.

the clawfoot tub—suggests early morning or late afternoon, a time of stillness and solitude. The fact that it is difficult to tell whether the day is beginning or ending is significant, because it symbolizes the psychological and physical disorientations produced by the sheer number of people getting sick and dying each day in these communities. The brilliant yellow sunlight on the windowsill suggests that life continues outside, while inside time stands still, as time itself is transcended by a love that exceeds the principles of reciprocity, affinity, and selection. In a posture of intense observation, of grooming and caretaking, the seated subject cups the bather's hand, palm facing upward, while his other hand tenderly strokes the tips of the fingers. Perhaps we are witnessing the caretaker searching purposefully for the deep bruise-like spots of Kaposi sarcoma, or he might be lost in grief, engaging in the only action he has left—to gaze with compassion at the body of a loved one who is clearly in pain and slipping out of existence.

Through depicting both caretaker and person with AIDS as masculine and vulnerable (even the curve of the seated figure's spine suggests flexibility rather than rigidity), Steers resists the biological essentialism that secures supposedly true masculinity as by nature hard, autonomous, and welded to power and control. He presents masculinity as soft and caring within a contemplative scene, the opposite of most paintings of men throughout the history of Western art, where youthful, idealized male bodies compose "the canon of beauty," in the paintings of Thomas Eakins, for example, who was rumored to be gay.[14] During the pandemic, young, healthy men became caretakers, then undertakers, and often died of complications related to the disease themselves. The timelessness of the scene blurs the boundary between life and death, a distinction that is necessary for nation-states to preserve so-called biopolitical sovereignty.[15] In Foucault's terms, "to make live and to let die," the state must demonstrate its jurisdiction over the biological functioning of the body.[16] In this painting, however, the dying body and the brilliant sunlight mesh together, as life and death become integrated phases of the same process.

Steers's work provides a poignant visual introduction to the unruly alliances that developed during this reactionary historical moment. Beginning in the 1970s and '80s, but acutely after the election of Ronald Reagan, the Republican Party was, according to Nikhil Pal Singh, the most entrenched—and white—far-Right political party in the Western world.[17] With the help of anti–Equal Rights Amendment activists like Phyllis Schlafly, the GOP mobilized and fused social conservatism and religiosity with an equally evangelical commitment to upward wealth distribution. They dedicated themselves to climate-change denial, the destruction of the social safety net, and the lowering of taxes for the wealthiest. In "Race, Capitalism, and the Anti-democracy," Cedric J. Robinson describes how, from 1980 to 1989, trillions of dollars were added to the national debt while billions were cut from numerous social services, including Social Security, unemployment insurance, food stamps, and housing assistance.[18] The movement gained support through images and rhetoric that distinguished between hardworking citizenry and those who gained rights through elite condescension, minoritarian maneuvering, special interests, and activist jurists.[19] This era extended the neoliberal restructuring project that began after the global economic downturn of the 1970s. As Robinson reports, between 1977 and 1989, according to the Congressional Budget Office, the wealthiest 1 percent amassed 60 percent of the growth in after-tax income, while the poorest 40 percent experienced income declines.[20]

After the late 1960s and '70s collapse of the postwar ideological consensus and a series of economic and political crises, Reagan also strengthened Cold War rhetoric. As Foner adds, "The Great Communicator effectively united into a coherent whole the elements of cold war freedom—negative liberty (that is, limited government), free enterprise, and anticommunism—all in the service of a renewed insistence on America's global mission."[21] Economic policies and their concurrent international crimes occurred against the backdrop of escalating public fears about race, crime, and national security, incited by racially coded refrains about the importance of law and order. The ramp-up of coercive policing, punishment, and confinement were key social policy instruments and legitimating frameworks for securing popular consent for a minority agenda.[22]

Within this economic and political climate, the unfolding HIV/AIDS crisis in the United States provided the fuel for anti-gay hate speech. During the 1980s, accusations of judicial activism, social engineering, and reverse discrimination (i.e., affirmative action) became part of the rallying cry of neoconservatives. They used racially inflected public contestation of affirmative action, tirades against bilingual education, the supposed abuse of public services by the undocumented, and the refusal of data from racial classification to redress past inequality as part of their platform.[23] These developments obviously affected poor, Black, and Indigenous people living with HIV/AIDS disproportionately, and increased violent homophobia, at a time when politicians and public figures could outrightly state that homosexuals were pathological and unworthy of receiving care. This hate speech occurred, at least in part, because of gay men's perceived penetrability, both sexual and emotional, and their association with the feminine. The state, by contrast, demonstrated its impenetrable defenses against the supposed disease of homosexuality, now manifest in the form of HIV/AIDS.

President Reagan neglected to even address the pandemic until late 1985, which reflects, in historian Sean Wilentz's words, less Reagan's personal animosity and more the "deep-seated public antagonism toward homosexuality and a political determination by the White House not to rile its supporters in the religious right."[24] Republican commentator Pat Buchanan snidely remarked, "The poor homosexuals; They have declared war on nature and now nature is exacting an awful retribution."[25] Conservatives called it the "gay plague," the wrath of an angry God who intended to punish all the perverts. As Sean Wilentz reports, finally, in 1987, after Reagan had defended levels of funding that medical experts found totally insufficient, he declared AIDS to be "public enemy number one."[26] However, he left it up to Congress to appropriate these substantial funds to research, disappointing even members of his own family. At the start of Reagan's second term, AIDS had killed 5,600 Americans—mostly young gay men—and four years later, the death toll reached 50,000. People living with HIV/AIDS found themselves in the crosshairs of the "culture wars," as neoconservatives attacked both feminism and gay rights as "products of a subversive counterculture."[27]

Gay men relied on their communities, which was a wonderful demonstration of how friendship becomes a way of life. In a 1981 interview with the French magazine *Gai Pied*, Foucault offered his view on the "multiplicity of relationships" that male–male homosexuality creates and sustains:

> Our rather sanitized society can't allow a place for [homosexuality] without fearing the formation of new alliances and the tying together of unforeseen lines of force. I think that's what makes homosexuality "disturbing": the homosexual mode of life, much more than the sexual act itself. . . . Institutional codes can't validate these relations with multiple intensities, variable colors, imperceptible movements and changing forms.[28]

Gay men continued to "to live together, to share their time, their meals, their room, their leisure, their grief, their knowledge, their confidences," all while in close proximity to death and dying.[29] Sharing the moments before death, a most vulnerable and penetrable time, gave rise to care practices that challenged gender and relational norms within and beyond queer communities. From teddy bears for dead lovers to the buddy system, gendered codes of behavior were unable to continue as before, and masculinity began to expand beyond the narrow parameters of both heteronormative masculinity and stereotypical gay masculinism. Even in mainstream media and on the news, images of men caring for one another unsettled the typical image of gay men "grabbing each other's asses and getting each other off in a quarter of an hour."[30] The idea that gay men can form unruly alliances based on "affection, tenderness, friendship, fidelity, camaraderie, and companionship," I believe, continues to rattle heteronormative society, especially in the violent backlash of the 2020s occurring around the world.[31] Foucault's understanding of friendship as a way life creates diagonal lines across the social fabric, erasing differences in age, class status, social standing, national belonging, etc., outside of any institution.

Foucault believes that the pederastic practices of the ancient Greeks can and do transfer not only to modern gay life but to societies of men more generally, blurring distinctions between homo- and heterosexual. Such intimacy between men is a form of "desire-in-uneasiness," in which men stand "naked" with one another outside of institutional relations, of family, professional, and obligatory camaraderie.[32] For Kadji Amin, friendship as a way of life expresses the utopian potential of "uninstitutionalized relations to generate reconfigured and antidisciplinary bodies, selves, and collectivities."[33] Amin recalls that the central binding for this way of life was pederasty, as it was practiced by French men in the 1980s (not the ancient Greek relation between pubescent boys and adult men).[34] As far as Foucault's remarks on the "canon of beauty," Amin notes that he is not only critiquing a familiar gay male obsession with youth, but he is also defending cross-generational relations, "increasingly, though not exclusively portrayed as monstrous and ugly in the French popular press."[35] By "new alliances" and "unforeseen lines of force," Foucault refers to the energies resulting from dissymmetry and inherent inequality in pederastic friendships across generations rather than between young, gay men of the same class status.[36] This erasure of pederasty from queer theorizations on friendship as a way of life indicates the degree to which the practice has been an embarrassment for some.

Aside from these erasures and Foucault's own intentions, I want to ask how friendship as a way of life reaffirms misogynistic attitudes. His utopian universalization of "homosexual ascesis" places assigned male bodies in an exceptional position. He even likens male homosexual repression to war and suggests lesbians are much better off (he says nothing about bisexuals or trans people). Citing Lillian Faderman's *Surpassing the Love of Men*, he comments—astonishingly—that at least women have access to one another's bodies without fear of reprisal (his stereotypical examples include doing each other's hair, helping one another with makeup, dressing each other, etc.).[37] By essentializing queer women's experiences, and promoting the idea that men have a "special" claim on homophobia, he runs the risk of remasculinizing friendship and creating a shadow brotherhood. Do women, and the feminine-identified, have a place in this friendship as a way of life, or are they again invisible, haunting the periphery of another fraternity?

For these reasons, I turn again to *The Politics of Friendship*, in which Jacques Derrida insists that the concepts of fraternity and democracy cannot simply be "enriched" with what is foreign to them. This includes any reinvestment in Greek asceticism. Women are doubly excluded from the canon of friendship, both in their relationships with each other and with men. In Foucault's failure to consider women's experiences meaningfully, he repeats the mistake of every major philosopher Derrida encounters. Here, the role of fraternity, and its portability as a construct, needs attention. Derrida writes that the exclusion of women is intimately related to "the movement that has always 'politicized' the friendship model at the very moment when one strives to rescue it from thoroughgoing politicization. The tension is here on the inside of the political itself. It is at work in all the discourses that reserve politics and public space to man, domestic and private space to woman."[38] This double exclusion of women is so complete that traditional friendship is best articulated through the "sublime figure of virile homosexuality."[39] In all forms of government, there exists some form of friendship that is coterminous with the relations of justice, but the brother relation is most salient in democracy (by contrast, in tyranny, friendship and justice become insignificant). Homosociality may be the foil for the installment of this sublime figure in politics, as even white gay men must be neutralized to be included (in other words, sexless).

Precisely how did gay men depart from normative masculinity during the HIV/AIDS crisis, when this potentially sublime figure of virile homosexuality was severely compromised by disease? For many, masculine impenetrability and the narcissism that constitutes male–male friendship became undesirable or no longer possible. This shift disturbed subject–object relations, leading to what Derrida describes as *lovence*. Lovers and friends experienced a connection that endured beyond death, not in the service of manly state power and the perpetuation of the patronym, but to dissolve into unknown forces. As discussed in chapter 4, to love someone beyond the grave, and to leave oneself behind, requires lovence—the ultimate act of selflessness, vulnerability, and penetrability. Love beyond death does not require reciprocity, affinity, election, or like-mindedness, nor is it solely confined to relations with men. In *Masculinity in Transition,* such a loving and shared masculinity becomes the condition of possibility, or the theoretical chain, which is held by the concept of alliance, or the performative chain. Unruly alliances in this chapter, guided by the *unheimlich* hand of lovence, welcome uncertainty, inviting a world in which masculinity is no longer welded to dominance and the habit of needing to be "on top" in every situation. Loss of self and identity in lovence makes it possible to love the world beyond narrow identitarian attachments.

Well after Foucault's death of AIDS in 1984 at the age of fifty-seven, gay men commemorated lives that were of no public consequence or political value. They were excluded from the trope of the epitaph, which ensures the continuation of fraternal power through the endurance of the proper name. Here, we can track the experience of mourning across the Western philosophical canon—from Cicero's *De Amicitia,* to Michel de Montaigne's "On Friendship," to Maurice Blanchot's *L'amitié*. As Derrida argues, in all these discourses, "through the irreplaceable element of the named they always advance in testimonial order to confide and refuse the death of the unique to a universalizable discourse [to which 'O My Friends' also belongs]."[40] In other words, friends become symbols rather than beings, which is how the canon is concretized and passed down. The importance of the name precedes the encounter with the dead, structuring "the testamentary survival stance," which ensures that the name continues to be invoked, a priori of the bearer and the person to whom the name refers. The name is always framed within a history, and it includes the chance of filiation, of the inherited name, as well as of renown—the chance to become legendary, "great men."[41]

Of course, in the contemporary retelling of the HIV/AIDS crisis, some names have persisted and attained legendary status, but as the many documentaries on the subject suggest, these are more often than not white men of means. This erasure from practices of remembrance should remind us of how exclusion and inclusion actually operate—not through brute force, or through a simple *yes* and *no* but through a more differential *more* or *less*. As Derrida conveys, total exclusion is never possible, for repression enacts the return of the repressed.[42] The works in this chapter offer this return—namely, through images of men who were sick, dying, and broken, yet also sexual beings.

Death and dying introduced an unheimlich energy into the heart of friendship, paradoxically causing its unraveling, and this energy compounds through the constant funerals at the time memorializing deaths that were not honorable. Derrida relates how, for Blanchot, the loss of Foucault to AIDS-related complications allows him to really consider a type of male friendship that could resist canonization:

> Friendship, this relation without dependence, without episode, into which, however, the utter simplicity of life enters, implies the recognition of a common strangeness which *does not allow us to speak of our friends, but only to speak to them*.[43]

Blanchot insists that friends are not themes or subjects to be spoken about. Instead, this recognition of "common strangeness" leads to infinite singularity and distance. Within this distance, Derrida recommends embracing the "pure interval," which allows us to relate to the other through a "non-negative neutrality": "Such a neutrality calls into question not only the memory of the friend, or fidelity *to him*, but the memory of what 'friendship' has always meant."[44] Blanchot invokes, for Derrida, the lovence that accompanies one beyond death, into a space where "'without sharing' and the 'without reciprocity' come to sign friendship, the response or the responsibility of friendship."[45]

Dying in common through separation, or infinite singularity, insured ironically by a lack of "honor," a new vision of what is common emerges. Derrida insists that through lovence, friendship is carried "beyond being-in-common . . . or sharing, beyond all common appurtenance (familial, neighborhood, national, political, linguistic, and finally generic appurtenance), beyond the social bond itself."[46] This community would be stripped of all the attributes of canonical friendship in Western philosophy. The HIV/AIDS pandemic did accomplish this, which gave rise to the reclamation of the word *queer* to express a radical, anti-identitarian politics. These alliances of the future would form through the desire to bridge the distance with *all* the others and would not be connected to facile motifs of community, or even to a particular way of life for men.

Disability theory becomes a necessary companion to queer theory for the analysis of this archive, particularly because it invites rather than resists interdependence and mutual aid. Disability scholar Lennard J. Davis proposes a move away from humanistic political frameworks that "mak[e] all identities equal under a model of the rights of the dominant, often white, male, 'normal' subject." In his view, we must create a "new category based on the partial, incomplete subject whose realization is not autonomy and independence but dependency and interdependence."[47] By necessity, this subject would revise those masculine practices that associate care and the body with the feminine. Recovering desire and forming relationship and community within systemic conditions of oppression and disease requires incredible emotional flexibility and fortitude. The survival of intimacy and care attests to the strength of the body, mind, and spirit to thrive within adverse conditions.

Through caring relationships of various kinds, queer-crip subjects dying of AIDS-related complications in the 1980s and early '90s, before the viability of lifesaving treatments, gave and received validation of their existence when no one else would do so. They dispelled what Abby Wilkerson calls "the folly of relying on atomistic visions of self-determination, which are based on autonomy at the expense of interconnection."[48] The importance of both sexuality and disability in public life cannot be underestimated. As Wilkerson states, it is crucial that we conceive of our *"sexual-political* interdependence," which gives way to a politics of coconspiratorship between queer and crip subjects, who are interdependent *through* the sexual.[49] However, while the convergence of sex and disability was addressed in activism and in cultural theory about HIV/AIDS (for example, in Michael Callen and Richard Berkowitz's *How to Have Sex in an Epidemic* and scholarly essays like Douglas Crimp's "How to Have Promiscuity in an Epidemic"), "this work tends to remain at an uneasy distance from disability scholarship."[50]

This distancing occurred even though AIDS activists knew they were indebted to the disability rights movement, particularly in the fight to include people living with HIV/AIDS in the 1990 Americans with Disabilities Act. HIV-positive serostatus is classifiable as a disability, but in queer theory people living with HIV are often grouped together with those who have less socially acceptable disabilities: schizophrenia, psychosis, or alcoholism. Robert McRuer rightly questions why people living with HIV/AIDS are named "queer subjects" rather than "crip" or "queercrip" subjects. In his seminal text *Crip Theory*, McRuer establishes the overlapping concerns of queerness and disability. The chapter "Capitalism and Disabled Identity" makes two key points that I want to highlight here: "First, that queer communities could acknowledge that the political unconscious of debates about normalization (including debates about marriage) is shaped, in large part, by ideas about disability; second, that disability communities, primed to enter (or entering already) some of the territory recently charted by queers, could draw on radical queer thought to continue forging the critical disability consciousness that has emerged over the past few decades—what I am calling in this book crip theory or crip culture."[51] In this chapter, I offer how the separation of sex and disability has occurred at the expense of a more sustained theorization of masculinity and its fraught relationship to vulnerability and precarity.

In this archive, queerness and disability do appear together, particularly in scenes of what I am calling "sick sex." Discomfort and uneasiness arise, which further suggests how masculine impenetrability, sexual dominance, and able-bodiedness are intertwined as cultural and political currency. Theorizing sick sex moves us away from the stereotype of relentless self-fashioning for which gay men are (often wrongly) associated. Practices of care develop out of the crumbling of subjective coherence, providing the ground for an entirely new relationship to masculinity. Disability scholarship tells us how any sex outside of the ableist imaginary, like sick sex, becomes "tragic deficiency or freakish excess."[52] This may help to explain why sexy, militant activism and not images of sick sex are often the focus of cultural theory on HIV/AIDS, which renders the dying or sick body asexual. The sick, asexual body is also no longer a danger to the public, making it a safe vehicle for the elicitation of sympathy, versus compassion (which would require identification and care). More sanitized imagery assumes that gay men died or got sick in the same ways and experienced the same kinds of feelings and thoughts about their illnesses.

By denying the presence of sex in death and dying, gay men as sexual subjects are assigned the social position of victim (in place of pervert, which both gay men and disabled men are apt to be labeled as well). To be an innocent victim, the cause of death (which is often sex) must be removed from the lives of the dying. This sanitization, which sometimes occurs through self-censorship by gay men and activist communities themselves, alerts us once again to the polarization of sex and disability and its corollary, the polarization of masculinity and care. Sex and disability are often polarized because, in Mollow and McRuer's words, they "often threaten to unravel each other."[53] If there is masculinity, then there cannot be care, and similarly if there is disability, which includes sickness, dying, or old age, then there cannot be sex. By contrast, where sex is present, disability must be absent. As Mollow and McRuer point out, a postidentity disability politics keeps these categories fluid, which means that masculinity, sex, and disability can be located together in unexpected settings (as Steers's paintings so powerfully reveal). By depicting the body as decaying and dying, writers, artists, and filmmakers express resistance to masculine calcification and the habitual aversion to care and mutual aid.

Sick Sex and the Queer Time of Disease

In the Australian memoir *Holding the Man* (1995), which later became a play and a movie in 2015, Timothy Conigrave invites his readers to share his grief over the death of his lover, John Caleo, as he himself is dying of AIDS-related illnesses. He details the various complications each experiences, the supposed remedies they experiment with, and their debilitating side effects, as well as scenes of sick sex.

While in *Masculinity in Transition*, I focus on U.S. cultural production, I include the Australian works *Holding the Man* and *Take Me to Paris, Johnny* because they were created within similar conditions of social and political exclusion. As Kelley writes, the United States, Canada, and Australia were not the result of plucky pioneers seeking better lives but the products of violent capitalist expansion and racial ideology. The ranks included "armed settlers backed by joint stock companies, a colonial state apparatus, and capital in the form of kidnapped labor."[54] Australia is not different from the United States in many respects, including its brands of toxic masculinity, but particularly when it comes to the pervasiveness of state-sponsored violence. To this point, minoritized populations in Australia, particularly Indigenous peoples, are also disproportionately represented in the nation's prisons, in similar or larger ratios than the United States.[55]

Tim first describes falling in love with John and how, despite their differences (John is a jock, he is an artist), they develop a multi-dimensional friendship and sexual relationship over the course of more than a decade. However, despite John being a jock, Tim's descriptions of his gender performance are nuanced from the beginning. He describes John's personality as straight-passing, typically masculine, and athletic but also vulnerable and caring, more so than himself. Tim writes in his college newspaper in response to a homophobic incident: "My boyfriend was captain of the football team at school. He is strongly built and masculine, and if you were to meet him you wouldn't know he was gay. He isn't like the stereotype."[56] Tim falls for John because of his soft/hard combination and because he is not like other men: "I saw the body of a man with an open, gentle face: such softness within that masculinity. He was beautiful, calm. I was transfixed" (31). John's vulnerability appears in tiny portraits and fleeting moments, which foreshadows the queer time of disease.

As both find themselves in close proximity to death and dying, Tim values even more John's softness, and in response Tim develops his own caring masculinity. They struggle first with the shame of coming out to their families as gay, and then later as people living with HIV, which they discover after being separated for several years. Tim receives a letter from the Red Cross telling him that blood he donated in June 1981 has transmitted HIV to someone he does not know, which also means that it is he who has transmitted HIV to John and not the other way around. He reflects, painfully, "*I have killed the man I love*" (208).

Compassion for one another increases as they view the illness from the other's point of view. Being part of the theater world becomes another way to access this compassion, such as when they view the play *Blood and Honour*, by Alex Harding, in which a man from China named Michael watches his lover Colin, a newsreader, die from AIDS-related complications. This compassion encourages

Tim and John to speak about their fears of dying and their separate ruminations on who will die first. Tim asks: *"I wonder what the moment of death will be like? Will I be so bombed on morphine that I won't even notice? Or will my soul crack open making its escape? And when John dies, what will it be like, life without him? I want it all to go away"* (202). Increasingly, care occurs in the context of hospitalization, further demonstrating how queer theory and disability theory need one another. Masculinity and care tend to sever from one another, but disease makes their separation impossible. When John is first diagnosed with *Pneumocystis* pneumonia, Tim brings him food and chamomile tea and wheels the TV into the bedroom to watch videos. Later in the hospital as the pneumonia worsens, he brings him bird-of-paradise flowers, which ironically symbolize freedom, joy, and oasis, as well as anticipation and excitement. These flowers suggest unruly alliances based not on strength and the cult of beauty but on lovence.

While tenderness and caring do not remove their sorrow, they find a way to connect through it, showing that their bond does not rely on elusive notions of wellness. After John is diagnosed with lymphoma, Tim cries so violently he nearly runs their car off the road: "When we got home we lay down on the bed and cuddled, just holding each other. *John is here in my arms.* But the sorrow rose up again" (219). With unusual directness and honesty, he recalls the rounds of chemotherapy, hair loss, endless pleurodeses for refilling lungs, toxoplasmosis in the brain, clipping each other's hair. They even spend time in the hospital in adjoining rooms. At times their roles switch, so that John takes care of Tim. On a trip to Bali they take despite illness, John witnesses Tim's struggle with uncontrollable diarrhea from campylobacter, which causes him to pass out, and come to, sitting among little piles of his own shit.

Sensual scenes of sick sex are not surprising, since their intimacy is presented throughout as distinct from the brief, violent fucking Foucault describes as the representational default for gay men. In one of their first clandestine moments together at school, John puts his hand on the back of Tim's seat and begins rubbing his muscles softly. He uses his back to caress John's hand: "My spine melted into his fingertips. When Alan Bates and Julie Christie spooned on the screen [in the movie/book *The Go-Between*] they were John and me" (80). In a sex scene (ironically, in an alley) they look at each other in a way that Tim recognizes as strange and beautiful, deviating from the normative masculinity they have been conditioned to perform: "We were standing holding hands, looking. I think this was the first time that we had ever really looked at each other. Boys do not look at each other like that" (89). Their ability to see one another—something boys do not do—underscores their betrayal not only of heteronormativity but of masculinity.

During a religious retreat for school, where all the "poofters" (gay boys) are sharing the floor, John and Tim begin the kind of exploration that would echo later in scenes of sick sex. All body parts are envisioned as erotic, and sex becomes an art of exploration:

> Lips caressing lips. Exploring. Our lips slightly parted, exchanging breath. Hands slipping into each other's sleeping-bags. His warm body in cotton PJs. Running my hand up his spine, feeling the muscles in his back. His hand going in under my pyjama shirt. Skin of his hand against the skin of my back. (93)

Innocent, deeply curious, and searching, their sex expresses Audre Lorde's notion of the erotic as a source of power.[57] The image of skin touching skin, hand touching back, reimagines masculine sexuality, infusing relations with the kind of care reserved in heterosexist patriarchies for cisgender men and their female partners.[58]

Toward the end of the memoir, they invent together a form of intimacy that includes death and dying. In a total reversal of what is expected, where sex *must* sever from the disabled body, Tim gets sexually excited by the idea of John having a lung operation: "I would love to know what my boyfriend looked like inside, a privilege that most couples don't get. Slug and snail and puppy-dogs' tails" (243). In death, both men return to the innocence evoked by the earlier scene when the "skin of his hand [was] against the skin of my back," but it is not an innocence devoid of eroticism, even as their relationship becomes haunted by the realization that they will not last "forever"—"*Either we break up or one of us dies*. There was no relief from this thought" (219). They get in bed together again at the hospital, which was itself a struggle, not only physically but because they have to confront the homophobia of a startled and disturbed nurse who quickly draws the curtain around them. Despite the institutional setting, they are encouraged by the approach of death to maintain their physical connection:

> I could smell the vanilla of the drip-feed as our tongues mingled. I put my hand under his T-shirt and was struck by how thin he was. I could feel the outline of his ribs, and my spine tingled. . . . I undressed him, revealing his skeletal body, his skin hanging loose. I tried hard not to let him see that I was shocked. I hugged him and we rolled around the bed naked, his tube swinging and getting caught up in our bodies. . . . When he came there was very little fluid, another reminder of how unwell he was. I withdrew, pulled the condom off and brought myself to orgasm, my come splashing onto my belly. John smeared it and then licked his fingers clean. "Mmm." We lay there. I felt sad. *That was such a gift, giving of himself. I love him for it.* We drifted off to sleep, content. (246–47)

Tim perceives this experience as a gift, one that brings spiritual peace and contentment. While he does express to himself shock at seeing John's body, instead of feeling repulsed, he experiences desire. Life and death become intertwined, as they engage in a lovence that already transcends their final moments.

Images of sickness arrive more rapidly, and a different form of care and attentiveness emerges, as sex sets the stage for death. In the last scenes, Tim tracks John's death through his breathing, the rhythm becoming like a spiritual mantra: "He moaned with every breath, like a wind through a piece of bamboo" (269). Witnessing John's last moments brings its own kind of climax, an experience of being together that only proximity to death and dying can provide: "John and I were alone again, alone with him groaning. I placed my head on his chest and put my arm across him as though I was holding him to this world. The moaning vibrating through his chest sounded like our sex, emotional, the end of climax as we drift off to sleep" (271). He experiences John's gentleness as his groans become whispers, his breathing now shallow and quiet, while the last signs of life depart. He begins to blow saliva bubbles, which start to run down his chin. Even the smell of feces in the air becomes an opportunity for a connection: "*Not a lot of dignity in death, eh?* John stopped breathing. He was dead" (275). Tim performs here the ultimate act of lovence. Instead of allowing his fear (of his own death, too) to overtake him, he eases John's passage, literally "holding the man," as the word *man* undergoes a radical revision.

Immediately after these sick sex scenes, Tim presents the startling contrast of John's parents' homophobia and Tim's erasure from any kind of public commemoration of John's life. Tim's father commands that no one will make a statement about AIDS or the "gay thing" in the Catholic Church during John's funeral. Tim's name does not appear in the obituary.

In *Take Me to Paris, Johnny* (1993), John Foster, another Australian writer and academic, also depicts, through unsentimental and unflinching prose, an intimate perspective on sex, disability, and masculinity. The work is an elegy for his lover Juan Céspedes, a Cuban national living in New York, who died of AIDS-related complications in the early 1990s. John is by turns angry, because of the callous degree of inaction by the Reagan administration, and tender, embracing the possibility of living more interdependently. He published the book shortly before his own death in 1994, two years before the arrival of the lifesaving, triple-drug viral suppression therapy. Symptoms were treated, but with severe side effects and bureaucratic red tape, especially for stateless persons like Juan. John's account shows how the disease became a creative outlet for the expression of variation in sexual practices and gender expression.

John describes Juan's suffering in vivid detail, as well as his own struggles to make sense of these memories. He enacts this struggle through contrasting short, suffocating sentences with excessive polysyndeton, which conveys a feeling of being out of control. Part of this struggle over memory has to do with the nature of the disease itself, which plunged people living with HIV/AIDS into a kind of negative queer presentism that could be both liberating and self-destructive:

> The virus makes you obsessive. It settles in your head. It distorts your vision. In the first flood of knowing—and believing—it can make you regard your own body with horror. The blood that is in you is lethal. It could drive you crazy if you dwelt on that knowledge, if you said to yourself, "I am the embodiment of death."[59]

The political and social climate of the time encouraged gay men to see themselves as contaminated, unclean, and shameful. By exposing this battle within himself through literature, and connecting with readers, he staves off self-annihilation.

As the relationship becomes more and more based on being with death and dying, John turns his writing into a meditation on Juan's qualities—his moods, joys, obsessions, and triggers—to the point where John himself disappears into the background. The body's frailties become part of these meditations, and part of the tragedy that the life they would have had together never arrives. What is more, due to "bureaucratic complications," Juan never becomes a citizen of Australia and is denied official forms of care. By choosing to tell the story of Juan's life before they met, he infuses Juan's memory with the scent of the gardenias of his native Cuba, in resistance to the hysterical Cold War attitudes against Communism. Through all the twists and turns of their separations and reunion, he tells a story of two people who were neither enmeshed nor remote but who gave one another a gift of lovence that yielded numerous lines of mutual aid and support.

John invites readers into the most harrowing scenes of Juan's illness, communicating his own vulnerability as a writer and his trust that his audience will hold these images without judgment. In one scene, when John sees Juan naked for the first time in a long while, he does not hide his shock:

> [The] weeping red eye of his *culi*, as he affectionately called his arse; stunned by the loose dark Buchenwald folds of skin that were all that was left of his buttocks. Searching for words, I found none. I said nothing, just as I said nothing when he told me he could no longer get an erection. But he seemed not to expect words. He simply took my hands and guided them, as if I were a blind man, to the points on his spine and shoulders and his neck where I could knead away the pain.[60]

The loss of language John experiences is quite common for those in traumatic situations, such as assault, war, or climate-change-related disasters, as the reference to "Buchenwald" suggests. These gaps in speech insulate the person from what they are seeing. What is most profound about this passage is the way Juan guides him, instead of the other way around. Juan intuitively understands that John's speechlessness is completely normal in this circumstance. He patiently instructs John on how to care for him, which shows Juan to trust in John's ability to perform caring masculinity. There is also an erotic tone to this scene, even though Juan can no longer get an erection. The act of guiding another person's hands to parts of the body that need attention is deeply sensual, and profound in this case because the body itself is slipping out of existence.

I discover in these memoirs a lovence that opens outward and recognizes supposedly failed masculinity and shared alienation as part of the neoliberal condition, particularly during acute moments of systemic neglect. However, these depictions are not enrichments and resignifications of any past masculinity or projections of any predetermined future. The queer temporality of this shared alienation (being alone while being together) is one of the present, with all that the present brings, expressing the in-betweenness of self and other rather than converging intimacies as they are commonly understood. Death creates relations that demand space and distance for perceiving the other, such as when Tim offers John the gift of himself in their last sexual encounter. These men shed the compulsion to become ideal masculine subjects, and move toward processes of subjectivation, which are always ongoing. Tom Roach describes these processes as "the undoing of socially, historically determined selves and the creation of new ones."[61] This state of being makes room for what Todd W. Reeser describes as masculinity-in-motion.[62] Sick sex values singularity and strangeness, compelling the question, "Can we care for those with whom we have nothing in common?" These communal forms of masculinity—integral to unruly alliance—have the capacity to transform gender and relationality on a collective level.

Sick sex as a generative ground for unruly alliance grates against queer scholarship that elevates "political progress, sexual egalitarianism, and muscular and volitional resistance to norms that are all indebted to liberal theories of the political subject."[63] In their brutal honesty, these images could be disturbing rather than politically invigorating. They are not the most celebrated or the most widely theorized aspects of queer rebellion in the period. Sick sex is not heroic like the art-based resistance of Gran Fury or the widely documented protests of ACT UP, famous for their bravado and humor. However, the unease that sick sex generates reminds readers of their own precarity and vulnerability to disability and disease, revealing how some aspects of queer sexualities are illegible or insufficiently political to "count" as legitimate sites of inquiry.[64]

Nation, Exile, and the Art of Life

As gay men of color persecuted both within and outside of their communities, Reinaldo Arenas and Marlon Riggs are uniquely positioned to connect masculinity, sex, and disability to historical trauma and social injustice, addressing issues of racism, exile, and national borders. They also suggest that masculinities in HIV/AIDS self-writing and autoethnographic film do not only express care in the couple form or in networks of close friends but toward entire communities rendered expendable. Arenas's memoir *Before Night Falls* and Riggs's autoethnographic film *Black Is . . . Black Ain't* reach toward undiscovered forms of unruly alliance, waiting just beyond the horizon. As their longevity and staying power confirm, both artists welcome audiences beyond the present moment of the AIDS crisis, audiences who may not have encountered this disease but who may apply their struggles to their own contexts. To reach, trembling, toward unruly alliance is by necessity to reach toward the unknown community based in lovence—to love those you have not yet met but who will perhaps encounter you after your death.

Racial and gender formations are produced in relations with others, not in a vacuum. As Hong argues, racialized masculinities "have the potential for unexpected forms of alliance" with other nonnormative gender formations, particularly those of color. However, they do not emerge with the same access to property, citizenship, and "self-will" as white masculinities, regardless of sexual or gender identity.[65] Arenas and Riggs resist "normative reading practices"—of texts as well as bodies—that produce racialized and gender meanings, which legitimate "racialized dispossession and white property rights, to enact the protection of white domesticity, and to ensure racialized labor exploitation."[66]

In *Before Night Falls,* the relationship between the United States and Cuba brings forward the discussion on impenetrability as the quality of a highly mobile, and ultimately fragile, form of masculine currency. When Cuba is pictured today, the shadow of Guantánamo comes into view, recalling a long history of U.S. intervention and imperial strong-arming, rendering penetrable the island of Cuba, much like the rest of Latin America and the Caribbean. The American gulag at Guantánamo Bay, featured in Arenas's memoir, is a territory secured over a century ago by gunboat diplomacy, and it exposes ongoing extralegal rendition and torture. The prison has lurked there as a mainstay even during Obama's presidency, and when he had the chance to dismantle it, he did not act.[67]

Cuba has been the object of desire for more than one imperial power since Spain first colonized the island in 1492, embroiling the country in numerous wars of independence. The Spanish–American War and U.S. occupation and intervention during the first years of the twentieth century meant that Cuba had not yet achieved its independence from foreign powers. In 1912, Afro-Cuban nationalists were subjected to "near-genocidal war under the direction of U.S. officials."[68] However, the 1959 Cuban Revolution promised a break with this legacy, but it took place in the context of the rise of the Soviet Union, which suggests how socialism can also be imperialist in its tendencies. For Quijano, the Cuban Revolution was a product of the radicalization of Latin American populist tendencies, which introduced new complications but also marked a point of departure.[69] The 26th of July Movement led by Fidel Castro was largely responsible for the overthrow of Fulgencio Batista in January 1959. The movement included a broad base of middle-class reformers, students, workers, and those like Che Guevara, with more openly Communist and anti-imperialist views. Their main proposals were land redistribution, the nationalization of public services, and other political and economic reforms. The new provisional revolutionary government, made up of 26th of July members, was not initially at odds with the United States. However, relations deteriorated when the Cuban government radically restructured Cuba's economic, political, and social system through revolutionary decrees that attempted to address disparities in wealth and access to social services. By 1959, U.S. officials were indignant and alarmed by Castro's audacity in the face of U.S. empire. Cuba simultaneously developed ties with the Soviet Union, signing the first treaty agreement in February 1960 and establishing formal diplomatic relations later that year.

As Katherine A. Gordy explains, in January 1961, the United States and Cuba broke diplomatic relations, CIA-trained exiles were defeated at the Bay of Pigs, and Castro declared the revolution socialist, though Che Guevara hinted at the Marxist nature of the Cuban Revolution before then.[70] This represented a threat to U.S. interests, because, as Quijano argues, "neo-colonial dependence requires a suitable state [read: penetrable]—a national-dependent state in which dependence predominates over nationalism."[71] Toward the end of 1961, President Kennedy authorized Operation Mongoose (commissioned earlier by Eisenhower in 1960 as a covert CIA operation). In 1962, in response to U.S. Jupiter missiles in Italy and Turkey, the Soviet Union installed ballistic missiles in Cuba, and the United States imposed a naval blockade. Kennedy and Nikita Khrushchev reached an agreement, however, and the missiles were removed from Turkey and Cuba. Not surprisingly, the Cuban government was mostly absent from these discussions, signaling their ongoing dependence (read: penetrability) rather than their liberation from larger powers. While the United States signed a nonaggression pact following the missile crisis, small-scale invasions through Miami-based, anti-Castro paramilitary groups like Alpha 66 continued. As Gordy shows, in 1963, U.S. policy shifted from supporting direct attacks to inciting revolt from inside, and the United States moved its bases of operations to other countries to avoid being held accountable.

Cuban officials, from Castro to Che Guevara, thought economic relations with the Soviets were advantageous and qualitatively different from those with the United States. The Soviets promised a guaranteed market for their sugar quota, and in return Cuba would receive mostly manufactured products or raw materials, rather than cash, which would allow them to bypass the world market. Critics warned that the geographical distance made Soviet imports expensive, but the Soviets' commitment to sell oil to Cuba at 33 percent cheaper than U.S. monopoly companies showed the agreement offered supposed economic liberation. Guevara felt that at least they would be simply selling merchandise instead of their own national sovereignty, as in the old days with the United States or Spain. This would, according to Gordy, be a kind of "pragmatic" anti-imperialism that would benefit Cuba. Privately, Cuban officials were frustrated, but this did not suggest Cuba's unquestioned subservience to the Soviets. In fact, Cuban foreign policy in the 1960s and '70s often covertly countered the Soviet Union. Cuban leaders viewed Cuba as distinct from the Soviet Union and China and, as a result, better positioned to understand and to aid in the struggles of the developing world. As Gordy explains, while anti-imperialist movements have used anti-imperialist rhetoric, in practice, these struggles in Cuba have looked less to disassociate themselves altogether from imperial power and instead have focused on producing results that weaken empire more broadly as a logic of European dominance and capitalist expansion.

Imperialism in its U.S. form operates not just through control of a nation-state's land, labor, raw materials, capital, and markets but also through the colonization of domestic struggles, which in Cuba have had to rely, in some way, on an imperial power. After 1959, while both Cuban and Soviet governments rejected the claim that their relations were a new type of imperialism, Cuban revolutionaries were still concerned with Cuba's compromised autonomy within this relationship. Some exile groups in the United States focused their attention on Cuba's relations with the Soviet Union, while a few maintained an anti-imperialist stance by criticizing both the Soviet presence in Cuba and the nefarious policies of the U.S. government, as well as the overdependence of many exile groups on the United States. For example, Cubans have, since the revolution, relied on the United States as a place of exile, a journey that Arenas finally succeeds in making after numerous failed attempts—but with very mixed results. Cubans disillusioned with the revolution came to Miami and, as rabid anti-Communists, supported U.S. efforts to take down Castro. However, as Gordy conveys, U.S. involvement compromised Indigenous Cuban resistance to Castro, since it meant that counterrevolutionaries and, later, dissidents could be "dismissed as lackeys of U.S. imperialism eager to return Cuba to its neo-colonial status."

By the start of the 1970s, as revolution in Cuba was institutionalized, exile plans for immediate return of the island faded, and the United States abandoned more aggressive actions, which left room for new groups of younger Cubans to organize. Both anti-Communist and anti-imperialist, they drew from Cuba's historic nationalist canon to criticize the older generations of exile leaders for their subservience and corruption with the United States. They were also critical of the U.S. failure to topple Castro, but unlike most they traced this failure back to the first half of the twentieth century when the United States failed to respect and support Cuban sovereignty. They opposed Castro not because of the Cuban government's decision to nationalize U.S. properties but because they were subservient to the Soviets. This indicated that Communism's flaw in Cuba was that it had been imported from abroad. Their anti-Communism was distinct from the exiles and from Marxism-Leninism because they formed alliances with civil rights groups, social democrats, pro-labor and other center-left organizations whose philosophies inspired their vision of Cuba's future economy. Consequently, Gordy explains, "Agrupación Abdala called for the withdrawal of *both* the Soviets *and* the United States still lodged at the U.S. naval base at Guantánamo Bay." However, combining these threads proved difficult in practice, as they struggled over tactics and the expediency of certain alliances.

Arenas's struggle as a gay man and a writer in pre- and postrevolutionary Cuba and as an exile in the United States shows the impossibility of a pure anti-imperialism, even if it was a part of a political platform on the level of ideology and rhetoric. His experiences as an internally displaced and stateless person also show that marginalization occurred for gay men in both Cuba and the United States, which disturbs the image of the United States as less hostile than socialist countries. Arenas's arrival in Miami was met with indifference or even rancor from anti-Castro Cubans. He experienced profound economic marginalization as he realized that each aspect of U.S. society is privatized and inaccessible. He also criticized the highly individualized gay scene in the United States—another effect of privatization. When Arenas finally made it to New York, he expected to find the friendly and open home he was looking for, but he quickly realized that the difference between capitalist democracy and Communism may be only a difference in kind.

When he was writing *Before Night Falls,* Arenas was very close to dying from AIDS-related complications, and the introduction to his memoir includes a suicide note, which he fulfills. He begins writing his memoirs under the title *Before Night Falls* while he is still in Cuba and in hiding from the police:

> I would write all day until dark, waiting for the other darkness that would come when the police eventually found me. I had to hurry to get my writing down before my world finally darkened, before I was thrown into jail. That manuscript, of course, was lost, as was almost everything I had written in Cuba that I had not been able to smuggle out, but at the time, writing it all down was a consolation; it was a way of being with my friends when I was no longer among them.[72]

"Being with [his] friends" through writing becomes a critical survival strategy in both contexts. He tells a story of how vulnerability, penetrability, and care are in conflict with racial capitalism in the United States and the often lethal anti-gay persecution in Cuba. His writing also countered the demand that writers in Cuba only pursue socialist themes. After the revolution, any book that was "ideological diversionism" disappeared from libraries and bookstores. Writers who did not follow this edict were arrested, but Arenas found a way to publish his novels outside of Cuba. He also hid literature to read in plastic bags so that he always had something to occupy his time when he was hiding from the police. He therefore never had the opportunity to write fully supported by either country as a gay male writer who took the "passive" role, and he longed all his life for that freedom, which makes his writing about his (many) erotic adventures even more important. In his dying moments, he describes himself as full of "erotic rage" (90).

Even though *Night* in the title of his novel is a euphemism for his own death, the memoir celebrates sexuality and unruly alliance, often within a complicated world of nationalist masculinities in Cuba. In Cuba, according to Arenas, the worst that can happen to you is that you will be publicly labeled a "faggot." He can connect this "faggot" label to the pushing away of femininity by the men in the government and in the army, who ironically become his sexual partners. Many of the young, virile men who marched in Revolutionary Square applauding Fidel Castro, "rifle in hand and with martial expressions, came to our rooms after the parades to cuddle up naked, and show their real selves, sometimes revealing a tenderness and true enjoyment such as I have not been able to find again anywhere else in the world" (101). During these casual sexual encounters, Arenas forms unruly alliances with these soldiers, based in tenderness and enjoyment, something unavailable in the public realm.

In the beginning of Castro's revolution there were still gay bars, even in small towns like Arenas's hometown of Holguín, but they disappeared when both homosexuality and friendships of a supposedly questionable nature were severely repressed. Gay men were sent to UMAP (Military Units to Aid Production)—concentration camps—unless you were close to the administration and could get away with having a gay "lifestyle." The new, revolutionary man was virile, hypermasculine, and able-bodied, propped up through punishment of "faggots," who were always already disabled and sick. Both women and gay men were considered inferior beings, which meant that it was perfectly acceptable for "macho" men to use violence against them. He watched this take place as a child in his own household, where the women suffered and cared for the children, while men took the abusive role. His narcissistic grandfather, a sadistic and cruel man, "did not talk to God as [his] grandmother did; he talked to himself." Sometimes women and gay men married each other to secure the protections of the state, something that was also quite common in the United States at the time (144).

Arenas has a depressive episode when he realizes that the difference between the capitalist and the Communist state is only slight: "Although both give you a kick in the ass, in the communist system you have to applaud, while in the capitalist system you can scream. And I came here to scream" (273). He even muses how the "the rulers of the world, that reactionary class always in power, and the powerful within the system, must feel grateful to AIDS because a good part of the marginal population, whose only aspiration is to live and who therefore oppose all dogma and political hypocrisy, will be wiped out" (xxvi). His writing threatened the dictatorship because it pointed to an art of life beyond the daily banal traditions and cruelties of a hypermasculine world. Authoritarian leaders cannot tolerate creativity or humor, which Arenas explains is the reason why many Cuban writers were ostracized and abandoned by everyone, including their friends tasked with the job of spying to save their own lives (85). Writers, particularly gay men, became alcoholics, were executed, died by suicide, or were left to die in institutions, while others simply became what Arenas calls "enslaved ghosts" (123). This gave rise to a kind of repressed dual masculine personality in Cuba. On one side, Cuba embodied the worst qualities of masculine normativity (shared by the United States as well)—betrayal, conspiracy, riot, coup fueled by infinite ambition, abuse, despair, false pride, and envy—while on the other side were the rebels, often gay men who experimented with the force of creativity but who eventually became extinct (87).

In telling the story of his life, he captures the erotic memories of his childhood—climbing trees, for example—through which he suggests that gay sex and alternative ways of being masculine are a part of the natural world around him. Trees had secret lives all their own, which gave him special communion with them. He also rejects the idea that the poor are sexually innocent. "In the country," he writes, "we were attached to the earth in an ancestral way; we could not do without it. The earth was there when we were born, in our games, in our work, and of course at the moment of our death" (27). By contrast, he describes Castro's farms as run by inept managers unskilled in animal reproduction or raising crops, which turned men into pathetic, sexless machines totally lacking in care.

After many failed attempts to leave Cuba—one involving a small inner tube, a can of beans, and a bottle of rum tied to his waist with a rope—he leaves the country after a scandal at the Peruvian embassy on April 4, 1980. During that scandal, ten thousand Cuban citizens occupied the embassy in hopes of receiving diplomatic protection. This event eventually led to the so-called Mariel boatlift and the mass emigration of around 125,000 Cubans to the United States. Some of these emigrating people, many of whom were incarcerated people from Cuban prisons and jails, became undercover agents in Miami. Others were "undesirables," such as neurodiverse and homosexual people. The homosexual exiles were, importantly, the penetrable-seeming ones, the passive "faggots," because in Cuba those who took the active role were not considered gay. Arenas escapes as an explicit "homosexual"—but only by changing his name to "Arinas," which allows him to allude the authorities who are already after him for his literary and social crimes against the regime.

Reaching the United States, and specifically Guantánamo, became Arenas's life goal. However, he quickly realizes that the life of the exile is one of perpetual homelessness: "In exile one is nothing but a ghost, the shadow of someone who never achieves full reality. I ceased to exist when I went into exile; I started to run away from myself" (277). What makes Arenas's memoir unique is his ability to capture the persecution of homosexuality in a transnational context. Not surprisingly, given the political conservatism and social backlash in the United States, he does not find the "scream" he is looking for, either creatively or sexually, because he discovers that everything is so regulated and identitarian, and "groups and societies have been created in which it is very difficult for a homosexual to find a man, that is, the real object of his desire" (103). He blames this reality on the fact that in more "advanced" societies, the homosexual becomes a recluse, separated out from the supposedly "nonhomosexual society."

In the end, new conceptions of masculinity in this memoir arrive through unruly alliances with people like his friend Lázaro, who becomes his only connection to his past while he is in exile, the only "witness" and link to the "irretrievable world" of his memory (292). This alliance persists even though, according to Arenas, one of the most grotesque things that Castro's regime accomplished was the breakdown of bonds between men. It is Lázaro who takes him to the hospital in New York when he is dying, but he discovers he cannot receive care in the United States because he is a foreign national. The only thing he has in his pocket is a handwritten copy of his will. He spends his entire life trying to get out of Cuba and into the United States, only to discover that his Cuban friends, to whom he owes his life, are still the only ones able and willing to help him: "I was practically dying," he writes, "but hospitals refused to admit me because I did not have the means to pay" (xx). He pointedly captures in a single sentence the erosion of the social safety net and the backlash in the United States in the 1980s and '90s, which echoes similar attacks against LGBTQIA+ people in the renewed culture wars of the 2020s.

In Marlon Riggs's *Black Is . . . Black Ain't,* masculinity, sex, and disability are also presented in tension with the U.S. backlash against queers and state-sponsored racism.[73] Riggs made the film in 1994 as part of a new movement of "history from below."[74] However, during this period of "perceived national fragmentation," particularly in regard to mass immigration, conservatives questioned whether the "new history" was promoting a less than uplifting version of the nation's development.[75] As Foner reports, people like Lynne Cheney, the former head of the National Endowment for the Humanities, asked whether the "new history" was paying too much attention to "obscure" minority groups, erasing American leaders, and offering a dreary and inaccurate account of the nation's founding and development.[76]

Riggs's second major work, *Tongues Untied* (1989), received a $5,000 grant from the now eliminated National Endowment for the Arts (NEA) regional regranting program, and the PBS series POV that aired the documentary received both NEA and Corporation for Public Broadcasting funding. *Tongues Untied* dealt a blow to the standards for representing Black masculinity because Riggs rejected both the assimilationist politics of civil rights and the nationalism of the Black Power movement. The film also catapulted him into the debate over public funding for the arts. The first honest depiction of gay male experience on television, it became a symbol of why public funding should be withdrawn from such supposedly obscure creators. The Christian Coalition sent to every member of Congress a highly edited and sensationalized seven-minute clip from the film, drawing the attention of Senator Jesse Helms, who somewhat humorously mistook the title as *Tongues United*.[77] Infringing upon the film's copyright, Pat Buchanan reedited a twenty-second clip for a TV ad hit piece condemning the NEA during the 1992 presidential primary.[78]

Riggs responded with a *New York Times* op-ed entitled "Meet the New Willie Horton," referring to a racist ad George Bush aired in the 1988 election.[79] Riggs pushed back, claiming the far-reaching effects of these attacks: "The insult extends not just to blacks and gays, the majority of whom are taxpayers and would therefore seem entitled to some means of representation in publicly financed art. The insult confronts all of us who witness and are outraged by the quality of political debate." In 1988, Riggs spoke before a U.S. Senate committee in support of the campaign to launch the Independent Television Service (ITVS), which would support representation of controversial independent voices on public television. On June 15, 1992, he spoke with David Mills of the *Washington Post* on the importance of ITVS: "The ITVS is supposed to shake you up, to address areas of deep taboo no one is willing to talk about. . . . America needs to realize the value of having a communicative institution designed to challenge us and upset us. . . . There is value in doing something more than making culture answerable to the marketplace."[80] In 1991, Riggs started his own nonprofit production company, Signifyin' Works, which produced *Black Is . . . Black Ain't*. Riggs's engagement with Blackness, within his own personal story of HIV/AIDS, captures how "new histories" refused to treat American history as "an unalloyed saga of national progress toward liberty and equality."[81]

The film finished production after Riggs died and debuted on PBS to a nationwide audience, despite fierce resistance. Riggs's film is a part of a larger archive of Black queer filmmaking of the 1990s, which includes Cheryl Dunye's *The Watermelon Woman* (1996), the first feature-length film by a Black lesbian. With Dunye, he began the project of launching Black queer critiques of the whitewashed exclusivity of LGBT and queer studies. As Kara Keeling observes, Riggs and Dunye countered "existing stereotypes and [broke] the silences that have characterized 'black lesbian and gay' representation and existence prior to that generation's hard-earned access to film and video making."[82]

Riggs's explorations of Black gay masculinity during this period occurred in the context of increased criminalization of Black bodies. After the extension of formal rights of liberal democracy to Black Americans and the end of national-origin strictures in U.S. immigration policy in 1965, fighting crime became a core feature of national security. In 1967, Lyndon B. Johnson described this fight as a "war within our borders," which President Nixon renamed the "war on crime." The enemy needed to be fought "from within," which recalls the history of slavery and the idea that enslaved people were "by nature" criminals with murderous intent, requiring constant surveillance and vigilance. As Singh explains, the metastasizing of "a carceral state of walls and cages directly paralleled the weakening of the support mechanisms of the social-welfare state. Together, these phenomena represent the most significant political and institutional development in American life since the late 1960s."[83] The limits of inclusion of Black people in the welfare-state framework, and the dismantling of that framework, would result in far more than supposed benign neglect of the undeserving but would give rise to ambitiously coercive institutional forms. The most extensive period of prison construction in human history occurred in the last two decades of the twentieth century.

Within an increasingly hostile system of state violence, the HIV/AIDS crisis affected Black gay men and undocumented people disproportionately, exposing them to death at higher rates than white men, strongly echoing the present-day Covid-19 pandemic. As Hong asserts, men of color are always already estranged from normative masculinity because for them the public sphere is always already a space of violence and abjection rather than self-possession.[84] In truth, the plurality of racialized masculine formations threatens white masculinist nationalisms, both democratic and socialist, and their various deployments of impenetrability.

In *Freedom Dreams*, Robin D. G. Kelley writes about his mother's compassion for the world and how she taught him to care for others, despite having so little for themselves. Growing up in Harlem, he learned to take care of injured animals and people, the misfits of society. His mother encouraged him to see with his "third eye," which would undo the patriarchal control of Black men within the family. She helped him to resist the self-centeredness that belongs to the "atomized, individualistic world of consumer capitalism."[85] Like Kelley, Riggs takes inspiration from the mostly female, renegade Black intellectuals, activists, and artists who helped him to craft his own dreams of freedom. Because Riggs engages in this kind of dreaming from his death bed, his project is totally dedicated to communicating with future generations, with those young people whose dreams are most at risk of being co-opted by the marketplace and by state-sponsored neglect and criminalization.

Riggs's film also becomes an opportunity to think about, in Sharpe's words, the "meanings of care and disaster as problems for thought in relation to black non/being."[86] Riggs discovers movement as a place of possibility within both gender and racial categorizations, which allows for what C. Riley Snorton calls an understanding of Blackness as that "vestibularizing paradigm that is both within and outside the nation-as-home, and in which black people find no home but a loophole of retreat—in life and within the symbolics of gender."[87] Riggs discovers within "the ungendering of blackness" an invitation to think about Black masculinity as "an infinite set of proliferative, constantly revisable reiterations figured 'outside' of gender's established and establishing symbolic order."[88] This revised understanding of Blackness requires what Hortense Spillers calls "the power of 'yes' to the female within." As Spillers writes, Black American men make up "the only American community of males handed the specific occasion to learn who the female is within itself, the infant child who bears life against the could-be fateful gamble, against the odds of pulverization and murder, including her own. It is the heritage of the mother that the African American male must regain as an aspect of his own personhood—the power of 'yes' to the 'female' within."[89] In response to Spillers, Snorton notes how the status of the Black man, "as both a cultural and a legal being," was bound in slavery and afterward to the status of his mother.[90] This connection to the mother replaces the search for an "authentic" Black masculinity, which for Frantz Fanon can never really occur since the "black man cannot be a man" within an anti-Black patriarchal formation.[91] While masculinizing power in Fanon remains tethered to the normative and patriarchal, for Spillers, power is derived from access to the Black mother, both spiritually and in the flesh (in *Black Is . . .*

Black Ain't, Riggs surrounds himself with surrogate "mothers").[92] Through the medium of filmmaking, Riggs captures Snorton's observations on how Black manhood is "orchestrated through a series of centrifugal and centripetal movements in relation to his mother."[93]

For queer of color theorist E. Patrick Johnson, by juxtaposing misogynist speeches by Louis Farrakhan with interviews by bell hooks and Angela Davis, Riggs "undermines the historical equation of 'real' blackness with black masculinity."[94] He expresses the identity politics of the Combahee River Collective, which theorized in the 1970s that the cultural investment in normative white femininity plays a role in racializing Black men and Black women.[95] However, as Hong argues, they were also critical of "Black male paternalism" and its concomitant patriarchal domesticity—the idea of the Black man as protector of the Black woman.[96] By establishing a link between himself and Black women, who are often the keepers of the archives and of the family albums and heirlooms, Riggs also shows his rejection of Black paternalism.

Riggs engages a variety of queer masculinities, proposing the possibility of unruly alliances. He disputes what Johnson calls both the "hegemonic constructions of black masculinity" and "the sexism found within the black community."[97] Riggs's film also exemplifies what Johnson calls "quare theory," a "a theory in the flesh" that "grants space for marginalized individuals to disidentify with mainstream definitions of Black masculinity" and to enact bell hooks's conception of "'radical black subjectivity.'"[98] Riggs "unhinges the link between hegemonic masculinity and authentic blackness" through vulnerability rather than hypermasculine nationalist rhetoric.[99] He speaks against the early twentieth-century sociological view of people like Robert E. Park, who believed that Black men were less than masculine due to their "racial temperament."[100] Park felt that the logical nature of the Jew, the contemplative countenance of the East Indian, and the adventurousness of the Anglo-Saxon were all masculine potentialities that the Black man supposedly lacked. The creation of vulnerable Black masculinities, desiring unruly alliance, occurs despite pervasive cultural stereotypes of hypermasculinity, negative impenetrability, and violence.

AIDS was the central catalyst that pushed Riggs to deal with his identity on a larger scale. In the process, he instructs both Black and white viewers to care for and identify with his image. As Riggs conveys, "The connection between AIDS and Blackness is metaphorical, as both AIDS sufferers and non-infected Black people are in a struggle against the odds, in the face of adversity and the possibility of extinction."[101] Riggs establishes himself from the opening shot as a totally different kind of masculine authority, as a man who will not back down in the face of adversity and oppression, but who is also vulnerable and willing to risk stigmatization as a Black "faggot." By ending with the line "black is you" and invoking biopolitics, he also conveys the importance of the "HIV/AIDS is *you*" message for audiences in the early 1990s and today. He directly confronts the homophobia often found in Black communities by proposing that their struggles are his, while his are also theirs. Riggs took great personal risk in allowing himself to be filmed as he was dying of AIDS-related complications in the hospital, but like *Before Night Falls,* the film is fundamentally about reclaiming life amid dying, through techniques of flashback and juxtaposition. As Riggs sings "Swing Low, Sweet Chariot" from his hospital bed, he calls back through history to remember both the pain Black people have endured and the joys of being and eating together. In scenes of himself running naked through the woods, he remembers his able body while not disavowing his illness—showing the world that affective communication across differences depends upon exposing ourselves to one another.[102]

With the camera at eye level, Black voices sing and chant, "Black is . . . Black ain't." Here Riggs connects various forms of friendship and community to issues of safety for Black people and to education and political and social justice. These are not connections that adhere through institutionalized forms of belonging. Interviewees discuss kinship ties in the Black community and how the desire for closeness and family does not need to be fulfilled by a blood-related mother and father. Such a person could even be your "next door neighbor's grandmomma." This form of relating opens the door to new ways of thinking about masculinity as well. White voices of authority reciting dictionary definitions that supposedly speak the truth about Black experience are drowned out by voices chanting, "Black is . . . Black ain't," widening the circle of mutual aid and of unruly alliance.

In shifting from past to present, Riggs intersperses images of his own body and voice with recent political atrocities against his community, such as the 1992 Rodney King riots in Los Angeles. Riggs employs a mixed temporality, which, in Keeling's words, offers a

Marxian "poetry of the future." She argues that documentary film content can exceed the grasp of the director, "exceeds its expression," and through these dislocated queer temporalities, the future might be "perceived yet not recognized."[103] While Riggs makes perceptible what "does not fit" present logics, he also insists that the poetry of the past still lives on, becoming the source material for the poetry of the future. This unfixed temporality that refuses heteronormative common sense is stitched together, using Nina Simone's "To Be Young, Gifted, and Black" and references to Black feminist critiques, giving the impression of a patchwork of text, images, historical photographs, scenes of Riggs in the hospital, and scenes of his friend Bill T. Jones dancing. Jones, Riggs, and poet Essex Hemphill abandon the code of silence for Black men that represses the feminine, and instead the Black male body becomes associated with movement—with dancing, dreaming, and hoping for a future.

Even in a country where one feels such hostility, where you are practically hunted down from the moment of birth, Riggs, a young Black gay boy growing up in the American South, and Arenas, a young Brown boy growing up among the trees in Cuba, discover in nature and specifically in water a tremendous life force and courage. There is an uncanny similarity in the way these creators of completely different contexts choose to talk about living and dying, and of the future of their people. Arenas writes of the singularity of afternoons by the sea in Havana, "where the sun falls into the sea like a giant balloon; everything seems to change at dusk, cast under a brief and mysterious spell. There is the smell of brine, of life, of the tropics" (106). Water might represent for both an escape from the nation in which they are repressed: "perhaps in floating on waves we escaped our cursed insularity" (109). What is doubly tragic is the fact that in Cuba, even the sea becomes privatized, available only to people who can pay—mainly foreign tourists. If you were caught swimming in the ocean, you would be arrested: "How could you live on an island and have no access to the sea? I always thought that in Cuba the only thing that saved us from absolute insanity was that, being surrounded by water, we had the chance to go to the shore and swim" (217).

Like Riggs, Arenas gets his sense of spirituality from his ancestors, specifically from his grandmother, who would fall devotedly on her knees and ask God for this or that, which she generally never got, but it was the practice of prayer that kept her alive (5). Riggs creates a river of storytelling and documenting with no beginning and no end. Water becomes a fitting metaphor for queer temporality and for the exploration of the shifting contours of unruly alliances. Water symbolizes the unpredictable movement of time and history, placing Riggs's struggle to survive in a larger context. Later scenes of Riggs speaking from his hospital bed are interspersed with images of himself fishing with an elderly woman who raised fifteen children on a farm in Dublin, Mississippi, in the 1930s. Her suffering becomes a part of the story of a Black gay man dying of AIDS-related complications in the late twentieth century. Water flows through scenes of masculine embodiment, sexuality, and care, as the fulfillment of sexual desire also becomes a form of resistance and an art of life.

A female voice in the documentary becomes a more active witness as Riggs becomes too weak to speak, tracking Riggs's storytelling until his very last moments of life. At the end of the film, Riggs develops an imagined connection to Harriet Tubman, who allows him to access his "yes" to a Black female source of power who will guide him to the afterlife.[104] Riggs tells his female witness about a dream he recently had about Tubman in which she came to him and stood by him quietly (Figure 14). Riggs gradually becomes aware of her presence, and they stand together in a dark forest, with a bubbling, lively river running through it. This is a similar river to the one Arenas discovers in his own dying moments. Arenas writes:

> I did not know where that river was headed, where that frenzied race would end, but something was calling me to go with it, saying that I too had to throw myself into those raging waters and lose myself, that only in that torrent, always on the move, would I find some peace. (17)

Tubman looks into Riggs's eyes and then looks at the river, and they proceed to walk together, across the water. Through Tubman, he performs a final, posthumous refutation of Black maternal nonbeing. It is also a reversal of the conventional religious ritual of baptism, cleansing in the moment of death rather than birth. Diasporic spiritual practices that circulate in Black communities are firmly rooted in a belief in the enmeshment of life and death, giving expression to a continuity of Black sociality in the form of communing with the ancestors.[105] Together, Riggs and Tubman become embodiments of

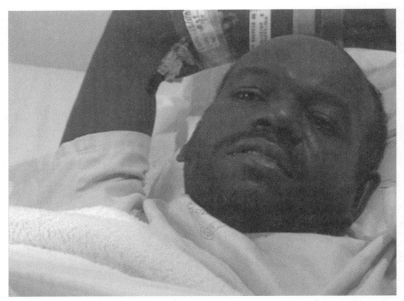

FIGURE 14. As he is dying, Riggs has a dream about Harriet Tubman, which shows how he said "yes" to the feminine within. *Black Is... Black Ain't,* directed by Marlon Riggs, featuring Bill T. Jones, Essex Hemphill, and Marlon Riggs (Signifyin' Works, 1995).

hope. In a voice slurring from medication and exhaustion, yet still retaining depth and power, Riggs tells the witness, "I'm going to cross that river." Riggs and Tubman walk side by side, toward the unknown, transcending the worldly limitations placed upon them. Even though he never got to see the final film, his spirit so infuses every scene that each viewer who encounters this film can access lovence. Riggs sends the message to viewers of the future that masculinity can transcend corrosive individualism and access lovence—enter the river and be transformed.

Toward Unruly Alliance as a Way of Life

In the twenty-first century, we live with the daily consequences of the ongoing Reagan revolution. As Foner insists, the very idea of freedom has been co-opted by libertarians and conservatives: "Once the rallying cry of the dispossessed, freedom is today commonly invoked by powerful economic institutions to justify many forms of authority, even as on the individual level it often seems to suggest the absence of authority altogether."[106] Advocates of unimpeded market economics continue to ramp up their war on the poor, while militia groups aggressively demand their right to bear arms against those with whom they disagree. In their refusal to wear masks or to take the vaccine during the Covid-19 pandemic, we see how freedom has come to mean a series of negations that erode any sense of social responsibility or common public. The freedom to say whatever you want—to mock so-called wokeism and encourage hate speech, to view freedom as solely a matter of consumer choice—all reveal how the Reagan revolution is lengthening at the time of this writing.

However, the masculine ideal of impenetrability—both a cause and effect of this "revolution"—is not inevitable. These works were created under the most hostile conditions imaginable, as people watched an entire generation vanish, with very little public outcry or even the most basic forms of care. However, the literary and filmic traces left behind offer potent testimonials of the power of unruly alliances and mutual aid, particularly during times of disease. The story of Covid-19 is still being written, but this latest crisis makes clear once again something these writers and filmmakers came to understand: without doubt, no less than the survival of humanity depends upon masculinity's transformation.

Chapter 6

"A Man Is a Worker"
Economic Penetrability, Labor Abuses, and Landlessness

> Within this novel I planted a flag: Here I am—does anyone want to discuss these important issues? I wrote it not as an expression of individual "high" art but as a working-class organizer mimeographs a leaflet—a call to action. . . . My life's work is about elevating collective organizing, not elevating individuals.
> —Leslie Feinberg, *Stone Butch Blues* (1993)

> A man is a worker. If he is not, then he is nothing.
> —Joseph Conrad, *Notes on Life and Letters* (1921)

In the late nineteenth and early twentieth centuries, as Joseph Conrad's words convey, masculine identity depended on the ability to work, own property, and maintain economic stability. However, with the evisceration of organized labor in the United States since World War II and the effects of global capital and mechanization, working-class people and people experiencing poverty have fewer opportunities to resist these conditions and less of a chance to harness a sense of identity in their work. In this chapter, I explore penetrability in terms of labor and property ownership, both of which are central to the development, and subversion, of normative masculinity. There is a deep need to understand how queer and trans masculinities have historically navigated and resisted economic realities and workplace abuses. While the ability to enter a workplace, to earn a living, and to sustain that employment are central issues, they are often ignored in queer and trans theorizing. When labor is addressed, it is usually not through a sense of job consciousness, which New Labor historian

David Brody advocates is the only way to achieve the political goals of a coalitional labor movement.[1]

Telling stories about work allows a glimpse of how masculinity is learned and unlearned, broken and reformed, in community with others. Literature acts as a suture for the categories of class, labor, sexuality, and gender, bringing together elements of masculine "lives lived" that are often critiqued separately. In the short story collection *Blue Collar, White Collar, No Collar*, editor Richard Ford contemplates how writing about work arrives at the heart of a lived life, putting into "imaginative play" the "provident concerns" of masculinity that become a source of both pride and suffering.[2] However, trans and queer laboring masculinities, and their "provident concerns," are all too often left out of these kinds of collections. Through *Stone Butch Blues* (1993), by Leslie Feinberg, and the short story "Brokeback Mountain," by Annie Proulx, published in the *New Yorker* in 1997, I propose the possibility of class and labor resistance based on unruly alliances, with queer and trans masculinities at the center. The effects of neoliberalism double for marginalized masculinities—particularly for people experiencing poverty, people who do not own land, and those with no options outside of the least desirable kinds of work. Both stories take place between the end of World War II and the 1980s, during the transition from the liberal institutions of citizenship and civil rights in the 1960s and '70s, to capital's global phase. They occur within a United States increasingly characterized by economic recession and stagnation and the deterioration of the quality of life in both cities and rural areas. As discussed in chapter 5, transnational capital restructured, but did not dismantle, the nation-state and led to the weakening of national boundaries that ensured the flow of capital (increased penetrability) and a ramp-up of repressive state militarism (impenetrability). The movement of goods, labor, and capital has been guaranteed through politically strong, consolidated, and hegemonic nation-states in control of the terms of this global restructuring.

Adored and critiqued by many, these stories have become what Miriam J. Abelson terms "amplified sites," cultural locations where categorizations and norms "play out in heightened ways."[3] Abelson uses this term to talk about public restrooms and doctors' offices, where transphobia is often encountered, but the term can also apply to stories that function as access points for broad encounters with trans and queer masculinity. Part of what makes these works extraordinary is their ability to reach marginalized audiences outside of mainstream, urban LGBTQIA+ communities and academic circles. To approach these amplified sites from a class and labor perspective, I pursue a process of what I call "reading again," which requires a deeper engagement than rereading, opening space for new insights. Through reading again, trans and queer scholars can interrogate their own selective vision through which labor and class struggles are often erased.

By addressing labor politics, property, and capitalist accumulation in the United States, this chapter participates in what David L. Eng calls a "renewed queer studies," which resists neoliberal economic practices that produce both commodity genderisms and labor-based inequalities.[4] Representation, and the critical interpretation of culture, is a part of this renewed queer studies, which opposes any liberalism that installs, and reinstalls, heteropatriarchy and the docile citizen. As Karl Marx observes, capitalism enlists culture as a kind of moral agent, separating fit subjects from the unfit all under the cover of aesthetic practice.[5] Through reading again, I discover what is suppressed in these stories, particularly because they are so often cast solely as tales of hard-won romantic love.

As labor leader, political activist, and author Sidney Lens reports, in the 1970s when these stories take place, the U.S. government moved closer to state-managed capitalism, which meant that federal, state, and local governments now controlled a third of the nation's income.[6] Decisions made on regulation, subsidies, taxes, and more "helped shape the economy as never before."[7] This means, in Lens's view, that labor's difficulties became increasingly tied to politics. While the international distribution of wealth accumulation has increased modestly, the conditions of life for billions of people experiencing poverty around the world have not changed and have even worsened because of catastrophic environmental degradation. These trans and queer characters are victims of this state of things. In addition to suffering pervasive workplace abuses, the characters in *Stone Butch Blues* and "Brokeback Mountain" are denied domestic security—a supposed hallmark of capitalist development. At the same time, work becomes a space where sexual identity and gender nonconformity are discovered, sometimes through a shared experience of alienation. In contrast to masculine normativity that traffics in the so-called virtues of autonomy, self-control, independence, and physical strength, trans and queer masculinities in these stories forge unruly alliances, despite incredible odds.[8]

In the 2020s, there has been a promising resurgence of labor organizing. The excitement around the 2020 campaign of Vermont senator Bernie Sanders; the success of unions in Starbucks franchises, Amazon warehouses, and Chipotle restaurants during the Covid-19 pandemic; and the "great resignation"—during which many folks quit their jobs due to oppressive working conditions, low wages, lack of child and elder care, and no paid time off for illness, among other factors—all suggest a moment of great potential. The critically acclaimed film adaptation of Jessica Bruder's *Nomadland* (2020) and the Obama-funded documentary *American Factory* (2019) suggest that mainstream cultural production has begun to pay attention. To this end, I read these stories alongside the work of New Labor historians, concluding with possibilities for the future.

"Remember Me as a Revolutionary Communist"

Stone Butch Blues is often remembered for its tender depictions of butch/femme couples in suit jackets and dresses, slow dancing to a jukebox in the back of a working-class dive bar. Feinberg's writing allowed butches and trans people to feel seen and heard for the first time. As Jay Prosser adds, the text represented the beginning of a new transgender movement, one that refused the terms of binary transition and invited the presence of "liminality on all fronts."[9] Feinberg spanned identity categories, turning *trans* into both a verb and an adjective, as she/zie strongly asserted that the rights of trans people are tied to everyone's right to define themselves.[10]

After its publication, Feinberg received hundreds of thousands of letters, emails, and phone calls in which people shared their heartfelt responses. These letters came not only from rallies, universities, and book readings but from people who were incarcerated or whom Feinberg happened to meet in gas stations in rural Iowa, for example: "These people many of whose life battles do not seem to be related in any way, shape, or form to oppression based on sexuality, gender or sex, took time and care to explain to me the impact the book had on their thinking, their decisions, their actions."[11] These responses "from below" resulted from the fact that Feinberg places economic oppression at the forefront, as Jack Halberstam observes in a blurb for the book, in the tradition of 1930s proletarian literature. To those being "ground up in economic machinery," Feinberg offered hope that they, too, could join the march toward liberation (307). Feinberg dedicated hir life to activism. Partner Minnie Bruce Pratt shares Feinberg's lasts words to her before she/zie died: "Remember me as a revolutionary Communist." In a personal interview, Pratt remembered how she used to tell Feinberg that she/zie had no idea how much of the appeal and success of *Stone Butch Blues* was due to hir having "imbued it with her communist, rank and file labor politics. They [hir readers] read it as a queer novel or a prescient trans novel—not realizing that she was able to write this and her other work because of decades of training in Marxist-Leninist analysis and organizing as well as (of course) her own life experience and brilliant insights."[12] Pratt is commenting here that Feinberg's readers often miss the class analysis in this novel, which is a point of departure for my own work in this chapter.

Feinberg and Pratt, who has dedicated her own life's work to preserving Feinberg's memory, inspire action through the living intersection of sexuality, gender, race, class, and labor. To this end, she/zie portrays the instability of trans and queer masculinity as it pivots between crisis and hegemony, or, in other words, hops from job to job. For these reasons, the novel is unique not only within the LGBTQIA+ canon but within late twentieth-century American literature more generally.[13]

Within liberal elite circles, butch lesbians and trans men of the working and lowest-income classes, particularly older adults, are often dismissed as uneducable "white trash" or "antiquated throwbacks" to an earlier political moment, easily defeated obstacles to mainstream rights agendas.[14] Detailed accounts of working conditions for people like Jess Goldberg, Feinberg's protagonist in *Stone Butch Blues,* often fall outside of the purview of queer and trans theory, even while these aspects have been the most compelling for so many readers.[15] Applying Kadji Amin's insights, these parts of the story may be implicitly dismissed as "'merely documentary,' of gay and lesbian history."[16] Their everyday lives may appear "retrograde," or too tedious and outside the lived experiences of theorists and critics to be taken seriously. The scenes of work and resistance described in the novel become "invisible or inaudible in the present."[17]

The story may also produce a sense of hopelessness for those who are dedicated to sustaining a mass labor movement. Feinberg addresses a part of the political and historical past and present in the United States that feels most intractable—the lack of a robust, cross-racial, and coalitional labor movement. With what Brody calls an acute job consciousness, Feinberg takes us inside the workplace, showing how trans and queer masculinities succeed or fail to become viable subjects of American manhood. Unruly alliances form in the novel across masculinities and identity categories, suggesting the potential for a horizontal and heterogeneous workers' movement founded upon a shared sense of economic penetrability.

The masculinity and resistance of Jess Goldberg is contextualized within a diverse group of laborers. This novel shares ground in this respect with Kale Bantigue Fajardo's 2011 interdisciplinary ethnography *Filipino Crosscurrents: Oceanographies of Seafaring, Masculinities, and Globalization*. For Fajardo, tomboys disrupt the idea that all Filipino seamen were "heterosexual, geographically and sexually mobile, heroically nationalistic, simultaneously family-oriented or heteronormative, and usually 'macho.'"[18] Living below the poverty line or being working class is central to how Filipinos understand tomboy practices and identities in the Philippines and in some immigrant communities in the United States.[19] In fact, his subjects were more likely to interact with him and discuss tomboy subjectivity if he talked about his working-class roots in the Philippines; when he brought up his career as a U.S.-based academic (which implies elite status), he was treated as a "woman."[20] Folded into the landscape of the workplace, the tomboy is not "routed or rooted through or in lesbianism, womanhood, and even femaleness (again because sex/gender is often fluid in Filipino contexts)."[21] Cultural representation in the Philippines also depicts tomboys as having income below the poverty line, being working class, being unemployed, working in low-wage and service industry positions (such as bus conductors, security guards, and factory workers), or being overseas migrants.[22] Like Filipino/a tomboys, butches in the factory suggest that social and interpersonal contexts have the capacity to displace (though perhaps only temporarily) any rigid anatomical understandings or biological readings of "the body."[23] However, while Fajardo's study of tomboys shows the centrality of class for some masculinities, this intersection is often overlooked in favor of individual sexual or gender identity.

Feinberg's protagonist, Jess Goldberg, grows up in Buffalo, New York, in former army barracks known as "the projects," which housed military-contracted aircraft workers and their families. The residents are still haunted by a fierce strike that was settled in 1949, the year Jess was born: "I overheard descriptions of such bloody strike battles, I thought WWII has been fought at the plant. At night when we'd drive my father to his shift, I used to crouch down on the back seat of the car and peek past the plant gates out over the now quiet fields of combat" (16). The strike occurred six years after the more conservative American Federation of Labor (AFL) and the more radical Congress of Industrial Organizations (CIO) merged, beginning a bleak period for labor organizing in the United States.[24] Yet, in the novel, fathers still argue about the strike in kitchens and at backyard barbecues. Feinberg shows through Jess's family that there has always been resistance—sometimes violent resistance—to coercive control in industrial work in the United States. The desire for workers to determine their own lives has taken many forms but has always been rooted in an informal social order on the shop floor, which not even the conveyor belt or the most persistent managerial control could eliminate.[25]

Feinberg begins this story, therefore, during a crucial turning point in labor history. After a half-decade of war, industrial unions gained a central place in the American economy, and by the end of the war, there were fourteen million union members.[26] As Brody reports, the movement had become, in the 1947 words of Walter Reuther, former president of the progressive United Auto Workers (UAW), "'the vanguard in America . . . the architects of the future.'"[27] After Franklin Delano Roosevelt's death, there were waves of strikes, spurred by the fear of postwar unemployment, that rivaled the 1936–37 scale. Working conditions and opportunities reversed for a time when the war ended and the transition began from a state of full employment to increasing precarity, even though both businessmen and economists warned that full employment would not continue. Cutbacks in production ended overtime work and bonus pay, and nearly one-quarter of war workers temporarily lost their jobs as factories transitioned to civilian production.[28]

Frustrated by government and business collusion during the war, postwar workers created their own instruments of democracy, using mass demonstrations and disruptions to go around so-called legitimate but nonresponsive channels.[29] Though they were focused primarily on wages and working conditions and the needs of the moment, these strikes made radicals hopeful and conservatives angry. As George Lipsitz writes, "Their opposition to authority, to work, to hierarchical power drew upon deep currents of resistance embedded in American working-class history."[30] The general strikes of 1946 that Feinberg references early in the novel were serious threats to both business and government authority, showing how when the state tries to impose labor peace, working-class demands automatically become challenges to state power.[31] This militant moment could not be converted, however, into legitimate programmatic alternatives because their real demands were radical and could not be satisfied within the system.[32] To fulfill those aspirations, workers needed to project a worldview "in which their desires for freedom and community were legitimate and in which the imperatives of work, hierarchy, and exploitation were illegitimate."[33] However, subsequent protest movements, including feminist and gay liberation, modeled themselves after working-class labor.

As a result of the chaos of the 1946 strikes, repressive measures were enacted to take political leadership away from the working class, "so that the powerful could go on reorganizing the postwar world on terms favorable to big business."[34] The Taft-Hartley Act was particularly disastrous, and it passed in 1946 thanks to a Republican Congress and an electoral trend away from New Deal ideology. The act banned tactics used in the 1946 strikes, including secondary boycotts, mass picketing, and sympathy strikes. It made unions responsible for damage caused during wildcat strikes (those that occurred in violation of contractual obligation not to strike), which the sponsors of the act hoped would encourage better policing of the rank and file. The Taft-Hartley Act allowed states to ban the union shop, and it increased the power of the president to obtain injunctions against strikes.[35] The act also denied foremen collective bargaining rights, which meant the widespread integration of first-line supervisors into the management structure.[36]

To be certified with the National Labor Relations Board (NLRB), unions now had to show that no members were Communists or sympathizers.[37] The FBI, and the unions themselves, engaged in harassment and destruction of interracial Communist-led unions and put pressure on non-Communist radicals who raised racial issues of power distribution within organized labor.[38] As historian Paul Buhle notes, the expelled unions represented the "racially variegated American industrial working class that the AFL and CIO had, on the whole, failed to reach," or did not even want to reach.[39] After the McCarthy era, antiradicalism became a mainstay in labor politics, not just for excising Communists but for shaping the general political character of organized labor (which is to say, utterly dependent on the Democratic Party, racially segregated, hostile to women and LGBTQIA+ groups, and very limited in its social and policy vision).[40]

However, outside of these memories of postwar strikes, Jess's suburb is an example of what Buhle calls the postwar "crabgrass pastorale."[41] The civil rights movement would not have been visible to Jess if were not for *Life* magazine with its images of segregation on the living room coffee table. However, as a gender nonconforming child, Jess suffers similar abuse, setting the stage for future interracial friendships and labor organizing. For her failure to feminize, Jess is sent to live in a psychiatric hospital for three weeks at eleven years old and then forced to attend charm school. Her high school might be desegregated in theory, but within the school is a fiercely maintained set of rules to keep Black and white students separate. Jess breaks these rules by sitting with Black students at lunch and is kicked out of school. She never returns.

As a teenager, Leslie Feinberg discovered the bar scenes in Niagara Falls, Buffalo, and Toronto, what she/zie vividly recalls as the electric world of drag queens, butches, and femmes.[42] However, she/zie found the answers to hir questions about history and discrimination not in school or in the bar but rather in the working-class factories and political movements for justice. As Feinberg acknowledges, growing up blue collar changed hir consciousness but did not make hir progressive or actively resistant to what W. E. B. Du Bois calls the public and psychological wages of whiteness, not without intensive study on the topics of race and class.[43]

Similarly, work becomes a way for Jess to fortify herself against abuse (in high school, she is gang raped by boys she has known her whole life, foreshadowing repeated rape by the police). Through work, she gets the chance to experience "what freedom meant," though within the constraints of the workplace itself. Jess does not initially enter the plants but first becomes involved in the lesbian bar scene, which is where she meets a Black butch named Edwin. Ed is a part of a younger generation of Black workers, some who were Black Power advocates with no faith in the integration of unions or the "jobs training" programs created by AFL-CIO and praised by in-house Black spokesmen.[44] Ed's character shows how Black political militancy spilled into factories and shops, as Black nationalism and integration drew heavily upon worker unrest at the point of production, creating a number organizations.[45] As historian Manning Marable notes, both the civil rights and the Black Power movements were "fundamentally working-class and poor people's movements."[46] This is Jess's first encounter with someone who is marginalized by race, gender, and sexuality.

Early in 1965, Ed stops coming to the white gay club, and Grant (a white butch who is a known racist) spreads the word that Ed "had a chip on her shoulder" after Malcolm X was killed in New York City. The butches at the auto plant report that Ed is very angry, and they instruct Jess to leave Ed alone. However, Jess ignores this advice, and, as a result, after hanging out at a club with Ed, endures a brutal beating by police. Jess receives some of the backlash of racist cops, who spit on her and call her a "traitor." After this incident outside of the bars, Jess decides to heed the advice of a femme:

> Get yourself a factory job so you don't end up spending your whole life in the bars. Life in the Tenderloin's like lickin' a razor blade. . . . I'm not saying the plants are heaven, or anything, but maybe you can get into a plant with the other butches, pay your bills, settle down with a girl. (69)

The femme expresses how dependent the butches are on the factories, for money and a sense of identity, especially considering that other trades, like construction work, are closed to "he-shes" (the term for butches at the time). Work becomes a source of cross-racial solidarity: "We clapped each other on the back in the bars and watched each other's back at the factory" (7).

The factory work Jess describes in the 1960s and '70s carries the history of revolutionary changes brought about by Fordism and Taylorism. Ford applied the moving belt in 1913, exponentially increasing industrial efficiency. The time to assemble a Model T fell to under two hours, while the output per worker per hour quadrupled in the auto industry between 1909 and 1919. Brody describes how the factory worker became a servant of the machine that performed the actual work; if the worker was responsible for the repetitive jobs on the assembly line, they actually became part of the machine.[47] Control over the pacing of the job was handed over to supervisors, as "the power over their working lives receded far into distant central offices and into the hands of men probably unknown to them even by name."[48]

Frederick W. Taylor, an idiosyncratic, upper-class Philadelphian, carried to an extreme the methods of earlier management reformers. He attempted to apply a "scientific" method of getting the maximum efficiency out of each worker.[49] "Brain" work was placed more and more into the hands of managers. Management could subject each task to "time-and-motion" study, which allowed hiring and training the "right man" for each job. Taylor considered his unique contribution to be fixing a differential rate that would give each worker the financial incentive to work at the speeds dictated to them. Taylorism was never fully implemented, however, and the few that tried paid dearly for it, but his influence has endured. As Grace Kyungwon Hong adds, Taylor's "scientific management" and Henry Ford's assembly line came together "to produce an undifferentiated, homogeneous worker whose embodied, human differences and particularities are foreclosed in the workplace and relegated to the space of the home, which then was to accrue new significance as the site for consumerist individualism."[50] Feinberg communicates the dangers and alienation in this type of work, as the production process was broken down into reducible parts, dividing production, management, and design, deskilling the worker and hierarchizing social relations within the factory.

The conditions of the factory required that butches develop masculine impenetrability in the form of "stone." *Stone butch* originally described a butch lesbian who refuses penetration by a lover, though *stone butch* can also refer to an interiorizing of emotion where feelings are shown through absence.[51] Emotional reserve in the public sphere and an aggressive stance become part of a historically constructed stone butch response to a wide variety of labor- and class-related abuses. Feinberg celebrates what Ann Cvetkovich calls "the hard-won experience of sexual pleasure without denying its roots in pain and difficulty."[52] What Cvetkovich still finds powerful about pre-1970s working-class, butch writings is the "raw, confrontational, and even sexy" attitude of these trauma stories.[53] Stone butch is shaped by personal and psychic reconciling of trauma and loss, but it also has transformative and revolutionary potential. As Halberstam observes, because of this stoic quality, working-class butch lesbians have been associated exclusively with "loss and lack," but *stone butch* actually holds the power to challenge the binary sex-gender systems at their roots.[54]

However, stoneness is a quality that all working-class people in Jess's community, regardless of sex and gender, embrace to some degree. Feinberg communicates the overall lack of protections for workers in the factories after Taft-Hartley, but particularly for butches. Through the factory foreman, modes of surveillance both produced and regulated racial, gender, and sexual difference, elevating and rewarding normative whiteness, masculinity, and heteronormativity, but unevenly. While this abstract space of the factory was supposed to be secured against any violence, it is inherently violent. At her first job, Jess unloads trucks at a frozen food plant and notices immediately the microaggressions against butches. However, Jess also learns from Grant how to ignore it: "Unloading trucks was male turf. It meant a lot to have another butch watch your back" (75). You could go along to get along by shaking the foreman's hand or, learning to work "with dignity," not showing that you were in physical pain. This is grueling labor, in frigid temperatures, with little rest in between trucks. Jess notices that some of the men are missing pieces of their ears and, in some plants, missing fingers down to the second joint, or a thumb: "Out here on the docks, which butt up against the frozen lake, the men gave up little exposed pieces of their bodies. It frightened me. I wondered what I would be forced to sacrifice in order to survive" (76).

The butches prefer to work in steel or auto, because of the strength of the unions in those industries and the increased masculine currency these jobs provide. Ed is even more direct about the benefits of a union job: they safeguard job security, which was invaluable. Unlike in a nonunion shop, if one of the butches has a run-in with a male worker or the foreman on the floor, it does not mean they will be fired automatically: "With union protection, all the butches agreed, a he-she could carve out a niche, and begin earning valuable seniority" (75). There was, however, the strong possibility that a butch would not last long enough on the job to join the union, as she would "conveniently" receive a pink slip before the ninety-day probation period. The older butches warn Jess that sometimes the men pressure one of the women to sleep with a butch as a joke and then come back and tell everyone about it. This always meant a butch would have to quit, in shame, along with the woman. As New Labor historian Barbara Mayer Wertheimer writes, sexual harassment became more widely discussed in the workplace in the 1970s and '80s, but harassment was particularly hard for women moving into nontraditional jobs in skilled trades, or in work like coal mining, truck driving, or dock laboring.[55] For butches, this harassment was rarely discussed and was still considered to be an unfortunate feature of the job.

In her next job, at the bindery, she learns the importance of solidarity with other marginalized workers. As the only butch in the plant, she befriends an older Indigenous woman, Muriel, who shares her food and coffee from her thermos. They even get up early to hang out with each other: "These moments before the whistle blew in the morning were precious because they were ours. Only the *kerchunk* of the time clock stole the last one from us. . . . We drank coffee and ate rolls, talked and laughed. . . . The owners only rented our hand, not our brains" (77). However, if the foremen saw they were enjoying themselves too much, he would come up behind them and slam the wooden worktables with a lead pipe, growling, "Get to work." His brutality signaled the fear of any workplace solidarity, particularly given the context of the postwar strikes.

In this multinational, multiracial crew at the bindery, half were from the Six Nations near Buffalo, most were Mohawk or Seneca, and they quickly became part of one another's lives, sharing pains and family crises, using song on the job to pass the time and to assert their humanity. The assembly line is where they worked side by side or facing each other, and the pastime of singing harkens back to other periods of organizing, such as the early twentieth-century Industrial Workers of the World movement, who called themselves the Wobblies. On this assembly line, Jess learns the value of what Lisa Lowe terms "horizontal community," which gives Jess the strength to resist gender conformity in the service of whiteness.[56] These scenes also show how, in Hong's words, "capital's exploitation of racialized and gendered difference leads to alternative modes of knowing and being."[57] Jess eventually becomes encouraged by the women to lead one of the songs herself, but after she does so, the foreman hands her a pink slip—because of this growing solidarity among the women but also because she is so close to getting into the union.

However, within this violence exist what Michel Foucault calls "heterotopias," which, in contrast to utopias, are "real sites" within the culture that are "simultaneously represented, contested, and inverted."[58] The factory floor becomes such a "real site" where unruly alliances are discovered and used to further resistance to capitalism. In the 1970s, butches sometimes formed their own subgroup within a hostile workplace, revealing how wildcat strikes continued to occur after Taft-Hartley. Whenever factory workers came into contact with one another, wherever they recognized a common alienation or abuse, they could potentially bond, legislate group work standards, and enforce informal rules on fellow workers and supervisors.[59] This did not wither in the postwar years of labor-management settlement, and contracts did offer protection from employers' arbitrary reprisals. Forming a subgroup was possible during the Vietnam War era because so many of the men from the plants were being drafted and killed in the war. Jess is not at all aware of the politics behind unions at this point, but she does begin to understand—the hard way—the importance of organized labor. At another bindery, Jess nearly makes grade five in the trimming and folding division, an impossible feat for both butches and men of color. Giant machines fold huge sheets of paper stock, which are then trimmed into pages. The stacks of pages are loaded on skids near the massive collating machine. Women are responsible for running the skids to feed fresh pages into the pockets of the collator. The pages drop onto a moving belt, and women at the end add cover sheets and staple them. Jess's job is to stack the finished booklets onto the skids, but occasionally she is called to work in the "men's terrain," unloading trucks and bringing in fresh skids of paper, which means she gets to drive a forklift.

However, tensions in the bindery come to a head over the battle for the union. The foreman, Jack, tries to set Jess up by teaching her how to do an apprentice job, which would give her the promotion to grade five. Jack and his racist pal Jim Boney actually use Jess to prevent Leroy, a Black man, from getting the job. Feinberg introduces us to Duffy, a shop steward and rumored Communist, who is modeled after Feinberg's friend, teamster Milt Neidenberg, who was "Duffy to her Jess." Duffy tells Jess that he will help her get a higher-grade job, but it is important for the union that Leroy be given a grade five first. The contract is set to expire, and the company wants to split the floor, making it harder to strike. Jess and the other butches deeply resent Duffy's response, which highlights both their own white privilege and the difficulties of coalitional organizing. Duffy is ready to help them, however, and when he learns that butches are not allowed to attend union meetings, he promises that after Leroy's promotion and the strike he will bring together the stewards and the butches to demand change.

Shop stewards like Duffy played an essential role in shop-floor organizing. However, union-imposed discipline removed the need for union delegates to appeal to workers' loyalty, and labor leaders got rid of the shop steward system that would have given ordinary workers the ability to address their concerns to union leadership.[60] In the shop steward, they had a designated leader with formal standing in the factory and with political reasons for supporting them. However, the ability to organize through the shop steward was highly dependent on "the technology of the given plant and, to some degree, to the ethno-cultural composition of the workers."[61] Whenever group cohesion was high on the floor, and the ability to exert pressure was intense, informal groups could leverage their employers in industrial settings.[62]

As Fajardo shows in *Filipino Crosscurrents*, while dominant masculinities may be naturalized, they are always "culturally, politically, and economically created, and/or in tension (with other masculinities)."[63] The analytic of "crosscurrent" shows how masculinities flow into one another, which in *Stone Butch Blues* occurs on the shop floor. Jess complies with Duffy's advice at first, but the other butches get upset that she has given up her grade five for a Black man, even after she tells them about Duffy's promise to get them into union meetings. Grant sneers, "Fuck that shit. I don't want to be part of no union that doesn't want me." However, Jess is insistent, "We can't just say 'fuck the union,' we're in it. The contract's up in October. What are we gonna do, go into the plant manager's office one at a time and negotiate? We don't have a choice. We've gotta make the guys see that they need us too" (84). Jess gives up, however, because of relentless abuse from Boney, who even pulls his penis out of his pants and rubs it on her jeans, laughing all the while. In a potential moment of solidarity between marginalized groups, Leroy calls him an asshole—tells him to put his dick back in his pants—and the whole shop floor breaks into a fight. Duffy also comes to Jess's rescue yelling, "She's a better union man than you are, Boney!" (85). Some of the other guys, like Walter the repairman, back her up as well, which suggests that not all cisgender white men were capable of the same levels of cruelty. However, Jack removes the safety from the die cutter, which punched school flashcards into the shape of decks, and she nearly loses her finger. Duffy tells Jess that he is going to prove to management what Jack did and threaten a walk out if they do not fire him. Jess is shocked by Duffy's solidarity: "I marveled at the idea that straight people would stand up for me, or for any he-she" (93).

    Coalitional solidarity is difficult to achieve for Jess, and yet Feinberg proves its necessity. Jess and her community put themselves in a precarious employment position when they refuse to help Duffy win the contract, a refusal that speaks to the ability for toxic masculinity to appear across embodiments. Duffy calls Jess after the accident and tells her that the ratification meeting is the next evening, and he invites the butches to come to the union meeting to vote. However, the steel plant is accepting applications. Duffy tells Jess this is a mistake, and he questions her motives for working at the steel plant: "What the hell is this about, looking tough?" (100). Jess yells back something that she will soon regret: "Yeah . . . in a way. But not like you're saying it. All we got is the clothes we wear, the bikes we ride, and where we work, you know? You can ride a Honda and work in a bindery or you ride a Harley and work at the steel plant. The other butches are gonna leave sooner or later, and I don't want to get stuck in that sweatshop with that rinky-dink union" (100). Duffy reminds her that if the vote passes, she should at least punch in Wednesday morning or she will be automatically fired, but she does not listen.

    Nothing could have prepared Jess for what she encounters at the steel plant. Jess and her butch friend Jan wander in a daze through the plant, which looks like a "rusty corrugated planet. Sounds, muffled and loud, startled us. The blast furnace lit up the sky orange and red" (100). The foreman instructs them to shovel snow off the railroad tracks, but when they ask how much they are supposed to shovel, he tells them with a shrug: "'You can shovel all night long and never get to the end'" (101). This is obviously an attempt to force the butches to quit, and later Jess apologizes to Duffy. He gives Jess an autobiography of Mother Jones, wrapped in an AFL-CIO newsletter, with the inscription: *"To Jess, with great expectations"* (102).

At this point in the novel, in the late 1960s, the new world system—fed for two decades by the reconstructions of Europe and Japan and the hegemony of American-based capital—began to unravel. The economic situation became increasingly dire in the 1960s, at which time the idea that the federal government could manage the economy successfully was completely discredited. Increased spending, first on Johnson's Great Society and then on the Vietnam War, sustained the economic boom but also increased inflation. Rising oil prices combined with poor economic management made inflation worse, even as the boom slowed, and unemployment rose. Inflation eliminated the gains of the professional and middle classes and created anxiety about the future. Attendance at union meetings dropped after 1950, but wildcat strikes like the one at the bindery kept going, expressing ongoing shop-floor discontent. As Lipsitz offers, "In their belief in direct decision-making, their use of small-group and mass mobilization, and their perception that bureaucracy actually made the system more vulnerable to disruption, they led the way for subsequent movements for social change."[64] Capitalists passed the indirect costs of production on to consumers and taxpayers, which caused traditionally working-class forms of resistance to spread; the tactics and aspirations of this postwar moment, in fact, influenced the civil rights, student, antiwar, women's, and LGBT movements. With the Paris May 1968 civil unrest and increasing rank-and-file militancy, some speculated by 1969 that the United States was on the verge of a new form of class politics, one that would pit consumers against producers, with labor at its core.[65] Opposition to established union leadership rose, even among highly disciplined units like the miners, steelworkers, and teamsters, which was virtually unheard of in the 1950s. The sources of the dissidence are complex, but it was a consequence of protections of the Landrum-Griffin Act (which provided some relief from Taft-Hartley), the social and racial pressures of the Vietnam War era, generational change in the workforce, and general resentment against oppressive work. Strikes occurring with a contract increased from one thousand in 1960 to roughly two thousand in 1969.[66]

However, this new class politics would never arise, for several reasons. The labor movement, though important to Democrats, did not want to share in governance, within the party or in office (except maybe over the Department of Labor, over which AFL-CIO asserted some claim).[67] As Brody explains, "The AFL-CIO, strong as it was, still felt a [historical] anxiety for asserting labor's separateness and independence. This in turn rested on labor's conception of how it was regarded by the larger American society, the final determinant of labor's maximum place in American politics."[68] Emanating from the leadership of Samuel Gompers (AFL president from 1886 to 1924), the AFL-CIO continued to assert that labor's sphere was limited, circumscribed in the nation's industrial and political life. The labor movement was "essentially a passive agent in relation to its surrounding environment."[69] While the radical moment passed, it injected a "syndicalist enthusiasm" that has redefined the terms of historical study of industrial unionism.[70]

After the steel plant, Jess and her friends go from job to job, working shifts here and there, often receiving a pink slip at the end of just one shift. Eventually Jess starts working the night shift at a plastic pipe factory in South Buffalo. The job involves dumping twenty-five-pound bags of powder into extrusion machines, allowing the finished plastic pipe to push out the other end. After ten minutes on the job, powder fills her pocket watch and coats her body from head to foot. Temp jobs force her and her friends to board company buses at four in the morning, often two hours each way, unpaid. However, the presence of the other butches on the bus—passing around a bottle of whiskey—remind Jess that this is the only real family she has ever known.

Jess meets her future partner, Theresa, at a cannery job in Buffalo. The foreman separates them, however, after he sees their flirtation, immediately taking Jess to another part of the plant where the actual canning is done. He points to a Y-shaped conveyor belt high above her, running close to the ceiling, where Jess sees the man she will replace, straddling a giant pipe near the point where the conveyor belt split in two. Every few seconds, a carton came speeding down the single belt, and it would be Jess's job to divert the cartons one way or another: "The cartons were packed with heavy cans of applesauce. They hurtled at me with tremendous velocity, and I had to hit them to divert them. I nearly fell off. I learned to hit the boxes from an angle, not head-on." The height gives Jess an overview of the factory, symbolizing the space as inherently violent but also providing a source of structure: "After I got the hang of it I realized what an interesting vantage point I had. I'd never seen the life of a factory from a bird's-eye view. The arrangement of the machines, the sequence and interrelatedness of tasks, the organized scurrying of workers" (120). However, this trance breaks when Jess sees Jan facing off with two women and a man over entering the women's restroom, an all-too-familiar occurrence. This scene foreshadows the events that unfold due to increasing competition for jobs, the hostility of some in the feminist movement toward butches and femmes, and the increasing economic problems in the United States in general.

Feinberg splits the novel almost in two halves, the second half beginning when Theresa takes a job at the university and starts bringing home Black Power and women's liberation leaflets, pamphlets, and underground newspapers: "The world was exploding with change. Everywhere, that is, except in the factories where I worked. Every morning at dawn we punched in as usual. We only dreamed at night" (124). Jess only knows about the war through the absence of draft-age guys and the grief in the faces of those left behind. The apolitical atmosphere of the factories reveals how the Vietnam War fractured the labor movement from within, for while union organizers, union members, and AFL-CIO President George Meany were in favor of the war, they were in direct conflict with young and queer people, and the Black community.[71] The AFL-CIO also had close ties to the American Friends of Vietnam (AFVN), a CIA-linked agency run by Cold War liberals close to labor leadership, who in the 1950s and early 1960s played a role in convincing Congress and liberal intellectuals of the need for war. The factory became increasingly intolerant to peaceniks, feminists, and those fighting for gay liberation.

Jess finds herself needing to choose sides after a fight at the bar involving Grant and Ed. After Grant's brother is killed in the war, close to the time of Martin Luther King Jr.'s assassination, Grant gets drunk and tells the crowd that the United States should drop a nuclear bomb on Vietnam, echoing a statement made by future president Ronald Reagan in October 1965; he stated, smiling all the while, "'It's silly talking about how many years we will have to spend in the jungles of Vietnam when we could pave the whole country and put parking stripes on it and still be home by Christmas.'"[72] The bar breaks out in a fight and everyone joins in along racial lines, which leads the bar owner to ban Black people.

While Jess smooths things over, and Grant apologizes, this scene depicts a shifting political map that splits Jess's community. By 1968, Richard Nixon was able to take advantage of several developments at once: Vietnam, widening divisions among Democrats, rebellion in Black urban neighborhoods, and the Republicans' strong comeback in the congressional elections of 1966. Upwardly mobile, conservative white southerners and southwesterners were persuaded to the Republican side, along with northern Catholics and working-class voters who were against both Johnson's civil rights program and the radical Left. Nixon was able to bring together a new Republican majority that would unseat the New Deal coalition and Johnson's Great Society.[73] As Brody adds, "Alabama's George Wallace made heavy inroads in a number of northern industrial states during the 1968 campaign."[74] As Republican pollsters later observed, this was a "logical and historically blessed alliance coming of age."[75]

The shift in working-class ideas, from liberal to conservative, Democrat to Republican, was in line with Harry Truman's assorted programs, because of its focus on both property (with minimum taxes) and racial insulation. From the 1930s to the 1950s, massive expenditures successfully provided welfare to the white working class (and its children), but these same white families did not want these social programs to be applied to the "undeserving" people of color living below the poverty line in the inner cities, which white families had abandoned.[76] Conservatives were well financed and had an abundance of think tanks (run by some noted intellectuals, both former Cold War liberal favorites of unions and future intimates of the Ronald Reagan White House).[77] Nixon appealed to white middle-aged, middle-income people who felt threatened by Black militancy and who sought revenge on young radicals.[78] The cultural and political instincts of the old liberal order, shaped by the Great Depression and World War II, were forged in the once-great cities, with effective political machines, masses of pro-Democratic workers, and vibrant immigrant neighborhoods.[79] As Sean Wilentz gravely states in *The Age of Reagan,* once again echoing the 2020s, "a struggle had begun over the nation's soul."[80]

Nixon was elected in part because he claimed he had a secret plan to end the war in Vietnam, but once in office, he escalated the war, "as an agonizing face-saving prelude to an American withdrawal that would begin his second term." Interestingly, his masculinist administration attacked critics of the war, even liberal Republicans whom he called "effeminate bums and defeatists."[81] At the same time, Nixon introduced patently antilabor legislation and punishing wage controls, but he calculated correctly that he could gain labor's approval by leveraging AFL-CIO President George Meany's desire for victory in Vietnam and hatred of domestic dissent.[82] Shockingly, Nixon also used orchestrated labor violence against young activists during a planned student demonstration down Broadway toward Wall Street in New York City, and he accomplished this with the help of the New York building trades and construction workers who were willing to brutally assault protestors.[83] As Buhle notes, there were also Vietnam veterans across racial categories who returned to working-class life rageful and often with substance use disorders: "It was this generational force, within a relative vacuum of other organized forces, which led to a politics of race, culture, and protest, more than factors of economics as such or even structural changes in unions."[84]

Despite the tragic events that unfolded in the late 1960s, the world only starts changing for Jess and her friends around 1973, when everyone is laid off. Men were returning to the factories from their service in Vietnam while the recession was deepening, and the big motor companies—Ford, Chrysler, and General Motors—were announcing massive labor cuts. It becomes clear to the butches they will need to transition to male to secure employment. While that is the primary reason for some in her community to transition, for Jess, transition proves more complicated. She dreams that she has a flat chest and a beard, but she still feels alienated from binary gender, which means she is embarking on a journey of self-discovery rather than undergoing a clear-cut binary transition.

However, when Jess begins to pass as a cisgender man, she has an immediate sense of euphoria that her body is now closer to what she expected before puberty confounded her. Most importantly, she can finally get work at a bindery as a mechanic's apprentice. Ironically, the man who hires her remarks, after some scrutiny, that she looks "like a clean-cut young man" (174). As Prosser writes, Jess discovers after transition an "unambivalent place" for accomplishing everyday activities—getting a haircut, using a public restroom—in short, becoming both less economically penetrable and more "culturally locatable."[85] However, Jess's world is expanding and at the same time shrinking. She tells a femme friend, "'I feel like a ghost. . . . Like I've been buried alive. As far as the world's concerned, I was born the day I began to pass. I have no past, no loved ones, no memories, no me. No one really sees me or speaks to me or touches me'" (213). She is also enraged that she is treated so much better as a man than as a butch woman: "Acceptance of me as a he felt like an ongoing indictment of me as a he-she" (178).

However, despite the impossibility of disclosing herself to the other men on the job, she shares their common goal of organizing. When Jess and a group of men are hired by a temp agency to be scabs, several of the workers pull out their UAW cards in protest. Jess and the others are furious that they have been put on the job under false pretenses. The conversation between the men makes clear the economic frustrations: "'There's more hard times coming, mark my words,'" one of the men exclaims; "'Yeah, but you bet the rich are still gettin' richer,'" another says. "'It wasn't just Nixon—they're all a bunch of crooks. This new peanut man in the White House isn't going to change anything.'" On the bus back to the temp agency, the men share how layoffs completely derailed their lives: "'Harrison, Chevrolet, Anaconda. Fifteen years seniority, twenty years, thirty years'" (182). Jess cannot escape the growing sense of economic precarity, even if she passes as a man.

The decline of the industrial workforce and the emergence of "rust bowls" in the 1970s deprived the AFL-CIO leadership of resources even before the severity of the 1970s oil crisis fully hit home.[86] As this scene reveals, the Carter administration was the final blow for many workers, as well as the AFL-CIO, dashing hopes for any revival of the liberal legislation that marked the Kennedy-Johnson years. Carter was an outsider whose commitment to a party platform was superficial, and he quickly abandoned labor under pressures of an inflationary spiral and a severe energy crisis.[87] Carter offered only symbolic gestures, like a modest array of antipoverty pilot programs, in the midst of a retreat from the promises of the Great Society.[88] Not only was labor losing with Carter and with Congress, it was also losing its public standing. Voters who were turning rightward—or becoming politically active for the first time (like evangelical conservatives)— thought unions were obstacles to free enterprise, and they supported a new wave of state right-to-work laws.[89] The magic phrase of "economic reform" had begun in the Carter years, which became a dog whistle in the 1980s and '90s, and beyond.[90] The massive cutbacks of social programs were accomplished by both parties since Johnson, and at this point in the novel, these cutbacks take place within the logics of 1970s-style "shared austerity."[91]

Massive plant shutdowns disrupted and displaced communities previously stable for generations. Thirty-eight million workers lost their jobs during the 1970s, as investments in plants and equipment declined sharply, and the industrial working class lost its numerical strength in the workforce.[92] And, beyond the employer-made problems, there were other impersonal forces at play: foreign competition consuming union jobs, computer technology replacing workers, the expansion of white-collar work in manufacturing, the long-term shrinkage of the economic sector represented by industry, mining, construction, and transportation (from half of nonagricultural employment in 1950 to barely a third in 1980).[93] Automation, outsourcing, the growth of multinationals, and the shift of investment from basic and mass production to high tech cut the numbers of union members in the old centers of industry. Tax cuts and other bribes delivered by corporations to cities and states either had no effect or gave companies the chance to gather the capital for a total reorientation. Corporations accelerated their move south and west and to the suburbs, if not abroad—in part to escape unions, as well as "restive minority workers."[94]

American business formed a united front, as nearly the entire spectrum came together, from the National Right to Work Committee to the corporate liberals in the prestigious Labor-Management Group.[95] What took shape in this period was the formation of a new bloc—a well-financed, well-organized coalition between big business and right-wing extremists.[96] Assault on labor reform went beyond the political arena: the move toward the open shop was again on the march (e.g., groups like the National Association of Manufacturers' Committee for a Union-Free Environment, in the booming area of labor-management consultant firms, and in resistance organizers regularly found in new plants even of un-unionized firms). For example, GM tried to keep the UAW away from new plants it was opening in the South.[97] In the 1970s, management became very sophisticated, launching surveys of employee attitudes, training and promotion programs, and "conflict resolution systems" modeled on union grievance procedures: "Open-shop firms took the stance of the enlightened employer who, in the words of one consultant, wants to 'remain union-free because he prefers to deal with you directly in our concern for your welfare.'"[98] However, this was only a veneer: in 1977, the NLRB received 42,802 complaints, a figure six times higher than that of the mid-1950s. Despite the efforts of unions, during the migration of industry to the Sunbelt, organization fell to half the level of the rest of the country by the end of the 1970s. The service economy largely replaced the industrial economy, which meant less unionization overall; just 12 percent of service workers and 20 percent of government workers were organized.[99]

Within this historical moment of dwindling labor power, Jess experiences one last failed moment of union activity before she decides to leave Buffalo and settle in New York City. The continued dangers on the job mean that Jess has no choice but to bid for a better one and try to become a union organizer. The old-timers remind Jess about the importance of a union: "'All us old-timers are UAW,' he said. 'I'll be a union man on the day they lower my casket into the ground. You gotta have a union, young fella. If you don't have a union, you better fight to get one'" (201). When yet another accident occurs at the plant and someone is severely injured, Jess agrees to show up at a meeting, also attended by Duffy, who has come to help build the union. However, Duffy publicly misgenders Jess at the union meeting, which means she has to leave Buffalo entirely, since she will likely be fired the next day and run out of town.

Duffy's mistake initiates for Jess a deeper questioning of her gender beyond the binary. She begins to claim an inner experience not determined by passing, and, as Prosser argues, "the masquerade" of binary masculinity fails to constitute her identity.[100] In fact, it is the masquerade that conceals her sense of self, which she discovers is liminal and in between. She seeks a new life in New York City, where, according to a temp agency, there are jobs, and maybe a sense of personal anonymity. In the 1970s, with the old way of life vanished, the factories and bars gone, there is nothing left, and everyone goes their separate ways or goes into hiding: "Loneliness had become my environment—the air I breathed, the spatial dimension in which I was trapped. I sat in a boat on a deathly calm sea, waiting for a breeze to fill my sails" (221).

Landing "in between" gives her the feeling of wanting to know herself more deeply, and this includes a sense of meaningful and stable work. As the train moves closer to the city, she reflects on the poverty upstate:

> Sleepy rural towns turned their shabby backs toward the railroad tracks. Block-long main drags: five and dime, hardware, auto parts, gasoline, home-cooking. Lime, lemon, peach pastel homes. Sagging porches. Pick-up trucks and children's swings rusting in the backyards. Trailer parks—yesterday's dreams of mobility stripped of wheels. Abandoned factories, familiar as a lover's sigh. Ribbons of roads, trestle, and track tied all of our lives together like a gift. (226)

Here, love and work life are intimate with one another as the abandoned factory conjures the feeling of a "lover's sigh," which is the opposite of what is expected, given how much the factory also stripped her of dignity. By revealing the extent of Jess's losses, Feinberg resists the homo- and transnormative solution of moving to an upwardly mobile urban environment. For a while, Jess is finally able to do vital identity work. She reads trans and labor history and even discovers in the archives an aunt who became a union organizer in the 1910s and '20s for the International Ladies' Garment Workers' Union. However, even after Jess becomes a skilled typesetter, she never regains union security and is often relegated to the overnight shift.

At the end of the novel, Jess discovers a large LGBTQ demonstration, where for the first time she hears the words *lesbian* and *gay* as rallying cries rather than as slurs. However, this rally is different because it is attended by lower-income and working-class folks from Brooklyn and Queens—and people of color, some of whom are butch or femme, telling stories of being raped and harassed. Jess summons the courage to speak to the crowd about what it was like to be a butch in Buffalo: "'There's lots of us who are on the outside and we don't want to be. We're getting busted and beaten up. We're dying out here. We need you—but you need us, too'" (296). Through Jess's presence at this rally, Feinberg makes an important historical statement about the trans-exclusionary and classist practices of the gay and lesbian movement from the 1970s forward, rendering Jess without a place in their world.

The rally inspires her to call Duffy, who now works at the union office in New York City on 17th Street, after being red-baited out of his last job. Jess tells him she is working for a typesetter—nonunion: "'Yeah. When the computers came on the scene, the owners could see first how it was going to transform the old hot-lead industry. So they hired all the people the old craft union didn't realize were important to organize. That's how they broke the back of Local 6'" (298). At the rally, she wanted to talk about the plants, "'how when a contract's almost up management works overtime trying to divide everybody. I didn't know if they'd get what I meant if I said it took the whole membership to win the strike'" (299). Duffy replies that today, it takes more than one union to win, but he reassures her that it is possible to change the world; in fact, working conditions will demand a fight. He encourages her to join him and to dare to *"imagine a world worth living in"* (301).

As Prosser notes, Feinberg completes Jess's narrative through a series of dreams that include a range of people she has encountered in the factories, in the bars, and in New York City, whom she carries with her as part of her internal trans community.[101] For Prosser, the dreams suggest Jess's desire for a transgender home that refuses the more contained queer space of the West Village rally. I believe there is a lot of value in considering how Jess wants to differentiate from those at the rally to discover a home in gender liminality and in trans-as-process. However, I also want to think through the ways that these dreams intersect with Feinberg's utopian vision of a formidable, coalitional labor movement, one that never comes to pass in this period or at any point up to the time of this writing. New Labor historians agree that unions remain central to any labor justice movement. I would add that the novel powerfully demonstrates how unions also remain central to the viability of queer and trans masculinities in workplaces of all kinds. As Wertheimer insists, the union is the only institution through which workers can challenge authority on a systemic, day-to-day basis.[102] Overall, however, coalitional labor organizing has been challenged by a recurring set of problems. Even during Democratic administrations, the Taft-Hartley Act has never been repealed, and the right to common situs picketing or reforms in health care are still denied. However, most of all, unions have had very little influence on government decisions that affect workers' lives, and further, as Buhle argues, business unionism has had its own inherent laws of centralization and power.[103]

Ultimately, Brody believes that the labor movement has been a victim of economic forces beyond its control, part of a global phenomenon affecting all advanced industrial economies, though not in the same ways or to the same degree. In Jess's time, a new stage of late capitalism had already set in, characterized by the displacement of regulated national economies and the installment of a global economic order characterized by capital mobility and competitive labor markets. However, while this was and is a global phenomenon, the U.S. labor movement was particularly hard hit in this period. With 17 percent of workers organized in 1985–1986, it stood in a class by itself, eleven points behind the next most slowed movement; as compared to other countries (e.g., Germany and Britain), the American economy was becoming distinguished by the fact that it is a "union free environment."[104] While it is true that in the 1980s, the political standing of the AFL-CIO went into a tailspin, with the hostile Reagan administration on one side and the "impotent" Democrats on the other, Brody insists that labor's decline was not a contingent event.[105] The decline could not have been avoided with better leaders or bolder policies. Rather, given the changes to the U.S. economy, it was historically determined: "In short: no other labor movement—not even one otherwise so alike [such as Canada] in its institutional characteristics—stands so exposed to the forces of its economic environment."[106] The key elements of the labor movement that supported collective bargaining—the legal framework, the market regulation, an agreed-upon workplace regime—broke down, which accounts for labor's decline in this period. By extension, he argues, these are the elements that will need to be brought back in the next expansionist period.[107]

Brody insists that what made trade unionism compelling for American workers in the past—and what will make it so in the future—is a job-conscious capacity to link itself to the aspirations for labor justice.[108] No labor movement can define itself without those aspirations derived from job consciousness or influence the processes that gave rise to them. This was true in the 1930s, when the labor movement joined the New Deal, advocated market regulations, and participated in the workplace struggles of 1933–36, but these events were not of labor's making, nor can we expect that they will be if another moment like the 1930s arises. A vital continuity between late capitalism and the 1930s needs reviving, in Brody's view. What we can hope is that the labor movement will know how to seize that moment should it present itself, but that will depend, as it did in the 1930s, on a sure sense of its job-conscious character.[109]

Unlike in other stories about labor and masculinity, in *Stone Butch Blues,* trans and lesbian characters are the ones best positioned to develop a sense of job consciousness. Feinberg's detailed descriptions of actual working conditions, of jobs performed, jobs won, and jobs lost, can be used to revive what Brody calls this sense of job consciousness, healing the fatal fracture between the industrial order and the labor movement located in the workplace itself.[110] Feinberg continually returns to the need for workers to seek their own freedom. According to Lipsitz, "if class is to have meaning as more than a code word for one set of interests, it lies in the way one group can make its own interests synonymous with the emancipation of others."[111] There needs to be a turn toward an independent politics from below, which has been revived to a certain extent since 2020 with the recent unionization push at Amazon and many Starbucks franchises across the country, as well as the "great resignation" of 2021. Such a turn would require unruly alliances, a form of what Sidney Lens calls "coalitionism," the act of uniting with outside groups for specific objectives, which would move us toward an independent labor politics.[112] As Buhle argues, one of the unrealized goals of the 1960s–1980s was the networking and communicating among workers themselves, both within and outside of traditional union channels and across state, country, or world.[113] Unions would also have to become horizontal rather than top-down.

Racism and a lack of sustained interracial labor activity is another factor in labor's continual loss of traction. Historian Eric Foner recalls how in the 1930s, the Communist Party was the only largely white organization to make antiracism central to its political program.[114] However, labor leaders, including Communists and Socialists, gave their consent willingly in the 1940s in the establishment of more bureaucracy, which insulated the crude, racist AFL-CIO President George Meany and, later, Lane Kirkland.[115] Labor leaders have largely been obstacles who sided with the supposed winners of history. Even at the time of Feinberg's writing in 1993, the distance between bureaucracy and ordinary members had not been bridged, nor had the historic dependence on the Democratic Party been significantly questioned: "Ultimately, the problem of labor bureaucracy cannot be isolated from the labor politics of exclusionism and imperial commitments."[116]

Marable believes that the only prescription for unions going forward is "a multiracial program for social transformation forged in industrial and public service unions," with the very existence of the union as, of course, a prerequisite for this transformation.[117] Unionization is clearly the route to better working conditions and upward mobility. A large body of research supports the idea that unionization has an egalitarian effect on dispersion of fringe benefits, particularly in capital-intensive industries where Black and white workers cooperate and keep the spirit of unions alive.[118] Marable insists from the perspective of the 1980s that it was essential for Black progressives and activists to support unions, even with the obvious racist contradictions, or they would alienate themselves from the Black working class and "participate in that class's ultimate destruction."[119] Marable is adamant that without this coalition, the gains of labor would be reversed. He warns: "Make no mistake: the organic crisis afflicting the black working class will extend to workers of all descriptions." In 2022, his remarks are prophetic.

When Jess contemplates joining the labor movement, the New Right was advancing its agenda, and they continue to do so in the 2020s with terrifying precision. Within these economic changes, in addition to reductions in social services and benefits, the "social wage" can only be achieved by "intensifying long-standing divisions among the poor and the angry."[120] The main tactic of the New Right remains to push cultural issues with special appeal for white ethnic voters and many lower-income groups, "diverting attention from economics and focusing instead on abortion, school prayer, de facto segregation, defeat of the Equal Rights Amendment, prevention of gay rights legislation and of all affirmative action statutes."[121] Then as now, the New Right aims to concretize fixed hierarchies and to dissolve social values that unions have represented at many points in history.

One of the most promising organizations for national renewal is Jobs with Justice, which as of 2022 has coalitions in over thirty cities and states in all regions of the country. Founded in 1987, Jobs with Justice brings together community-labor coalitions of activists, environmentalists, and consumer groups. Historically, they have rallied around the rights of janitors and others through picket, civil disobedience, rallies, and fundraisers. Union members sign pledge cards committing each signer to "be there" regularly and to "fight for someone else's fight as well as [your] own." As Buhle notes, "No better sustained example of the Industrial Workers of the World slogan, 'An Injury to One is an Injury to All,' could likely be found today."[122] However, Buhle is also pessimistic, with good reason: "Abandonment of the bureaucratic vertical style, akin to corporate or military models, will not be easy and is not likely to come soon."[123] Substantive change will also require a "decisive reversal" and a "mental leap" away from the idea that Americans are the aristocrats of the planet, who can flagrantly waste resources in pursuit of evermore luxurious suburban lifestyles.[124]

The American working class has changed dramatically in structural terms since the CIO or the earlier era of AFL's greatest influence, and "the millions of old industrial jobs lost will not return," while at the same time, "the millions of new jobs in fast foods or similar merchandizing or the white-collar business sector all seem daunting prospects at best for unionization."[125] This will continue to be true, despite the promises of both Democratic and Republican administrations. Feinberg presents a clear and accurate understanding of when labor briefly became a social movement, during the postwar strike years, and during the small moments when a range of union activists reached out, mainly at the local level, to peace, environmental, feminist, and LGBTQIA+ and other social movements, creating alliances that could have changed the course of the future.[126] For many historians, and for Feinberg, the answer clearly lies in the old Wobbly attitude: "Ordinary working people acting as their own leaders."

Gay White Trailer Trash

Annie Proulx's "Brokeback Mountain" has often been referred to as that "gay cowboy story," especially after the release of the film adaptation in 2005, which was inducted into the National Film Registry in 2018, revealing its continued status as a watershed moment for LGBTQIA+ filmmaking.[127] However, Proulx's short story differs greatly from the film in many ways, but particularly in its treatment of "white trash" status, landlessness, and labor abuses. Well before "Brokeback Mountain," Proulx showed her sensitive, firsthand knowledge of the unforgiving wind and weather on the Wyoming plains and the people who live there. Her stories depict with intimate familiarity greedy newcomers from the coast wanting cheap land, as well as the locals' unemployment, gambling, and substance use disorders. At the same time, in their pursuit of new sites for fracking and other pillages, gas companies show blatant disregard for the land and its people. Homosexuality hovers like a dirty secret at the edges of these stories, in the form of rumor, suspicion, and innuendo. Gay masculinities become effeminized and ersatz counterpoints to the gruff, weather-beaten, salt of the earth straight masculinities. However, given the tendency of men in Wyoming to appear impenetrable, Proulx was surprised when she received, over a period of a decade, an overwhelming number of letters written not by "outraged religio-moral types" but by Wyoming ranch hands, cowboys, and fathers admitting, "You told my story," or, "I now understand what my son went through."[128]

Diminished life chances wrap through and around queerness in the lives of her characters, Ennis Del Mar and Jack Twist, two young men who eke out a living in the summers as sheepherders. In the world of Wyoming work, sheepherders are the lowest of the low. Neither one of the men is likely to earn enough to buy their own place, a fact that haunts their relationship, and ultimately precipitates its ending. However, for a time, the land—like the factory floor—provides Ennis and Jack with a sense of grounding, both for their labor and their sexuality. Despite hostilities, Ennis and Jack refute the rough-hewn masculine impenetrability of Wyoming men and develop care for one another.

Through characters who are both queer and landless, Proulx's story recalls how the United States has historically privileged the white male propertied subject. Possessive individualism during the national phase of capital is part of a liberal humanism that erases the very hierarchies of power on which it depends. In the nineteenth century, American exceptionalism grew out of the claim that European feudal structures of inequity had been vanquished and replaced by a society composed of (white male) individuals who make their own fortunes in a horizonal societal structure.[129] The U.S. nation-state based itself on liberal political theory that sees the protection of property as the only justification for the formation of the state. For example, John Locke began his *Second Treatise of Government* with the following revealing statement: "*Political Power,* then, I take to be a *right* of making laws with penalties of death, and consequently all less penalties, for the regulating and preserving of property."[130] Fraternity took on a new form in the United States, but with deep ties to the European context, rendered invisible through the liberal social contract.

Consequently, differential access to property structures social relations of rule, creating in its wake cycles of poverty that are used to justify economic stratification.[131] Nikhil Pal Singh offers how racial differentiation changes "an idealized game of merit and chance into a stacked deck: racially disparate fates have been manifested as devalued land, degraded labor, permanent indebtedness, and disposability."[132] Racial domination consistently weaves into the management of a capitalist society throughout the history of the United States. However, class and sexuality racialize whiteness in this story, which places Jack and Ennis in the same material condition as the Black and Brown folks whom they may disavow.

In the eighteenth and nineteenth centuries, free labor was only an entitlement for white people, but capitalism relies on increasing differentiation, which explains the poverty and landlessness for "white trash," and in this case, "gay white trailer trash." According to Annalee Newitz and Matt Wray, beginning in the 2010s, *white trash* became a term that is "good to think with," because it disrupts the stereotyping of white and Asian American people as always middle class and Black and Latinx people as always "poor."[133] *White trash* allows cultural critics to imagine the categories of whiteness and working-class or underclass poverty as closely related. Proulx presents two gay white men who are considered by their communities to be "white trash," a term I extend to include sexuality.

Brokeback Mountain the film continues the tradition of lyrical pastoralism, the dominant mode for depicting the American West, but the short story provides a window into the loneliness, isolation, and poverty on the plains that shapes the lives and desires of Ennis and Jack. Within these intersections, a caring and penetrable masculinity emerges, one that is closely attuned to the land, animals, and other men. However, this caring is swiftly and adeptly truncated by suffering and death. The short story emphasizes how class and landlessness play a large role in this suffering, while the film thoroughly privileges their love story, in solidarity with mainstream liberal LGB agendas (Figure 15). Clyde Taylor theorizes on the problems of adaptation in "The Ironies of Palace-Subaltern Discourse":

> By lining up an adapted text diachronically behind its model, we can clearly see the difference that, when read as discursive ironies, matter in the politics of representation. Lay viewers from repressed communities are right on target in decoding the politics of adaptation by indexing what was added, changed, or left out in the transition from one telling to another.[134]

As a result of what is "left out" of the film, viewers wrongly perceive Ennis's loss of interest in his own life as a result of his inability to come out rather than as a complex effect of low-wage work and a particular kind of rural Wyoming masculine normativity. The adaptation presents instead a grand picture of the West and of the redemptive quality of queer sexuality, one that features a thousand ewes and their lambs dutifully marching through the sublime flowering meadows, without sustained confrontation with the living conditions of these men (Figure 16). Such lyrical pastoralism is evident in the long history of photography of the West, from Ansel Adams's *Moonrise, Hernandez, New Mexico,* to the Richard Avedon series *In the American West*. Director Ang Lee and screenwriters Larry McMurtry and Diana Ossana present an idealized gay romance in which sex is literally hidden from view, without sweat or dirt, things that would be visible when two men have sex with each other out in the country after working with animals all day. Identity triumphs over economic equality, even among the liberal Left, who would still consider themselves enlightened consumers of films like *Brokeback Mountain*.

What the film depicts with visual splendor, the story takes up in much more modest terms, for while the thousand ewes and their lambs are also present in the story, they instead "flowed up the trail like dirty water through the timber and out above the tree line into the great flowery meadows and the coursing, endless wind."[135] The story is compact and rich with Proulx's knowledge of the landscape and the very specific affect produced by living in Wyoming, the least populous state, having the second lowest population per square mile (after Alaska). The wind becomes like an additional character, one that could be "fresh and warm and perfumed with pine resin" or "erratic, inimical . . . falling on the house with ferocity."[136] Gaining ground on the wind becomes a sign of one's masculine prowess and

FIGURE 15. In the movie adaptation *Brokeback Mountain,* their romantic love is privileged without addressing the cycles of poverty that shape their desire. *Brokeback Mountain,* directed by Ang Lee, featuring Heath Ledger and Jake Gyllenhaal (Universal Studios Home Entertainment, 2006), DVD.

impenetrability. The wind also adds to the feeling of "no future," of disenfranchisement and isolation, that stalks Ennis and Jack at every turn.

In the story, they are high school dropouts, country boys just shy of twenty years old, raised on small, poor ranches on opposite sides of the state. They are already accustomed to multiple forms of lack: "hard work and privation" (2). "Rough-mannered, rough-spoken, inured to the stoic life," they take jobs as sheepherders and camp tenders for Farm and Ranch Employment (1–2). In contrast to the film (featuring the ridiculously attractive actors Heath Ledger as Ennis and Jake Gyllenhaal as Jack), the boys are worn-down-looking with boots that need replacing and bellies swollen from too much beer and whiskey. The foreman quickly sizes them up as "a pair of deuces going nowhere" (3). What the foreman means by this phrase is that they are akin to the twos, the lowest-ranked playing cards in the deck. He knows they are "white trash" even before he catches them fooling around through a pair of binoculars, an act that surely marks them as such, considering that sexual deviance is often part of the epithet's meaning. The treatment of Jack and Ennis by hypermasculine superiors mirrors the treatment of Jess and her friends on the factory floor.

Brokeback Mountain itself is not a tourist destination but is rather

FIGURE 16. The movie conforms to the lyrical pastoralism that dominates photography and filmmaking about the West. *Brokeback Mountain,* directed by Ang Lee, featuring Heath Ledger and Jake Gyllenhaal (Universal Studios Home Entertainment, 2006), DVD.

drab and dirty, much like the land in Proulx's story "The Half-Skinned Steer," which resembles a brutalized human body, vulnerable to the elements and to man-made interference (in the form of speculators looking for gas, oil, and minerals): "Then the violent country showed itself, the cliffs rearing at the moon, the snow smoking off the prairie like steam, the white flank of the ranch slashed with fence cuts, the sage-brush glittering and along the creek black tangles of willow bunched like dead hair."[137] Proulx describes the men who populate the state as "bone-seasoned, tireless workers accustomed to discomfort, took their pleasure in drink, cigarettes, getting work done . . . brass-nutted boys, sinewy and tall, nothing they liked better than to kick the frost out of a horse in early morning."[138] With severe prose, Proulx depicts the unending cycles of desperation, which exist long before and continue long after Ennis and Jack appear on the scene. In telling their story, Proulx applies searing intensity to the emotional and economic deprivation in the rural West more generally, making more visible and audible the queerness that is stifled there. The sublime grandeur of the American West in the film version, set to an orchestral soundtrack, contrasts against this scene of pebbles and "crumbs of soil" casting shadows in the air, lodgepole pines "massed in slabs of somber malachite" (4).

Proulx describes herself as a "geographical determinist," someone who writes out of their belief that region, climate, and topography shape culture and identity, which directly structures sexual relationships. As she explains in the essay "Getting Movied," she feels an allegiance to the Wyoming landscape and to depicting with rigorous honesty how people make a living in "hard, isolated livestock-raising communities dominated by white masculine values, but also holding subliminal fantasies."[139] Real cowpokes despise not only homosexuality but the kind of sheepherding that Ennis and Jack engage in on Brokeback Mountain. In other stories, Proulx's sheepherders are "mangy" and not worth marrying—nobodies—which provides context. Men like Ennis and Jack work livestock in big territory and even feel contempt for those who do not, which partially explains Ennis's resentment toward Jack when he marries "up" and leaves their way of life behind.[140]

When Proulx first shows their attraction to one another, she does so through themes of distance, showing how loneliness and poverty shape their desire: "[Ennis] sometimes saw Jack, a small dot moving across a high meadow as an insect moves across a tablecloth; Jack, in his dark camp, saw Ennis as night fire, a red spark on the huge black mass of mountain" (4). However, in silence, they tend to the land and the animals, transforming masculinity and work through care. Gay masculinity built on care disrupts the category of "rural worker" and the image of the straight, brawny, working man, which creates in its wake multiple categories of masculine-identified people with lower life chances. Jack's and Ennis's practices of care wrap through their sexuality and become foundations for unruly alliance, even while the dialogue between the two men is, like the landscape, sparse. They avoid emotions but talk profusely about work, horses, radio, roughstock events, wrecks and injuries, dogs each had owned, needing to leave high school when the transmission on the pickup fails, sisters marrying roughnecks in Casper, brothers abandoning them—the mundane details of their lives.

When Ennis and Jack fuck on the mountain, after a day of performing work routines largely in silence, their sex is automatic: "No instruction manual needed. . . . They never talked about the sex, let it happen . . . saying not a goddamn word except once Ennis said, 'I'm not a queer,' and Jack jumped in with 'me neither. A one-shot thing. Nobody's business but ours'" (7). However, as the story unfolds, both realize that this is anything but a "one-shot thing." Moments of care shift the image of rural working men as inured and calloused to the wind and to the emotions of others: "They were respectful of each other's opinions, each glad to have a companion where none had been expected. Ennis, riding against the wind back to the sheep in the treacherous, drunken light, thought he'd never had such a good time, felt he could paw the white out of the moon" (6). When they start having sex, they lose track of the sheep, and their defenses, and everything begins to feel, in a disquieting way, "mixed" (8). Further showing his vulnerability, when Ennis leaves Jack at the end of the summer, he feels like "someone was pulling his guts out hand over hand a yard at a time" (9). They both resist in their own ways the heteronormative mandate that keeps capitalism in place, for even while they marry other people, have children, and ostensibly move on with their lives, they lack the same tenderness and care for their families that they show one another (as proof of this lack of care, Ennis calls both his horses and daughters "little darlin") (10).

However, Ennis and Jack must prove occasionally that while they enjoy sex with one another, they are not "soft." When Jacks hurts his face on a rock after seeing a bear and losing track of the mules, Ennis initially recoils from Jack's tender touch. Ennis shows the ways he protects himself from abuse and violence. On their last day together on the mountain, Ennis punches Jack hard, drawing blood and leaving his jaw "bruised blue" (8). Their sex is hypermasculine, which shows how femininity is pushed away as a defense mechanism. Four years later when Jack meets Ennis in Riverton, Wyoming, they retreat to a seedy hotel, each still covering his emotion; only trembling reveals the intensity of care. The scene is meanwhile butch to its core, hypermasculine and infused with the smell of sex and hard labor, "semen and sweat and whiskey, of old carpet and sour hay, saddle leather, shit and cheap soap" (12).

For Ennis in particular, the caring masculinity he develops fails to survive, which strongly suggests the multiple forms of disenfranchisement he experiences. While Jack wants a life with Ennis, Ennis has hardened to the point where he cannot bear to take the risk, in part because he is haunted by memories of his dad taking him to see the dead body of a gay rancher killed by a tire iron, his penis dismembered. Ennis impresses on Jack in the hotel room, "'We do that in the wrong place we'll be dead'" (13). And yet, as a testimony to the strength of their bond and of their caring masculinity, the relationship stumbles onward, toward a blank future: "Nothing ended, nothing begun, nothing resolved" (22). It is not just the sex that haunts Jack in particular but rather the memory of Ennis's care, coming up behind and pulling him close, "the silent embrace satisfying some shared and sexless hunger" (22). It was this memory that Jack nurtures, "that dozy embrace solidified in his memory as the single moment of artless, charmed happiness in their separate and difficult lives" (22). Jack admits to Ennis that he misses him so badly, "enough sometimes to make him whip babies," but the fantasy Jack nurtures of a future life with Ennis has as much to do with sex and romance as it does with a love for the work and the land: "'Tell you what, if you and me had a little ranch together, little cow and calf operation, your horses, it'd be some sweet life'" (19, 14). Their sexuality and their livelihood *are* Brokeback, and over the years, though they never return to that particular mountain, it becomes the place that haunts their dreams and waking lives.

Ennis turns him down, claiming he is "caught in [his] own loop," but as a consequence, Ennis's work and sexual life become less and less satisfying, and out of a nostalgic desire to relive Brokeback, he develops a "yearning for low-paid, long-houred ranch work" (16). Jack, as a result of Ennis's rejection, essentially trades in his queerness for a normal, white, middle-class life, complete with a wife from an upwardly mobile family, a home, and stable employment. However, Ennis never fully represses his memories of Brokeback Mountain and remains unassimilable. He exists only in a state of semicalcification because he allows these memories to penetrate his consciousness. Given Jack's suicide, it seems, ironically, that Ennis's inability to move on saves his life, while Jack's propertied lifestyle and false marriage make him more vulnerable to premature death. He buys in to the American ideal of possessive individualism and the institutionalization of whiteness and masculinity, undergirded by feminized, bourgeois domesticity. Jack wanted to build a life with Ennis, with some land and a place of their own, which would demand that both claim this domestic space for themselves. This is something Ennis is completely unwilling to do, which leaves Jack devastated.

Ennis's downward spiral shows how much internalized homophobia and class-based shame work together to keep him from living. Ennis refuses to engage the caring masculinity he once discovered with Jack. His wife, Alma, divorces him and Ennis turns to alcohol, suffering a death of the soul. After Jack's death, Ennis distances himself from his daughters and from the world. The story ends where it begins: Jack is dead, and Ennis is living in the miniature space of a trailer out on a lonely plain, stalked by a wind that "hisses in around the aluminum door and window frame . . . strikes the trailer like a load of dirt coming off a dump truck" (1). Ennis's despair develops in sympathy with the "huge sadness of the northern plains" that "rolled down on him" after he learns of Jack's death, and it intensifies beyond measure after he learns Jack would not be buried at Brokeback as he requested but instead on some "grieving plain" (27).

Ennis still does not own the land, which means that because the ranch he is working for is sold, he must move on again. Ennis still finds pleasure in the temporary, in-between silences, which hold his dreams about Jack that sweeten the taste of stale, reheated coffee. Proulx shows the tragedy of Ennis's life as white trash, but without blaming him for his problems or turning his existence into a joke. The shirts that he and Jack wore, which Ennis covets, end up hanging like an elegy on the wall of his trailer below a postcard of Brokeback. This refusal and/or inability to move forward depicts the psychic space of stuckness due to class, sexuality, and geographic isolation, in which the lack of emotional movement combines with the scripted, hard, sometimes brutal physical gestures of masculinity. There is a palpable feeling of despair and giving up in the last lines of the story: "There was some open space between what he knew and what he tried to believe, but nothing could be done about it, and if you can't fix it you've got to stand it" (28). The shirts hung together on the trailer wall also shows the inability, or unwillingness, to read class and sexuality together in "Brokeback Mountain," as sexuality often subsumes class even in so-called intersectional analysis. Proulx witnesses scenes through a fictionalized gaze that would otherwise have gone undocumented and unaccounted for, demonstrating sociologist Michael Harrington's assertion that the marginalization of people experiencing poverty needs to be invisible in order for American exceptionalism to march onward.[141]

In *Stone Butch Blues* and "Brokeback Mountain," trans and queer masculinities are denied both job security and the safety of the domestic sphere, which was supposed to function as a "repository of the affective and the emotional[,] . . . the site that compensates for the alienation experienced in the public space of work."[142] However, for Jess Goldberg and Ennis Del Mar especially, it is a space continually under threat, relegating them to "uneven and unruly modes of life."[143] Even when Jess finds a livable apartment in New York City, the landlord burns the building to the ground to collect the insurance, a common occurrence in an era of intensifying gentrification. Their economic precarity occurs within conditions when more and more workers became unable to consume the goods they produced—the supposed goal of Fordism and Taylorism.[144]

The construction of the normative, white worker/consumer actually produced contradiction and incommensurability. Even ethnic European immigrants and rural white working-class subjects were not evenly or completely included as part of the white working class, and many still are not. Hong argues that these uneven integrations demonstrate the crises of U.S. capitalism, which, while different from those produced in colonized sites and by racialized populations, must be read as allied to them.[145] Property comprises not only actual homes, objects, and consumer goods but "a complex social network that relates each subject to the state and to each other."[146] As Hong writes on Locke, "The subject is defined by *his* ability to own, and indeed, the first and foremost thing he owns is himself. Subjectivity, then, is a possession."[147] For Ennis, and for Jess "dispossession" is akin to social death.

While Black poverty is depicted as supposedly natural or endemic, white poverty is atypical or accidental, which means that neither journalists nor sociologists have shown much interest in depicting lower-income white people as a class. As Andrew Hacker contends from the perspective of the early 1990s, "At times, it almost appears as if white poverty must be covered up, lest it blemish the reputation of the dominant race. . . . As has been the case throughout American history, the majority of the American poor are white but now they are absent."[148] "White trash" as an analytic allows cultural critics to imagine the categories of whiteness and working-class or underclass poverty as closely related, undoing damaging depictions of "white trash" as the "unbred perverse" responsible for halting American progress.[149] Dehumanizing images of "white trash" strip masculinities, in particular, of their humanity within racial capitalism, reducing white poverty to a caricature, images that compound when the supposedly wrong kinds of sexual deviance are introduced—or, in other words, outside of the sanitized, romantic film image. The American tradition of making stories of white trash into "lies, jokes, or dirty secrets" extends to perceptions of queer and trans masculinities as lower-class, "ersatz," and doubly "perverse."[150]

While they are not marketed as romance narratives, "Brokeback Mountain" and *Stone Butch Blues* are powerful political tracts that bridge divides on the Left, where class is opposed to race and gender politics. According to Singh, to bridge this divide, the Left would need to establish a more "politically generous" conception of how racism is activated. Race and racial animus are not fixed characteristics of an already defined group but rather "a situational dimension of our common political life that is repeatedly mobilized."[151] As *Stone Butch Blues* suggests, white people and white workers can be encouraged toward a nonracist politics centered on economic justice, but this requires active, intentional constituency building.[152] More Americans identify as working class than at any other time since the 1930s and '40s, which makes this a large potential bloc of activists. However, Singh writes about the term *white working class* in way that indicates a path forward:

> [White working class] reifies the link between whiteness and the material interests of working and unemployed people. It makes less and less sense in the context of the most hopeful and vibrant movement of today: the multiracial fight for the $15 hourly minimum wage; the organization of legions of home workers and domestic caregivers, the least visible and most diverse sectors of the working class (mostly women); the battles to present the poisoning of vital resources at Standing Rock, across Indian lands, and in the national commons, where ancient struggles for decolonization continue; the demands to be protected from arbitrary force and premature death at the hands of police; and the creation of sanctuary for those facing summary deportation and destruction of their kinship and neighborhood ties.[153]

The possibility of cross-racial alliance has always been there. Examples of solidarity can be found in W. E. B. Du Bois's *Black Reconstruction in America,* as well as fugitive gatherings of escaped enslaved Africans, white bondsmen, and Indigenous communities.[154]

A "unified white caste" is not the natural order of things. White supremacy is fragile and racial capitalism depends upon both the violent subjugation of the other and "keeping whites in line."[155] As Robin D. G. Kelley pointedly conveys, white solidarity is a lie, but a terribly seductive lie.[156]

Unruly alliances are the kinds of coalitional bonds that open outward to recognize shared alienation as part of the neoliberal condition. They can be a response to racial capitalism, as the primary guarantor of wealth and power for the overwhelmingly white, heteronormative fraternity in the Global North. Unlike film or visual media, literature and storytelling illuminate more deliberately and with less gloss the ways sexuality and gender have at times diminished the actual public and psychological wages of whiteness. Both should be considered labor narratives that detail the struggles of those who deviated from the heteropatriarchal mandate during an important transition to capital's global phase in the 1970s. However, liberal trans and queer agendas force cultural criticism to congeal around trans- and homonormativity and the ideal of the liberal, assimilable subject. Through the practice of reading again, we can resist this tendency to view labor and class as subordinate categories.

Vulnerable expressions of masculinity derive their contours from the pleasures and hardships of work, perhaps more powerfully and directly than any other factors, and these aspects of the everyday should not be overlooked. The workplace becomes a powerful location for the denaturalization and transformation of masculinity and whiteness and for the development of unruly alliances that work against the norm of masculine impenetrability. They embrace a sense of a common world that Tom Roach characterizes as "movement, always becoming, never finite, impossible to share, grasp, or 'rule in the name of' in every way that private property is."[157] The bonds these masculinities enjoy often solidify because of, not despite, working-class alienation. They create temporary and fleeting connections through their outsider status and shared activity, which should be read as a hopeful sign of the implacable, unstoppable movement of the heart and the spirit toward mutual aid.

Conclusion
Toward the Future of Masculinity and Relationality

At the time of this writing, the world is witnessing accelerating brutality, perpetrated by both authoritarian regimes and so-called democratic societies. In such a world, where gender, sexuality, and race become primary ways to rationalize direct and covert annihilation, what remains is a state of psychic and material starvation. As sociologist of masculinity R. W. Connell writes, if unchallenged, the centralization across the world of "competitive and dominance-oriented masculinity" will make the trends of military technology, environmental degradation, and increasing economic inequality extremely threatening.[1] To be masculine means in many contexts to uphold the kinds of sexual domination, nationalism, and impenetrability that this book explores.

However, ultimately, normative masculinity is a fragile positionality, resulting from the oscillation between the two poles of hegemony and crisis.[2] Todd Reeser claims that masculinity itself can never be stable because it swings between these two extremes even while it might parade, in a counterfeit fashion, as "free" of gender and "free" of constraint.[3] In this regard, masculinity and capitalism resonate with one another, as both are endowed with the "freedom" to accumulate, to move in and out of neighborhoods through a "right" to gentrify, to dominate in public spaces, etc.[4] However, its inherent fragility means that masculine normativity often disrupts itself, as no subject position or group formation can maintain this kind of drive to be on top in all situations without rupture and contradiction, especially as precarity becomes more and more the norm for nearly everyone. Through exploiting these ruptures and contradictions, cultural forms can play a role in collective efforts to make masculinity more mobile across embodiments and more intent on refusing the seductive lie of gender stasis.

In the first part, the penis/phallus equation conveys not the strength of normative masculinity but rather its weakness, as men become mired in anxiety over the inevitable failure to approximate the phallic ideal. Male anxiety over their phallic prowess is acutely visible in the film *The Crying Game,* in which the character Fergus vomits in response to seeing his girlfriend's penis. This reaction—this loss of bodily control, this sign of penetrability—suggests Fergus's own doubts about his masculinity, for if a woman can also have phallic potential, then the racial and gender categories on which domination depends are collapsible rather than fixed. Fergus's reaction led to a spate of similar media portrayals in which men vomited when trans women's penises came into view, suggesting the power of cultural forms to take control of the narrative and to perpetuate marginalization, ad infinitum. However, culture can play a healing role, as explored through trans and nonbinary poets, who develop mentoring relationships and invent their own imagined boyhoods, challenging the supposed naturalness of boyhood narcissism and sadism, predicated on whiteness. There is no ontological truth to the superiority ascribed to the assigned male penis; rather, those meanings are relentlessly constructed in a range of ways. The question of phallic power, then, must be reassessed as a possibility for all embodiments, gender identifications, and sexualities, which would lead to a universalization of its creative and sexual potential, outside of aggression and total dominance.

In the second part, masculine-nationalism is both challenged and reified in twentieth-century literature and film, suggesting this back-and-forth movement between the poles of hegemony and crisis. Like in so many other genres, the Western acts as both an elixir for this anxiety and its perpetuator, as nationalism is demythologized and revealed to be haunted in some postrevisionist films. In the postwar period, even John Wayne cannot continue the seamless performance of masculine hegemony without being cast in some respects as fraudulent or flawed. However, normative masculinity's staying power and ability to shape-shift are well-captured in the 2016 limited series *Godless.* Even after Frank Griffin's posse is dead, the masculine-presenting Mary Agnes cannot stop shooting at the bodies. I see this not as an irrational or paranoid response but rather as Mary Agnes's recognition that normative masculinity cannot be simply killed off, in part because of its remarkable ability to adapt across time. The archive I have created addresses the possibilities of resisting normativity and allowing something new to take its place. "Killing" normative masculinity does not automatically signal its defeat; rather, there must be emergent forms of care and mutual aid to take its place. In chapter 4, we see how normative masculinity is not a historically homogeneous category, nor is it consistently embodied and performed. However, within the contradictions of their lives and works, Gertrude Stein and Willa Cather connected their own suffering and humiliation to the wounded body-minds of the soldiers returning from World War I, who in turn became avid readers and supporters.

Given the Covid-19 pandemic, and its complex, disabling effects, chapters 5 and 6 are particularly relevant for the current moment, as they offer forms of unruly alliance developed in times of disease and precarity. As Judith Butler wrote in *The Psychic Life of Power* during the height of the AIDS crisis, "The emergence of collective institutions for grieving are thus crucial to survival, to reassembling community, to rearticulating kinship, to reweaving sustaining relations," a fact that is evident in the archive of chapter 5.[5] However, I interpret *institutions* here to mean forms of coming together that do not rely on so-called official forms of support but instead are flexible, nonhierarchical, and responsive to changing conditions and crisis under racial capitalism and white political fraternity. Masculinity, sexuality, and disability exist in dynamic tension with each other in literature, film, and painting of the time, offering how disease and outrageous governmental neglect and victim-blaming force a reckoning with masculine normativity. In *Stone Butch Blues*, the relationship between the shop steward, Duffy, and Jess suggests the need for heterogeneous groups of laborers who understand the necessity of collective organizing. *Stone Butch Blues* makes clear that one single individual cannot fight the abuses of multinational corporations, nor can any single political figure undo centuries of fraternization. The men who expressed their gratitude to Annie Proulx for writing "Brokeback Mountain" offer the ways in which such stories can have a broad impact, potentially influencing heterosexual men as well to admit their own fragility and penetrability. Communities of expression arise around these works, which confirm variability rather than homogeneity. Perhaps after all, masculinity and femininity exist in fractal-like combinations, in fluctuating proportions that are subject to the movement of time and history.

The Covid-19 pandemic has revealed the importance of femininity and the qualities of receptiveness, tenderness, and care with which it is associated, particularly through the life-and-death difference between masculine- and feminine-styled policymaking. As Katie Tyner and Farida Jalalzai reported in the *Washington Post* in December 2022, research has confirmed an earlier narrative in the Covid-19 pandemic that traits associated with female leadership have led to better overall handling of the crisis. These so-called feminine traits include "consensus-oriented governance; honest and frequent communication; enabling agile and adaptive institutions; deference to the advice of scientific experts; collective and decisive action; and guiding policies through empathy and humility."[6] Meanwhile, the United States under former president Donald Trump adopted the exact opposite approach, with the tragic result that many of Trump's own supporters believed that whiteness and masculinity provided a wall of immunity from the virus. Recall the moment Trump declared his own personal victory over Covid-19 in October 2020. In a promotional video, Trump stood on the Truman Balcony and ceremoniously ripped off his mask.[7] Hiding his symptoms and the severity of his condition throughout this period, he convinced the public that only the weak die of Covid-19. On a global level, when white and wealthy countries of the Global North decide that the pandemic has been largely eradicated, marginalized global populations still struggle to obtain adequate amounts of vaccine, which renders these communities feminized and penetrable. Personal triumph over disabling conditions denies intersectional realities and bolsters the hegemony of white, class-privileged masculinity, suggesting they were the ones capable of overcoming while others could not.

As Nikhil Pal Singh observes, Trump is not an anomaly on American soil, nor is he unique in American history. Instead of being seen as a foreign agent that must be defeated, fascism—and its associated masculinities—is the doppelgänger of Democratic liberalism. Manifestations of a fascist mentality have endured across time in the form of plantations, reservations, ghettos, and prisons, and in the more overtly political evasion of constitutional constraints on the frontier, in the colony, in the state of emergency, occupation, and counterinsurgency.[8] As Singh reports, Trump kept Hitler's speeches by his bedside, which confirms the homegrown nature of his brand of fascism as a kind of postmodern pastiche, in line with his—many hoped hyperbolic—admiration for authoritarian leaders like Jair Bolsonaro, Viktor Orbán, Kim Jong-Un, and Vladimir Putin.[9] Certainly, increased militarization domestically, permanent war, and a frontier mentality regarding the "rest of the world" supports Singh's doppelgänger thesis. Trump and his predecessors extended a Jacksonian idealization of democracy, nourished in Jackson's time by racist individualism and settler freedom, a weakened central government, and an increase in violence on the borders and margins.[10] In this respect, the January 6, 2021, assault on the U.S. Capitol, enacted by largely white (and male), organized and semiorganized paramilitary, suggests the worst may be yet to come.

During the global pandemic, a large percentage of women have left careers to take care of children and the home, as some families and companies defaulted to what were considered outdated gender norms.[11] This pervasive default, even in younger, supposedly more progressive groups of people, underscored the actual position of women within a patriarchal civil society, reflected in structural barriers such as lack of access to day care and unfair wages. Meanwhile, it has become obvious how a larger percentage of women of color perform frontline work and are more likely to be exposed to the virus and, further, terminated from their jobs when these positions are (falsely) deemed no longer necessary.[12] Race continues to structure this separation of public and private, and women of color are more likely to be in domestic service positions, jobs that vanished or became more dangerous during the crisis. As Aníbal Quijano notes, this is a historically enduring situation in which, for Black people in particular, "the racial inferiority of the colonized implied that they were not worthy of wages. They were naturally obliged to work for the profit of their owners."[13] Extending his argument to the twentieth century, Quijano writes that it is "not difficult to find, to this very day, this attitude spread out among the white property owners of any place in the world." As shown in chapters 5 and 6, unruly alliances, forged during times of crisis and economic stress, become ways of approaching all relationality during future pandemics and epidemics, as well as economic crises, which are increasing in intensity and speed.

Ultimately, there needs to be a political Left that is not content with postracial bland intellectualizing, thin attempts at representation in television and film, repressive tolerance, and "small-ball, progressive tinkering," which so far have not been able to withstand or deter the forces of repression and social decay that Trump inflicted, culminating in the coup attempt. Trump's election—and his masculinity—were not "unprecedented" but rather the logical next step in a long history of abuses, not least of which is our toxic contribution to the planet's "ecological commons."[14] Trump was not a departure—as many hoped—but a continuation and an attempt to "bring the war home."[15]

However, with all this scrutiny of masculine normativity in the popular press and social media, particularly surrounding Trump and his supporters in the United States, it becomes necessary to ask what really needs critiquing and dismantling. To create lasting change, we need to hold accountable those political, cultural, and familial systems that produce and are produced by masculine normativity, which necessitates an analysis of how these norms are reproduced in social relations and in cultural production. What is needed is an expansion of what relationality can mean, across embodiment, gender identification, and sexuality. The question of care must be a part of this conversation, with the past as resource for the future. Care webs and mutual aid projects suggest their overlapping concerns, but there must be continuing efforts to untether care from the feminine.

Clearly, toxic masculinity is one of many symptom-effects of white supremacy and the hegemony of global capital. The fraternal bond is seductive, and it is difficult, perhaps impossible, to refuse its terms entirely within the current conditions and the bounds/binds of racial capitalism, within its insidious dependence on money, wealth, accumulation, and private property. Dismantling these intertwined power structures may never occur in our lifetimes, but understanding them and responding collectively in whatever way possible can ease the suffering of the moment. The critique of culture, as an ideological conduit, can lead to greater comprehension of these conditions, as well as to the recognition, and further creation, of alternative ways of being. However, these ways of being should not be confused with gender freedom—the idea that one can become free to choose one's gender as an individual and become a free spirit. Rather, by becoming acquainted with uncertainty and chance, we become responsible for collectively thinking and sustaining the future, and capable of enduring, in Jacques Derrida's words, "the intolerable, the undecidable and the terrifying."[16] Sustaining the future can only occur when these devastating realities are confronted head on.

Acknowledgments

Thank you to all the unruly alliances who helped shape the vision of this book. I would not have written this book without my MA thesis committee members and friends at the University of Wyoming: Jeanne Holland, Danielle Pafunda, and Michelle Jarman. You believed in me before I could believe in myself. To the Graduate Center of the City University of New York, Robert Reid-Pharr, and my dissertation committee, Wayne Koestenbaum, Steve Kruger, and Nancy K. Miller: Wayne, you gave me your love of early twentieth-century butches, your spirit of generosity, and an invitation to unruliness in all my work. Steve, thank you for helping put together the archive of chapter 5 on HIV/AIDS and for giving time to early drafts. And to Nancy K. Miller, thank you for urging me to think masculinities and feminism together. Our many spirited conversations continue to inspire and challenge.

I am so grateful to my colleagues, friends, and especially my students at Vanderbilt, who have been my biggest sources of encouragement over the years. Thank you for building community with me in the classroom and for the laughter and intensity you bring into my life. A special thank you to research librarian Melinda Brown, who talked me down from many crises and was always there with a new resource and a listening ear. You have been a dear friend and co-conspirator. Thank you to all who shared their work and time with me, especially Cynthia Cyrus, Gilbert Gonzales, Tara McKay, and Rob Nelson. Thank you to the Department of Gender and Sexuality Studies and to the Vanderbilt School of Medicine and Blair School of Music for inviting me to share across the disciplines on masculinities, disability, and HIV/AIDS.

Thank you to other mentors and guides who have come along at exactly the right time, including Robert McRuer, Alexandre Baril, Greta Olson, and especially Christopher Breu, whose scholarly zeal and attentive reading brought the book to its final form. I am grateful to all the critiques and encouragement from journal editors who published my work: Keri Watson, Timothy W. Hiles, Kimberly M. Jew, Trace Peterson, Maura Sheehy, Lucas Gottzén, Wibke Straube, Francisco J. Galarte, Karen Weingarten, Maria Rice Bellamy, Esther D. Rothblum, LaShawn Harris, and Erin McKenna. I am blessed to have found humanities editor Leah Pennywark at the University of Minnesota Press, who understood my vision from the beginning, and editorial assistant Anne Carter, who patiently answered my many queries.

And to the folks outside academia who cared for me body, mind, and heart. To Edwin, you have been there through it all, and our talks are imprinted everywhere in this book. To Jascha, thanks for the good vibes, the guitar playing, and the scholarly and comedic riffs over the past decade. To Jen and Liz, who introduced me to the work of Andrea Gibson, and to Nat and Bil, I'm honored to have heard your firsthand stories about New York during the HIV/AIDS pandemic in the 1980s and '90s. To Maria, and the rest of my tribe, who show me every day that the future is friendly, even when it does not seem so. And to my mom, and in memory of my dad, Brad Stroup, who passed right before this book's publication. Brad, your presence infuses these pages, and I know you are still with me, smiling from that field beyond binaries, which you spoke of so often. To folks who so freely contributed their work and encouragement in the final stages: Samuel Ace, Nao Bustamante, Minnie Bruce Pratt, Tanesha Tyler at Button Poetry, and Wade Nobile at Alexander Gray Associates, who found the exact right image to pay tribute to artist Hugh Steers, who died of AIDS in 1995.

And most of all, to Carmen and my dog Knox, for sharing life with me and for making so many sacrifices as I labored away on this manuscript over the past few years. Knox, I owe you some walks, buddy.

And to the unruly alliances of the future whom I have yet to meet. I hope this book provides hope in a dark time.

Notes

Introduction

1. Dean Spade and Ciro Carrillo, "What Is Mutual Aid (Classroom Version)," March 25, 2017, YouTube Video, 7:37, https://youtu.be/rYPgTZeF5Z0.

2. Bobby Noble, *Sons of the Movement: FtMs Risking Incoherence on a Post-Queer Cultural Landscape* (Toronto: Women's Books, 2006), 32.

3. Noble, *Sons of the Movement*, 33.

4. Jasbir Puar, *Terrorist Assemblages: Homonationalism in Queer Times* (Durham, N.C.: Duke University Press, 2017), xxiii.

5. Puar, *Terrorist Assemblages*, xxiv.

6. *Hegemonic masculinity*, a term that evolved from sociological studies to describe power dynamics within the workplace and institutions, does not mean that men have total control, as hegemony may be disrupted or disrupt itself. Sociology, together with psychoanalytic work on character and ideas from social movements, allowed sociologists to understand that recognizing diversity in masculinity was not enough; one needed to understand dialectal dynamics, which "do not correspond to the one-way causation of a socialization model." R. W. Connell, *Masculinities*, 2nd ed. (Berkeley: University of California Press, 2005), 37.

7. Robin D. G. Kelley, preface to *Freedom Dreams: The Black Radical Imagination* (Boston: Beacon Press, 2002), xiv–xvii.

8. Robin D. G. Kelley, foreword to *Border and Rule: Global Migration, Capitalism, and the Rise of Racist Nationalism*, by Harsha Walia (Chicago: Haymarket Books, 2021), xv.

9. Kelley, foreword, xv.

10. C. Riley Snorton, *Black on Both Sides: A Radical History of Trans Identity* (Minneapolis: University of Minnesota Press, 2017), 57.

11. Hortense Spillers, "Mama's Baby, Papa's Maybe: An American Grammar Book," *Diacritics* 17, no. 2 (1987): 67.

12. Snorton, *Black on Both Sides*, 96.

13. Angela Davis, "Reflections on Race, Gender, and Class in the U.S.A," in *The Politics of Culture in the Shadow of Capital*, ed. Lisa Lowe and David Lloyd (Durham, N.C.: Duke University Press, 1997), 322.

14. Kale Bantigue Fajardo, *Filipino Crosscurrents: Oceanographies of Seafaring, Masculinities, and Globalization* (Minneapolis: University of Minnesota Press, 2011), 5.

15. Fajardo, *Filipino Crosscurrents*, 31.

16. Jack Halberstam, *Female Masculinity* (Durham, N.C.: Duke University Press, 2011), 9.

17. Halberstam, *Female Masculinity*, 43.

18. Lesbian and trans masculinity have been influenced by their historical connection to available assigned-male masculinities, and it would seem natural and beneficial that masculine-identified people learn from each other.

19. Linda Martín Alcoff, *The Future of Whiteness* (Cambridge: Polity Press, 2015), 157.

20. Alcoff, *Future of Whiteness*, 157.

21. Alcoff, 9.

22. Sara Ahmed, *Queer Phenomenology* (Durham, N.C.: Duke University Press, 2006), 126.

23. Alcoff, *Future of Whiteness*, 8–9, 81.

24. Halberstam, *Female Masculinity*, 3.

25. Lisa Duggan, "The New Homonormativity: The Sexual Politics of Neo-liberalism," in *Materializing Democracy: Toward a Revitalized Cultural Politics*, ed. Russ Castronovo and Dana D. Nelson (Durham, N.C.: Duke University Press, 2002), 190.

26. Miriam J. Abelson, *Men in Place: Trans Masculinity, Race, and Sexuality in America* (Minneapolis: University of Minnesota Press, 2019), 56.

27. Connell, *Masculinities*, 41.

28. As Lauren Berlant insists, masculinity is tied to the symbolic and comes with both the privilege and burden of identifying with/as the Law, offering what Berlant calls a "mirage of identity," a "fixed and monumental presence." "Desire," in *Critical Terms for the Study of Gender*, ed. Gilbert Herdt and Catharine R. Stimpson (Chicago: University of Chicago Press), 88–89.

29. Jack Halberstam, *Queer Art of Failure* (Durham, N.C.: Duke University Press, 2011), 167.

30. Jacques Derrida, *The Politics of Friendship* (New York: Verso, 2006), ix.

31. Nikhil Pal Singh, *Race and America's Long War* (Berkeley: University of California Press, 2017), 165.

32. Grace Kyungwon Hong, *The Ruptures of American Capital: Women of Color Feminism and the Culture of Immigrant Labor* (Minneapolis: University of Minnesota Press, 2006), 17.

33. Hong, xxvi–xxvii; "The Combahee River Collective: A Black Feminist Statement," in *Women's Liberation! Feminist Writings That Inspired a Revolution & Still Can*, ed. Alix Kates Shulman and Honor Moore, 443–52 (New York: Library of America, 2021).

34. Patricia Hill Collins, "What's in a Name? Womanism, Black Feminism, and Beyond," *Black Scholar* 26, no. 1 (Winter/Spring 1996): 14.

35. Michel Foucault, *Ethics: Subjectivity and Truth*, ed. Paul Rabinow, trans. Robert Hurley and others (New York: New Press, 1997), 166.

36. Foucault, *Ethics*, 166.
37. Foucault, 166.
38. Roderick Ferguson, *Aberrations in Black: Toward a Queer of Color Critique* (Minneapolis: University of Minnesota Press, 2004), 14; Dean Spade, *Normal Life: Administrative Violence, Critical Trans Politics, and the Limits of Law* (Durham, N.C.: Duke University Press, 2015), 1; Cathy J. Cohen, "Punks, Bulldaggers, and Welfare Queens: The Radical Potential of Queer Politics?," in *Black Queer Studies: A Critical Anthology*, ed. E. Patrick Johnson and Mae G. Henderson (Durham, N.C.: Duke University Press, 2007), 26.
39. Robert McRuer and Anna Mollow, introduction to *Sex and Disability*, ed. Robert McRuer and Anna Mollow (Durham, N.C.: Duke University Press, 2012), 14.
40. Robert McRuer, *Crip Times: Disability, Globalization, and Resistance* (New York: New York University Press, 2018), 45.
41. Kadji Amin, *Disturbing Attachments: Genet, Modern Pederasty, and Queer History* (Durham, N.C.: Duke University Press, 2017), 113.
42. Amin, *Disturbing Attachments*, 120.
43. Amin, 10.
44. Amin, 11.
45. Leslie Feinberg, *Stone Butch Blues* (1993; Los Angeles: Alyson Publications, 2004); Annie Proulx, "Brokeback Mountain," in *Brokeback Mountain: Story to Screenplay*, ed. Annie Proulx, Larry McMurtry, and Diana Ossana (New York: Scribner, 2005), 2. "Brokeback Mountain" was first published in the *New Yorker* on October 13, 1997.
46. Colleen Lye, *America's Asia: Racial Form and American Literature, 1893–1945* (Princeton, N.J.: Princeton University Press, 2009), 7.
47. Lye, *America's Asia*, 8.
48. Lye, 8.
49. Amin, *Disturbing Attachments*, 13.
50. Leah Lakshmi Piepzna-Samarasinha, *Care Work: Dreaming Disability Justice* (Vancouver: Arsenal Pulp Press, 2018), 18.
51. Hil Malatino, *Trans Care* (Minneapolis: University of Minnesota Press, 2020), 24.
52. Piepzna-Samarasinha, *Care Work*, 44.
53. Piepzna-Samarasinha, 42.
54. Dean Spade, *Mutual Aid: Building Solidarity during This Crisis (and the Next)* (New York: Verso, 2020), 1.
55. Spade, *Mutual Aid*, 2.
56. Dean Spade, "Shit's Totally FUCKED! What Can We Do? A Mutual Aid Explainer," July 9, 2019, YouTube video, 7:54, http://bigdoorbrigade.com/what-is-mutual-aid/.
57. Aren Aizura, "Communizing Care in *Left Hand of Darkness*," *Ada*:

A Journal of Gender, New Media, and Technology, no. 12 (November 2017): https://adanewmedia.org/2017/10/issue12-aizura/.

58. Malatino, *Trans Care,* 71.
59. Malatino, 4–5.
60. Malatino, 2.
61. Spade, *Normal Life,* xvi.
62. Cedric J. Robinson, *Cedric J. Robinson: On Racial Capitalism, Black Internationalism, and Cultures of Resistance,* ed. H. L. T. Quan (London: Pluto Press, 2019), 75. Robinson makes clear how Plato's "episteme" has served to "fertilize and dominate the conceits masqueraded as American democracy" (128).
63. Derrida, *Politics of Friendship,* viii.
64. Derrida, viii.
65. Carole Pateman, "The Fraternal Social Contract," in *The Masculinity Studies Reader,* ed. Rachel Adams and David Savran (Malden, Mass.: Blackwell, 2002), 120.
66. *The Crying Game,* directed by Neil Jordan, featuring Jaye Davidson and Stephen Rea (1992; Los Angeles: Miramax, 2013), DVD.
67. Derrida, *Politics of Friendship,* 79.
68. Martin Legassick and David Hemson, *Foreign Investment in South Africa: A Discussion Series,* No. 2 (London: Anti-Apartheid Movement, 1976), 1–16.
69. Robin D. G. Kelley, foreword to *Black Marxism: The Making of the Black Radical Tradition,* by Cedric J. Robinson (Chapel Hill: University of North Carolina Press, 2020), xiv.
70. Robinson, *Cedric J. Robinson,* 79. This view is still prominent among some neo-Marxists, like Michael Walzer, Walter Benn Michaels, and David Harvey.
71. Eric Foner, *Who Owns History? Rethinking the Past in a Changing World* (New York: Hill and Wang, 2002), 155.
72. Robinson, *Cedric J. Robinson,* 76.
73. Derrida, *Politics of Friendship,* 275.
74. Snorton, *Black on Both Sides,* 10.
75. Robinson, *Cedric J. Robinson,* 112.
76. Robinson, 112.
77. Robinson, 113.
78. Robinson, 112. The full quote from Robinson appears as an epigraph in Alberto Toscano, "Black Sansculottes and Ambitious Marionettes: Cedric J. Robinson, C. L. R. James and the Critique of Political Leadership," *Viewpoint Magazine,* February 16, 2017, https://viewpointmag.com/2017/02/16/black-sansculottes-and-ambitious-marionettes-cedric-j-robinson-c-l-r-james-and-the-critique-of-political-leadership/.
79. *Black Is . . . Black Ain't,* directed by Marlon Riggs, featuring Bill T. Jones, Essex Hemphill, and Marlon Riggs (1995; Signifyin' Works, 2004).

80. Robinson, *Cedric J. Robinson*, 355.
81. Hong, *Ruptures of American Capital*, xxi.
82. Snorton, *Black on Both Sides*, xi.
83. Snorton, 2.
84. Snorton, 7.
85. Snorton, 8.
86. Halberstam, *Queer Art of Failure*, 167.
87. Noble, *Sons of the Movement*, 4.
88. Singh, *Race and America's Long War*, xi.
89. Singh, 106.
90. Singh, 109.
91. Langston Hughes and Christopher C. De Santis, *Let America Be America Again: Conversations with Langston Hughes*, ed. Christopher C. De Santis (Oxford: Oxford University Press, 2022), 46.
92. Robinson, *Cedric J. Robinson*, 150; John Weiss, ed., *The Fascist Tradition* (New York: Harper & Row, 1967); Stein Ugelvik Larsen, Bernt Hagtvet, and Jan Petter Myklebust, ed., *Who Were the Fascists? Social Roots of European Fascism* (New York: Columbia University Press, 1980).
93. Robinson, 150; Stuart Woolf, *Fascism in Europe* (London: Methuen, 1981), 1.
94. Robinson, 152.
95. Robinson, 152.
96. Robinson, 155.
97. Oliver C. Cox, *Caste, Class, and Race* (New York: Monthly Review, 1970), 198.
98. Hong, *Ruptures of American Capital*, xvii.
99. *Godless*, directed by Scott Frank (Netflix, 2017), https://www.netflix.com/title/80097141; *Westworld*, aired October 2, 2016, on HBO, https://play.hbomax.com/player/urn:hbo:episode:GV7xwpQbVEMMbwgEAAAHt.
100. Jessica Nydia Pabón-Colón, *Graffiti Grrlz: Performing Feminism in the Hip Hop Diaspora* (New York: New York University Press, 2018), 72.
101. Singh, *Race and America's Long War*, 165.
102. Hong, *Ruptures of American Capital*, xii.
103. Hong, 69.
104. Aníbal Quijano, "Coloniality of Power, Eurocentrism, and Latin America," *Nepantla: Views from South* 1, no. 3 (2000): 576, https://muse.jhu.edu/article/23906.
105. Todd Reeser, *Moderating Masculinity in Early Modern Culture* (Chapel Hill: University of North Carolina Press, 2006), 30–31.
106. Todd W. Reeser, *Masculinities in Theory*, 1st ed. (Chichester, U.K.: Wiley-Blackwell, 2010), 25.
107. Reeser, *Masculinities in Theory*, 40.
108. Reeser, 40.

109. Halberstam, *Female Masculinity*, 16, emphasis added.
110. Reeser, *Masculinities in Theory*, 10.

1. "She's a Pistol"

1. Todd W. Reeser, *Masculinities in Theory*, 1st ed. (Chichester, U.K.: Wiley-Blackwell, 2010), 16.
2. Reeser, *Masculinities in Theory*, 84–86.
3. Lillian Faderman, *Surpassing the Love of Men: Romantic Friendship and Love between Women from the Renaissance to the Present*, 2nd ed. (New York: HarperCollins, 2001), 29.
4. Faderman, *Surpassing the Love of Men*, 36.
5. Faderman, 29.
6. Reeser, *Masculinities in Theory*, 28.
7. Reeser, 73–74.
8. Kadji Amin, *Disturbing Attachments: Genet, Modern Pederasty, and Queer History* (Durham, N.C.: Duke University Press, 2017), 110.
9. Amin, *Disturbing Attachments*, 110.
10. Aníbal Quijano, "Coloniality of Power, Eurocentrism, and Latin America," *Nepantla: Views from South* 1, no. 3 (2000): 554.
11. Quijano, "Coloniality of Power," 555.
12. Quijano, 555.
13. Jacques Derrida, *The Politics of Friendship* (New York: Verso, 2006), 277.
14. Derrida, *Politics of Friendship*, 237.
15. Derrida, 240.
16. Derrida, 237. This exemplarist logic is apparent in the last words of Jules Michelet's *L'Amour*: "'All I have in this world—my friendships—I offer them up to her, and give to my country the beautiful name handed down by ancient France. I lay them all at the altar of the *Great Friendship*'" (Michelet quoted in Derrida, 238).
17. Derrida, 278.
18. Derrida, 238.
19. Paul B. Preciado, *Countersexual Manifesto* (New York: Columbia University Press, 2018), 5.
20. Preciado, *Countersexual Manifesto*, 5.
21. Jacques Lacan, "The Moral Goals of Psychoanalysis," in *The Seminar of Jacques Lacan, book 7, The Ethics of Psychoanalysis, 1959–1960*, ed. Jacques-Alain Miller, trans. Dennis Porter (New York: W. W. Norton & Company, 1992), 308–9.
22. Judith Buter, "The Lesbian Phallus and the Morphological Imaginary," in *Bodies That Matter: On the Discursive Limits of "Sex"* (New York: Routledge, 1993), 57–92.
23. Judith Butler, *Bodies That Matter: On the Discursive Limits of "Sex"* (New York: Routledge, 1993), 90.

24. Butler, *Bodies That Matter*, 81.
25. Butler, 90.
26. Butler, 74.
27. Viviane K. Namaste, *Invisible Lives: The Erasure of Transsexual and Transgendered People* (Chicago: University of Chicago Press, 2000), 10.
28. Jack Halberstam, *Female Masculinity* (Durham, N.C.: Duke University Press, 1998), 235.
29. Halberstam, *Female Masculinity*, 235.
30. Tom Roach, *Friendship as a Way of Life: Foucault, AIDS, and the Politics of Shared Estrangement* (Albany: State University of New York Press, 2012), 74.
31. Butler, *Bodies That Matter*, 84.
32. Lacan, "Moral Goals of Psychoanalysis," 308–9.
33. K. Allison Hammer, "'Doing Josephine': The Radical Legacy of Josephine Baker's Banana Dance," *WSQ: Women's Studies Quarterly* 48, no. 1/2 (2020): 167, https://doi.org/10.1353/wsq.2020.0010.
34. Hammer, "'Doing Josephine,'" 165.
35. Reeser, *Masculinities in Theory*, 31.
36. Nao Bustamante, *Silver & Gold*, performed by Nao Bustamante et al., 2009, Sundance Film Festival, 45:00, http://naobustamante.com/archive/silver-gold/.
37. Bustamante, *Silver & Gold*.
38. Butler, *Bodies That Matter*, 234.
39. Juana María Rodríguez, *Sexual Futures, Queer Gestures, and Other Latina Longings* (New York: New York University Press, 2014), 6.
40. Amelia Jones, "The Now and the Has Been: Paradoxes of Live Art in History," in *Perform, Repeat, Record: Live Art in History*, ed. Amelia Jones and Adrian Heathfield (Bristol, U.K.: Intellect Books, 2014), 18.
41. Jones, "Now and the Has Been," 12.
42. Jones, 14.
43. Jones, 13.
44. Nao Bustamante, "The Personal Evolution of the Performance Object (Or, What to Do with Leftovers)," in *Perform, Repeat, Record: Live Art in History*, ed. Amelia Jones and Adrian Heathfield (Bristol, U.K.: Intellect Books, 2014), 294.
45. Bustamante, "Personal Evolution of the Performance Object," 297.
46. Bustamante, 298; Rodríguez, *Sexual Futures*, 5.
47. Rodríguez, *Sexual Futures*, 11.
48. Grace Kyungwon Hong, *The Ruptures of American Capital: Women of Color Feminism and the Culture of Immigrant Labor* (Minneapolis: University of Minnesota Press, 2006), 108.
49. Hong, *Ruptures of American Capital*, 108.
50. Hong, 108.
51. Hong, 108.

52. Hong, 109.
53. Hong, xxiv.
54. Guy Debord, *Society of the Spectacle and Other Films* (London: Rebel Press, 1992).
55. Hong, *Ruptures of American Capital*, 133.
56. Hong, 115.
57. Hong, 142.
58. Mel Watkins, *On the Real Side: Laughing, Signifying—The Underground Tradition of African-American Humor That Transformed American Culture, From Slavery to Richard Pryor* (New York: Simon and Schuster, 1999), 25; Bambi Haggins, *Laughing Mad: The Black Comic Persona in Post-Soul America* (New Brunswick, N.J.: Rutgers University Press, 2007).
59. Haggins, *Laughing Mad*, 1.
60. Nao Bustamante, *Indigurrito*, performed by Nao Bustamante et al., 1992, digital recording of a videocassette, 14:32, https://hdl.handle.net/2333.1/m0cfxpz3.
61. Bustamante, "Personal Evolution of the Performance Object," 296.
62. Rodríguez, *Sexual Futures*, 23.
63. Bustamante, "Personal Evolution of the Performance Object," 295.
64. Bustamante, 295.
65. Bustamante, 298.
66. Phillip Auslander, "The Performativity of Performance Documentation," in *Perform, Repeat, Record: Live Art in History*, ed. Amelia Jones and Adrian Heathfield (Bristol, U.K.: Intellect Books, 2014), 49.
67. Jones, "Now and the Has Been," 14.
68. Auslander, "Performativity of Performance Documentation," 47.
69. Auslander, 54.
70. Hammer, "'Doing Josephine,'" 178–79.
71. Hammer, 178–79.
72. Preciado, *Countersexual Manifesto*, 73.
73. Preciado, 135; Hammer, "'Doing Josephine,'" 170.
74. Preciado, 7.
75. Hammer, "'Doing Josephine,'" 172.
76. Preciado, *Countersexual Manifesto*, 66.
77. However, Bustamante refuses Preciado's clear-cut distinction between the penis, as "organic embodiment" of the hegemonic tradition, and the dildo as cyborgian intervention. Such a distinction could have negative consequences for trans women who either decline gender affirmation surgery or are preoperative, or otherwise suffer from shame. Different theorizations of the penis are needed that do not automatically assume its hegemony. I also disagree with Preciado's idea of the dildo as new "origin," wherein the penis becomes a copy of the dildo. The idea of an origin conflicts with his otherwise horizontal schematic of sex and gender possibilities. Preciado, 22.

78. Preciado, 121; Hammer, "'Doing Josephine,'" 177.
79. Preciado, 72, 7; Hammer, 179.
80. Héctor Domínguez-Ruvalcaba, *Translating the Queer: Body Politics and Transnational Conversations* (London: Zed Books, 2017), 12.
81. Domínguez-Ruvalcaba, *Translating the Queer*, 5.
82. Rodríguez, *Sexual Futures*, 2.
83. Butler, *Bodies That Matter*, 89.
84. Anne Anlin Cheng, *Second Skin: Josephine Baker and the Modern Surface* (Oxford: Oxford University Press, 2011), 48.
85. Cheng, *Second Skin*, 47.
86. Hammer, "'Doing Josephine,'" 177.
87. Hammer, 177–78.
88. Preciado, *Countersexual Manifesto*, 73.
89. *Disclosure*, directed by Sam Feder (Netflix, 2020), https://www.netflix.com/title/81284247; *The Crying Game*, directed by Neil Jordan, performed by Jaye Davidson and Stephen Rea (1992; Los Angeles: Miramax, 2013), DVD.
90. *M. Butterfly*, directed by David Cronenberg, performed by Jeremy Irons and John Lone (1993; Burbank, Calif.: Warner Home Video, 2009), DVD.
91. C. Riley Snorton, *Black on Both Sides: A Radical History of Trans Identity* (Minneapolis: University of Minnesota Press, 2017), 185.
92. Miriam J. Abelson, *Men in Place: Trans Masculinity, Race, and Sexuality in America* (Minneapolis: University of Minnesota Press, 2019), 56.
93. Snorton, *Black on Both Sides*, 140.
94. Snorton, 160.
95. Emily Skidmore, "Constructing the 'Good Transsexual': Christine Jorgensen, Whiteness, and Heteronormativity in the Mid-Twentieth-Century Press," *Feminist Studies* 37, no. 2 (2011): 270–300.
96. Snorton, *Black on Both Sides*, 142.
97. Snorton, 143.
98. Snorton, 144.
99. Snorton, 144.
100. Namaste, *Invisible Lives*, 9. Butler's theory of gender performativity relies on the central example of the drag queen but fails to account for sexism within gay male clubs and bars where these drag shows take place. Butler decontextualizes drag and the fact that "elements of femaleness and femininity are highly regulated within gay male consumer culture" (Namaste, 21). Drag queens are entertainment, not lived reality for many. Because it becomes from this viewpoint a kind of "spectacle," the real reasons why one might perform in drag are obscured, which might include exploration of gender identity, gesture of political intervention, creative solution to boredom, or to pay rent, which might not be mutually exclusive (21).

101. Namaste, 12.
102. Namaste, 13.
103. Namaste, 14.
104. Joy Ladin, "Diving into the Wreck: Trans and Anti-trans Feminism," *EOAGH* 9 (2019): https://eoagh.com/diving-into-the-wreck-trans-and-anti-trans-feminism/.
105. Jay Prosser, *Second Skins: The Body Narratives of Transsexuality* (New York: Columbia University Press, 1998), 171.
106. Bobby Noble, *Sons of the Movement: FtMs Risking Incoherence on a Post-Queer Cultural Landscape* (Toronto: Women's Books, 2006), 19.
107. Noble, *Sons of the Movement*, 19–20.
108. Noble, 20.
109. Viviane K. Namaste, *Sex Change, Social Change: Reflections on Identity, Institutions and Imperialism* (Toronto: Women's Press, 2005), 4.
110. Loren Cameron, *Our Vision, Our Voices: Transsexual Portraits and "Nudes,"* 1993, reproduced in Leslie Feinberg, *Transgender Warriors* (Boston: Beacon Press, 1996), 117.
111. Julia Serano, *Whipping Girl* (New York: Seal Press), 229.
112. Dead Spade, *Normal Life: Administrative Violence, Critical Trans Politics, and the Limits of Law* (Durham, N.C.: Duke University Press, 2011), 161.
113. Spade, *Normal Life*, 161.
114. Hil Malatino, *Trans Care* (Minneapolis: University of Minnesota Press, 2020), 26.
115. micha cárdenas, "Shifting Futures: Digital Trans of Color Praxis," *Ada: A Journal of Gender, New Media, and Technology* 6 (2015): https://doi.org/10.7264/N3WH2N8D.
116. Hong, *Ruptures of American Capital*, xxviii.
117. Butler, *Bodies That Matter*, 79.
118. Spade, *Normal Life*, 12.

2. "When I Was a Boy"

1. I place "boyhood" in quotation marks here to indicate the instability of the category, but to avoid confusion, I do not place the term in quotations elsewhere.
2. Emma Pérez, "Gloria Anzaldúa: La Gran Nueva Mestiza Theorist, Writer, Activist-Scholar," *NWSA Journal* 17, no. 2 (2005): 1.
3. Gloria Anzaldúa, *Borderlands/La Frontera: The New Mestiza* (San Francisco: Aunt Lute Foundation, 1987), 19.
4. B. Cole, "Persistence," in *Persistence: All Ways Butch and Femme*, ed. Ivan Coyote and Zena Sharman (Vancouver: Arsenal Pulp Press, 2011), 128.
5. C. Riley Snorton, *Black on Both Sides: A Racial History of Trans Identity* (Minneapolis: University of Minnesota Press, 2017), 175.

Notes to Chapter 2

6. Emma Pérez, "Gloria Anzaldúa: La Gran Nueva Mestiza Theorist, Writer, Activist-Scholar," *NWSA Journal* 17, no. 2 (2005): 3.

7. Trace Peterson, "Becoming a Trans Poet: Samuel Ace, Max Wolf Valerio, and kari edwards," *TSQ: Transgender Studies Quarterly* 1, no. 4 (November 2014): 537. This is the first scholarly journal article to invoke "trans poet" as a unique and specific category.

8. Hil Malatino, *Trans Care* (Minneapolis: University of Minnesota Press, 2020), 68.

9. Sigmund Freud and Jane Temperley, "The Analysis of a Phobia in a Five-Year-Old Boy," in *Freud: A Modern Reader*, ed. Rosine Jozef Perelberg (New York: Routledge, 2005), 68.

10. Ken Corbett, *Boyhoods: Rethinking Masculinities* (New Haven, Conn.: Yale University Press, 2009), 25.

11. Corbett, *Boyhoods*, 48.

12. David Eng, *The Feeling of Kinship: Queer Liberalism and the Racialization of Intimacy* (Durham, N.C.: Duke University Press, 2010), 16.

13. Victor Turner, *Blazing the Trail: Way Marks in the Exploration of Symbols* (Tucson: University of Arizona Press, 1992), 132.

14. Turner, *Blazing the Trail*, 148.

15. Victor Turner, *The Ritual Process: Structure and Anti-structure* (Ithaca, N.Y.: Cornell University Press, 1969), 143.

16. Turner, *Blazing the Trail*, 49.

17. Jacques Derrida, *The Politics of Friendship* (New York: Verso, 2006), 166.

18. Aimé Césaire, "Poetry and Knowledge," in *Refusal of the Shadow: Surrealism and the Caribbean*, ed. and trans. Michael Richardson and Krzysztof Fijalkowski (London: Verso, 1996), 134–46.

19. Robin D. G. Kelley, "'When History Sleeps': A Beginning," in *Freedom Dreams: The Black Radical Imagination* (Boston: Beacon Press, 2002), 45–57.

20. Susan Sontag, "The Third World of Women," *Partisan Review* 40, no. 2 (1973): 181.

21. Peterson, "Becoming a Trans Poet," 523.

22. Peterson, 524.

23. Viviane K. Namaste, *Invisible Lives: The Erasure of Transsexual and Transgendered People* (Chicago: University of Chicago Press, 2000), 1.

24. Jay Prosser, *Second Skins: The Body Narratives of Transsexuality* (New York: Columbia University Press, 1998), 176.

25. Susan Stryker and Paisley Currah, introduction to "Postposttranssexual," *TSQ: Transgender Studies Quarterly* 1, nos. 1–2 (2014): 8.

26. Stryker and Currah, introduction, 8.

27. Grace Kyungwon Hong, *The Ruptures of American Capital: Women of Color Feminism and the Culture of Immigrant Labor* (Minneapolis: University of Minnesota Press, 2006), 58.

28. Gillian Brown, *Domestic Individualism: Imagining Self in Nineteenth-Century America* (Berkeley: University of California Press, 1990), 3.

29. Sandra M. Gilbert and Susan Gubar, *The Madwoman in the Attic: The Woman Writer and the Nineteenth-Century Literary Imagination* (New Haven, Conn.: Yale University Press, 2020), 583.

30. Derrida, *Politics of Friendship*, 78.

31. Emily Dickinson, "Poem VII," in *The Poems of Emily Dickinson*, ed. R. W. Franklin (Cambridge, Mass.: Harvard University Press, 1999).

32. Alfred Habegger, *My Wars Are Laid Away in Books: The Life of Emily Dickinson* (New York: Random House, 2001), 117.

33. Joanne Dobson, *Dickinson and the Strategies of Reticence: The Woman Writer in Nineteenth-Century America* (Bloomington: Indiana University Press, 1989), 13.

34. Dobson, *Dickinson and the Strategies of Reticence*, 10.

35. Dobson, 19.

36. Dobson, 2.

37. Dobson, 9.

38. Gilbert and Gubar, *Madwoman in the Attic*, 6.

39. Gilbert and Gubar, 8. However, I disagree with Gilbert and Gubar that "the phenomenon of male mimicry is itself a sign of female dis-ease, a sign that infection . . . 'in the sentence breed[s]'" (71). Women writers who performed masculinity do not automatically become "males *manques*, mimics who disguised their identities and, denying themselves, produced most frequently a literature of bad faith and inauthenticity" (72).

40. Habegger, *My Wars Are Laid Away in Books*, 229.

41. Emily Dickinson and R. W. Franklin, "Poem 271," in *The Poems of Emily Dickinson*, ed. R. W. Franklin, Variorum ed. (Cambridge, Mass.: Belknap Press of Harvard University Press, 1998), 289. All future direct references to Emily Dickinson poems come from the same source.

42. Here I am consciously referencing the title of the collection *Troubling the Line: Trans and Genderqueer Poetry and Poetics*, ed. TC Tolbert and Trace Peterson (Callicoon, N.Y.: Nightboat Books, 2013).

43. Martha Nell Smith and Ellen Louise Hart, eds., *Open Me Carefully: Emily Dickinson's Intimate Letters to Susan Huntington Dickinson*, 1st ed. (Ashfield, Mass.: Paris Press, 1998), xxiv.

44. Paula Bennett, *Emily Dickinson: Woman Poet*, 2nd ed. (Brighton, U.K.: Edward Everett Root Publishers, 2019), 28.

45. Bennett, *Emily Dickinson*, 85.

46. Sharon Cameron, *Choosing Not Choosing: Dickinson's Fascicles* (Chicago: University of Chicago Press, 1992), 24.

47. Cameron, *Choosing Not Choosing*, 25.

48. Habegger, *My Wars Are Laid Away in Books*, 159.

49. Habegger, 161.

50. Robert McClure Smith, *The Seductions of Emily Dickinson* (Tuscaloosa: University of Alabama Press), 92.
51. Sara Ahmed, *Queer Phenomenology* (Durham, N.C.: Duke University Press, 2006), 78.
52. Eve Kosofsky Sedgwick, *Tendencies* (Durham, N.C.: Duke University Press, 1993), 4.
53. Smith, *Seductions of Emily Dickinson*, 87.
54. Dickinson, "Poem 272," 289.
55. According to Smith, this disruption occurs often enough "that the examination and dismantling of the power dynamic between speaker and her male addressee is the primary theme of the poems." Smith, *Seductions of Emily Dickinson*, 87.
56. Smith, 87.
57. Dickinson, "Poem 1263," 1,089.
58. Bennett, *Emily Dickinson*, 19.
59. Smith, *Seductions of Emily Dickinson*, 92.
60. Dickinson, "Poem 305," 326.
61. Smith, *Seductions of Emily Dickinson*, 95.
62. Smith, 99.
63. Smith, 100.
64. Sedgwick, *Tendencies*, 8.
65. Todd W. Reeser, *Masculinities in Theory* (Chichester, U.K.: Wiley-Blackwell, 2010), 40.
66. Robert McRuer, *Crip Theory: Cultural Signs of Queerness and Disability* (New York: New York University Press, 2006), 165.
67. Ahmed, *Queer Phenomenology*, 58.
68. Peterson, "Becoming a Trans Poet," 525.
69. Eric Foner, *Who Owns History? Rethinking the Past in a Changing World* (New York: Hill and Wang, 2002), 70–71.
70. Bobby Noble, "Our Bodies Are Not Ourselves: Tranny Guys and the Racialized Class Politics of Incoherence," in *The Transgender Studies Reader 2*, ed. Susan Stryker and Aren Z. Aizura, 248–57 (New York: Routledge, 2013).
71. Peterson, "Becoming a Trans Poet," 531.
72. Samuel Ace, *Meet Me There: Normal Sex and Home in Three Days, Don't Wash* (New York: Belladonna, 2020), 13.
73. Peterson, "Becoming a Trans Poet," 531.
74. TC Tolbert, "Prayer for Us, In the Wilderness," in *Meet Me There: Normal Sex and Home in Three Days, Don't Wash*, by Samuel Ace (New York: Belladonna, 2020), 170.
75. Peterson, "Becoming a Trans Poet," 531.
76. Cameron Awkward-Rich, "Linda Smukler's Trans Poetics," in *Meet Me There: Normal Sex and Home in Three Days, Don't Wash*, by Samuel Ace (New York: Belladonna, 2020), 161.

77. Joan Nestle, "My Letter of Appreciation," in *Meet Me There: Normal Sex and Home in Three Days, Don't Wash*, by Samuel Ace (New York: Belladonna, 2020), 164.

78. Peterson, "Becoming a Trans Poet," 525.

79. J. M. Barrie, *"Peter Pan" and "Peter Pan in Kensington Gardens"* (London: Arcturus, 2019); *Peter Pan,* directed by Clyde Geronimi, Wilfred Jackson, and Hamilton Luske (1953; Walt Disney Productions, 2018), DVD.

80. Samuel Ace in discussion with the author, August 2022.

81. Linda Smukler (Samuel Ace), *Normal Sex* (Ithaca, N.Y.: Firebrand Books, 1994), 29.

82. K. Allison Hammer, "Radical 'Boyhood' Futures for the Twenty-First Century, or Pinocchio (Finally) Gets His Phallus," *Studies in Gender and Sexuality* 20, no. 3 (2019): 182, https://doi.org/10.1080/15240657.2019.1641944.

83. Smukler (Ace), *Normal Sex,* 22.

84. Smukler (Ace), 22.

85. Smukler (Ace), 22.

86. Smukler (Ace), 24.

87. Smukler (Ace), 24.

88. Peterson, "Becoming a Trans Poet," 525.

89. Peterson, 530.

90. Awkward-Rich, "Linda Smukler's Trans Poetics," 162.

91. Smukler (Ace), *Normal Sex,* 41.

92. Ace, *Meet Me There,* 15.

93. Ace, 15.

94. Andrea Gibson, interview by Tig Notaro, "The Pioneering Poet," *Interview,* April 22, 2015, https://www.interviewmagazine.com/culture/andrea-gibson.

95. Lisa Tedesco, "Andrea Gibson: Behind the Words," *Curve* (blog), July 9, 2010, https://www.curvemag.com/blog/interview-culture/andrea-gibson-behind-the-words/.

96. Gibson, "Pioneering Poet."

97. Marcie Bianco, "Andrea Gibson: Speaking of Genderqueer—The Poet as Out Oracle," *Curve,* December/January 2018, 53.

98. "Tour," Andrea Gibson, accessed August 10, 2020, www.andreagibson.org/tour.

99. Andrea Gibson et al., "It's Okay to Fall Apart," Zoom, September 19, 2020.

100. Robert McRuer, "Composing Queerness and Disability: The Corporate University and Alternative Corporealities," in *Crip Theory: Cultural Signs of Queerness and Disability* (New York: New York University Press, 2006), 149.

101. Gibson, "Pioneering Poet."

102. Andrea Gibson, *Lord of the Butterflies: Poems* (Minneapolis: Button Poetry/Exploding Pinecone Press, 2019), 25.
103. Gibson, "Pioneering Poet."
104. Gibson, *Lord of the Butterflies*, 16.
105. Andrea Gibson, *Pansy*, 1st ed. (Austin: Write Bloody Publishing, 2015), 33.
106. Gibson, *Lord of the Butterflies*, 4.
107. Gibson, 67.
108. Gibson, 85.
109. Gibson, *Pansy*, 19.
110. Gibson, *Lord of the Butterflies*, 4–5.
111. Gibson, 5.
112. TC Tolbert, introduction to *Troubling the Line*, ed. TC Tolbert and Trace Peterson (Callicoon, N.Y.: Nightboat Books, 2013), 9.
113. Emma Pérez, *The Decolonial Imaginary: Writing Chicanas into History* (Bloomington: University of Indiana Press, 1999), xix.
114. Eileen Myles, "Poem," in *Troubling the Line*, ed. TC Tolbert and Trace Peterson (Callicoon, N.Y.: Nightboat Books, 2013), 177.

3. The "Not (Quite) Yet" of a New Collectivity

1. Bob Woodward, *Bush at War* (New York: Simon & Schuster, 2002), 168.
2. Barry Langford, "Revising the 'Revisionist' Western," *Film and History* 33, no. 2 (2003): 34; Nikhil Pal Singh, *Race and America's Long War* (Berkeley: University of California Press, 2017), 118.
3. Grace Kyungwon Hong, *The Ruptures of American Capital: Women of Color Feminism and the Culture of Immigrant Labor* (Minneapolis: University of Minnesota Press, 2006), 8.
4. Eric Foner, *Who Owns History? Rethinking the Past in a Changing World* (New York: Hill and Wang, 2002), 57.
5. Singh, *Race and America's Long War*, xvii.
6. Cedric J. Robinson, *Cedric J. Robinson: On Racial Capitalism, Black Internationalism, and Cultures of Resistance*, ed. H. L. T. Quan (London: Pluto Press, 2019), 76.
7. The Philippines was a U.S. colony from 1898 to 1946, which unsettles the U.S. claim to innocence. Bush's words suggest a recombinant state formation in which brute force can and must be used, at the same time that neocolonial global influence is disavowed. Hong, *Ruptures of American Capital*, 144.
8. Singh, *Race and America's Long War*, 118; Thomas Barnett, *The Pentagon's New Map: War and Peace in the Twenty-First Century* (New York: G. P. Putnam's Sons, 2004).
9. Mark E. Wildermuth, *Feminism and the Western in Film and Television* (Cham, Switzerland: Palgrave Macmillan, 2019), 147.

10. Jessica Nydia Pabón-Colón, *Graffiti Grrlz: Performing Feminism in the Hip Hop Diaspora* (New York: New York University Press, 2018), 46–47.

11. Homi K. Bhabha, "Are You a Man or a Mouse?," in *Constructing Masculinity*, ed. Maurice Berger, Brian Wallis, and Simon Watson (New York: Routledge, 1995), 55.

12. *OED Online*, s.v. "disturb, v.," https://www-oed-com.proxy.library.vanderbilt.edu/view/Entry/55820?isAdvanced=false&result=2&rskey=aggl4l.

13. Hong, *Ruptures of American Capital*, xi.

14. Hong, xvi.

15. Todd W. Reeser, *Masculinities in Theory*, 1st ed. (Chichester, U.K.: Wiley-Blackwell, 2010), 141.

16. Singh, *Race and America's Long War*, 17.

17. Benedict R. Anderson, *Imagined Communities: Reflections on the Origins and Spread of Nationalism*, rev. ed. (London: Verso, 2006), 7.

18. Aníbal Quijano, "Coloniality of Power, Eurocentrism, and Latin America," *Nepantla: Views from South* 1, no. 3 (2000): 557, https://www.muse.jhu.edu/article/23906.

19. Anderson, *Imagined Communities*, 7; Quijano, "Coloniality of Power," 557.

20. Quijano, 557–58.

21. Joane Nagel, "Masculinity and Nationalism: Gender and Sexuality in the Making of Nations," *Ethnic and Racial Studies* 21, no. 2 (1998): 244. This "renaissance" gave rise to the modern Olympic movement in 1896 and boys' and men's lodges and fraternal organizations, such as the Knights of Columbus.

22. Nagel, "Masculinity and Nationalism," 245.

23. Nagel, 251.

24. Nagel, 252.

25. Singh, *Race and America's Long War*, 158.

26. Singh, 158; John Lewis Gaddis, *Surprise, Security, and the American Experience* (Cambridge, Mass.: Harvard University Press, 2004).

27. David Lusted, *The Western* (Oxon, U.K.: Routledge, 2014), 4.

28. Mary Lea Bandy and Kevin Stoehr, *Ride, Boldly Ride: The Evolution of the American Western* (Berkeley: University of California Press, 2012), 5.

29. Bandy and Stoehr, *Ride, Boldly Ride*, 280.

30. Immanuel Kant, *Metaphysics of Morals* (1797), in *Political Writings* (Cambridge: Cambridge University Press, 1970), 170; Singh, *Race and America's Long War*, 143.

31. James Baldwin and William F. Buckley Jr., *Debate: Baldwin vs. Buckley* (Greenwood, Ind.: Educational Video Group, 1965).

32. Singh, *Race and America's Long War*, 119.

33. Singh, 171.

34. Carl Schmitt, *Political Theology: Four Chapters on the Concept of Sovereignty*, trans. George Schwab (Cambridge, Mass.: MIT Press, 1986), 5.

35. Singh, *Race and America's Long War*, 119. As the ACLU reports, the USA PATRIOT (Uniting and Strengthening America by Providing Appropriate Tools Required to Intercept and Obstruct Terrorism) Act violated five amendments of the Bill of Rights when it gave a secretive government the legal authority for unconstitutional powers. Robinson, *Cedric J. Robinson*, 169.

36. Adolf Hitler, *Mein Kampf* (Boston: Houghton Mifflin, 1939).

37. Hitler, *Mein Kampf*, 419.

38. Singh, *Race and America's Long War*, 120.

39. Quijano, "Coloniality of Power," 561.

40. Quijano, 541.

41. Jacques Derrida, "The Phantom Friend Returning," in *The Politics of Friendship* (New York: Verso, 2006), 75–111.

42. Carl Schmitt, *The Concept of the Political*, trans. George Schwab (Chicago: University of Chicago Press, 2007), 35.

43. Schmitt, *Political Theology*, 6.

44. Schmitt, 5.

45. Derrida, *Politics of Friendship*, 104.

46. Derrida, 105.

47. Schmitt, *Concept of the Political*, 29.

48. Derrida, *Politics of Friendship*, 87.

49. Derrida, 99–100.

50. Derrida, 104–5.

51. Schmitt, *Concept of the Political*, 35.

52. Derrida, *Politics of Friendship*, 129.

53. Schmitt, *Concept of the Political*, 35.

54. Schmitt, 35; Derrida, *Politics of Friendship*, 130.

55. Schmitt, 35.

56. Derrida, *Politics of Friendship*, 116.

57. Derrida, 117.

58. Carl Schmitt, *Theory of the Partisan: Intermediate Commentary on the Concept of the Political*, trans. G. L. Ulmen (Candor, N.Y.: Telos Press, 2007).

59. Schmitt, *Theory of the Partisan*, 10–11.

60. Derrida, *Politics of Friendship*, 148. The philosophical theory of the partisan is taken up in real time by Lenin, whom Schmitt admires, and later by Mao. Schmitt, *Theory of the Partisan*, 8.

61. Derrida, 138.

62. Schmitt, *Theory of the Partisan*, 28.

63. Schmitt, 11.

64. Derrida, *Politics of Friendship*, 148.

65. Derrida, 149.

66. Derrida, 150.

67. Derrida, 156.
68. Derrida, 157.
69. Schmitt, *Concept of the Political*, 9.
70. Derrida, *Politics of Friendship*, 165.
71. Derrida, 159.
72. Derrida, 92–93.
73. Jim Kitses and Gregg Rickman, *The Western Reader* (New York: Limelight Editions, 2010), 19.
74. André Bazin, "The Evolution of the Western," in *The Western Reader*, ed. Jim Kitses and Gregg Rickman, 49–56 (New York: Limelight, 1998); Bandy and Stoehr, *Ride, Boldly Ride*, 7.
75. Bandy and Stoehr, 185.
76. Bandy and Stoehr, 187.
77. Nancy Schoenberger, *Wayne and Ford: The Films, the Friendship, and the Forging of an American Hero* (New York: Nan A. Talese Doubleday, 2017), 27.
78. Reeser, *Masculinities in Theory*, 26.
79. Maureen T. Schwarz, "Searching for a Feminist Western: *The Searchers, The Hired Hand,* and *The Missing*," *Visual Anthropology* 27, nos. 1–2 (2014): 45.
80. Fran Pheasant-Kelly, "Gender Politics in the Revisionist Western: Interrogating the Perpetrator-Victim Binary in *The Missing*," in *Women in the Western*, ed. Sue Matheson (Edinburgh: Edinburgh University Press, 2020), 6.
81. Ron Lackmann, *Women of the Western Frontier in Fact, Fiction and Film* (Jefferson, N.C.: McFarland, 1997), 120.
82. Phil Hardy, *The Western* (Woodstock, N.Y: Overlook Press, 1994), 470.
83. Lusted, *Western*, 254; *Calamity Jane*, directed by David Butler, featuring Doris Day, Howard Keel, and Allyn Ann McLerie (1953; Warner Bros., 2005), DVD.
84. Pheasant-Kelly, "Gender Politics in the Revisionist Western," 5.
85. Bandy and Stoehr, *Ride, Boldly Ride*, 198; *The Man Who Shot Liberty Valance*, directed by John Ford, featuring John Wayne, James Stewart, and Vera Miles (1962; Paramount Pictures, 2005), DVD.
86. Bandy and Stoehr, *Ride, Boldly Ride*, 200.
87. Bandy and Stoehr, 201.
88. Bandy and Stoehr, 200.
89. Lusted, *Western*, 7.
90. Lusted, 250.
91. Lusted, 252.
92. Pam Cook, "Women in the Western," in *The BFI Companion to the Western*, ed. Edward Buscombe (London: British Film Institute/André Deutsch, 1988), 295.

93. Gaylyn Studlar and Matthew Bernstein, introduction to *John Ford Made Westerns: Filming the Legend in the Sound Era*, ed. Gaylyn Studlar and Matthew Bernstein (Bloomington: Indiana University Press, 2001), 11.

94. Lee Russell, "Budd Boetticher," in *The Western Reader*, ed. Jim Kitses and Gregg Rickman (New York: Limelight Editions, 1998), 200.

95. Bandy and Stoehr, *Ride, Boldly Ride*, 201.

96. Bandy and Stoehr, 202.

97. John Cawelti, *The Six-Gun Mystique Sequel* (Bowling Green, Ohio: Bowling Green State University Popular Press, 1999), 29.

98. Bandy and Stoehr, *Ride, Boldly Ride*, 205.

99. Eve Kosofsky Sedgwick, *Epistemology of the Closet* (Berkeley: University of California Press, 2008), 15.

100. Reeser, *Masculinities in Theory*, 49.

101. Reeser, 50.

102. Jasbir K. Puar, *Terrorist Assemblages: Homonationalism in Queer Times* (Durham, N.C.: Duke University Press, 2017), 50–51.

103. *Man Who Shot Liberty Valance*.

104. The audience would have recognized Jimmy Stewart in this role from previous films in which he plays men caught between dedication to civic justice and the possibility of the need for violence. He played the gun-wary lawman of *Destry Rides Again* (1939), an idealistic senator in Capra's *Mr. Smith Goes to Washington* (1939), and psychologically and morally complex protagonists in Mann's Westerns (e.g., *Bend of the River* [1952], *The Naked Spur* [1953], and *The Man from Laramie* [1955]) and in Hitchcock's thrillers (e.g., *Rear Window* [1954] and *Vertigo* [1958]). Bandy and Stoehr, *Ride, Boldly Ride*, 208.

105. Bandy and Stoehr, *Ride, Boldly Ride*, 208.

106. Bandy and Stoehr, 209.

107. Bandy and Stoehr, 209.

108. *Man Who Shot Liberty Valance*.

109. Bandy and Stoehr, *Ride, Boldly Ride*, 212.

110. *Man Who Shot Liberty Valance*.

111. Bandy and Stoehr, *Ride, Boldly Ride*, 213.

112. Bandy and Stoehr, 204.

113. *Man Who Shot Liberty Valance*.

114. Bandy and Stoehr, *Ride, Boldly Ride*, 214.

115. Bandy and Stoehr, 214.

116. Bandy and Stoehr, 214.

117. Langford, "Revising the 'Revisionist' Western," 28.

118. *Johnny Guitar*, directed by Nicholas Ray, featuring Joan Crawford, Mercedes McCambridge, and Sterling Hayden (1954; Republic Pictures, 2012), DVD.

119. Cook, "Women in the Western," 298.

120. Cook, 299.

121. Cook, 299.

122. Jack Halberstam, *Female Masculinity* (Durham, N.C.: Duke University Press, 1998), 194–95.

123. Jennifer Peterson, "The Competing Tunes of 'Johnny Guitar': Liberalism, Sexuality, Masquerade," *Cinema Journal* 35, no. 3 (1996): 4–6.

124. Lusted, *Western*, 258.

125. Lusted, 258.

126. Jennifer Peterson, "'Maybe He's Tough but He Sure Ain't No Carpenter': Masculinity and In/competence in *Unforgiven*," in *The Western Reader*, ed. Jim Kitses and Gregg Rickman (New York: Limelight Editions, 1998), 334.

127. *Johnny Guitar*.

128. Peterson, "Maybe He's Tough," 336.

129. Molly Haskell, "The Woman's Film," in *Feminist Film Theory: A Reader*, ed. Susan Thornham (New York: New York University Press, 1999), 29.

130. Catherine Russell, "Johnny Guitar (Video Recording Review)," *Cineaste*, March 22, 2017, 61.

131. Reeser, *Masculinities in Theory*, 53.

132. Iris Marion Young, *On Female Body Experience: "Throwing like a Girl" and Other Essays* (New York: Oxford University Press, 2010), 32.

133. Sara Ahmed, *Living a Feminist Life* (Durham, N.C.: Duke University Press), 235.

134. Derrida, *Politics of Friendship*, 99.

135. Derrida, 100.

136. Derrida, 244.

137. Christopher Wicking and Barrie Pattison, interview with Anthony Mann, in *The Western Reader*, ed. Jim Kitses and Gregg Rickman, 201–8 (New York: Limelight, 1998); Bandy and Stoehr, *Ride, Boldly Ride*, 1.

138. Derrida, *Politics of Friendship*, 165.

139. Sophocles, *Antigone*, trans. Reginald Gibbons, and Charles Segal (Oxford: Oxford University Press, 2003), 78.

140. Sophocles, *Antigone*, 102.

141. Judith Butler, *Antigone's Claim: Kinship between Life and Death* (New York: Columbia University Press, 2000).

142. Martin Holtz, "The Female Avenger in Post-9/11 Westerns," *Women in the Western*, ed. Sue Matheson (Edinburgh: Edinburgh University Press, 2020), 1.

143. *Deadwood*, directed by David Milch, aired March 21, 2004, on HBO, https://play.hbomax.com/page/urn:hbo:page:GVU2b2A6ZF47DwvwIAT34:type:series.

144. Langford, "Revising the 'Revisionist' Western," 34.

145. Singh, *Race and America's Long War*, 28.

146. Robinson, *Cedric J. Robinson*, 165.

147. Singh, *Race and America's Long War*, 13.

148. Singh, 15.
149. Singh, 100.
150. Wildermuth, *Feminism and the Western*, 46.
151. Lynn Spigel, "Entertainment Wars: Television Culture after 9/11," *American Quarterly* 56, no. 2 (2014): 246.
152. Susan Faludi, *The Terror Dream: Fear and Fantasy in Post-9/11 America*, 1st ed. (New York: Metropolitan Books, 2007), 148.
153. Rebecca Bell-Metereau, "Crazy Like a Prof: Mad Science and the Transgressions of the Rational," in *Bad: Infamy, Darkness, Evil, and Slime on Screen*, ed. Murray Pomerance (Albany: State University of New York Press, 2004), 143; Holtz, "Female Avenger," 14.
154. Holtz, "Female Avenger," 13.
155. Pheasant-Kelly, "Gender Politics in the Revisionist Western," 6. As Pheasant-Kelly also suggests, Westerns dominated by women persisted and are increasing in output in the 2020s, but they tend to feature a single female lead (5).
156. Pheasant-Kelly, 10.
157. Maria Cecília de Miranda N. Coelho, "Horses for Ladies, High-Ridin' Women, and Whores," in *Iconography and Archetypes in Western Film and Television*, ed. Sue Matheson (Jefferson, N.C.: McFarland, 2017), 113.
158. Pheasant-Kelly, "Gender Politics in the Revisionist Western," 10.
159. *Godless*, directed by Scott Frank, aired November 22, 2017, on Netflix, https://www.netflix.com/title/80097141.
160. Stella Hockenhull, "Women Gotta Gun? Iconograpy and Female Representation in *Godless*," in *Women in the Western*, ed. Sue Matheson (Edinburgh: Edinburgh University Press, 2022), 2.
161. Richard Slotkin, *Gunfighter Nation: The Myth of the Frontier in Twentieth-Century America* (Norman: University of Oklahoma Press, 1998), 270.
162. Sabine Sielke, *Reading Rape: The Rhetoric of Sexual Violence in American Literature and Culture, 1790–1990* (Princeton, N.J.: Princeton University Press, 2009), 2.
163. Phillip R. Loy, *Westerns in a Changing America, 1955–2000* (New York: McFarland, 2015), 277, 276.
164. Maria Cecília de Miranda N. Coelho, "'We Been Haunted a Long Time': Raped Women in Westerns," in *Women in the Western*, ed. Sue Matheson (Edinburgh: Edinburgh University Press, 2022), 187–200.
165. Coelho, "'We Been Haunted a Long Time,'" 196.
166. *Godless*, episode 1, "An Incident at Creede," directed by Scott Frank, aired November 22, 2017, on Netflix, https://www.netflix.com/title/80097141.
167. Ann Cvetkovich, *An Archive of Feelings: Trauma, Sexuality, and Lesbian Public Cultures* (Durham, N.C.: Duke University Press, 2003), 119.
168. Nagel, "Masculinity and Nationalism," 256.

169. Terry Gross, "*Godless* Creator Scott Frank/Allison Janney," August 29, 2018, in *Fresh Air*, produced by WHYY and NPR, podcast, 48:00, https://www.npr.org/2018/08/29/643020122/godless-creator-scott-frank-allison-janney. Scott Frank was inspired by spaghetti Western director Sergio Leone.

170. *Godless*, episode 4, "Fathers & Sons," directed by Scott Frank, aired November 22, 2017, on Netflix, https://www.netflix.com/title/80097141.

171. Hockenhull, "Women Gotta Gun?," 9.

172. *Godless*, episode 7, "Homecoming," directed by Scott Frank, aired November 22, 2017, on Netflix, https://www.netflix.com/title/80097141.

173. Gross, "*Godless* Creator." Host Terry Gross remarks on how Mary Agnes's character seems to be offering a powerful vision of what it would have been like if the Magnificent Seven had been women.

174. Hockenhull, "Women Gotta Gun?," 5.

175. *The Ballad of Little Jo*, directed by Maggie Greenwald, featuring Suzy Amis, Bo Hopkins, and Ian McKellan (1993; New Line Home Video, 2003), DVD.

176. Lusted, *Western*, 238.

177. Lusted, 244.

178. Hockenhull, "Women Gotta Gun?," 4–5.

179. Young, *Throwing like a Girl*, 43.

180. Hockenhull, "Women Gotta Gun?," 6.

181. Coelho, "Horses for Ladies," 116.

182. Hockenhull, "Women Gotta Gun?," 6.

183. Hockenhull, 7.

184. Hockenhull, 8.

185. Hockenhull, 5.

186. *Westworld*, created by Lisa Joy and Jonathan Nolan, aired October 2, 2016, on HBO (HBO Entertainment, Kilter Films, Bad Robot Productions, Warner Bros. Television).

187. *Westworld*, directed by Michael Crichton, featuring Yul Brynner, Richard Benjamin, and James Brolin (1973; Warner Home Video, 2000), DVD.

188. Brian Tallerico, "The Long, Weird History of the Westworld Franchise," *Vulture*, September 3, 2016, https://www.vulture.com/2016/09/westworld-franchise-long-weird-history.html.

189. Lusted, *Western*, 237–38.

190. Homi K. Bhabha, *The Location of Culture* (London, U.K.: Routledge, 2004), 2.

191. Sigmund Freud, *The Uncanny* (London, U.K.: Penguin, 2003).

192. Bhabha, *Location of Culture*, 2.

193. Bhabha, 19.

194. Langford, "Revising the 'Revisionist' Western," 28.

195. William Shakespeare, *Romeo and Juliet* (Auckland: Floating Press, 2009), 100.

196. Bhabha, *Location of Culture*, 13.

197. *Unforgiven*, directed by Clint Eastwood, featuring Clint Eastwood, Gene Hackman, and Morgan Freeman (1992; Warner Bros., 2010), DVD.

198. *Westworld*, season 1, episode 4, "Dissonance Theory," directed by Vincenzo Natali, aired October 23, 2016, on HBO.

199. Bhabha, "Are You a Man or a Mouse?," 57.

200. Hong, *Ruptures of American Capital*, 20.

201. *Buck the Preacher*, directed by Sidney Poitier, featuring Sidney Poitier, Harry Belafonte, and Ruby Dee (1972; Sony Pictures Home Entertainment, 2000), DVD.

202. Singh, *Race and America's Long War*, 21.

203. H. L. T. Quan, foreword to *Cedric J. Robinson: On Racial Capitalism, Black Internationalism, and Cultures of Resistance*, by Cedric J. Robinson, ed. H. L. T. Quan (London: Pluto Press, 2019), 4.

204. Victoria Hesford and Lisa Diedrich, "Thinking Feminism in a Time of War," in *Feminist Time against Nation Time: Gender, Politics, and the Nation-State in an Age of Permanent War*, ed. Victoria Hesford and Lisa Diedrich (Lanham, Md.: Lexington Books, 2011), 9.

205. Snorton, *Black on Both Sides*, 195.

206. *Godless*, episode 2, "The Ladies of La Belle," directed by Scott Frank, aired November 22, 2017, on Netflix, https://www.netflix.com/title/80097141.

207. Leah Lakshmi Piepzna-Samarasinha, *Care Work: Dreaming Disability Justice* (Vancouver: Arsenal Pulp Press, 2018), 42.

208. Dean Spade, *Normal Life: Administrative Violence, Critical Trans Politics, and the Limits of Law* (Durham, N.C.: Duke University Press, 2011), 161.

4. Virtue Is Divided

1. Jasbir K. Puar, *The Right to Maim: Debility, Capacity, Disability* (Durham, N.C.: Duke University Press, 2017), 34.

2. Jacques Derrida, *The Politics of Friendship* (New York: Verso, 2006), 159; 42.

3. K. Allison Hammer, "Epic Stone Butch: Transmasculinity in the Works of Willa Cather," *TSQ: Transgender Studies Quarterly* 7, no. 1 (2020): 81, https://doi.org/10.1215/23289252-7914528.

4. Kadji Amin, *Disturbing Attachments: Genet, Modern Pederasty, and Queer History* (Durham, N.C.: Duke University Press, 2017), 4.

5. Amin, *Disturbing Attachments*, 9.

6. Amin, 11.

7. Amin, 9.

8. Derrida, *Politics of Friendship*, 42.

9. Michel Foucault, "Friendship as a Way of Life," in *Ethics: Subjectivity, and Truth*, ed. Paul Rabinow, trans. Robert Hurley et al. (New York: New Press, 1997), 137.

10. Ulla E. Dydo, *Gertrude Stein: The Language That Rises, 1923–1934* (Evanston, Ill.: Northwestern University Press, 2008), 13.

11. Gertrude Stein, "If I Told Him: A Completed Portrait of Picasso (1923)," in *A Stein Reader*, ed. Ulla E. Dydo (Evanston, Ill.: Northwestern University Press, 1993), 466.

12. See Sharon O'Brien, *Willa Cather: The Emerging Voice* (Oxford: Oxford University Press, 1987); Hammer, "Epic Stone Butch," 82.

13. Jean E. Mills, "Gertrude Stein Took the War like a Man," *Gay and Lesbian Review Worldwide* 10, no. 2 (2003): 17.

14. Mills, "Gertrude Stein," 18.

15. Gertrude Stein, *Tender Buttons*, ed. Seth Perlow (1914; San Francisco: City Lights Press, 2014), 31.

16. Diana Souhami, *Gertrude and Alice* (London: Pandora, 1991), 288.

17. Carl Van Vechten and Gertrude Stein, *The Letters of Gertrude Stein and Carl Van Vechten, 1913–1946*, ed. Edward Burns (New York: Columbia University Press, 2013), 4.

18. O'Brien, *Willa Cather*, 121.

19. Nikhil Pal Singh, *Race and America's Long War* (Berkeley: University of California Press, 2017), 94.

20. Singh, *Race and America's Long War*, 94.

21. W. E. B. Du Bois and Mack H. Jones, *Black Reconstruction in America: Toward a History of the Part of Which Black Folk Played in the Attempt to Reconstruct Democracy in America, 1860–1880* (London: Routledge, 2017), 626.

22. Singh, *Race and America's Long War*, 140–41; Aníbal Quijano, "Coloniality of Power, Eurocentrism, and Latin America," *Nepantla: Views from South* 1, no. 3 (2000): 561.

23. Singh, 140–41.

24. Singh, 96.

25. Grace Kyungwon Hong, *The Ruptures of American Capital: Women of Color Feminism and the Culture of Immigrant Labor* (Minneapolis: University of Minnesota Press, 2006), viii.

26. Cheryl I. Harris, "Whiteness as Property," *Harvard Law Review* 106, no. 8 (June): 1,729.

27. Emily Skidmore, *True Sex: The Lives of Trans Men at the Turn of the Twentieth Century* (New York: New York University Press, 2017), 60.

28. Miriam J. Abelson, *Men in Place: Trans Masculinity, Race, and Sexuality in America* (Minneapolis: University of Minnesota Press, 2019), 203.

29. Jasbir Puar, *Terrorist Assemblages: Homonationalism in Queer Times* (Durham, N.C.: Duke University Press, 2017), 8.

30. Linda Martín Alcoff, *The Future of Whiteness* (Cambridge: Polity Press, 2015), 103.

31. Hammer, "Epic Stone Butch," 81; David L. Eng, *The Feeling of Kinship: Queer Liberalism and the Racialization of Intimacy* (Durham, N.C.: Duke University Press, 2010), 13.

32. Christopher Nealon, *Foundlings: Lesbian and Gay Historical Emotion before Stonewall* (Durham, N.C.: Duke University Press, 2001), 92.

33. Lisa Ruddick, *Reading Gertrude Stein: Body, Text, Gnosis* (Ithaca, N.Y.: Cornell University Press, 1990), 127.

34. Gertrude Stein, "An Instant Answer or a Hundred Prominent Men," in *The Geographical History of America or the Relation of Human Nature to the Human Mind* (1936; Baltimore: Johns Hopkins University Press, 1995).

35. Ruddick, *Reading Gertrude Stein*, 23.

36. Otto Weininger, *Sex and Character* (Bloomington: Indiana University Press, 2005), 276.

37. Weininger, *Sex and Character*, 231.

38. Barbara Will, *Unlikely Collaboration: Gertrude Stein, Bernard Faÿ, and the Vichy Dilemma* (New York: Columbia University Press, 2015), 37.

39. Weininger, *Sex and Character*, 231.

40. Weininger, 231.

41. Barbara Will, *Gertrude Stein, Modernism, and the Problem of "Genius"* (Edinburgh: Edinburgh University Press, 2000), 4.

42. Lucy Daniel, *Gertrude Stein* (London: Reaktion, 2009), 15.

43. Henry Miller, *The Cosmological Eye* (1961; Norfolk, Conn.: New Directions, 2013), 120.

44. Iris Marion Young, *On Female Body Experience: "Throwing like a Girl" and Other Essays* (New York: Oxford University Press, 2010), 129.

45. Gertrude Stein, *The Making of Americans* (1925; Normal, Ill.: Dalkey Archive Press, 1995), 609.

46. Derrida, *Politics of Friendship*, 22.

47. Derrida, xi.

48. Derrida, xi.

49. Aristotle and Peter L. P. Simpson, *The Eudemian Ethics of Aristotle* (Somerset: Taylor & Francis Group, 2013), 1239a26–33, 150.

50. Derrida, *Politics of Friendship*, 7.

51. Derrida, 7.

52. Derrida, 7.

53. Derrida, 7.

54. Derrida, 10.

55. Derrida, 10. Derrida notes that the "reciprocalist or *mutualist* schema of requited friendship" is found in both *Eudemian Ethics* (1239a 4, 20) and in *Nicomachean Ethics* (1159b, rev. Oxford trans.).

56. Aristotle and Simpson, *Eudemian Ethics of Aristotle*, 144.

57. Derrida, 42.

58. Aristotle and Simpson, *Eudemian Ethics of Aristotle*, 1234b18–b21.
59. Derrida, 8.
60. Siegfried Sassoon, *The War Poems of Siegfried Sassoon* (London: W. Heinemann, 1919), 40.
61. Susan Sontag, *Regarding the Pain of Others* (New York: Picador, 2003), 25.
62. Willa Cather, "The Namesake," *McClure's*, March 28, 1907, https://cather.unl.edu/ss003.html.
63. O'Brien, *Willa Cather*, 258.
64. Willa Cather, *The Selected Letters of Willa Cather*, ed. Andrew Jewell and Janis Stout (New York: Knopf, 2012), 66.
65. Cather, *Selected Letters of Willa Cather*, xi.
66. Cather, xi.
67. Cather, 561.
68. Willa Cather and Janet Sharistanian, *My Ántonia* (1918; Oxford: Oxford University Press, 2006), 17.
69. "#2256: Willa Cather to Meta Schaper Cather, December 27 [1918]," in *The Complete Letters of Willa Cather*, Willa Cather Archive, accessed January 23, 2018, https://cather.unl.edu/writings/letters/let2077.
70. Hammer, "Epic Stone Butch," 90.
71. Cather, *Selected Letters*, 256.
72. Hammer, "Epic Stone Butch," 87.
73. O'Brien, *Willa Cather*, 240.
74. Cather, *Selected Letters*, 336–37.
75. Cather, 318.
76. Hermione Lee, *Willa Cather: Double Lives* (New York: Vintage, 1989), 173.
77. Willa Cather, *One of Ours* (New York: Knopf, 1922), 244.
78. Cather, *One of Ours*, 335.
79. Cather, 453.
80. Hammer, "Epic Stone Butch," 90.
81. Cather, *Selected Letters*, 309–10.
82. Hammer, "Epic Stone Butch," 90.
83. Lee, *Willa Cather*, 180; Hammer, "Epic Stone Butch," 90.
84. Lee, 177.
85. Hammer, "Epic Stone Butch," 90.
86. Hammer, 90.
87. Lee, *Willa Cather*, 180.
88. K. Allison Hammer, "Doing Josephine: The Radical Legacy of Josephine Baker's Banana Dance," *Women's Studies Quarterly* 48, no. 1/2 (2020): 170, https://doi.org/10.1353/wsq.2020.0010.
89. Bennetta Jules-Rosette, *Josephine Baker in Art and Life: The Icon and the Image* (Urbana: University of Illinois Press, 2007), 151–52.
90. Jeremy Braddock and Jonathan P. Eburne, introduction to *Paris,*

Capital of the Black Atlantic: Literature, Modernity, and Diaspora, ed. Jeremy Braddock and Jonathan P. Eburne (Baltimore: Johns Hopkins University Press, 2013), 4.

91. Terri Francis, "Embodied Fictions, Melancholy Migrations: Josephine Baker's Cinematic Celebrity," in *Paris, Capital of the Black Atlantic: Literature, Modernity, and Diaspora*, ed. Jeremy Braddock and Jonathan P. Eburne (Baltimore: Johns Hopkins University Press, 2013), 142.

92. Braddock and Eburne, introduction, 5.

93. Dydo, *Gertrude Stein*, 161.

94. Gertrude Stein, *Everybody's Autobiography* (New York: Random House, 1937), 133.

95. Will, *Unlikely Collaboration*, 96.

96. Barbara Will, *Unlikely Collaboration: Gertrude Stein, Bernard Faÿ, and the Vichy Dilemma* (New York: Columbia University Press, 2011).

97. Singh, *Race and America's Long War*, 113.

98. Singh, 113.

99. Gertrude Stein, *Useful Knowledge* (1928; Barrytown, N.Y.: Station Hill Press, 2001), 80.

100. Ruddick, *Reading Gertrude Stein*, 189.

101. Carl Van Vechten and Gertrude Stein, *The Letters of Gertrude Stein and Carl Van Vechten, 1913–1946*, ed. Edward Burns (New York: Columbia University Press, 2013), 29.

102. Stein and Van Vechten, *Letters*, 28.

103. Ulla E. Dydo, introduction to "Pink Melon Joy," in *A Stein Reader*, ed. Ulla E. Dydo (Evanston, Ill.: Northwestern University Press, 1993), 280.

104. Gertrude Stein, "Pink Melon Joy," in *A Stein Reader*, ed. Ulla Dydo (Evanston, Ill.: Northwestern University Press, 1993), 288.

105. Stein, "Pink Melon Joy," 288.

106. Stein, 297.

107. Gertrude Stein, *Lucy Church Amiably* (1930; Normal, Ill.: Dalkey Archive Press, 2000), 171. Future citations to this work will be in text.

108. Janet Malcolm, *Two Lives: Gertrude and Alice* (New Haven, Conn.: Yale University Press, 2007), 8.

109. Gertrude Stein, *The Autobiography of Alice B. Toklas* (New York: Penguin, 2001), 8. In addition, the income she garnered from family investments was dwindling, and she needed the money in order to continue living the upper-middle-class lifestyle to which she and Toklas had become accustomed.

110. Stein, *Autobiography of Alice B. Toklas*, 144.

111. Stein, 13.

112. Stein, 203.

113. Gertrude Stein, *Wars I Have Seen* (1945; London: Brilliance Books, 1984), 77.

114. Ruddick, *Reading Gertrude Stein*, 179.

115. Dydo, *Gertrude Stein*, 172.
116. Gertrude Stein, *Stanzas in Meditation: The Corrected Edition*, ed. Susannah Hollister and Emily Setina (1933; New Haven, Conn.: Yale University Press, 2012), 61.
117. Ulla Dydo, "Stanzas in Meditation: The Other Autobiography," *Chicago Review* 35, no. 2 (1985): 14.
118. Jean Mills, "Gertrude on the Block: Writing, Love, and Fame in *Stanzas in Meditation*," *Philological Quarterly* 83, no. 2 (2014): 197.
119. Dydo, "Stanzas in Meditation," 14.
120. Dydo, *Language That Rises*, 511.
121. Dydo, "Stanzas in Meditation," 18.
122. Stein, *Stanzas in Meditation*, 76.
123. Stein, *Wars I Have Seen*.
124. Will, *Unlikely Collaboration*, 48.
125. Will, 22.
126. Cather, *Selected Letters*, 359.
127. Carole Pateman, "The Fraternal Social Contract," in *The Masculinity Studies Reader*, ed. Rachel Adams and David Savran (Malden, Mass.: Blackwell, 2002), 120.
128. Derrida, *Politics of Friendship*, 302.
129. Derrida, 302.
130. Heather Love, *Feeling Backward: Loss and the Politics of Queer History* (Cambridge, Mass.: Harvard University Press, 2010).
131. Amin, *Disturbing Attachments*, 108.
132. Jack Halberstam, *Queer Art of Failure* (Durham, N.C.: Duke University Press, 2011), 164.

5. "Skin of His Hand against the Skin of My Back"

1. Aníbal Quijano, "Coloniality of Power, Eurocentrism, and Latin America," *Nepantla: Views from South* 1, no. 3 (2000): 561. The coloniality of power based on race as an instrument of domination has always been a limiting factor for constructing nation-states based on a Eurocentric model. The degree of limitation depends upon the proportion of colonized races within the total population and on the density of their social and cultural institutions (570).
2. Grace Kyungwon Hong, *The Ruptures of American Capital: Women of Color Feminism and the Culture of Immigrant Labor* (Minneapolis: University of Minnesota Press, 2006), 134.
3. Hong, *Ruptures of American Capital*, 135.
4. Eric Foner, *Who Owns History? Rethinking the Past in a Changing World* (New York: Hill and Wang, 2002), 170.
5. As a historian, Foner contends that "whether one believes in the jurisprudence of original intent or in a vision of the Constitution informed by a broad understanding of our nation's past, an appreciation of history

is essential for anyone attempting to confront the continuing racial dilemmas of our society." Foner, *Who Owns History?*, 188.

6. Foner, 68. Foner cites a 1958 essay in which Sir Isaiah Berlin sharply criticizes the U.S. perspective on freedom, as promotion of a "negative freedom" as the absence of external obstacles to satisfy desires. Isaiah Berlin, *Four Essays on Liberty* (New York: Oxford University Press, 1969), xliii–xlix.

7. Robin D. G. Kelley, foreword to *Border and Rule: Global Migration, Capitalism, and the Rise of Racist Nationalism*, by Harsha Walia (Chicago: Haymarket Books, 2021), xv.

8. Jasbir K. Puar, *Terrorist Assemblages: Homonationalism in Queer Times* (Durham, N.C.: Duke University Press, 2017), xxiii.

9. Puar, *Terrorist Assemblages*, xxiii. Patriotic masculinities must first identify the terrorist and either discipline, incorporate, or expel this "true [feminine] queer" (xxiii).

10. Anne Fausto-Sterling, *Sexing the Body: Gender Politics and the Construction of Sexuality* (New York: Basic Books, 2000), 311.

11. Christina Sharpe, *In the Wake: On Blackness and Being* (Durham, N.C.: Duke University Press, 2016), 38.

12. Michel Foucault, "Friendship as a Way of Life," in *Ethics: Subjectivity and Truth*, ed. Paul Rabinow, trans. Robert Hurley and others (New York: New Press, 1997), 135–40.

13. Hugh Steers, *Bath Curtain*, 1992, oil on canvas, 64½ × 72½ in (163.8 × 184.2 cm), Alexander Gray Associates, New York.

14. Michel Foucault, *Ethics: Subjectivity and Truth*, ed. Paul Rabinow, trans. Robert Hurley and others (New York: New Press, 1997), 136.

15. Tom Roach, *Friendship as a Way of Life: Foucault, AIDS, and the Politics of Shared Estrangement* (Albany: State University of New York Press, 2012), 139.

16. Michel Foucault, "Society Must Be Defended, 17 March 1976," in *Cultural Theory: An Anthology*, ed. Timothy Kaposy and Imre Szeman (West Sussex, U.K.: Wiley-Blackwell, 2011), 125.

17. Nikhil Pal Singh, *Race and America's Long War* (Berkeley: University of California Press, 2017), 153–54.

18. Cedric J. Robinson, "Race, Capitalism, and the Anti-democracy," in *Cedric J. Robinson: On Racial Capitalism, Black Internationalism, and Cultures of Resistance*, ed. H. L. T. Quan (London: Pluto Press, 2019), 332–33.

19. Singh, *Race and America's Long War*, 129.

20. Robinson, "Race, Capitalism, and the Anti-democracy," 333.

21. Foner, *Who Owns History?*, 69.

22. Singh, *Race and America's Long War*, 127.

23. Singh, 129.

24. Sean Wilentz, *The Age of Reagan: A History, 1974–2008* (New York: Harper Perennial, 2009), 185.

25. Patrick J. Buchanan, "Homosexuals and Retribution," *New York Post*, May 24, 1983.
26. Wilentz, *Age of Reagan*, 185.
27. Wilentz, 186.
28. Foucault, "Friendship as a Way of Life," 136–37.
29. Foucault, 136.
30. Foucault, 136.
31. Foucault, 136.
32. Foucault, 136.
33. Kadji Amin, *Disturbing Attachments: Genet, Modern Pederasty, and Queer History* (Durham, N.C.: Duke University Press, 2017), 15.
34. Amin, *Disturbing Attachments*, 15.
35. Amin, 22.
36. Amin, 22. In 1970s and '80s France, French gay liberationists embraced pederasty as a challenge to the bourgeois family, parents' possessive attitudes toward their children, and minors' rights to express their sexuality (23).
37. Foucault, "Friendship as a Way of Life," 138.
38. Jacques Derrida, *The Politics of Friendship* (New York: Verso, 2006), 281.
39. Derrida, *Politics of Friendship*, 279.
40. Derrida, 290.
41. Derrida, 292–93.
42. Derrida, 293.
43. Maurice Blanchot, *L'amitié* (Paris: Gallimard, 1971), 328–29, emphasis added by Derrida.
44. Derrida, *Politics of Friendship*, 295.
45. Derrida, 295–96.
46. Derrida, 299.
47. Lennard J. Davis, *Bending Over Backward: Disability, Dismodernism, and Other Difficult Positions* (New York: New York University Press, 2002), 30.
48. Abby Wilkerson, "Normate Sex and Its Discontents," in *Sex and Disability*, ed. Robert McRuer and Anna Mollow (Durham, N.C.: Duke University Press, 2012), 205.
49. Wilkerson, "Normate Sex," 204.
50. Anna Mollow and Robert McRuer, introduction to *Sex and Disability*, ed. Robert McRuer and Anna Mollow (Durham, N.C.: Duke University Press, 2012), 3.
51. Robert McRuer, *Crip Theory: Cultural Signs of Queerness and Disability* (New York: New York University Press, 2006), 80.
52. Mollow and McRuer, introduction, 1.
53. Mollow and McRuer, 24.
54. Kelley, foreword, xv.

55. Callan Morse, "Global Expertise Called on to Reduce Indigenous Incarceration in South Australia," *National Indigenous Times*, October 4, 2022, https://nit.com.au/04-10-2022/4018/global-expertise-called-on-to-reduce-indigenous-incarceration-in-south-australia.

56. Timothy Conigrave, *Holding the Man* (1995; New York: Penguin, 1998), 127. All further citations to this work will be parenthetical in the text.

57. Audre Lorde, "Uses of the Erotic: The Erotic as Power," in *Sister Outsider: Essays and Speeches* (Trumansburg, N.Y.: Crossing Press, 1984), 53–59.

58. Foucault, *Ethics*, 136–37.

59. John Foster, *Take Me to Paris, Johnny*, 1st ed. (Melbourne: Text Publishing, 2016), 133.

60. Foster, *Take Me to Paris*, 148.

61. Roach, *Friendship as a Way of Life*, 129.

62. Todd W. Reeser, *Masculinities in Theory* (Chichester, U.K.: Wiley-Blackwell, 2010), 40.

63. Amin, *Disturbing Attachments*, 36.

64. Amin, 31.

65. Hong, *Ruptures of American Capital*, viii.

66. Hong, ix.

67. Singh, *Race and America's Long War*, 17. To link domestic and foreign war, it is important to understand that the military police involved in torture at Guantánamo were trained in onshore U.S. prisons.

68. Cedric J. Robinson, "Fascism and the Response of Black Radical Theorists," in *Cedric J. Robinson: On Racial Capitalism, Black Internationalism, and Cultures of Resistance*, ed. H. L. T. Quan (London: Pluto Press, 2019), 153.

69. Aníbal Quijano, *Nationalism and Capitalism in Peru: A Study in Neo-imperialism*, trans. Helen R. Lane (New York: Monthly Review Press, 1971), 6–7.

70. Katherine A. Gordy, "Strategies of Imperialism and Opposition in Cuba: Reflections on the Purity of Anti-imperialism," *Viewpoint Magazine*, February 1, 2018, https://viewpointmag.com/2018/02/01/strategies-imperialism-opposition-cuba-reflections-purity-anti-imperialism/.

71. Quijano, *Nationalism and Capitalism*, 49.

72. Reinaldo Arenas, *Before Night Falls*, trans. Dolores M. Koch (New York: Penguin Books, 2020), 165. All further citations to this work will be parenthetical in the text.

73. *Black Is . . . Black Ain't*, directed by Marlon Riggs, featuring Bill T. Jones, Essex Hemphill, and Marlon Riggs (1995; Signifyin' Works, 2004), DVD.

74. The works of E. P. Thompson, Eric Hobsbawm, and other British

scholars of "history from below" came to be called the "new social history." Foner, *Who Owns History?*, 11.

75. Foner, xii.

76. Foner, xii.

77. "Marlon Riggs—October 2007" (Q & A), Jim Crow Museum, Ferris State University, October 2007, https://www.ferris.edu/HTMLS/news/jimcrow/question/2007/october.htm.

78. "User Clip: Pat Buchanan Ad Featuring Tongues Untied," Presidential Campaign Commercials 1992, February 28, 1992, C-SPAN, 00:32, https://www.c-span.org/video/?c4679699/user-clip-pat-buchanan-ad-featuring-tongues-untied.

79. Marlon T. Riggs, "Meet the New Willie Horton," *New York Times*, late edition, East Coast, March 6, 1992, A33.

80. David Mills, "The Director with Tongue Untied," *Washington Post*, June 15, 1992, https://www.washingtonpost.com/archive/lifestyle/1992/06/15/the-director-with-tongue-untied/4ba20897-fa8c-4506-bffc-cc56e2fb1dd4/.

81. Foner, *Who Owns History?*, xv.

82. Kara Keeling, "'Joining the Lesbians': Cinematic Regimes of Black Lesbian Invisibility," in *Black Queer Studies: A Critical Anthology*, ed. E. Patrick Johnson and Mae G. Henderson (Durham, N.C.: Duke University Press, 2005), 215.

83. Singh, *Race and America's Long War*, 8.

84. Hong, *Ruptures of American Capital*, viii.

85. Robin D. G. Kelley, "When History Sleeps," in *Freedom Dreams: The Black Radical Imagination* (Boston: Beacon Press, 2002), 1–12.

86. Sharpe, *In the Wake*, 5.

87. C. Riley Snorton, *Black on Both Sides: A Racial History of Trans Identity* (Minneapolis: University of Minnesota Press, 2017), 74.

88. Snorton, *Black on Both Sides*, 74.

89. Hortense Spillers, "Mama's Baby, Papa's Maybe: An American Grammar Book," in *Black, White, and in Color: Essays on American Literature and Culture* (Chicago: University of Chicago Press, 2003), 101.

90. Snorton, *Black on Both Sides*, 103.

91. Frantz Fanon, *Black Skin, White Masks*, trans. Charles Lam Markmann (New York: Grove Press, 1967), 8. As Snorton writes, the Black man can never be the "Enlightenment man," but rather he results from the "antinomic projections that center him in a universe that requires his destruction." Snorton, *Black on Both Sides*, 105.

92. Snorton, 108.

93. Snorton, 129.

94. E. Patrick Johnson, "'Quare' Studies, or (Almost) Everything I Know about Queer Studies I Learned from My Grandmother" in *Black*

Queer Studies: A Critical Anthology, ed. by E. Patrick Johnson and Mae G. Henderson (Durham, N.C.: Duke University Press, 2005), 143.

95. "The Combahee River Collective: A Black Feminist Statement," in *Women's Liberation! Feminist Writings That Inspired a Revolution and Still Can,* ed. Alix Kates Shulman and Honor Moore (New York: Library of America, 2021), 443–52.

96. Hong, *Ruptures of American Capital,* xxxii–xxxiii.

97. Johnson, "'Quare' Studies," 143.

98. Johnson, 141; bell hooks, *Yearning* (Boston: South End, 1990), 26.

99. Johnson, 143.

100. Roderick Ferguson, *Aberrations in Black: Toward a Queer of Color Critique* (Minneapolis: University of Minnesota Press, 2004), 58.

101. *Black Is . . . Black Ain't,* directed by Marlon Riggs.

102. Johnson, "'Quare' Studies," 145.

103. Kara Keeling, "LOOKING FOR M—: Queer Temporality, Black Political Possibility, and Poetry from the Future," *GLQ* 15, no. 4 (2009): 566.

104. Spillers, "Mama's Baby," 101.

105. Snorton, *Black on Both Sides,* 185.

106. Foner, *Who Owns History?,* 70.

6. "A Man Is a Worker"

1. David Brody, *Workers in Industrial America: Essays on the Twentieth Century Struggle,* 2nd ed. (New York: Oxford University Press, 1993), 254–55.

2. Richard Ford, introduction to *Blue Collar, White Collar, No Collar: Stories of Work,* ed. Richard Ford (New York: Harper Perennial, 2011), x–xi.

3. Miriam Abelson, *Men in Place: Trans Masculinity, Race, and Sexuality in America* (Minneapolis: University of Minnesota Press, 2019), 23.

4. David L. Eng, *The Feeling of Kinship: Queer Liberalism and the Racialization of Intimacy* (Durham, N.C.: Duke University Press, 2010), 34.

5. Karl Marx, *Economic and Philosophic Manuscripts of 1844* (n.p.: Wilder Publications, 2018), 125.

6. Sidney Lens, "Labor and Capital Today and Tomorrow," in *Working for Democracy: American Workers from the Revolution to the Present,* ed. Paul Buhle and Alan Dawley (Urbana: University of Illinois Press, 1985), 141.

7. Lens, "Labor and Capital," 141.

8. Susan Sontag, "The Third World of Women," *Partisan Review* 40, no. 2 (1973): 181.

9. Jay Prosser, *Second Skins: The Body Narratives of Transsexuality* (New York: Columbia University Press, 1998), 177.

10. In this chapter, I use *she/zie* and *hir* pronouns for Feinberg. As partner Minnie Bruce Pratt explained when Feinberg died, Feinberg was very

agnostic about which pronouns she/zie wanted people to use, but hir preference when referencing hirself was *she/zie* and *hir*. See "Self," Leslie Feinberg, www.lesliefeinberg.net/self/.

11. Leslie Feinberg, *Stone Butch Blues* (1993; Los Angeles: Alyson Publications, 2004), afterword. All further citations to this work will be parenthetical in the text.

12. Minnie Brue Pratt in discussion with the author, August 2022.

13. In *Second Skins*, Prosser writes on how Feinberg fought against class bias in order to have the book read as a novel rather than an autobiography. Feinberg wrote to Prosser in an email that "an elitist class bias has been revealed to me by some who have conveyed their assumption that a blue-collar person, who lacks extended formal education, could not possibly write about anything except their own life." Jay Prosser, *Second Skins: The Body Narratives of Transsexuality* (New York: Columbia University Press, 1998), 199.

14. Feinberg, *Transgender Warriors*, 89.

15. I use *butch lesbian* to indicate Jess's identity, but the confusion over whether we are reading a trans or a butch lesbian body suggests the "unstable border" between these categories. For more on this instability, as well as the "border wars," see Feinberg, *Transgender Warriors*, 92; K. Allison Hammer, "Invited to Gaze: Butch Characters and the Trope of Mental Illness in American Postwar Film," *NORMA: International Journal for Masculinity Studies* 11, no. 4 (2017): 287–300; Patricia Elliot, *Debates in Transgender, Queer, and Feminist Theory: Contested Sites* (New York: Taylor and Francis, 2016), 48.

16. Kadji Amin, *Disturbing Attachments: Genet, Modern Pederasty, and Queer History* (Durham, N.C.: Duke University Press, 2017), 24.

17. Amin, *Disturbing Attachments*, 31.

18. Kale Bantigue Fajardo, *Filipino Crosscurrents: Oceanographies of Seafaring, Masculinities, and Globalization* (Minneapolis: University of Minnesota Press, 2011), 153.

19. Fajardo, *Filipino Crosscurrents*, 163.

20. Fajardo, 167.

21. Fajardo, 162.

22. Fajardo, 164.

23. Fajardo, 154.

24. The CIO emerged in the 1930s in response to the growth of a large, permanent class of industrial proletarians, who were eager to be organized since the 1910s. The CIO was also the first to include women on a large scale in the 1930s. As New Labor historian Barbara Mayer Wertheimer explains, women were on equal footing with men; they sat in and took over factories to win union recognition in garment plants, Pennsylvania coal towns, five-and-dime stores in New York, drug stores in Detroit, and pecan farms in Texas. Barbara Mayer Wertheimer, "Women Workers," in

Working for Democracy: American Workers from the Revolution to the Present, ed. Paul Buhle and Alan Dawley (Urbana: University of Illinois Press, 1985), 116.

25. Brody, *Workers in Industrial America,* 14.
26. Brody, 116, 121.
27. Brody, 121.
28. George Lipsitz, "Labor and the Cold War," in *Working for Democracy: American Workers from the Revolution to the Present,* ed. Paul Buhle and Alan Dawley (Urbana: University of Illinois Press, 1985), 104.
29. Lipsitz, "Labor and the Cold War," 106.
30. Lipsitz, 111.
31. Lipsitz, 106–7.
32. Lipsitz, 111.
33. Lipsitz, 111–12.
34. Lipsitz, 107.
35. Lipsitz, 108–9.
36. Brody, *Workers in Industrial America,* 183.
37. Paul Buhle, *Taking Care of Business: Samuel Gompers, George Meany, Lane Kirkland, and the Tragedy of American Labor* (New York: Monthly Review Press, 1999), 127.
38. Buhle, *Taking Care of Business,* 166.
39. Buhle, 128.
40. Buhle, 136.
41. Buhle, 186.
42. Feinberg, *Transgender Warriors,* 8.
43. Feinberg, 11; W. E. B. Du Bois and Mack H. Jones, *Black Reconstruction in America: Toward a History of the Part of Which Black Folk Played in the Attempt to Reconstruct Democracy in America, 1860-1880* (London: Routledge, 2017), 626.
44. Buhle, *Taking Care of Business,* 172.
45. Manning Marable, "Black Insurgency," in *Working for Democracy: American Workers from the Revolution to the Present,* ed. Paul Buhle and Alan Dawley (Urbana: University of Illinois Press, 1985), 125.
46. Marable, "Black Insurgency," 126.
47. Brody, *Workers in Industrial America,* 6. Brody's use of the word *he* throughout this work suggests how the masculine gender pronoun has been a default in this historical work more generally. To account for the fact that most factory workers today are young women of color in the developing world, I have changed the pronoun to the more neutral *they* whenever possible.
48. Brody, 8.
49. Brody, 11.
50. Grace Kyungwon Hong, *The Ruptures of American Capital: Women of*

Color Feminism and the Culture of Immigrant Labor (Minneapolis: University of Minnesota Press, 2006), 73.

51. Ann Cvetkovich, "Untouchability and Vulnerability: Stone Butchness as Emotional Style," in *Butch/Femme: Inside Lesbian Gender*, ed. Sally R. Munt (London: Cassell, 1998), 159.

52. Ann Cvetkovich, *An Archive of Feelings: Trauma, Sexuality, and Lesbian Public Cultures* (Durham, N.C.: Duke University Press, 2003), 4.

53. Cvetkovich, *Archive of Feelings*, 4.

54. Jack Halberstam, "Between Butches," in *Butch/Femme: Inside Lesbian Gender*, ed. Sally R. Munt (London: Cassell, 1998), 65; Jack Halberstam, *Female Masculinity* (Durham, N.C.: Duke University Press, 2011), 139.

55. Wertheimer, "Women Workers," 121.

56. Lisa Lowe, *Immigrant Acts: On Asian American Cultural Politics* (Durham, N.C.: Duke University Press, 1996), 36.

57. Hong, *Ruptures of American Capital*, 39.

58. Michel Foucault, "Of Other Spaces: Utopias and Heterotopias," trans. Jay Miskowiec, in *Architecture Mouvement Continuité*, October 1984, 3.

59. Brody, *Workers in Industrial America*, 189.

60. Buhle, *Taking Care of Business*, 204.

61. Brody, *Workers in Industrial America*, 189.

62. Brody, 189–90.

63. Fajardo, *Filipino Crosscurrents*, 14.

64. Lipsitz, "Labor and the Cold War," 112.

65. Brody, *Workers in Industrial America*, 218.

66. Brody, 193.

67. Brody, 219.

68. Brody, 220.

69. Brody, 221.

70. Brody, 138.

71. Buhle, *Taking Care of Business*, 182. Meany was known for gay-baiting as "fags" the Democratic "peacenik" delegates from New York City.

72. Ronald Reagan (candidate for Governor of California), interviewed in the *Fresno Bee*, October 10, 1965.

73. Wilentz, *Age of Reagan*, 20.

74. Brody, *Workers in Industrial America*, 226.

75. Buhle, *Taking Care of Business*, 185.

76. Buhle, 186.

77. Buhle, 200.

78. Buhle, 186.

79. Wilentz, *Age of Reagan*, 24.

80. Wilentz, 22.

81. Wilentz, 20.

82. Buhle, *Taking Care of Business*, 200, 186.

83. Buhle, 187.

84. Buhle, 188.
85. Prosser, *Second Skins*, 184.
86. Buhle, *Taking Care of Business*, 195.
87. Brody, *Workers in Industrial America*, 229.
88. Buhle, *Taking Care of Business*, 197.
89. Buhle, 198.
90. Buhle, 199.
91. Buhle, 215.
92. Buhle, 199.
93. Brody, *Workers in Industrial America*, 233.
94. Buhle, *Taking Care of Business*, 199.
95. Brody, *Workers in Industrial America*, 231.
96. Brody, 227.
97. Brody, 231.
98. Brody, 232.
99. Buhle, *Taking Care of Business*, 200.
100. Prosser, *Second Skins*, 186.
101. Prosser, 188.
102. Wertheimer, "Women Workers," 118.
103. Buhle, *Taking Care of Business*, 204.
104. Brody, *Workers in Industrial America*, 244.
105. Brody, 248–49.
106. Brody, 249.
107. Brody, 227.
108. Brody, 262.
109. Brody, 254–55.
110. Brody, 255.
111. Lipsitz, "Labor and the Cold War," 112–13.
112. Lens, "Labor and Capital," 142.
113. Buhle, *Taking Care of Business*, 256.
114. Eric Foner, *Who Owns History? Rethinking the Past in a Changing World* (New York: Hill and Wang, 2002), 6.
115. Buhle, *Taking Care of Business*, 204.
116. Buhle, 263.
117. Marable, "Black Insurgency," 133.
118. Marable, 130.
119. Marable, 133.
120. Marable, 132.
121. Marable, 132.
122. Buhle, *Taking Care of Business*, 260.
123. Buhle, 256.
124. Buhle, 262.
125. Buhle, 262.
126. Buhle, 263.

127. "National Film Registry Turns 30: 'Brokeback Mountain,' 'Jurassic Park,' 'My Fair Lady' among the Titles Added," Library of Congress, December 12, 2018, https://www.loc.gov/item/prn-18-144/library-of-congress-national-film-registry-turns-30/2018-12-12/; *Brokeback Mountain*, directed by Ang Lee, featuring Heath Ledger and Jake Gyllenhaal (2005; Universal Studios Home Entertainment, 2006), DVD.

128. Annie Proulx, "Getting Movied," in *Brokeback Mountain: Story to Screenplay*, ed. Annie Proulx, Larry McMurtry, and Diana Ossana (New York: Scribner, 2005), 133.

129. Hong, *Ruptures of American Capital*, 9.

130. John Locke, *Second Treatise of Government* (Indianapolis: Hackett, 1980), 8.

131. Hong, *Ruptures of American Capital*, 8.

132. Nikhil Pal Singh, *Race and America's Long War* (Berkeley: University of California Press, 2017), 79.

133. Annalee Newitz and Matt Wray, introduction to *White Trash: Race and Class in America*, ed. Annalee Newitz and Matt Wray (Florence, Italy: Taylor and Francis, 2013), 4.

134. Clyde Taylor, "The Ironies of Palace-Subaltern Discourse," in *Black American Cinema*, ed. Manthia Diawara (New York: Routledge, 1993), 186.

135. Annie Proulx, "Brokeback Mountain," in *Brokeback Mountain: Story to Screenplay*, ed. Annie Proulx, Larry McMurtry, and Diana Ossana (1997; New York: Scribner, 2005), 4. All further citations to this work will be parenthetical in the text. "Brokeback Mountain" was first published in the *New Yorker* on October 13, 1997.

136. Annie Proulx, *Bad Dirt* (New York: Scribner, 2004), 66.

137. Annie Proulx, "The Half-Skinned Deer," *Atlantic*, November 1997, https://www.theatlantic.com/magazine/archive/1997/11/the-half-skinned-steer/306168/.

138. Annie Proulx, *Close Range: Brokeback Mountain and Other Stories* (London: HarperCollins Publishers, 2012), 99.

139. Proulx, "Getting Movied," 129.

140. Proulx, *Close Range*, 101.

141. Michael Harrington, *The Other America* (New York: Scribner, 1997).

142. Hong, *Ruptures of American Capital*, 94.

143. Hong, 105.

144. Fordism and Taylorism attempted to construct a white working class as consumerist class on the premise that these workers would be paid well for their submission to scientific management. This shift in working class identity from producer to consumer was based on the concepts of living wage and the American standard of living, which constructed proper consumerism as American, masculine, white, and free—as opposed to undocumented, feminine, nonwhite, and enslaved. The high rate of pay would transform any irregularities in whiteness—such as irresponsibility,

drunkenness, sexual deviance, etc.—and people would also become more thrifty.

However, the actual conditions of factory life meant that many workers had to live in nonnormative domestic arrangements. In other words, capital's need to recruit heterogenous populations—the very people we see represented in these texts (European immigrants, rural workers, racialized workers, and women)—undercut the desire to create homogeneity. Hong, 90.

145. Hong, 75.

146. Hong, 11.

147. Hong, 11.

148. Andrew Hacker, *Two Nations* (New York: Charles Scribner's Sons, 1992), 100.

149. Nancy Isenberg, *White Trash: The 400-Year Untold History of Class in America* (New York: Penguin Books, 2017), 309.

150. Jillian Sandell, "Telling Stories of 'Queer White Trash,'" in *White Trash: Race and Class in America*, ed. Annalee Newitz and Matt Wray (Florence, Italy: Taylor and Francis, 2013), 232.

151. Singh, *Race and America's Long War*, 176.

152. Singh, 176.

153. Singh, 176–77.

154. Robin D. G. Kelley, foreword to *Border and Rule: Global Migration, Capitalism, and the Rise of Racist Nationalism*, by Harsha Walia (Chicago: Haymarket Books, 2021), xvi.

155. Kelley, foreword, xvii.

156. Kelley, xvii.

157. Tom Roach, *Friendship as a Way of Life: Foucault, AIDS, and the Politics of Shared Estrangement* (Albany: State University of New York Press, 2012), 132.

Conclusion

1. R. W. Connell, *Masculinities*, 2nd ed. (Berkeley: University of California Press, 2005), 216.

2. Todd Reeser, *Moderating Masculinity in Early Modern Culture* (Chapel Hill: University of North Carolina Press, 2006), 30–31.

3. Todd W. Reeser, *Masculinities in Theory* (Chichester, U.K.: Wiley-Blackwell, 2010), 50–51.

4. Reeser, *Masculinities in Theory*, 25.

5. Judith Butler, *The Psychic Life of Power: Theories in Subjection* (Palo Alto, Calif.: Stanford University Press, 1997), 148.

6. Katie Tyner and Farida Jalalzai, "Some Female Leaders Handled Covid and Other Crises Very Well," *Washington Post*, December 20, 2022.

7. CNN, "Contagious President Trump Removes Mask at White House,"

October 5, 2020, YouTube video, 10:15, https://www.youtube.com/watch?v=q6_sOuwGbm8.

8. Nikhil Pal Singh, *Race and America's Long War* (Berkeley: University of California Press, 2017), 109.

9. Singh, *Race and America's Long War*, 169.

10. Singh, 172.

11. Molly Kaplan, interview with Colleen Ammerman, "How COVID-19 Is Setting Working Women Back," November 12, 2020, in *At Liberty*, podcast, MP3 audio, 32:32, https://www.aclu.org/podcast/how-covid-19-setting-working-women-back-ep-127.

12. Chabeli Carrazana, "Most of the COVID-19 Workforce Were Women of Color: What Happens Now as Those Jobs End?," 19th, June 2, 2022, https://19thnews.org/2022/06/covid-19-workforce-women-of-color-jobs/.

13. Aníbal Quijano, "Coloniality of Power, Eurocentrism, and Latin America," *Nepantla: Views from South* 1, no. 3 (2000): 539.

14. Singh, *Race and America's Long War*, 159.

15. Singh, 158–59.

16. Jacques Derrida, *The Politics of Friendship* (New York: Verso, 2006), 37.

Index

Abdullah, King, 85
Abelson, Miriam J., 6, 47, 138, 212
Abernathy, Dolores, 124, 125, 126
ableism, 78, 82, 183
Abu Ghraib, 116
accumulation, 18, 258; capital, 138, 213; economic, 40; flexible, 40; logic of, 2; material, 116
Ace, Samuel, 20, 60, 196; boyhood of, 70–81; Dickinson and, 73; masculinity and, 82; photo of, 72 (fig.); on sexual abuse, 75; Tolbert and, 72
Ace Ventura: Pet Detective (film), 46
ACLU, USA PATRIOT Act and, 279n35
activism, 53, 183, 239
ACT UP, 191
Adams, Ansel, 243
Adams, Nick, 46
aesthetics, 24, 63, 77, 89, 93, 124, 213; Kantian ideal of, 42; trans poetry, 60
AFL. *See* American Federation of Labor
AFL-CIO. *See* American Federation of Labor-Congress of Industrial Organizations
African National Congress, 16
Afro-Cuban nationalists, 193
Age of Reason, The (Wilentz), 230
Agrupación Abdala, 196
Ahmed, Sara, 5, 113
AIDS. *See* HIV/AIDS
Alcoff, Linda Martín, 5
Alexander the Great, 134

alienation, 11, 66, 191, 213, 221, 224; working-class, 252
Alpha 66, 194
American Expeditionary Forces, 148
American Factory (documentary), 214
American Federation of Labor (AFL), 217, 219, 228, 240
American Federation of Labor-Congress of Industrial Organizations (AFL-CIO), 220, 227, 228, 229, 237, 238
American Friends of Vietnam (AFVN), 229
American Fund for French Wounded, 153
Americans with Disabilities Act (1990), 183
America, the Beautiful (film), 41, 42
Amin, Kadji, 9, 11, 134, 215; de-idealization and, 10; on friendship, 178; queer family and, 30; on queer time, 164
Amis, Suzy, 120, 284n175
Anderson, Benedict, 88
"Andrea/Andrew" (Gibson), text of, 79
androcentrism, 14, 24, 32, 104, 162
anti-Communism, 153, 176, 195
Antigone, 22, 97, 114–15, 121
Antigone (Sophocles), 85, 114
Antigone's Claim: Kinship between Life and Death (Butler), 22
anti-imperialism, 194, 196
antiracist movement, 22

antiwar movement, 227
antiwill, 127
anxiety, 25, 30, 50, 141, 227, 228, 254; castration, 34, 36, 42; male, 254
Anzaldúa, Gloria, 56, 71, 76; *Nepantla* and, 19; queer theory and, 55
April Twilights (Cather), 147
Arenas, Reinaldo: Mariel boatlift and, 199; memoir of, 172, 192–208; sense of spirituality of, 206–7; struggles of, 196
Aristotle, 14, 62, 143, 144; ethics of, 145
art of life, nation/exile and, 192–208
assimilation, 10, 66, 152, 200
"Attack" (Sassoon), text of, 145
authoritarianism, 3, 21, 76, 140, 253
Autobiography of Alice B. Toklas, The (Stein), 158–59, 160, 161
autonomy, 9, 11, 23, 60, 182, 195, 214
Avedon, Richard, 243
Awkward-Rich, Cameron, 73, 76

"Baby Woojums" (Stein), 136
Baker, Josephine, 152
Balboa, Rocky, 5
Baldwin, James, 90
Ballad of Little Jo, The (film), 119, 120, 284n175
Bandy, Mary Lea, 98, 100, 101, 107
Barney, Matthew, 42
Barrie, J. M., 73
Bates, Alan, 186
Bath Curtain (Steers), 174 (fig.)
Batista, Fulgencio, 193
Baudrillard, Jean, 36
Bazin, André, 98
Bechdel, Alison, 77
Before Night Falls (Arenas), 172, 192, 196, 197, 205
Belafonte, Harry, 284n201

Belladonna* Collaborative, 72
Bend of the River (film), 281n104
Benjamin, Richard, 284n187
Bennett, Paula, 64, 68
Berkowitz, Richard, 182
Berlant, Laurent, 264n28
Berlin, Isaiah, 291n6
Bernstein, Matthew, 101
Bersani, Leo, 40
Beyond Westworld (television series), 123
Bhabha, Homi K., 87, 123, 125
big brother/sister, trans, 56
Bill of Rights, 279n35
binary system, 2, 3–4, 66, 222; friend/enemy, 89
Bin Laden, Osama, 85
biological determinism, 29, 35, 52
Biology Is Not Destiny (Brandeis), 51
biopolitics, 173, 175, 205
bisexuals, 77, 179
Black bodies, criminalization of, 202
Black community, 131, 229, 230; crime against, 128; kinship ties in, 205
Blackdom, 127, 128, 129
Black Is . . . Black Ain't (film), 18, 172, 192, 200, 201, 203–4, 208, 266n79
Black Lives Matter, 20, 23, 128, 129
Black masculinity, 169, 202, 204
Black men, 204; patriarchal control of, 203
Blackness, 23, 203, 204, 205; denigration of, 137; transness and, 19
Black people, 18, 91, 176, 257; devaluing, 137–38; HIV/AIDS and, 177; marginalization of, 23; migration of, 128; securing existence of, 130; white privileged relationship to, 137
Black Power, 200, 220, 229
Black Reconstruction in America (Du Bois), 251

Black Trans Lives Matter, 129
Blanchett, Kate, 117
Blanchot, Maurice, 14, 62, 180, 181
Blaxploitation, 169
Blood and Honour (Harding), 185
Blue Collar, White Collar, No Collar (Ford), 212
Boetticher, Budd, Jr., 101
boi/boyhood, 56, 57, 59, 71
Bolsonaro, Jair, 2, 257
bonding, 13, 15, 162, 164; fraternal, 116; white male, 54
Boney, Jim, 224, 225, 226
Border and Rule: Global Migration, Capitalism, and the Rise of Racist Nationalism (Kelley), 171
Borderlands/La Frontera: The New Mestiza (Anzaldúa), 56
border wars, 296n15
Boy George, 48
boyhood, 66, 79; analysis of, 19; desire for, 81; experiencing, 76; gifts of, 55; imagined, 57, 60, 61, 70, 74, 81; liminality of, 76; normative, 58; phallic, 55; theory of, 58; transition and, 75–76; undecidable, 70–81; white, 56. *See also* boi/boyhood
"boys will be boys," 55, 57–60
Brady, Scott, 109
Brandeis, Tala Candra, 51
Brewster, Achsah Barlow, 149
Brewster, Earl, 149
Brodie-Sangster, Thomas, 120
Brody, David, 212, 216, 217, 220, 230, 297n47; on AFL-CIO, 228; labor movement and, 237
Brokeback Mountain, 10, 244–45, 246, 248, 249
Brokeback Mountain (film), 242–43, 300n127; still from, 244 (fig.), 245 (fig.)
"Brokeback Mountain" (Proulx), 212, 213, 240, 249, 251, 255; characters of, 10; publication of, 300n135
Brolin, James, 284n187
Brown, Gillian, 61
Browne, Kath, 4
Bruder, Jessica, 214
Brynner, Yul, 284n187
Buchanan, Pat, 177, 201
Buck and the Preacher (film), 128, 285n201
Buckley, William F., Jr., 90
Buhle, Paul, 219, 231, 236, 238, 240
Burden, Jim, 147
Burke, Tarana J., 117, 129
Bush, George H. W., 201
Bush, George W., 117, 277n7; swagger of, 85–86; Wild West and, 116
Bustamante, Nao, 16, 30–31, 37–46, 270n60; appearance of, 37–38; culture and, 40–41; dildo and, 43, 45, 54; female phallicism of, 44; performance art of, 39, 40, 42, 52; queer/transgender movements and, 54; sexual identity of, 45
butch, 4, 5, 52, 86, 221, 235, 247; term, 56
butches, 110, 214, 216, 219, 220, 221, 222, 225, 226, 229; reinscription of, 54; sexual harassment and, 223; as subgroup, 224
butch lesbians, 8, 215, 221, 222, 296n15
Butler, Judith, 22, 34–35, 44, 115; on collective institutions, 255; female phallus and, 35; gender performativity and, 39, 50, 271n100; phallus and, 34, 36; substitutability and, 54
Bylsma, Chris, 130

Calamity Jane (film), 99
Caleo, John, 184
Callen, Michael, 182
Cameron, Loren, 51–52

Cameron, Sharon, 66
capital: accumulation, 138, 213; difference and, 223–24; flow of, 212; mobility, 237; transnational, 170. *See also* global capital
capitalism, 12, 17, 25, 41, 42, 62, 86, 129, 137, 184, 195, 198, 237–38, 242; consumer, 203; development of, 138; hegemony of, 227; heteronormativity and, 247, 253; history of, 16; labor, 10; masculinity and, 253; resistance to, 224; state-managed, 213; U.S., 88, 250; white supremacy and, 1. *See also* racial capitalism
Capra, Frank, 281n104
cárdenas, micha, 53
Cardinal, Tantoo, 120
care, 3, 8, 164, 171, 184, 185, 186, 255; communization of, 12; forms of, 11; masculinity and, 186; meritocratic, 14
care webs, 11, 12, 258
Carrillo, Ciro, 1
Carter, Jimmy, 233
castration, 36, 42, 54; threat of, 34
Castro, Fidel, 172, 193, 197, 199, 200; resistance to, 195; Soviet relations and, 194
Cather, Grosvenor P., 148
Cather, Meta Schaper, 148
Cather, Willa, 152, 255; affection/care and, 8; conservatism of, 161, 162; feminist cause and, 139; lovence and, 143–44, 146; masculinity of, 136, 146–47; misogyny of, 139; normative masculinity and, 162; soldiers and, 144; Stein and, 7–8, 134, 135, 137, 138, 140–41, 142, 145; writing of, 136, 146, 149, 150, 151, 164
Cather, William, Jr. (Willa Cather), 136
Césaire, Aimé, 59

Céspedes, Juan, 189
Cheney, Dick, 85, 115
Cheney, Lynne, 200
Cheng, Anne Anlin, 44
Christian Coalition, 201
Christianity, 21, 93, 130
Christie, Julie, 186
Church, Lucy, 156, 158
CIA, 194
Cicero, 62, 180
CIO. *See* Congress of Industrial Organizations
cisgender women, 30; femme-presenting, 34
citizenship, 123, 192, 212; denial of, 17; foundation of, 93; women's, 17, 97
civilization, 90, 98, 102, 116, 120
civil rights, 137, 196, 200, 212, 219, 227, 230
civil society, 15, 257
Civil War, 128, 146, 159
class, 51, 61, 212, 215, 219, 242, 249; economic, 111; production of, 137; social, 111; socioeconomic, 25; status, 171; struggles, 213; whiteness and, 8, 138
Claude, 148, 149; death of, 151; war and, 150–51
Coburn, Alvin Langdon, 139
cock, girly, 16, 51
Coelho, Maria Cecilia de Miranda N., 117, 119
Cohen, Cathy, 9
Cold War, 49, 153, 176, 190, 229, 230
Cole, B., 56
Collins, Patricia Hill, 8
colonialism, 22, 23, 41, 44, 56, 76, 129, 152, 169
Combahee River Collective, 8, 204
Communism, 153, 172, 190, 195, 196
Communists, 193, 218–19, 224, 238
community, 12; Black, 128, 131,

205, 229, 230; forming, 182; freedom and, 218; gender and, 11, 258; horizontal, 223; Indigenous, 131, 251; individual and, 162; LGBTQIA+, 7, 213, 215, 219; motifs of, 182; term, 133
Concept of the Political, The (Schmitt), 94, 97
Congressional Budget Office, 176
Congress of Industrial Organizations (CIO), 217, 219, 240, 296n24
Conigrave, Timothy, 172, 184
Connell, R. W., 253
Conrad, Joseph, 211
conservatives, 177, 199, 230, 232
constitutional rights, rollback of, 170–71
consumerism, 6, 203, 239, 300n144; culture and, 40
Cooper, Gary, 86, 90, 111
Corbett, Ken, 57
Corporation for Public Broadcasting, 200
Countersexual Manifesto (Preciado), 42
counterterror, terror and, 96
Covid-19 pandemic, 3, 18, 19, 77, 171, 202, 209, 214, 255, 257; Trump and, 256
Cox, Oliver C., 22
Crawford, Joan, 99, 109, 111, 112
creative practices, 53, 71, 152
Cremaster (films), 42
Creon, King, 85, 114, 115, 125, 127
Crichton, Michael, 123, 284n187
crime, 176; interrelated, 89; political, 89
crimes against humanity, women and, 31
Crimp, Douglas, 182
crip theory, 11, 183
Crip Theory: Cultural Signs of Queerness and Disability (McRuer), 183
Crip Times: Disability, Globalization, and Resistance (McRuer), 9
critical whiteness studies, 5, 137, 252
Crockett, Davy, 20, 76
Cronenberg, David, 46–47, 271n90
"Crying Game, The" (Boy George), 48
Crying Game, The (film), 16, 46–47, 52, 254; still from, 49 (fig.); transmisogyny and, 50; transphobia and, 54
Cuban Revolution, 193, 195
Cubans, emigration of, 199
"cult of true womanhood," 61, 62
cultural criticism, 164, 252, 258
cultural production, 29, 31, 46, 171, 258
cultural theory, HIV/AIDS, 182, 183
culture, 3, 15, 24, 29, 43, 44, 48, 53, 59, 70, 81, 115, 231; American, 118; Black political, 129; consumerism and, 40; cowboy, 103; function of, 40–41; gay, 4, 271n100; minoritized, 41; Native American, 87, 117; patriarchal, 122; politics and, 50; popular, 17; struggle and, 24
culture wars, 31, 177, 200
Currah, Paisley, 61
Cvetkovich, Ann, 119, 221

Daniels, Jeff, 118
Davidson, Jaye, 47, 49
Davis, Angela, 3, 204
Davis, Lennard J., 182
Day, Doris, 99
Deadwood (television show), 86, 115; war on terror and, 116
De Amicitia (Cicero), 180
death, 158; friendship and, 144; trans, 19
Debord, Guy, 40
Decolonial Imaginary, The (Pérez), 82

decolonization, 42, 43, 44, 251
Dee, Ruby, 285n201
Del Mar, Ennis, 10, 244, 245, 250; Jack and, 241, 242, 246–47, 248, 249; loss of interest for, 243
democracy, 130, 139, 142, 217; capitalist, 17, 86, 88, 196; concept of, 179; fraternal contract and, 14; ideal of, 163; Jacksonian idealization of, 257; liberal, 91, 162, 202; totalitarianism and, 21
Democratic Party, 219, 230, 237, 238; labor movement and, 228
Department of Labor, 228
Derrida, Jacques, 7, 8, 14–15, 17, 18, 89, 94, 96, 102, 113, 114, 143, 148, 181, 259; on discourses, 180; enemy and, 93; fraternal friend/Schmittian enemy and, 92; fraternity and, 179; on friendship, 59; friendship and, 32, 144; liberal contract and, 13; lovence and, 135, 144; phallocentrism and, 14, 33; phallogocentrism and, 14, 33, 97, 162; politics and, 13, 95; racial capitalism and, 16; Schmitt and, 92, 95; Stein/Cather and, 142
Descartes, René, 32
Destry Rides Again (film), 281n104
development, 22, 148, 164, 171, 176, 200; boyhood, 58; capitalist, 138, 214; character, 89; economic, 8, 17, 61; historical, 39; institutional, 202; masculine, 58, 211; narratives of, 86
Devine, Andy, 101
Dickinson, Emily, 19–20, 69, 70, 74–75, 274n41; Ace and, 73; childhood scenes and, 63; deviations of, 67; fascicle of, 65 (fig.); gender nonconformity and, 60; imagined boyhood of, 61; male names of, 62; poetry of, 64; religion and, 66

Dickinson, Susan Huntington Gilbert, 62
Diesel, Vin, 29
difference: construction of, 18; gendered, 40, 223–24; racial, 40, 44, 51, 52, 222, 223–24; sexual, 17, 51, 52, 75, 222
Dil, 47, 48, 50; body of, 47; transphobic depiction of, 54
dildo, 16, 29, 43; anthropomorphized, 38; bedazzled, 30–31, 37, 44, 45 (fig.); living, 46; masculine voice of, 38; penis and, 30, 54, 270n77; as phallic signifier, 36; reconfiguring, 42; as sexual object, 36
disability, 191, 255; convergence of, 182; queerness and, 183; sex and, 184; theory, 182, 186
disability justice movement, 18
Disclosure (documentary), 46, 53
discrimination, 55, 162, 219; reverse, 176
disease, 18, 22, 24, 146, 172, 173; AIDS-related, 184, 186; queer time of, 18, 184–91
disenfranchisement, 18, 244, 247
disorientations, 70, 81, 159; historical, 23; psychological/physical, 174; queer, 68, 80
dispossession, 43; political/economic effects of, 3; racialized, 192
Disturbing Attachments (Amin), 9
Dobson, Joanne, 63
Dockery, Michelle, 118
domesticity, 6, 192, 204, 248
domination, 13, 25, 56, 180; European, 195; masculine, 2, 20, 21, 23; racial, 242; sexist, 113; sexual, 1, 183, 253
Domínguez-Ruvalcaba, Héctor, 44
Doniphon, Tom, 105, 107, 108, 127; butch swagger of, 104; funeral of, 109; Hallie and, 101–2; interven-

tion by, 104; justice and, 106; masculinity and, 101–2; Pompey and, 106; Ransom and, 99–100, 103, 106
Douglass, Frederick, 137
drag queens, 50, 219, 271n100
Drucker, Zachary, 53
drug abuse, 241
Du Bois, W. E. B., 137, 219, 251
Duel in the Sun (film), 119
Duffy, 224–25, 234, 235–36, 255; Jess and, 226, 227
Duggan, Lisa, 6
Dunye, Cheryl, 201
Duterte, Rodrigo, 3
Dydo, Ulla E., 135, 152, 155, 161; on lesbians/men's clothing, 152

Eakins, Thomas, 175
Eastwood, Clint, 105, 125, 284n197
ecological issues, 3, 239
economic issues, 3, 6, 22, 24, 62, 170, 176, 229, 232, 233, 237, 245, 250, 257, 258
economic systems, 13, 129, 131, 193, 209
edwards, kari, 60
Eisenhower, Dwight D., 194
"Elbows" (Gibson), 81
embodiments, 31, 37, 51, 254; boyish, 64; natural/artificial, 123; trans, 50, 56
Emma, 109, 110, 112, 121; Vienna and, 111, 113
employment, 18, 111, 137, 211, 217, 226, 231, 248; nonagricultural, 233
Eng, David L., 58, 139, 213
Enlightenment, 14, 130
environmental issues, 213, 239
environmental movement, 24
epistemology, 45; heteronormative/colonial/racialized, 33, 34; nationalist, 127

equality, 90, 113, 131, 143, 170–71, 201; economic, 243, 263; legal/civil/political, 88; universal, 13
Equal Rights Amendment, 175, 239
Eros, femininity and, 171
eroticism, 187, 197, 198
Eteocles, 114
ethnocentrism, 33, 104, 113
Eudemian Ethics of Aristotle (Aristotle and Simpson), 143, 144
eugenics movement, 138
Everybody's Autobiography (Stein), 153
exceptionalism, 151; American, 138, 139, 241, 249; butch, 7–8, 134, 138, 140, 160
exclusion, 2, 14, 31, 35, 51, 54, 90, 97, 115, 119, 145, 160, 179, 181; countering, 162; political, 184; social, 184; theater of, 98
exile, art of life and, 192–208
experiment, term, 82

Faderman, Lillian, 29, 178
Fajardo, Kale Bantigue, 4, 216
Faludi, Susan, 117
familial, term, 14
family, 59; masculinity of, 2
Family Guy (television show), 46
Fanon, Frantz, 203
fantasy, 3, 60, 75, 76, 116, 119, 248; sexual, 23
Farrakhan, Louis, 204
fascism, 3, 20, 21, 153, 162, 256; ascendancy of, 2; rise of, 22
Faÿ, Bernard, 140, 161
FBI, 218
Feinberg, Leslie, 10, 216, 211, 222, 224, 226, 229, 235, 236, 240; bar scenes and, 219; identity categories and, 214–15; pronouns of, 295–96n10; Prosser and, 296n13; strikes and, 218
female masculinity, 5, 29, 122

Female Masculinity (Halberstam), 4, 5, 25, 52, 109–10
female phallicism, 15–16, 30, 44; relationality and, 54; theory of, 31–37; trans theory of, 46–53
feminine, 74, 182, 216; repression of, 58; traditional, 52
femininity, 60, 69, 82, 247, 256; Eros and, 171; homosexuality and, 104; masculinity and, 101, 139–40; rejection of, 8
feminism, 51, 54, 58, 111; benefits of, 6–7; portrayal of, 117; transnational, 129; women of color, 22, 87, 129
feminist masculinity, 22, 87, 97–99, 110, 114, 117, 118, 120, 122, 123, 129, 130
feminist movement, 22, 240
feminists, 5, 51, 229; biological determinism and, 52; lesbian, 51, 73; radical, 77; women of color, 8, 24, 53. *See also* trans-exclusionary radical feminists
femme, 42, 214, 219, 229, 232, 235; presenting, 36, 38; vulnerability, 52; witnesses, 134, 145
Fergus, 46, 47, 48, 49 (fig.); masculinity of, 254
Ferguson, Roderick, 9
fetishes, 34, 43, 44, 45, 52
Filipino Crosscurrents: Oceanographies of Seafaring, Masculinities, and Globalization (Fajardo), 4, 216, 225
film noir, 98, 111
Finn, Huck, 66, 75
Fisher, Dorothy Canfield, 149
Fletcher, Alice, 118, 119, 120, 121, 122
Foner, Eric, 70, 170, 200, 208, 238, 290n5; on citizenship, 17; negative freedom and, 291n6; on Reagan, 176

Ford, Henry: assembly line and, 221
Ford, John, 103, 105, 108, 111, 280n85; revisionism and, 100–101; Wayne and, 98; Westerns and, 98–99
Ford, Richard, 212
Ford, Robert, 107
Fordism, 40, 220, 250, 300n144
Foreign Investment and the Reproduction of Racial Capitalism in South Africa (Legassick and Hemson), 16
Foster, John, 172, 189
Foucault, Michel, 18, 135, 173, 175, 177, 179; canon of beauty and, 178; death of, 180, 181; friendship and, 178; heterotopias and, 224; identity and, 9; pederastic practices and, 178; representational default and, 186
Foundlings (Nealon), 139
Franco, Francisco, 140, 153
Frank, Scott, 117, 120, 121, 128, 130, 284n169, 284n172, 285n206
fraternal bonds, 104; queer/trans, 141
fraternalist, term, 14
fraternity, 3, 7, 10, 25, 87, 89, 96, 111, 113, 114, 125, 145, 151, 242; concept of, 14, 33, 179; counterfeit currency of, 13–20; deconstruction of, 127; friendship and, 15, 97; future of, 130; heteronormative, 252; hyperbolization of, 32–33; language of, 33; laws of, 142; logics of, 16; masculine, 141; patriarchal, 139; political, 15, 17, 133, 255; rejection of, 143, 173; revolutionary, 32; universality and, 33, 142; white, 170
fraternization, 12, 31, 32, 97, 104; empire and, 22; process of, 14, 17; reproduction of, 59
Frazer, Tess, 118

freedom, 1, 21, 25, 32, 253; community and, 218; creative, 71, 152; gay, 50, 197; gender, 258; globalization and, 70; negative, 70, 171, 291n6; positive, 71, 171; sexual, 152
Freedom Dreams (Kelley), 2, 202
free enterprise, 1, 71, 176
Freeman, Morgan, 284n197
Freud, Sigmund, 34, 67; boyhood and, 58; feminine/failure and, 58; phobic dread and, 57; pseudo-biological interpretation and, 58
friend/enemy concepts, 15, 93, 94, 145
friendship, 143, 178, 185; death and, 144; discourses on, 32; first, 145; fraternal contract and, 15; fraternity and, 97; gay men and, 173, 177; homosexuality and, 197; male–male, 13–14, 31, 173; masculine, 13, 14, 16, 24, 59, 151, 179; poetic, 59; politics and, 142, 179; primary, 144; queer theorizations of, 178; reciprocalist/mutualist schema of, 287n55; responsibility of, 181; standard interpretation of, 142
"Friendship as a Way of Life" (Foucault), 135
Fuller, Bert, 151
Fun Home (musical), 77
Futureworld (film), 123

Gaddis, John Lewis, 89
Gai Pied, 177
gap, term, 55
gay, term, 235
Gay, Roxanne, 77
gay liberation, 218, 229, 292n36
gay male clubs/bars, sexism within, 271n100
gay men, 172, 176; Black, 202; death of, 183–84; friendship and, 173, 177; image of, 178; lives of, 180, 201; marginalization of, 196; normative, 50; ostracization of, 18; protections for, 198; representation default of, 186
gay plague, 177
gender, 2, 19, 25, 31, 37, 44, 48, 50, 82, 87, 131, 158, 212, 215, 252, 253; binary, 66; biological concepts of, 3–4; colonial, 39; community and, 11, 258; desire and, 56; discourses of, 110; essence of, 51; explaining, 81; fluid, 110; hegemony and, 129; idea of, 79; masculine, 10, 137; natural laws of, 75; "No-Man's-Land" of, 20; normative alignments of, 7; as political, 6; pronouns and, 69; race and, 19; sex and, 29, 52, 56, 69, 70; stagings of, 39; World War I and, 8
gender affirmation, 52, 56, 75–76
gender categories, 35, 47, 54
gender conformity, 57, 78
gender confusion, 110–11
gender expressions, 25, 189, 192
gender nonconformity, 60, 76, 213
gender norms, 68, 177, 257
gender performativity, 35, 39, 50, 271n10
genderqueer, 77, 78, 82
gender relations, 127, 138
genocide, 90, 120, 142, 145, 148
Gertrude Stein: The Language That Rises (Dydo), 135
"Gertrude Stein Took the War like a Man" (Mills), 136
"Getting Movied" (Proulx), 246
Gibson, Andrea, 20; boyhood of, 70–81; masculinity and, 82; tomboy past of, 80
Gilbert, Sandra M., 63, 274n39
Ginsburg, Ruth Bader, 77–78
global capital, 7, 18, 62, 211; formations of, 40; hegemony of, 258

Global North, 171, 252, 256
Go-Between, The (film), 186
Godless (television show), 22, 23, 87, 97, 111, 115, 117, 119, 127, 128–29, 130, 254, 284n172, 285n206; analysis of, 114; criticism of, 122; female cast of, 118; scarring/historical amnesia and, 120; sexual assault and, 118; still from, 121 (fig.), 128 (fig.)
Goldberg, Jess, 215, 216, 217, 250
goldilocks man, 6, 25, 47
Gompers, Samuel, 228
Goode, Roy, 118
Good, the Bad, and the Ugly, The (film), 105
Gordy, Katherine A., 193, 194, 195, 196
Gran Fury, art-based resistance of, 191
Great Society, 227, 230, 232
Green, Jameson, 4
Greenwald, Maggie, 284n175
Griffin, Frank, 118, 121, 254
Gross, Terry, 284n173
Guantánamo, 116, 192, 196, 199, 293n67
Gubar, Susan, 63, 274n39
Guevara, Che, 193, 194
Guitar, Johnny, 109, 110, 111, 113
Gyllenhaal, Jake, 244, 245, 300n127

Habegger, Alfred, 63–64, 66–67
Hacker, Andrew, 250
Hackman, Gene, 285n197
Haggins, Bambi, 41
Halberstam, Jack, 5, 25, 52, 109–10, 164–65, 215, 222; on dildo/phallic signifier, 36; masculinity and, 6; queer theory and, 4; unfettered masculinism and, 7, 19
"Half-Skinned Steer, The" (Proulx), 245
Hallie, 99, 100, 103, 104, 106, 108; Ransom and, 102, 105; Tom and, 101–2
Hangover: Part II, The (film), 46
Harding, Alex, 185
Harrington, Michael, 249
Harris, Cheryl I., 138
Harris, Ed, 125
Hart, Ellen Louise, 64
Harvey, David, 40, 266n70
Haskell, Molly, 111
hate speech, 176, 209
Hawks, Howard, 98
Hayden, Sterling, 109, 112
health care, 12, 18
Heaven's Gate (film), 116, 123
hegemony, 24, 35–36, 153, 215, 253, 254; crisis, 25; cultural, 85; gender and, 129; masculine, 46, 115, 130; textual, 33
Heidegger, Martin, 93
heimlich/unheimlich, 59, 124, 135
Helms, Jesse, 201
Hemphill, Essex, 206, 208, 266n79
Hemson, David, 16
Herthum, Louis, 124
heteronormativity, 43, 49, 172, 178, 187, 206, 222; capitalism and, 247; white, 57
heteropatriarchy, 115, 252
heterosexuality, 4, 5, 9, 22, 57, 61, 101, 178, 255
heterotopias, 224
Hey Galaxy, 77
Hickok, Wild Bill, 99
hierarchy: national sociology of, 17; racial, 17, 20, 39, 62; sexualized, 37
High Noon (film), 111
history, 16, 24, 219; gay, 215; great men of, 141; lesbian, 215; natural, 17; philosophical, 31; queer, 164; transgender, 60
Hitchcock, Alfred, 281n104
Hitler, Adolf, 91, 153, 257

HIV/AIDS, 172, 175, 198, 201, 202, 204, 205, 207; cultural theory about, 182, 183; death from, 173, 180; living with, 177, 183, 185, 189; pandemic, 11, 13, 18, 176–77, 179, 180–81, 182, 192, 195; transmission of, 185
Hobbes, Thomas, 93
Hockenhull, Stella, 121–22
Holding the Man (Conigrave), 172, 184
Holtz, Martin, 117
Home in Three Days, Don't Wash, 72
Homer, 139
homicide, 90, 142
homonormativity, 6, 7, 133, 171, 235
homophobia, 129, 138, 139, 177, 179, 185, 187, 189, 205, 248
homosexuality, 2, 60, 69, 82, 103, 104, 178–79, 199, 241; antagonism toward, 177; femininity and, 104; friendship and, 197; male-male, 177; persecution of, 199; virile, 179
homosexuals, 97, 177, 178, 199
homosociality, 113, 179
Hong, Grace Kyungwon, 24, 40, 41, 192, 250; antiwill and, 127; on capital/difference and, 223–24; individualism and, 8; on national boundaries, 170; racial capitalism and, 87; on Taylor, 221; white masculinity and, 106; women of color feminism and, 22
hooks, bell, 204
Hopkins, Anthony, 107
Hopkins, Bo, 284n175
How to Have Sex in an Epidemic (Caller and Berkowitz), 182
Hughes, Langston, 21
humanism, 152, 241
human rights: breaches of, 116; counterfeiture of, 116
Human Rights Campaign, 6

Huntington, Samuel P., 90
Hwang, David Henry, 47
hypermasculinity, 52, 169, 204, 247

identity, 7, 8, 31, 107, 137, 172, 180, 182; categories, 214–15; cross-gendered, 58; disguising, 274n39; domesticating, 9; economic equality and, 243; formation of, 1; gay male, 50; gender, 2, 17, 37, 53, 87, 192, 216, 254, 258, 271n100; markers, 60; masculine, 211; national, 113, 138; personal, 164; racial-historical, 17; sexual, 45, 53, 192, 213, 216; trans, 60
Iliad (Homer), 119
immigration, 162, 200, 202
imperialism, 8, 21, 129, 193, 194, 195; economic, 97; Western, 123
Independent Television Service (ITVS), 201
Indian Wars, 87, 89, 91
Indigenous people, 11, 95, 98, 176, 185, 195, 223, 251; devaluing, 137–38; marginalization of, 23; slaughter/relocation of, 91; Westerns and, 100, 101, 120, 121, 131. *See also* Native Americans
Indigurrito (video), 41
individualism, 248; American ethos and, 8; consumerist, 221; corrosive, 208; masculine, 130–31, 161; neoliberal, 6; possessive, 241; rational, 86
industrial economy, 228, 234
Industrial Workers of the World (IWW), 223, 240
insecurity, 141; conveying, 39; debilitating, 7
interdependence, sexual-political, 182
International Ladies' Garment Workers' Union, 235
intersex scholarship, 41

IRA, 47, 48
Irons, Jeremy, 271n90
isolation, 13, 244, 246; geographic, 249
IWW. *See* Industrial Workers of the World

Jalalzi, Farida, 256
Jameson, Fredric, 40, 41
Jefferson, Thomas, 161
Jess, 219–20, 222–26, 228–32, 234, 235, 236, 237, 239, 250; Duffy and, 226, 227; Jack and, 224; Jan and, 229; Leroy and, 224; Theresa and, 228
Jim Crow, 49
Jobs with Justice, 239
John Mary, 157–58; neuroatypicality of, 157
"Johnny Appleseed" (Gibson), text of, 80
Johnny Guitar (film), 99, 109, 111, 121; lesbianism and, 110; still from, 112 (fig.)
Johnson, E. Patrick, 204
Johnson, Lyndon B., 202, 230, 232, 233; Great Society and, 227
Johnson County War, 116
Jones, Amelia, 39
Jones, Bill T., 206, 208, 266n79
Jones, Mother, 227
Jordan, Neil, 49
Jorgensen, Christine, 48–49, 50
Joy, Lisa, 284n186
justice, 106, 145; economic, 251; labor, 237; meanings of, 19; political, 205; social, 130, 205; vigilante, 86

Kant, Immanuel, 14, 62, 89
Keel, Howard, 99
Keeling, Kara, 201, 205–6
Kelley, Robin D. G., 2, 59, 171, 184, 202, 203, 252

Kelly, Grace, 111
Kennedy, John F., 194, 232
Khrushchev, Nikita, 194
Kim Jong-Un, 257
King, Martin Luther, Jr., 229
King, Rodney, 205
kinship, 58, 134, 205, 251; patriarchal, 114; queer, 3, 9; rearticulating, 255
Kipling, Rudyard, 136
Kirkland, Lane, 238
Kitses, Jim, 98

La Belle, 117, 130; racist indifference of, 127
labor, 211, 212, 215, 231, 239; abuses, 10; exploitable, 19; interracial, 238; politics and, 228; queer, 10; separateness/independence of, 228; struggles, 213; trans, 10; working-class, 218
Labor-Management Group, 233
labor movement, 219, 236, 237–38, 239; coalitional, 216; Democrats and, 228; goals of, 212; mass, 216. *See also* unions
Lacan, Jacques, 34, 36
Ladin, Joy, 51
L'amitié (Blanchot), 180
LaMotta, Jake, 5
L'Amour (Michelet), 268n16
Landrum-Griffin Act (1959), 227
Latin@ body, "too muchness" of, 38, 44
law and order, 106, 108, 176
Law of the Father, 127
Ledger, Heath, 244, 245, 300n127
Lee, Ang, 152, 243, 244, 245, 300n127
Lee, Hermione, 150, 152
Legassick, Martin, 16
Lens, Sidney, 213, 238
Leone, Sergio, 284n169
lesbians, 4, 110, 179, 216; Black, 202;

men's clothing and, 152; normative, 50; phallic, 36; punishment of, 29; term, 235
Lewis, Richard J., 126, 153
LGBTQIA+ community, 7, 200, 213, 215, 219, 235
LGBTQIA+ movement, 227, 240
liberalism, 18, 19, 90, 256; queer, 30; racial, 18
liberty, negative, 176
Life magazine, 219
"Lifting Belly" (Stein), 133
liminality, 58–59, 66, 69, 70, 76, 214, 234, 236
Lipsitz, George, 218, 227, 238
Locke, John, 241, 250
Lone, John, 271n90
Longmire (television show), 115
Lorde, Audre, 187
"Lost Boyhood" poems, 72, 75
Louis XIII, 136
Love, Heather, 164
lovence, 135, 164, 181, 186, 192, 208; expressions of, 145–61, 188, 191; incommensurability and, 144; self/identity in, 180; subject-object relations and, 144; transformative power of, 136–45
Lowe, Lisa, 223
Lowell, Amy, 162
Lucy Church Amiably (Stein), 156, 157, 158, 160, 161
Lusted, David, 100, 110
Lye, Colleen, 10

Machiavelli, 93
Magnificent Seven, as women, 284n173
Making of Americans, The (Stein), 141
Malatino, Hil, 11, 12, 56
Malcolm, Janet, 140, 158
Malcolm X, 220
male authority, structures of, 30

maleness, 4
Man from Laramie, The (film), 281n104
manhood, 4, 15, 216; penis and, 29
Manifest Destiny, 23, 127, 153
manliness, 88, 117, 146, 171
Mann, Anthony, 114
Man Who Shot Liberty Valance, The (film), 98, 99, 110, 280n85; still from, 103 (fig.), 108 (fig.)
Marable, Manning, 220, 239
marginalization, 10, 23, 24, 124, 196, 213, 249, 254
Mariel boatlift, 199
Martin, Mary, 73
Marty, Samuel, 120
Marvin, Lee, 100
Marx, Karl, 213
Marxism-Leninism, 196
Mary Agnes, 118, 120, 121, 122, 130, 254, 284n173
masculine normativity, 4, 25, 198, 243, 258; defining quality of, 169; transferability of, 80; trans/queer masculinity and, 213–14
masculine of center, term, 56
masculinism, 1, 10, 202; fascist, 20, 22; gay, 178; unfettered, 7, 19
masculinity: boyish, 78; commodified, 70; conceptions of, 115, 191, 199–200; concerns for, 98, 102, 212; cross-pollinating, 87; decaying, 172; desire for, 146; dreams of, 137; hegemonic, 138, 139, 263n6; interpretation of, 78–79; male, 5; materiality of, 136; nationalist, 197; phallic, 35, 82; protecting, 150; psychic drama of, 60; racialized, 192; reimagining, 127; standards of, 47; tension with, 225; term, 52; theorization of, 183; white, 106, 171, 192. *See also* Black masculinity; female masculinity; feminist

masculinity; hypermasculinity; normative masculinity; queer masculinity; toxic masculinity; trans masculinity
masculinity-in-motion, 191
masochism, 58, 59
materialism, 2, 152
M. Butterfly (film), 47, 271n90
McCambridge, Mercedes, 109, 112
McCarthy era, 172, 219
McClung, Isabelle, 147
McClung, Sharon, 148
McKellan, Ian, 284n175
McLerie, Allyn, 99
McMurtry, Larry, 243
McNairy, Scott, 118
McNue, Bill, 118
McRuer, Robert, 9, 70, 78, 183, 184
Meany, George, 229, 238, 298n71
Mein Kampf (Hitler), 91
melting pot, myth of, 169–70
Men in Place (Abelson), 6, 138
Men of Mark (Coburn), 139
mentorship, 11, 55, 56, 57, 59, 71, 75
Metaphysics (Kant), 89
Me Too movement, 117, 118, 129
Michaels, Walter Benn, 266n70
Michelet, Jules, 268n16
Milano, Alyssa, 129
Milch, David, 115
Miles, Vera, 99, 103, 108, 280n85
militarization, 21, 170, 212, 257
Military Units to Aid Production (UMAP), 197
Millay, Maeve, 125, 126
Miller, Henry, 141
Mills, David, 160, 201
Mills, Jean E., 136
misogyny, 35, 80, 129, 178
Missing, The (film), 117
modernity, 140, 147, 152–53
Modi, Narendra, 2
Mollow, Anna, 9, 184
Monaghan, Jo, 120

Montaigne, Michel de, 14, 62, 180
Montez, Maria, 37, 45–46
morphology, 47; gender, 37; masculine/feminine, 36; sexual, 34
Mr. Smith Goes to Washington (film), 281n104
Muslims, 23, 93
Mussolini, Benito, 153
mutual aid, 3, 78, 131, 164, 182, 184, 205, 252, 255; impersonal and, 13; as survival work, 12
My Ántonia (Cather), 133, 147, 148
My Darling Clementine (film), 100
Myles, Eileen, 82

Nagel, Joane, 88
Naked Spur, The (film), 281n104
Namaste, Viviane K., 50, 51, 60
"Namesake, The" (Cather), 146
Napoleon Bonaparte, 134, 147
Napoleonic Wars, 156
narcissism, 54, 131, 180, 198; boyhood, 254; masculine, 97
nation, 51, 137; art of life and, 192–208; masculinity and, 22, 87
National Association of Manufacturers' Committee for a Free-Union, 233
national belonging, 152, 178
National Endowment for the Arts (NEA), 200, 201
National Endowment for the Humanities, 200
National Film Registry, 240
nationalism, 20, 21, 33, 41, 85, 104, 194, 200, 253, 254; Black, 220; hegemonic, 139; masculine, 87, 254; nostalgic, 21; patriarchal, 129; right-wing, 2; white androcentric, 24
National Labor Relations Board (NLRB), 218, 234
National Right to Work Committee, 233

nation-state, 94, 97, 119, 133, 151; hegemonic, 212; male connection to, 151; normative masculinity and, 88, 89; politics of, 114; preservation of, 150; resisting, 87
Native Americans, 89, 121, 128; dispossession of, 17; HIV/AIDS and, 177; as ontological enemies, 90; tropes for, 120; white privileged relationship to, 137. *See also* Indigenous people
nativism, white, 170, 270
NEA. *See* National Endowment for the Arts
Nealon, Christopher, 139
Neidenberg, Milt, 224–25
neocolonialism, 56, 195, 277n7
neoliberalism, 6, 7, 9, 10, 11, 13, 39, 130, 213, 252; extension of, 2
Nepantla, 19, 56, 57, 61, 71, 77, 82; Nahuatl concept of, 55
Nestle, Joan, 73
neutrality, 92; non-negative, 181
New Deal, 162, 218, 230, 237
Newitz, Annalee, 242
New Labor, 211, 214, 223, 296n24
New Right, 239
Newton, Esther, 5
Newton, Thandiwe, 125
New York Daily News, 48
New Yorker, 212, 300n135
New York Times, 201
Nietzsche, Friedrich, 14, 62
Nixon, Richard, 202, 230–31, 232
NLRB. *See* National Labor Relations Board
Noble, Bobby, 1, 20, 51, 71
"No Filter" (Gibson), text of, 80
Nolan, Jonathan, 284n186
Nomadland (Bruder), 214
Nordmarken, Sonny: photo by, 72 (fig.)
Normal Sex (Ace), 71, 75–76
normative masculinity, 8, 10, 23, 24, 30, 58, 115, 130, 131, 169, 187, 202, 208, 211, 254–55; able-bodied, 29; aspirational, 133; capitalism and, 253; caring, 247, 248–49; class-privileged, 256; construction of, 26, 250; countering, 16, 32; crises for, 4; deconstruction of, 150; definition of, 2, 11, 20, 103; disloyalty to, 165; dominance and, 13; envisioning, 25; expressions of, 252; feminine, 108, 131; gay, 241, 246; kinder/gentler, 7; naming/refusing, 3; nation-state and, 22, 88, 89; naturalness of, 126; new relationships to, 26; penis and, 29; physical gestures of, 249; queer, 4, 55; reconceptualization of, 13; scripts of, 1–2; social relations and, 6; straight, 241; subverting, 54, 120; terrorist, 2; transformation of, 5, 6, 11, 12, 209, 246, 252; as universal signifier, 25–26; as virile virtue, 31; Western, 17, 62; white, 2–3, 108; white trash, 242, 250
normativity: capitalist, 71; resisting, 255. *See also* masculine normativity
North, Alfred, 154
North American Free Trade Agreement (NAFTA), 170
nostalgia, 141, 147, 164; masculine, 108, 138
Notaro, Tig, 78, 79
Notes on Life and Letters (Conrad), 211

Obama, Barack, 193
O'Brien, Edmund, 104
O'Brien, Sharon, 148
O'Connell, Jack, 118
Odysseus, 147, 152
Odyssey, The, 150
Oedipus, 58, 114

Oedipus Rex, 114
One of Ours (Cather), 139, 148, 152
Open Range (film), 115
Operation Mongoose, 194
Orbán, Viktor, 2, 257
Orpheus, 147
Ossana, Diana, 243
other, 31, 171; denigration/exclusion of, 2; self and, 191
Our Vision, Our Voices: Transsexual Portraits and "Nudes" (Cameron), 51
"Over the Fence" (Dickinson), 65 (fig.)

Pabón-Colón, Jessica Nydia, 22, 87
Pansy (Gibson), 79
Park, Robert E., 204
partisans: theory of, 96; ultimate, 88–98, 102, 113
Pascoe, C. J., 4
Pateman, Carole, 15, 162
paternalism, Black, 18, 204
patriarchy, 22, 66, 70, 113, 114; capitalist, 34; dismantling, 7; heterosexist, 187; homophilic version of, 15
patriotism, 2, 33
PBS, 200, 201
Peabody, Dutton, 104, 105
peaceniks, 229, 298n71
pederasty, 14, 178
pedophilia, 2
penis, 35, 38, 53, 57, 75, 225; battle with, 45; dildo and, 30, 54, 270n77; estrogenized, 52; girly, 16, 51; manhood and, 29; normative masculinity and, 29; as "organic embodiment," 270n77; phallus and, 15, 30, 34, 36, 42–51, 51–52, 254; power of, 63; white, 44
penises, swarm of, 38, 41, 44
Pérez, Emma, 55, 56, 82
performance, 78; art, 39, 40, 42, 52; document and, 42; gender, 50, 185
personhood, 123, 127, 203
Pétain, General, 162
Peter Pan (musical), 73
Peterson, Jennifer, 110
Peterson, Trace, 73, 76; on Ace, 71, 75; on Anzaldúa, 56; trans poetry aesthetic and, 60; utopian vision of, 70
phallic, 29, 36, 37, 39, 46, 50, 54, 59, 82; potential, 35, 52
phallicism, 30, 32, 42. *See also* female phallicism
phallic power, 15, 29, 30, 31, 254; accessing, 56; radical conceptions of, 53
phallic supremacy, 24, 31, 32, 40, 56, 57, 78; absurdity of, 43; gift of, 33; white, 55
phallic woman, 30
phallocentrism, 14, 30, 31, 33, 68, 69; certainty of, 39
phallogocentrism, 14, 15, 69, 97, 104, 114, 162
phallus, 33, 37, 54; butch, 35; female, 35, 36, 45, 53; lesbian, 34; misplaced, 36; penis and, 15, 30, 34, 36, 42–51, 51–52, 254; as privileged signifier, 34; psychoanalytic terms for, 35; resignifying, 35, 42
Pheasant-Kelly, Fran, 99, 117, 283n155
Philadelphia Record, 147
philia, 113, 143, 145
phratrocentrism, 33
phusis, 113
Piepzna-Samarasinha, Leah Lakshmi, 11
"Pink Melon Joy" (Stein), 154; text of, 155
"Pink Melon Joy III" (Stein), text of, 155

Plato, 266n62
"Poem 271" (Dickinson), 66, 68; text of, 64
"Poem 272" (Dickinson), text of, 67–68
"Poem 305" (Dickinson), text of, 68–69
"Poem 1263" (Dickinson), 68
poetics, 59, 64, 66, 67, 69; trans, 60, 68, 70, 254
poetry, 64; cognitive maps and, 60; enigma, 68, 69; of the future, 206; of the past, 206; queer, 19; trans, 19–20
Poitier, Sidney, 128, 284n201
political systems, 13, 193
Political Theology (Schmitt), 92
politics, 11, 40, 48, 53, 59, 86, 92, 94, 115, 118, 176, 189; assimilationist, 200; class, 227–28; coalitional, 61; concrete, 95; culture and, 50; disability, 12; electoral, 18; feminist, 12, 51; fraternal, 15, 55, 131; friendship and, 142, 179; gender, 251; identity, 7, 8; independent, 238; labor, 213, 219; labor and, 228; nonracist, 251; production and, 61; race, 251; radical, 182; war and, 145
Politics of Friendship, The (Derrida), 13, 32, 179
Polyclinic Hospital, 148
Polynices, 114
poor people's movement, 220
POV (television show), 200
poverty, 50, 86, 216, 235, 246, 249; Black, 230, 250; white, 250; working-class/underclass, 242, 250
power, 11; dynamics, 59, 263n6; labor, 234; male, 43; masculine, 68, 104; political, 241; race and, 290n1; self-authorizing, 134. *See also* phallic power

Pratt, Minnie Bruce, 215, 295–96n10
precarity, 183, 191, 217, 253, 255; economic, 232, 250
Preciado, Paul B., 34, 42, 270n77
private/public life, 15, 62
pronouns, gender and, 69, 77, 297n47
propaganda, 116, 156
Prosser, Jay, 4, 51, 214, 231, 234; Feinberg and, 236, 296n13; transgender and, 61
Proud Boys, 57
Proulx, Annie, 10, 240, 242, 243, 245, 246, 249, 255, 300n135; letters to, 241
Psychic Life of Power, The (Butler), 255
Psycho (film), 46
Puar, Jasbir K., 2, 104, 133, 172
public enemy, private hatred and, 94
pugilism, 5, 155
Putin, Vladimir, 257

queer, 25, 30, 61, 172; agenda, 252; directionality, 66; icons, 9–10; inquiry, 134; term, 182; time, 164, 185
queer communities, 172, 177, 183
queer masculinity, 11, 20, 24, 36, 55, 164, 171, 213, 216, 236, 251; instability of, 215; job security/domestic sphere and, 249–50; masculine normativity and, 213–14
queer movement, 54
queerness, 44, 183
queer past, 133; critiquing, 161–65
queer people, 9, 53, 56, 179
queers of color, 9
queer studies, 30, 54, 134, 136, 191, 213
queer subjects, 18, 57, 59, 80, 182, 183

queer theory, 3, 4, 9, 23, 50–51, 54, 67, 135, 215
Quijano, Aníbal, 24, 32, 88, 137, 169, 193, 257; coloniality and, 91

race, 25, 37, 48, 51, 61, 87, 131, 176, 215, 219, 231, 251, 253, 257; categorization, 44, 47; colors of, 17; gender and, 19; power and, 290n1; production of, 137–38; quasi-scientific theories of, 32
racial capitalism, 10, 21, 41, 55, 71, 87, 131, 133, 137, 197, 250, 255; counterfeit currency of, 13–20; critiques of, 3, 13; logics of, 17; outgrowth of, 22; response to, 252
racialization, 13, 18, 56, 73
racism, 7, 18, 46, 55, 76, 82, 170, 200, 220, 251; historical, 20; issues of, 192; present-day, 20
Ray, Nicholas, 109, 112
Rea, Stephen, 46, 49
Reagan, Ronald, 175, 189, 208, 209, 229, 230, 237; AIDS pandemic and, 176–77
realism: photographic, 41; romanticism and, 107
Rear Window (film), 281n104
reciprocity, 143, 144, 174, 180, 181; spirit of, 131
Red River (film), 98
Reeser, Todd W., 37, 69–70, 105, 253; on film/television, 87; manhood/penis and, 29; on masculinity/capitalism, 25; masculinity-in-motion and, 191
Regarding the Pain of Others (Sontag), 146
relationality, 25, 177; securing, 59
relationships: caring, 182; masculine, 10; multiplicity of, 177; privileged, 137; queer, 11; sexual, 185
remembrance, 63, 101, 127, 141, 157, 181; practices of, 164

Republicans, 175, 230, 231
Reuther, Walter, 217
revisionism, 98, 100–101
rhetoric, 64, 67, 68, 130, 196; Cold War, 176
Rickmann, Gregg, 98
Riggs, Marlon, 18, 19, 172, 192, 200, 203, 204–5, 206, 208 (fig.), 266n79; Black manhood and, 204; death of, 201; political/social justice and, 205; on real, 204; storytelling/documenting and, 207; Tubman and, 207–8
Right Now, I Love You Forever (Gibson), 77
Roach, Tom, 191, 252
Robinson, Cedric J., 16, 18, 21, 86, 116, 175, 176, 266n78; capitalist democracy and, 17; on Plato's "episteme," 266n62; racialism and, 13
Rodríguez, Juana María, 39, 40, 41, 44
romanticism, realism and, 107
Romantics, 77, 140
Romeo and Juliet (Shakespeare), 124
Roosevelt, Franklin Delano, 153, 217
Rosie the Riveter, 156
Ruddick, Sara, 154, 160

sadism, 57, 58, 59, 70, 254
Sanders, Bernie, 214
Sargent, Elizabeth, 162
Sassoon, Siegfried, 145, 146
savage, 90; noble, 120; primitive, 120
Schlafly, Phyllis, 175
Schmitt, Carl, 14, 90, 91, 92, 93, 95–96, 97, 108, 123; Derrida and, 95; friend/enemy and, 94; political theory and, 96; on sovereign, 90; theorizing by, 95
Schoenberger, Nancy, 98
Schwarz, Maureen T., 99
Searchers, The (film), 98, 107
Second Skins (Prosser), 296n13

Second Treatise of Government (Locke), 241
Second Wave, 115
security: border, 171; as dog whistle, 171; job, 222, 249–50; national, 176
Sedgwick, Eve Kosofsky, 67, 69, 103
self, 82; biography and, 60; other and, 191
September 11th, 2, 85, 86, 90, 116, 117, 122; Westerns and, 115, 127
Serano, Julia, 52
sex, 2, 131; as art of exploration, 187; biological, 60; categories, 44, 54; convergence of, 182; death/dying and, 184; disability and, 184; gender and, 29, 52, 56, 70; hypermasculine, 247; normative alignments of, 7
Sex and Character (Weininger), 139, 140
sexism, 55, 271n100
sexual assault, 22, 119
sexual expressions, 25, 60
sexuality, 2, 14, 25, 31, 37, 44, 51, 87, 173, 189, 212, 215, 242, 249, 252, 253, 254, 255, 258; femme, 42; fluid, 110; gender and, 69; masculine, 10, 187; masculinity and, 136; phallic, 135; queer, 191, 243; women's, 69
sex workers, 123, 125
Shakespeare, William, 124, 139
Shane (film), 116
Sharpe, Christina, 173, 203
Sherman, Cindy, 42
"she's a pistol" (phrase), 29, 48
"Shower, The" (Ace), 75
sick sex, 172, 183; queer time of disease and, 184–91
Sielke, Sabine, 118
signified, signifier and, 42
Signifyin' Works (Riggs), 201
Silver & Gold (filmformance), 16, 37–46, 54; still from, 43 (fig.), 45 (fig.)
Simone, Nina, 206
Singh, Nikhil Pal, 7, 20, 23, 87, 88, 91, 116, 137, 175, 242, 251, 256; on social-welfare state, 202; on Trump/Hitler, 257; war on terror and, 22; on war/torture, 21
"Sister" (Ace), 76
Skidmore, Emily, 49, 138
slavery, 22, 87, 125, 137, 251
Slotkin, Richard, 118
Small, Emma, 109
Smith, Jack, 37
Smith, Martha Nell, 64
Smith, Robert McClure, 67, 68, 69
Smukler, Linda, 71, 72, 73
Snorton, C. Riley, 2, 47, 129, 203, 294n91; Black manhood and, 204; countermythology and, 50; on Jorgensen, 48–49; race/gender and, 19; on trans embodiment, 56; transversality and, 17; on trans women/freedom/unfreedom, 49
social connection, 39, 181
social contract, 14, 15, 33, 242
social institutions, 8, 67, 290n1
socialism, 15, 193
social movements, 13, 47, 129, 240; transformative change and, 12
social order, 115, 134, 217
social relations, 6, 24, 87, 221, 258
social safety net, 16, 175, 200
social service, 175, 193, 239
solidarity, 19, 20, 54, 220, 223, 224, 242, 251–52; coalitional, 226; feminist, 22; politics of, 3, 14; workplace, 223
Sontag, Susan, 146
Sophocles, 85, 114, 115
Soule, Samantha, 121
sovereignty, 90, 194, 195; biopolitical, 175; national, 153

Spade, Dean, 9, 53, 54, 131; on capitalism/white supremacy, 1; mutual aid and, 12
Spanish–American War, 193
Spigel, Lynn, 116
Spillers, Hortense, 2, 203
"Squirrelhorse" (Ace), 73
Stalin, Joseph, 153
Stallone, Sylvester, 29
Standing Rock, 20, 77, 251
Stanzas in Meditation (Stein), 160, 161
Steers, Hugh, 173, 184; painting by, 174 (fig.)
Stein, Gertrude, 133, 146, 155, 156, 157, 158, 160–61, 162, 255; affection/care and, 8; authoritarianism and, 140; butch exceptionalism of, 140, 160; career of, 152, 164; Cather and, 7–8, 134, 135, 137, 138, 140–41, 142, 145; Communism and, 153; conservatism of, 161; feminist cause and, 139; lovence and, 143–44, 161; masculinity of, 136, 140; normative masculinity and, 162; pacifism and, 154; photo of, 163 (fig.); sexual/textual presence of, 160; soldiers and, 144, 154; strangeness/disconnection and, 159; Toklas and, 140, 155, 158, 160; Weininger and, 139, 140
Stein Reader, A (Dydo), 155
stereotypes, 44, 122, 178, 179, 185, 201, 204
Stewart, Jimmy, 99, 103, 108, 280n85, 281n104
Stoddard, Ransom, 107–8; effeminacy of, 104; Hallie and, 102, 105; interview of, 101; Liberty and, 106; Tom and, 99–100, 103, 107
Stoehr, Kevin, 98, 100, 101, 107
stone butch, 221–22
Stone Butch Blues (Feinberg), 10, 211, 212, 213, 215, 225, 249, 251, 255; butch/femme couples and, 214
strikes, 218, 223, 224, 227, 236
Strode, Woody, 104
Stryker, Susan, 61
student movement, 227, 231
Studlar, Gaylyn, 101
subjectivity, 3, 7, 37, 81, 87, 123, 159, 250; femme, 42; phallic, 35; tomboy, 216
subordination, 17, 59, 124, 171, 195, 252; gendered, 173; racial, 173
Sullivan, Lou, 4
Surpassing the Love of Men (Faderman), 179

Taft-Hartley Act (1947), 218, 222, 224, 227, 236
Take Me to Paris, Johnny (Foster), 172, 184, 189
"Tales of a Lost Boyhood" (Ace), 71, 74
Taylor, Clyde, 243
Taylor, Frederick W., 221
Taylorism, 220, 221, 250, 300n144
technology, 109, 225; computer, 233; military, 253
temporality, 74; queer, 191, 206, 207
Tendencies (Sedgwick), 67
Tender Buttons (Stein), 136, 154
TERFS. *See* trans-exclusionary radical feminists
terror, 13, 24, 96, 154, 155. *See also* war on terror
Theory of the Partisan (Schmitt), 95
Toklas, Alice B., 136, 153, 289n109; Stein and, 140, 155, 158, 160
Tolbert, TC, 72, 82
tomboys, 79, 80, 216
Tongues Untied (film), 201; grant for, 199–200
torture, 21, 23, 116, 193, 293n67
totalitarianism, democracy and, 21

toxic masculinity, 20, 21, 57, 70–71, 130, 185; celebration of, 85; focus on, 1; spread of, 3, 171; using, 170; white supremacy and, 258
Toye, Frederick E. O., 126
trailer trash, gay white, 240–52
trans communities, 11
trans-exclusionary radical feminists (TERFS), 31, 35
trans feminist art, 16
transformation, 134; masculine, 58; social, 13, 239
transgender, 82, 236; as abstraction, 51; as analytical tool, 61, 137; coalitional politics and, 61; as identity marker, 137; studies, 41, 56; theory, 3, 4, 35
Trans Lives Matter, 129
trans masculinity, 11, 20, 24, 52, 55, 71, 77, 164, 171, 216, 236; influence of, 264n18; instability of, 215; job security/domestic sphere and, 249–50; lower-class, 251; masculine normativity and, 213–14; white, 6; whiteness and, 138
trans men, 8, 36, 54, 138
transmisogyny, 46, 50, 52
transnationalism, 133, 170
transness, 19, 23, 47, 68, 79
transnormativity, 6, 7, 8, 133, 235
trans past, 133; critiquing, 161–65
trans people, 35, 79; categories for, 53; lesbian feminists and, 73; securing existence of, 130
transphallomisogyny, 16, 31, 35, 37, 46, 53
transphobia, 16, 46, 54, 212–13
trans scholars, 54, 213
transsexual, 4, 50, 61
Transsexual Empire: The Making of the She-Male, The (Raymond), 51
trans subjects, 18, 57, 59, 80
trans theory, 9, 23, 135, 215

transversality, term, 17
trans women, 30, 46, 48, 52, 53; bias against, 51; Black, 50; category "woman" and, 31; degradation/omission of, 35; penis and, 34, 46, 47; sex/gender contradiction of, 34; sexual imaginary for, 54
Trap Door: Trans Cultural Production and the Politics of Visibility (Burton and Gossett), 53
Troubling the Line (Tolbert and Peterson), 82
True Sex: The Lives of Trans Men at the Turn of the Twentieth Century (Skidmore), 138
Truman, Harry, 230
Trump, Donald, 2, 23–24; Covid-19 victory of, 256; fascism and, 20, 21–22; Hitler speeches and, 257; repression/social decay of, 258; toxic masculinity and, 1, 20, 70–71, 256
TSQ: Transgender Studies Quarterly, 61
Tubman, Harriet, 207–8
Turner, Victor, 58
26th of July Movement, 193
Twist, Jack, 10, 244, 245; Ennis and, 241, 242, 246–47, 248, 249; suicide of, 248, 249
Two Lives (Malcolm), 140
Tyner, Katie, 256

UAW. *See* United Auto Workers
Ulysses, 134
unemployment, 175, 217, 241
Unforgiven (film), 125, 285n197
unions, 217, 218, 222, 225, 226, 227, 228, 231, 234, 235, 236, 237, 238, 240; industrial, 239; issues with, 232–33; politics behind, 224; public service, 239; social transformation and, 239. *See also* labor movement

United Auto Workers (UAW), 217, 232, 233, 234
Unlikely Collaboration: Gertrude Stein, Bernard Fay, and the Vichy Dilemma (Will), 153
unruly alliance, 3, 114, 208–9
USA PATRIOT Act, 279n35
U.S. Army, 154
U.S. Capitol, assault on, 257
U.S. Constitution, 170, 171
Useful Knowledge (Stein), 154
U.S. Immigration and Customs Enforcement (ICE), 170
U.S. Marine Corps, 154
U.S. Supreme Court, 170
utopia, 224; queer articulation of, 40

Valance, Liberty, 100, 105; death of, 106, 107; Pompey and, 104; Ransom and, 103, 106; Tom and, 102
Valerio, Max Wolf, 60
Van Cleef, Lee, 105
Van Vechten, Carl, 136, 155; photo by, 163 (fig.)
Vertigo (film), 281n104
Vienna, 99, 109–10, 112, 121; Emma and, 111, 113; gender trouble and, 110; masculinity of, 110
Vietnam War, 224, 227, 229–30, 230–31
violence, 13, 23, 50, 76, 88, 116, 157, 198, 204, 252; anti-Black, 19; anti-trans, 19, 47; biopolitical, 87; boyhood, 57; colonial, 152; gender-based, 68; gratuitous, 121; justifying, 86; lawless, 96; mob, 21; nature of, 15, 155; preemptive, 89; racial, 22; state, 18, 102, 185; Western, 86
virtue, 163; divided, 136–45; virile, 31, 37, 39, 97
Vox Feminista, 77
vulnerability, 25, 39, 52, 76, 78, 79, 161, 172, 180, 183, 185, 190, 191, 196, 204, 247; masculine, 10–11

Walia, Harsha, 171
Wallace, George, 230
Walzer, Michael, 266n70
war on drugs, 18
war on terror, 22, 24, 87, 88, 116
Wars I Have Seen (Stein), 161
Washington Post, 201, 256
Watermelon Woman, The (Dunye), 201
Watkins, Mel, 41
Wayne, John, 85–86, 99, 103, 106, 108, 121, 127, 254, 280n85; Ford and, 98; masculine physicality and, 109
Wayne and Ford (Schoenberger), 98
wealth distribution, 175, 213
Weeks, Mabel, 158
Weininger, Otto, 139, 140
Wertheimer, Barbara Mayer, 223, 236, 296n24
West, idea of, 89
Westerns, 86, 89, 98, 116; civilizing forces of, 102; feminist, 99; Indian Wars and, 91; Indigenous people and, 100, 120; low-budget, 101; normative masculinity and, 131; ontological enemies of, 90; political/cultural concerns and, 115; racial genocide and, 120; revisionist, 98–111, 113; September 11th and, 115, 127; shift in, 87; super-, 98; white masculine hegemony and, 115; women in, 100, 116, 283n155
West Village, queer space of, 236
Westward the Women (film), 99
Westworld (television series), 22, 23, 87, 97, 107, 111, 115, 125, 127, 130, 284n186, 284n187; analysis of, 114; marginalized and, 124; personhood/citizenship and, 123;

still from, 126; unhomely stirring in, 124
Wever, Merritt, 118
"when I was a boy," 60–65, 66–70
Whipping Girl (Serano), 52
Whitaker, Forest, 47
Whitehead, Evelyn, 154
white male: authority, 125; as normal, 182; wounded, 146
whiteness, 5, 19, 44, 45, 140, 171, 222, 223, 242, 250, 254; class and, 8, 138; denaturalization/transformation of, 252; institutionalization of, 248; irregularities in, 300n144; masculinity and, 71, 256; public/psychological wages of, 137; racialization of, 242; trans masculinity and, 138
white supremacy, 2, 5, 7, 16, 25, 71, 123, 153; political effects of, 3; toxic masculinity and, 258
white vanguardism, 5
Whitman, Walt, 66
Wild Bunch, The (film), 122
Wilde, Oscar, 139
Wildermuth, Mark E., 87, 116
Wild West, 109, 124

Wilentz, Sean, 177, 230
Wilkerson, Abby, 182
Will, Barbara, 153
Wizard of Oz (film), 44
"women as victim" trope, 117
women of color, 8, 24, 53, 129; performers, 46; resistance by, 123
women's liberation, 229
women's movement, 227
Wood, Evan Rachel, 124
working class, 211, 218, 221, 222, 227, 230, 233; Black, 239; white, 250, 251, 300n144
working-class movement, 22, 220
World War I, 8, 21, 95, 135, 142, 143, 153, 255; slaughter of, 145
World War II, 21, 32, 111, 134, 153, 159, 211, 212, 217, 230
Wray, Matt, 242
Wynonna Earp (television show), 115

xenophobia, 93, 94, 113

Yellowstone (television show), 115
Young, Iris Marion, 113, 122, 141
"Your Life" (Gibson), 79

K. Allison Hammer is assistant professor and coordinator of the Women, Gender, and Sexuality Studies Program, in the School of Africana and Multicultural Studies, at Southern Illinois University.